PERSONAL HISTORY

BOOKS BY

VINCENT SHEEAN

Personal History
The Tide
Gog and Magog
American Among the Riffi
Anatomy of Virtue
New Persia
Sanfelice

PERSONAL HISTORY~

Vincent Sheean

Garden City Publishing Co., Inc.

New York

PRINTED AT THE *Country Life Press*, GARDEN CITY, N. Y., U. S. A.

CL

1937
GARDEN CITY PUBLISHING CO., INC.

TO R. P.:

Neuer beleeue though in my nature raign'd,
All frailties that besiege all kindes of blood,
That it could so preposterouslie be stain'd,
To leaue for nothing all thy summe of good:

SONNET 109.

Due acknowledgment is made to the "Atlantic Monthly" *for permission to reprint such material as has appeared in their pages.*

Contents

Contents

PERSONAL HISTORY

I

The Modern Gothic

THE ARMISTICE came when I was eighteen. What it meant to the war generation I can only imagine from the stories they tell; to me it meant that we in the University of Chicago, that mountain range of twentieth-century Gothic near the shores of Lake Michigan, went out of uniform and into civilian clothes.

The world has changed so much that it seems downright indecent to tell the truth: I was sorry when the war ended. I fumed with disappointment on the night of the false armistice—the celebrated night when the American newspapers reported the end of the war some days before it happened. We were all patriots then. We knew nothing about that horror and degradation which our elders who had been through the war were to put before us so unremittingly for the next fifteen years. There were millions of us, young Americans between the ages of fifteen or sixteen and eighteen or nineteen, who cursed freely all through the middle weeks of November. We felt cheated. We had been put into uniform with the definite promise that we were to be trained as officers and sent to France. In my case, as in many others, this meant growing up in a hurry, sharing the terrors and excitements of a life so various, free and exalted that it was worth even such hardships as studying trigonometry. So we went into uniform and marched about the place from class to class like students in a military academy; listened to learned professors lecturing about something called 'War Aims'; lived in 'barracks'; did rifle drill. The rifles were dummies, and the 'barracks' were only the old dormitories rechristened, but such details made little difference. We played at being soldiers for a few months with tremendous seriousness, and then the glorious uproar to which we had been

1

preparing our approach suddenly died down. Our part of the war had been a prelude to something that did not take place.

And when demobilization came at last the prospect of returning to the regular life of the University had become repellent to me. I had nobody to persuade but my mother, who was still too thankful for the Armistice to make many objections. Consequently I went job hunting and spent three months as secretary to a millionaire builder and real estate operator in the Chicago financial district. It was there, hanging out a window above the crevasse of LaSalle Street, that I watched the Black Hawk Division come home. Waving flags and the thump of a military march were enough to stir me to any extravagance; we all shouted and waved and winked back the hysterical tears. Those were patriotic days.

My employer was an odious little man who had quarreled with his wife and disinherited his son because the latter wanted to go on the stage. He was a brilliant entrepreneur, the little man: he used to point with pride to the ceilings of the skyscraper in which he had his office, saying, 'That ceiling is a good six inches shallower than the law allows. You can always arrange things if you know how. I got eight extra storeys into this building by that little detail.' When I inquired if the building was likely to fall down he sniffed contemptuously. 'Buildings don't fall down,' he said. The building did start to fall down some years later, was condemned and demolished. By an unfortunate accident, its builder was not buried under the ruins.

He sent me on one occasion to collect rents from the impoverished tenants of a village he owned in Indiana. It was a horrible experience from which I escaped as quickly as I could, but the thought of it came back to me for years. The tenants of the wretched little Indiana town worked in a coal mine belonging to my employer when they worked at all, but they had not worked for many months. They lived in houses belonging to him (if you could call such hovels houses) and bought their food from stores belonging to him. I was to collect what I could of the back rent owed on the disgraceful shacks in which they were obliged to live. I was a failure at the job, for the sight of the life into which children were there being born disorganized whatever efficiency

2

I possessed as a secretary. That day in the little mining town was my introduction to capitalism at work, and it filled me, even then, with disgust. I blamed the busy little entrepreneur as well as the system of which he was a part, and it was not long before the idea of continuing to work for him became insupportable. 'Business' (if this was business) bored, irked and revolted me, and I determined to do whatever I could to avoid being involved in it again.

In the spring of 1919, therefore, I went back to the University and stayed on throughout the summer to make up for lost time. My education up to then had been a sorry failure. I had never made any headway with science, mathematics or the classical languages. Of the first two I remembered nothing; of the second I remembered just one Greek sentence, *enteuthen exelaunei* ('and the next day he marched onward')—this not because it had any stirring significance for me, but because it marked the welcome end of nearly every chapter in the Anabasis.

I had derived, it was true, considerable pleasure of a low order from some other academic pursuits in my first two years of college. I had come to the University knowing some Italian, German, and French (particularly French), and could easily make a better showing in these subjects than my contemporaries. My favourite trick had been to register for courses in which I was unlikely to encounter anything I did not already know. Such conduct was lazy and dishonest, but you could make out a good case for the theory that young people were all lazy and dishonest when they could be. Certainly what the undergraduates called 'snaps' (i.e., courses easy to get through without undue effort) were always crowded in my day at the University. The football players, the social lights, the pretty co-eds, and all the other students who regarded study as an inconvenient detail in college life, rushed to inscribe themselves for 'snap' courses. I was in a more advantageous position than some of my fellows for wasting time, since more courses were 'snaps' for me. I could go to a series of lectures on Victorian Prose, for example, and be confident of hearing nothing new; similarly, in French, with the novels of Victor Hugo or the plays of Molière. I had read altogether too much in the two languages, thanks to a bookish childhood. There was thus a group of studies open to me at the University in which I could, without working or learning, impress my instructors sufficiently to make a good record.

More than two years of my three and a half at the University of Chicago had already been wasted in this way. It was a kind of confidence game of which the victim was, of course, myself. I did well enough in the subjects I already knew to make up for my failures in the subjects I did not know and was too lazy to study. I was too undisciplined, too indolent, and too dishonest to force myself to learn what did not interest me. And it was not until that summer of 1919 that I began to realize the silliness of such an approach to what ought to be one of the great experiences of a life. The University of Chicago in summer was invaded by hordes of earnest men and women from the smaller colleges and schools of the Middle West, working towards their master's or their doctor's degree. These thin, spectacled myrmidons, hump-backed from carrying armfuls of books up and down academic steps for many years, filled the cool gray corridors and covered the green lawns I had always thought reserved for pretty girls and long-legged youths. The summer school, I discovered, was an altogether different affair from the ordinary academic year. If you tried to talk to a summer student during a lecture, a cold glance through glittering spectacles was the only reply. The brilliant hot sun of a Chicago July threw into merciless relief all the unloveliness of these dank visitors from the provincial colleges of Indiana, Wisconsin, Illinois, Iowa, and Minnesota. Their presence was somehow unbecoming, both to their surroundings and to the general fitness of things. I resented them for two or three weeks, and on the few occasions when I saw my vacationing friends, the undergraduates who had finished their college year in June, we were exceedingly witty about the looks, manners, lives, and minds of the pitiable summer students. There were probably not half a dozen of these bookworms, we calculated, who could dance the fox trot decently.

But as the summer study advanced I became more and more uncomfortable about them. They were not beautiful, but neither were they ignorant. They were always putting me to shame, some-how or other. I was not to remember much about most of the studies of that summer; only one was vivid in retrospect. It was a fairly advanced course in French—the poetry of Victor Hugo, all of it, including every pitiless line of *La Légende des Siècles*. The instructor was a visiting bigwig from one of the Eastern universities, a Frenchman with a German name. He used to conduct the course in an informal fashion, lecturing some of the time, reading occasionally, and starting discussions whenever the spirit moved him. It was assumed that students in a such a course as this would be mature and educated enough to know something besides the actual subject matter itself. Comparisons were always popping up, were constantly invited. Most of the students— there may have been twelve or fifteen, men and women—were well past thirty, and probably all of them taught French literature somewhere or other. In that company, through July and August, I first began to be ashamed of my evil ways, and no amount of smug scorn for the bookworms could disguise the fact.

'Vous trouverez ici sans doute que Hugo a beaucoup emprunté à Chateaubriand; n'est-ce pas, Mademoiselle?' the professor would inquire innocently, smiling across his desk at an eager spinster from Indiana. And then off she would go, talking about Hugo and Chateaubriand in a French accent that would have been incomprehensible to either of those gentlemen—but talking, just the same, with information and intelligence. The professor would argue with her; others would join in; and it appalled me that I could not even follow their battle from afar. I had never read a word of Chateaubriand; my interest in Christianity was almost nonexistent; I had no real idea why it had ever seemed intellectually important to Victor Hugo or to anybody else. And I looked at the summer students in amazement. Their excitement over such subjects actually brought colour to their wan faces; they could smile, make jokes, go through all the movements of living organisms when their attention was aroused.

My salvation was that the instructor was a Frenchman. If he had been an American or an Englishman he would have seen at once that my glibness in French was a sheer accident, and that I actually understood nothing of the turmoil through which Victor Hugo had lived and written. But, being French, the professor had a natural prejudice in favour of hearing his language pronounced correctly. In spite of all their knowledge and interest, most of the students in this course had abominable accents; it seemed to be a rule among American school teachers. I had learned French so young that all the laziness in the world could never rob me of a fairly good pronunciation. Consequently, when I had occasion to read some of Victor Hugo's detested verses aloud, the professor would lean back in his chair with satisfaction. This, combined with a prudent silence when the discussions were out of my depth, gave the good man the idea that I really knew something of the subject, and I finished the course with an unjustifiably handsome record.

But something important happened to me during the summer of 1919, thanks chiefly to the Hugo poems. I had been realizing with increasing clarity, week after week, the superficial character of my own mind. I was nineteen, and I knew nothing. The fact that I could speak a sort of French had nothing to do with me; what credit there might be for that should have gone to the devout and kindly Irish priest who had tutored me in it for years. Of the actual meaning of French literature I knew far less than the scrubbiest high-school teacher from Iowa. The struggles of men's minds—whether of contemporary minds or of those like Chateaubriand's and Hugo's, long gone to dust—meant nothing to me at all. I had existed without realizing that it seriously mattered to anybody what men believed, or under what form of government, in what structure of society, they lived. The summer's study gave me no love for the poetry of Victor Hugo: on the contrary, the mere thought of *La Légende des Siècles* made me feel slightly uneasy for years to come. But I did derive from it some idea of what the process of literature could be—some hint of the stormy sincerity in which minds like Hugo's sought for the truth. The suggestion, however dim, was sufficient reward for the boredom of reading what then seemed to me an intolerable quantity of pompous, overstuffed verse.

My ideas of what I might get out of the University thereafter submitted to rearrangement. Words could no longer suffice: I understood Hugo's words well enough, the upholstery of his mind, but it was the mind itself that escaped me. If a mind of Hugo's quality was incomprehensible, how could I expect to know anything about the rarer minds that did (even then) seem to me most worth the effort of comprehension: Molière, Racine, Shakespeare? And, even in a world I found tiresome beyond my powers of resistance, the world of the 'Victorian Prose Writers,' what could I hope to understand by words alone? It was clear, after the Hugo experience, that literature involved something at once more complex and more ordinary, more closely related to the whole life of mankind, than the science of stringing words together in desirable sequences, however fascinating the contemplation of such patterns might seem to a bookish and word-conscious nature.

Nothing could be learned about literature by studying literature: that was what it came to. Courses in literature seldom took on the vitality of that special Hugo course with its special participants. In general, they were either arranged to suit average students with no interest in the subject, or specialists with an interest so minute that it was (in my view) equivalent to no interest at all. I had no desire to count the feminine endings in the lines of the Canterbury Tales. What I wanted to know—in so far as I really wanted to know anything about them—was why the Canterbury Tales were written; what mysterious springs existed in the mind and heart of a man named Geoffrey Chaucer to bring forth such a particular stream of articulated language; what the world was like for which he wrote, in which he lived, and what was his particular struggle with it. Professors did sometimes try to convey this sort of information; but it was obvious that they had obtained it elsewhere and were passing it on in capsule form. Where had they obtained it?

History, perhaps, was the answer; philosophy might be part of it.

That autumn, when the regular academic year began, I switched from the faculties of English literature and Romance languages to those of history and philosophy. And perhaps if this had been the arrangement two years before I might not have wasted quite so much time.

I am not suggesting that I became a model of industry and scholarship promptly at nine o'clock on the morning of registration day in October, 1919. I still frittered away a good three quarters or four fifths of my time, still registered for an occasional course of lectures that could be treated cavalierly as a 'snap' (History of Venetian Art, for instance). But at least I was not behaving altogether as if the University were a country club. Both in history and in philosophy I learned something—not much, but something. There was a course in Plato that conveyed meaning to me; another, on the German idealists, I found as exciting as a romantic novel. But perhaps the most interesting of all—the one to be recalled most often in subsequent life—was a term of lectures and reading on the Decline of the Ottoman Empire.

This—an 'advanced,' and therefore a rather small, class—was in charge of an inspired teacher. I never knew what made the difference between a good and a bad teacher, but I did know that Ferdinand Schevill was a superlatively good one. He was a German, short and rather formidable in appearance, with eyeglasses and a neatly trimmed Vandyke beard. His university was Heidelberg or Bonn, I believe, and yet he had none of that pedantry which is supposed to be the vice of German scholarship. When he led us through the immense and complicated story of the decay that fell upon Suleiman's empire after the seventeenth century he did not try to treat it microscopically as an isolated phenomenon. He talked about the Arabs, the Turks, the Balkan peoples, as if they were alive; and they soon began to come to life for me. Schevill's system was to allow his students to read at will through the whole literature of the subject, and therefrom to choose, halfway through the course, a particular aspect for further reading and a final paper. I began to read everything I could find about the Asiatic empire of the Turks. Almost from the first day that side of the Bosphorus seemed to me of greater interest than this. I extended my researches to the files of newspapers and magazines, and when it came time to choose, I took for my term paper the history of the Wahabite movement.

An odder choice for a nineteen-year-old undergraduate at the University of Chicago would be hard to imagine. Ibn es-Sa'ud was then almost unknown to the Western world, and the literature on the Wahabi was scarce indeed. I read everything I could find in English, French, or German, and performed the best piece of honest work I had ever done. For a few weeks, while I was reading in the library, I nearly persuaded myself that I was living in Arabia, and sometimes the vast cloaks and camel turbans of the Bedawin seemed more real than the swishing skirts of the co-eds going by. Later on I obtained permission to go down into the stacks of that huge library—steel stacks with glass floors running among them, layer upon layer. The world's knowledge lay there like a sunken continent swimming in subaqueous light, and through its fields I ranged more or less at will. My interest in Islam, such as it was, began that year, and what I learned in Schevill's course was never wholly forgotten. If other teachers had been like him, other subjects as vivid to me as the disintegration of Turkey became, I might have learned more in my long sojourn under the sham-Gothic towers.

But the social system of the undergraduate world in which I lived was the villain of the piece. No teacher could have compelled full attention from a mind preoccupied with elaborate details of social relationship. The University of Chicago, one of the largest and richest institutions of learning in the world, was partly inhabited by a couple of thousand young nincompoops whose ambition in life was to get into the right fraternity or club, go to the right parties, and get elected to something or other. The frivolous two thousand—the undergraduate body, the 'campus' —may have been a minority, for the University contained a great many solitary workers in both the undergraduate and graduate fields; but the minority thought itself a majority, thought itself, in fact, the whole of the University. And it was to the frivolous two thousand that I belonged.

Chicago was by no means the worst American university in this respect—it was supposed, on the contrary, to be one of the best; but even at Chicago 'campus activities' were the most serious part of life. Freshmen chose, on the advice of their elders, which of these 'activities' to pursue throughout the four years. Some 'went out for the *Maroon*' (i.e., worked for the college's daily newspaper), some 'for the team' (i.e., football), some for other organized athletics, and some for 'class politics.' Rare and wonderful freshmen 'went out for' everything at once.

There were hierarchies in the *Daily Maroon*, in the Dramatic

Club, which made productions every two or three months and in the Blackfriars. This last was an association of undergraduates interested in producing an operetta (original, more or less) in the spring of every year with men in all the parts. Freshmen were graduated through the successive steps in all these organizations until the survivors, by natural selection and incredibly hard work, stood out in their senior year, immortal: the editor of the *Maroon*, the president of the Dramatic Club, the abbot (and other officials) of Blackfriars. Football and track athletics had their four-year plans as well, but they were not my line of country, and I knew little about them.

Organized 'activities,' as occupation for the energies of youth, could have done no harm if they had not been supplemented, and to some extent even controlled, by a social life of singular ferocity. The women undergraduates had a number of clubs to which all the 'nice' girls were supposed to belong. Four or five of these clubs were 'good' and the rest 'bad.' Their goodness and badness were absolute, past, present and future, and could not be called into question. They had no houses or rooms of their own, but they maintained a rigid solidarity and succeeded in imposing upon the undergraduate society a tone of intricate, overweening snobbery.

The men were grouped in Greek-letter fraternities with houses for residence. Half a dozen of these were 'good' and the rest 'bad'; but their goodness and badness were not quite so irremediable as the similar qualifications among the women's clubs. The fraternities were national organizations, with chapters in most of the American universities, and it was well known that the same fraternity might be 'good' at the University of California and 'bad' at Yale. The salutary effect of this consideration was supported by the fact that the men did not seem to have the same high degree of social cruelty as the women. Men often joined a fraternity because their brothers or fathers had belonged to it, because they had friends in it, because they liked some one person in it, or even because its house or its food or its heating system appealed to them. Such homely, sensible reasons weighed little with the women. All of them, true to the great tradition of American womanhood, took the very 'best' club to which they could possibly be elected, and the logic of their behaviour kept their club system rigid throughout my four years at the University.

My experience with the fraternity system was a weird one. It was in no way typical, but it exhibited some of the cannibalistic character of the institution and the intensity with which its importance was felt among the undergraduates. I entered the University ignorant of even the names of the Greek-letter societies. On my first or second day I was asked to lunch at a fraternity house and went. On the next day I discovered that that godlike creature, the editor of the *Maroon*, was a member of this very fraternity. When, on about the fourth day, I was asked to pledge myself to join it, I accepted at once.

Followed what has since appeared to be a grand tragicomic episode. I moved into the fraternity house, where lived the friends, ready-made, among whom I was supposed to pass four years. My roommate was Alan Le May, a dour, dark and silent freshman with a sharp intelligence. He afterwards took to making vast sums of money by writing about the wild and woolly West, but at the time he was more concerned with such effete Eastern matters as French composition and English literature. There were a number of other brothers-in-the-bond who loomed particularly large. Above them all, in a kind of hazy splendour like that which crowns a high mountain in the sun, there dwelt the supreme god, A.B., the editor of the *Maroon*. He was kind to me, suggested books to read, talked to me about the scraps of verse I used to write. I never saw anybody afterwards who possessed quite his Olympian quality, and two or three kings, with a pope and a president thrown in, could not possibly have awed me so much in later days as he awed me then. In all, I was happy in that life; but it was not prolonged.

On the day of our initiation into the fraternity, three months after the taking of the pledge, a girl asked me to cut my classes and take a long walk with her. She was a pretty girl, a freshman, whom I had met in the office of the *Daily Maroon* and with whom I was conducting a shy and tentative flirtation. It was bitter cold that day; she was wrapped in furs, and I decidedly was not; but we walked for many hours through the snowy streets, down to

PERSONAL HISTORY

Jackson Park with its trees hung in ice, and out to the wintry lake. After we had been chattering about ordinary things for ten or fifteen minutes she suddenly opened up on me.

'I've been talking to various people around the *Maroon* about you,' she said. 'We all think you're a pretty good freshman. You might amount to something if you had any sense. I don't think you know what you're doing. I realize it's none of my business, but I've made up my mind to talk to you about it before it's too late.'

This meant nothing to me, and I said so.

'Oh, don't pretend that you don't understand,' she said. 'It's that damned fraternity. You can't possibly belong to it and make anything at all out of your college life. You'll be miserable in another year, when you know where you are. No girl will go out with you—no nice girl, that is. And you're barred from everything that makes college life what it is. Of course, I know you're not Jewish, but everybody doesn't realize that, and I think it's a terrible shame.'

In my entire life I had never heard a more surprising series of statements.

'But what are you talking about, anyway?' I asked. 'Why on earth should anybody think I was Jewish?'

'Because you belong to a Jewish fraternity,' she said.

Ensued a ludicrous, painful, silly and melancholy conversation. In the course of it I made acquaintance with (a) the social system of the University of Chicago; (b) the Jewish problem; (c) the way of the world; (d) my own colossal ignorance. Incredible though it seemed afterwards, I had never known a Jew in my life and had no idea that there were so many of them growing there under my eyes. I had only the romantic and provincial notions about Jews: thought of them as bearded old gentlemen with magic powers and vast stores of gold. Except for Rebecca in *Ivanhoe*, I had never made the acquaintance of a *young* Jew even in literature. I suppose I must have thought they had sprung full grown into the Middle Ages and thence vanished into the oblivion of eastern Europe. At any rate, the fact was that I had never thought of the Jews as a possibility in the here and now: my contemporaries in America, in Chicago. To Lucy, my pretty little girl-friend—a wise little girl indeed, striding along in her muskrat coat—I must have seemed an imbecile. At first she refused to believe that this was new to me.

'You're sixteen years old,' she scolded. 'You've got a fair amount of brains. My God, boy, do you mean to tell me you don't know a Jew when you see one? Look at them, idiot; look at them. They have noses, hair, eyes, features, mouths, all different from anybody else. Can you honestly tell me you didn't know that —— was a Jew?'

And then the melancholy catalogue began. One by one we ran through the list of every member of my fraternity. They were all, it seemed, Jews.[1] So were half the freshmen, male and female, on the *Daily Maroon*. The last name, the one I dreaded to pronounce, was that of the godlike senior, the editor of the *Maroon*. And he too, as Lucy proved by a merciless analysis of his name and appearance, was certainly Jewish.

After this I walked along for a long time in silence. Lucy kept on talking, but I scarcely heard what she said. I was trying to realize that I had been living for nearly three months in a houseful of Jews and had never known it. I was shocked, humiliated, and angry, not because my fraternity brothers were Jewish, but because I had not known about it. The shock would have been the same if they had all turned out to be Swedenborgians, or Spaniards, or vegetarians, or believers in the transmigration of souls. It made them a special caste, a marked and unvariable species, to which I could not possibly belong. To have failed to recognize a quality so singular was also a proof of abysmal ignorance on my part. I was naïf and provincial, of course, but I had never realized to what a degree. In the end I had recourse to the expedient we all come to at one time or another—I refused to believe the truth.

'Well, Lucy,' I said combatively, 'I don't believe a single thing you say, but let's just suppose for a minute that it's true. Then what? What's the difference? What possible harm can it do me to belong to a Jewish fraternity?'

---

[1]They weren't, but this was a detail I did not know for years. The undergraduate body called it a 'Jewish fraternity' because it contained Jews; and among the supposed Jews were a good many Gentiles.

She began a recital that horrified me. It horrified me more afterwards, as I came to know that the state of affairs described was by no means peculiar to the University of Chicago or to university life. The Jews, it seemed, could not possibly go to the 'nice' parties in college. They could not be elected to any class office, or to office in any club, or to any fraternity except the two they had themselves organized; they could not dance with whom they pleased or go out with the girls they wanted to go out with; they could not even walk across the quadrangles with a 'nice' girl if she could possibly escape. And so on. The picture was painted with violence, but it was true, as I was to learn before long. Hitler himself could not have invented a more savage and degrading system of anti-Semitism than that worked out by those little monsters, the undergraduates. The system had been operating all around me from the day I entered college, and I had never seen it. As Lucy explained, my position was peculiar. I was a non-Jewish freshman pledged to a Jewish fraternity. My own brothers-in-the-bond would naturally not explain these things to me, said she, and nobody else had the courage to do so.

It took another period of painful argument to convince me that such prejudices and restrictions existed. Having, finally, accepted them as true on Lucy's testimony, I then asked why they should apply to me.

'After all,' I argued, 'I've got the map of Ireland in my face. Not to speak of my name. How on earth could anybody think I was Jewish?'

'It doesn't make any difference,' she said. 'You belong to a Jewish fraternity. That's enough. Lots of Jews take Irish names, and lots of Jews don't look especially Jewish. You'll be marked as a Jew, all right, if you go on into the fraternity. Take my word for it: I know.'

After hours of explaining, exhorting and laying down the law, Lucy brought forth the suggestion to which all this had been a preparation. It was that I should break my pledge to the fraternity, spend two or three months living in a 'dormitory' (i.e., a college hall), and then, in the spring, join one of the better Gentile fraternities.

I repudiated the notion with vehemence. What? Leave the

place I liked best in the whole University? Abandon my friends? Desert the roommate who was the only person I knew foolish enough, and amiable enough, to sit up arguing with me until two or three in the morning? Above all, forsake the precincts hallowed by the presence of that saint, that prince of the world, the editor of the *Maroon?* Impossible!

And on that note the afternoon ended. We had walked from early afternoon until dark; we had ploughed through snow and shivered on the icy lake front; I had been more thoroughly upset than ever before in my seventeen years. Lucy entered the gates of Foster Hall without knowing whether her effort had been in vain or not, and I went on home to the fraternity house, which seemed to have been invested, between lunch and dinner, with mystery.

It is difficult to make out just what my idea of a Jew was. It seems probable that the word had no significance at all, except the dubious significance given it in the romances I had spent my childhood reading. But it must have set up some kind of reverberation in my mind, because all my friends began to seem a little mysterious to me from the moment I thought they were Jewish. The ideas that Jews are a terrifying people, that they deal in dark magic, that they belong to an especially gifted and especially tragic race, are scattered so widely through all the literature of Christian Europe that we take them in unconsciously, more or less as we absorb air and moisture, without troubling to notice the process. Unconscious anti-Semitism was here, as in larger issues, what made the problem so extraordinarily difficult. I was not knowingly anti-Jewish; I had never knowingly spoken to a Jew or thought about the Jewish problem; and yet the accumulated prejudices of two thousand years had so subtly and insensibly poisoned my mind that it came as a shock to hear that my particular friends, the most admired of my acquaintance, were Jews.

Such shocks are absorbed by time. Along with other oddments of superstition, the origins of which we cannot always trace, there disappears the notion that the Jews are a sinister race, gifted in the black arts or banded together in sorcery; we learn that when they are treated like anybody else they do not greatly differ from anybody else. But to dispel these ancestral fancies, clinging like vague vapours in the mind, we require the light and air of experience. And it was precisely experience that was most conspicuously lacking in the equipment of the freshman who ploughed through the snow that night, going home, for the first time in his life, with a Problem.

'Lemmy!' I said, coming into my room, 'I've got to talk to you. Do you think that A. B. is Jewish?'

'Of course,' he said. 'What's the matter?'

I told him as much as I could of the afternoon's discoveries, but there was little time. The dinner bell was ringing, and freshmen could not be late.

'It's all true enough,' he said. 'I've known it all the time. Haven't you?'

His glum face was glummer than ever; he frowned intently, scratched his close-cropped black head.

'After dinner,' he said, 'we can lock the door and talk it out. Let's eat.'

Lemmy completed the education Lucy had begun. After dinner, a nervous meal under the circumstances, we made for our room at once to 'study.' With the door locked we sat there and talked in the quiet voices of conspirators. He had learned, from his father probably, a great deal about the world we lived in.

Our fraternity, he told me, had been founded to include (and perhaps to reconcile) Jews and non-Jews; it had only succeeded in getting itself labelled as wholly Jewish; and a national convention the year before had restricted its membership in future to Gentiles. (I remember my feeling of relief when I learned that he too was a Gentile; I was never to be sure whether anybody else in the house was or not.)

Like Lucy a few hours earlier, Lemmy found my ignorance hard to believe. He said, patiently enough, that everybody knew these things; that the difference between Jews and Gentiles was as obvious as that between men and women, and that it would never occur to anybody to state it. He further corroborated everything Lucy had told me about the opprobrium, the ridicule, the complicated varieties of discrimination and prejudice, to which any Gentile who belonged to a Jewish fraternity would have to submit throughout four years in college. He had known all this when he was pledged, he said; and he had still taken the pledge because (in his humility) he supposed the 'bid' to join a fraternity to be a rare thing, and a Jewish fraternity to be better than none. He agreed that no house could be pleasanter than ours, no friends more satisfactory; but he was convinced that remaining in the fraternity meant accepting a kind of permanent ostracism from the life of the Gentile part of the undergraduate body.

We agreed, in a high state of hysterical agitation, to do 'something.' But that 'something' could not be long delayed. The informal initiation into the fraternity would take place in an hour, and the following day we were to take the solemn, irrevocable oaths of the formal initiation. We were still in turmoil when a solemn knock on our door summoned us to the ordeal.

'Informal initiation' into a fraternity was supposed to be a test for the courage or endurance of the freshman candidate for membership. The candidate was stripped naked and led, blindfolded, into a room where the elders of the fraternity exercised their strength and wits in an attempt to try his nerve. Actually no candidate, however poltroonishly he behaved during the tests, was ever refused admission to the brotherhood, and the 'informal initiation' was therefore merely an excuse for some rather rudimentary fun. The ordeal by fire, the ordeal by water, and a dozen other curious relics of savagery were brought into play, ostensibly to prove that a boy of sixteen or seventeen was made of the right stuff to be a brother in the bond.

I went into the initiation in a state of nerves that might have made the simplest trial difficult for me. Fortunately it worked the opposite way. No matter what the brothers had done I doubt if I should have cried out or betrayed my mortal terror. The only thing I can remember saying is a sudden and involuntary 'What's that?' when the brand of the fraternity's initial letter was put on my arm and I felt the searing of the flesh. That brand remained ever afterwards, faint but quite clear, to remind me of the fantastic episode of which it was a part.

My initiation was short and easy. In five minutes it was all over and I heard A. B.'s kindly voice saying, 'All right, Jim, you can go back to your room.' Trembling with relief, I raced down the corridor to my own place and got into my clothes. Lemmy was already there, dressing. The house was quiet with our door closed, but occasionally the loud laughter of the upper classmen came through from the continuing initiation. Lemmy sat on the edge of the bed and looked glum.

'We can pack a bag,' he said, 'and go to Aurora after everybody is asleep. We'll have to jump out the window. But that is only if you've made up your mind. You've got to make up your mind. If you want to do it, I'll stick.'

We agreed on the plan of escape. We both felt that it would be impossible to face the assembled brethren, headed by A. B., and tell them our decision. They could easily overwhelm us with arguments; and tomorrow, after the formal oaths of allegiance, it would be too late.

It was most unpleasant, after this, to receive congratulations on having passed through the horseplay initiation 'successfully.' I suppose we both felt like the lowest of traitors; I know I did. But the congratulations were over in half an hour; the whole house went to sleep; at some time after midnight, with the precautions and terrors of an elopement, we dropped a bag out the window and jumped after it. From the narrow garden side of the house it was a quick scramble to the street, to a taxicab, to the train. We arrived in the middle of the night at the house of Lemmy's astonished parents in Aurora and remained there for the next two days. It was Lemmy who wrote to the fraternity to explain what we had done.

On the following afternoon A. B. arrived to talk to us. In that painful interview, all the arguments were brought forth in their unrelieved ugliness. Lemmy and A. B. did most of the talking. In the end A. B. said that since our decision was not to be changed, he would accept it, and that it would make no difference to either of us on the *Daily Maroon*. In a state of suicidal gloom, all three of us then returned on the afternoon train to Chicago and to the University.

A. B. seemed to me, then and afterwards, the most admirable person I knew in Chicago. He could not have been more than twenty, but he was invested (in my eyes at least) with the wisdom of the ages. He had apparently founded great hopes for the fraternity on both of us, and our desertion was a blow to him; but he had a sense of justice. He could see that there was something to be said on our side, and having accepted the monstrous situation he made the best of it. During the rest of the year A. B. seemed to be little changed, and in the spring, when the freshmen were weeded out for the next step in the *Daily Maroon's* hierarchy, it was A. B. who made me night editor for the following year. I never took the job; my exploits in the democratic army, followed by three months out of college, kept me from going on in the scheme that was to lead (in A. B.'s plan) to the editorship-in-chief. But anybody who knows the fierce antagonisms and merciless injustice of the fraternity system can see that in treating a renegade so fairly A. B. was showing a character rare among undergraduates. There may have been other fraternity men with enough maturity of mind to rise above the system, but I never knew one.

The next three months were, for Lemmy and me, a taste of thoroughgoing ostracism from the normal 'campus.' In the fraternity system the offense of 'pledge stealing' (i.e., inducing a freshman pledged to one fraternity to break his pledge in order to join another) was rigidly condemned. Consequently nobody in any other fraternity would talk to us. The offense of 'pledge breaking' was regarded as equally heinous by our former brothers in the bond, and not one of them except A. B. ever spoke to us again. It was a curious and painful experience to pass them on the campus, as we did a dozen times every morning. After a few experiences we learned to look the other way, but the effort was not pleasant. We were, for the winter term, 'barbs' (i.e., 'barbarians,' since 'all who are not Greeks are barbarians'). But we were in a far worse position than other 'barbs,' because they, for the most part, cared nothing about the ordinary undergraduates, led their own lives, and had their own friends. We had none.

'Barbarians' included most of the Jewish students, who were a majority of the total enrolled; the 'grinds' and 'Christers' among the Christian students; and a few notably 'queer' ones who were too violently unlike the average to be desirable recruits to the campus life. Glenway Wescott, descending upon the University from a Wisconsin farm, frightened most of his classmates with his waving yellow hair and his floating black cape and his weirdly literary manner of speech. Elizabeth Roberts, austere and diligent, serious with a terrifying concentration, never showed the slightest interest in the frivolities of the ordinary undergraduates. These and other eccentrics came to be almost my only acquaintances in the University during that term of ostracism from the gayeties of the campus. They were (God save us all!) the 'Poetry Club.'

The Poetry Club had been formed early in the winter of my freshman year by professorial advocates of an intellectual life for undergraduates. It had started as a prize competition for student poetry. The prize was the sum of $25. I had sent in two bits of verse, neither of them much good, and had thereafter concealed my temerity from everybody, even from A. B. The prize was awarded to a senior whose name I forget, a medical student; but it was explained in the *Daily Maroon* that this had required two ballots, since on the first it was found that three undergraduates had tied for first place. The three were the aforesaid medical student, Glenway Wescott, and myself. The medical student got the $25 and we got the Poetry Club.

We used to meet solemnly in little padded drawing rooms in Ida Noyes Hall and discuss the productions of our colleagues. Glenway always had a sheaf of immortal poetry somewhere about him, which he was ready to read out at the drop of a hat. His poetry was exceedingly 'modern,' without rhyme or meter or capital letters or punctuation, and very often (to my untutored ear) without sense either. But I was conscious enough of my shortcomings to realize that this was probably my fault, not his; and I sat through many a long reading of which I could make neither head nor tail. His modern verse was eclipsed in modernity and incomprehensibility by that of a senior who was president of the Poetry Club. Indeed, the whole club was excessively modern, and it would have taken more courage than I possessed to affront its contemporary ears with such a deplorable throwback as a sonnet. And since, at that time, I was writing sonnets by the dozen, my contribution to the poetic feast was nil.

We used to enjoy, in our first year, a flattering amount of attention from literary personages not in the University. We were thought, for some reason, to be 'promising,' and consequently Miss Harriet Monroe, Mr. Carl Sandburg, and other notables from the Chicago *cénacle*, condescended to visit us and read us their own verse. Thus I formed the belief that all poets loved reading aloud and traveled about with reams of unpublished poetry in their pockets.

The solemnity of our gatherings at the Poetry Club would have stunned T. S. Eliot himself. It was sometimes difficult for me to keep from snickering, particularly when the young poets were carried away by the excitement of reading their own productions. More than once the president had to reprove me for undue levity in comment. No doubt the whole thing was funny, but not perhaps so uproariously funny as it seemed to me at seventeen. The whole fraternity-and-campus-collegiate side of me crinkled with hostile, unreasoning laughter at the sight of Glenway declaiming his impassioned verses, his yellow mane thrown back and his childish face uplifted. His later development into a sincere and sensitive artist would have seemed incredible to me then, if anybody had been so rash as to predict it.

The barbarians, the grinds, and the highbrows learned much more than I did at the University. Scornful of the 'campus life' that preoccupied the rest of us, they grew into intellectual maturity more rapidly than their fellows, and their interest in general ideas was aroused before most of us knew what an idea was. They knew nothing of the fraternities or clubs, went to no 'parties,' and ignored the existence of football. It might have been a good thing if I had remained one of them. But I was afflicted by a dichotomy that has never left me: I could not avoid trying to make the best of two worlds. The term of ostracism to which Lemmy and I had been submitted by interfraternity rules came to an end in the spring, and I soon forgot all about the Poetry Club in the excitement of readmission to the other, the average, world of the undergraduates.

No freshman who had broken his pledge to one fraternity could be 'rushed' for another for three months. But when the period of suspension ended, at Easter, a change came over the complexion of things. People who had avoided me like the plague all through the winter suddenly started asking me to lunch. In two or three weeks after the ending of the ban I had been pledged again to another fraternity—this time to a Gentile one, which I believe had been exceedingly 'good' and was afterwards 'good' again. At the precise moment of my admission it was not one of the most brilliant of the undergraduate houses, but it did contain two or three freshmen who were to be among my best and most lasting friends in Chicago. Lemmy—who was off to the wars that summer—joined me in it the following year.

But I was never what is called a 'good fraternity man.' After the bizarre introduction I had had to the system, it was impossible for me to take it with the literal seriousness it required of its adherents. The adolescent sentimentality that was supposed to be lavished upon the fraternity and the brothers in the bond had been pretty well burned out by my unorthodox experience. It was hard to get up enthusiasm for songs, rituals, and ceremonies when I knew they were being gone through in a couple of dozen other fraternity houses at the same time and by almost exactly the same people. Uniformity—the true uniformity of the good American undergraduate, who talked the same language and wore the same clothes and did exactly the same things as every other undergraduate—was not really accessible to me. It fascinated me for a long time, and I attempted for two years to achieve it; but the effort was useless and soon began to appear uninteresting as well. After about a year in the house (the new house) I moved away from it, to a college hall, and for the rest of my time in the University I lived alone, like a 'barb,' with the single difference that I did have a fraternity to go to when I pleased. The brothers did not like this attitude and said so more than once, but by the time I had been two years in the college I knew that the heavens would not fall if I went my own way, and their protests did not disturb me.

Christmas of 1920 was my last in the University. My mother was very ill; early in January, 1921, she died. The disaster would probably have made college life unbearable in any case, but there was also the question of money. There had been little enough before; there was none now. January passed in unrelieved gloom. I returned to Chicago lonely and helpless. There was a job for me (thanks to a friend) as a reporter on the Chicago *Daily News*, but I must have been phenomenally stupid at it, for I lasted only two or three weeks. When I received my congé I did, almost without thinking, something that had probably been floating about in the undergrowth of my mind for weeks or months. I walked out of the *Daily News* office, down to the old Dearborn Street station, and onto a train for New York—without luggage and with very little money. For hour after hour I sat at a train window and stared out through tears and dirt. It was a fairly typical departure, to be worked out during the next ten years into a system of going away. *Fuir, là-bas fuir*, could serve as a kind of epigraph for my youth, for it was spent in flight.

I was not to see Chicago again except on two short visits years later, in a world altogether different from that of the University. Those brief visits were sufficient to show me, in retrospect, how narrow my experience had been. For example, there were in Chicago some of the finest collections of modern pictures in the world: I never saw one of them while I was in the University. The Chicago Symphony Orchestra had a long season of concerts and was one of the best ensembles to be found in the United States: but the only concerts I heard in college were a few of the few (four or five a year) given in the University chapel. There were buildings, clubs, interiors, examples of modern art and architecture, and a thousand varieties of life to be seen in the lusty, sprawling, vulgar and vigorous town: I had seen only one. For the whole of my three years and a half beside Lake Michigan I was walled up in a world self-contained, self-governing and self-sufficient, the world of the college undergraduates. Ten years later I could not even remember my way about Chicago, and had to walk all the way to the lake front every time I wanted to distinguish north from south. So much for the people who believed that a university could not lead its own life in a great city! Youth, at least my variety of ignorant youth, built its own walls very high, and no city was powerful enough to batter them down.

Within those walls what, after all, had I learned? What did I take away from the pseudo-Gothic sanctuary of my pseudo-education? Not much. I had some vague idea of history and philosophy, a bowing acquaintance with English and French literature. I had learned a good deal about snobbery, cruelty, prejudice, injustice and stupidity. I had acquired half a dozen friends—perhaps. I had learned how to dance the fox trot.

It is stupefying to remember how little else I carried from

Chicago with me. I spent the next ten years learning the course of events in the world from 1917 to 1921, approaching them as one approaches the course of events in the Renaissance or the Middle Ages. I was a freshman when the Bolshevik Revolution took place, and I am certain that I did not even read the accounts of it that appeared in the Chicago newspapers. The Treaty of Versailles, the defeat and collapse of Woodrow Wilson, the crash of monarchies all through Europe, the revolution in Turkey and the whole bestirring of assorted nationalisms, Wilson's legacy to the world, were duly recorded in history while I went to class dances and wrote songs for Blackfriars. The bourgeois system insulated all its children as much as possible from a knowledge of the processes of human development, and in my case it succeeded admirably in its purpose. Few Hottentots or South Sea Islanders could be less prepared for life in the great world than I was at twenty-one. As I sat in that filthy day coach on the train to New York (filthy with a concentrated filth known only to American day coaches) I was the least respectable of passengers: my ticket went one way only, and I had no baggage of any kind.

II

Journalism

My introduction to the larger world outside the University was a baptism by total immersion, and in icy water at that. One day I was still thinking (when I thought at all) about books and characters. The next day I was the familiar friend of murderesses, the apologist of divorcées, a professional observer at the peep-show of misery: a reporter for the New York *Daily News*.

That paper, afterwards the largest and richest in the United States, was a struggling novice in its field, and was not above hiring a young reporter whose experience had almost all been obtained on a college newspaper. The *Daily News* was frankly interested in scandal above everything. As all good scandals revolved in some way about a lady, and as scandalous ladies were supposed to be more hospitable to the youth of the opposite sex than to other possible ambassadors, my job for the next few months consisted in dancing attendance on the heroines of *causes célèbres*. I approached them with respect: they were romantic heroines, they were Anna Karénina, Emma Bovary, Judith, Floria Tosca. But the moment they began to speak they dispelled such illusions, and it was sometimes difficult to keep up enough enthusiasm about their drab misdeeds to give their stories validity. I learned the formulas of the trade without delay, and in spite of my ignorance of New York, its people, and human behaviour in general, I had enough natural adaptability to shed the feeling of strangeness after the first week or two. New York, the most various and comprehensive of American cities, could not help arousing all the curiosities of inexhaustible youth: I sat at the feet of various 'radicals' in the old Liberal Club in Greenwich Village, listened to talk about Lenin and Trotzky, got drunk in small bars with men from my newspaper and other newspapers, went to concerts and the play, walked in the Park or surveyed existence from the top of a Fifth Avenue bus, as ardent a newcomer to the spectacle as any fledgling of the past. I had an immense amount of innocence to lose, and with the best will in the world I could not lose it quickly enough: the more I found out the more there seemed to be to find out. Becoming, for the first time, aware of a wide range of possibilities—sexual freedom; self-indulgence in such matters as drink; the pleasures of talk, particularly of political discussion; the pleasures of personal influence or expression, so essential to a developing confidence—all hitherto obscured or unknown, I grew, in the less measurable regions, inches every day. In the single possibility to which I have given the name 'political discussion,' the readiness to defend a point of view in matters of public concern, I discovered unsuspected resources. My interest here outran my information, and when I tried to make up the defects I felt in any such talk with older people than myself, I fell upon the astounding tale of the past few years, the years through which I had lived sealed up behind the walls of the University: the years of the war, of the Russian Revolution, of the Treaty of Versailles. In talk with people who had actually been present at the Russian Revolution (Louise Bryant, Albert Williams) or at the making of the Versailles treaty, these events, once as remote to me as if they had taken place five hundred years before and on another planet, came to have a meaning at least as immediate as that of my latest interview with the newest divorcée or murderess. They were soon to acquire more—much more.

2

I left New York for Paris in the spring of 1922. I had had almost a year of New York, enough to make that convenient metropolis the 'permanent residence' inscribed on a thousand hotel slips and steamship tickets for the next decade—enough, even, to make an occasional return there pass as a kind of homecoming. But the new curiosities aroused since I had left the University pushed me on towards Europe, and when I came into possession of enough money to be off, I went on my way. I think

I knew, even then, that it would be a long way, leading through regions not yet imagined; and the noisy departure from New York, the immense novelty of the sea, the Frenchness of the French boat—for, to make the jump quicker, I had taken a French boat—combined with my own mounting excitement to make the event seem final, overwhelmingly important: it was like the voyage of the *Santa Maria* in reverse.

Paris could never be a disappointment to anybody who approached it as eagerly as I did. The peculiarity of the place was that everybody felt at home there at once. It preëxisted in the memory, somehow, so that it began by being familiar even to those who had never seen it before: it was a *patrie* of the imagination. I did nothing for days but dawdle, look at people in the streets, look at pictures in the museums, go to theatres and sit in cafés. Then, through the kind offices of a fellow passenger, I found my place for the summer: a retreat in northern France where I remained for three months without hearing, speaking or reading a word of English. I was a paying guest at the most modest of rates, the country was smiling and peaceful, the house had no equal for feather beds and good cooking, and I had unlimited time for writing a bad novel in the intervals when I was not altogether drowned in the French language. My hosts were Papa and Maman, a pair of *petits bourgeois* who had once been merchants in the Quartier du Temple, and had now returned to the life of their peasant ancestors. After I had been an inmate of the comfortable old house for a week or two I learned, by pure accident, that Papa and Maman had lived together for forty years without ever going through a ceremony of marriage.

At the time I found this fact shocking beyond description. That Papa and Maman, those two elderly shopkeepers with the manners and ideas of peasants, should have lived in the state called 'sin' for forty years was something outside my faculty of comprehension. I cannot now fix upon the most shocking element: whether it was that they were old and outwardly so respectable; whether it was the vista of those forty years; or whether it was simply that I thought nobody had a right to live in 'sin' except myself. The conclusion, upon information and belief, that the unhallowed state of their union was due to Papa's politico-religious philosophy ('Papa est très-laïque!') was as puzzling as the original conundrum, and it was weeks before I had explored the mysterious articulation of Papa's ideas with his mode of life.

I had already found out that Papa was a true son of the French Revolution, with a deep hatred of priests, noblemen, the upper classes in general, the professional politicians, the diplomats and the tax collectors of the Third Republic. His bitter dislike for constituted authority was an old story: almost on the first occasion I talked to him I had found out that he was a *sans-culotte*. But it had never previously been shown to me that anybody could put into practise, in the ordinary arrangements of life, such a system of ideas. I devoted myself whenever possible to Papa, to find out how his theory and action were combined. It proved an interesting inquiry. For instance, Papa did not believe in war and said so with complete frankness. If he had been a young man he might have fought in the war anyway, as Frenchmen did; but he was already past middle age when the Germans marched into Amiens. He was there at the time—had retired there after he sold his shop in Paris. For a great part of the war he had lived under German occupation. He told me that he had seen nothing of 'atrocities' and did not believe they had existed, although he agreed that anything was possible in war time. The German soldiers had his complete respect and even a sort of admiration, based upon their size and their discipline.

'C'tait de grands gaillards,' he puffed away through his large, bristling moustaches, 'magnifiques! Et marchaient, tictac!'

The old man swung his arms and clicked his tongue to indicate the precision with which the German troops had marched into the cathedral town.

Papa, like all of his variety of Frenchmen, the true descendants of the Revolution, had an exaggerated respect for reason. The highest praise he could award anybody was to say he was *raisonnable*. Where he got his ideas I never determined. Certainly they did not come from books, for Papa never read anything but bits of the newspaper. I supposed that the French proletariat and *petite bourgeoisie* must have been saturated with such ideas all through the nineteenth century, and Papa must have learned them in his childhood, breathed them in with the air of Paris. For more than four years he had had the sound of the guns in his ears morning, noon, and night. He had seen some appalling things. But through it all he seemed to have kept his head, maintained his belief in reason, peace, and hard work. An industrious, ignorant, parsimonious old fellow, unworthy of the attention of the great men in Downing Street and the Quai d'Orsay, he had more common sense than many of his betters.

'Voyez-vous, monsieur,' he would say, 'la guerre, c'est pour emmerder le monde.'

Maman was less categorical about these matters. She agreed that war was a terrible thing, but she was inclined to believe it an ineluctable curse, like disease and death. At the same time she was secretly convinced that it took place as the result of nefarious conspiracies on the part of evil foreigners against France. She did not attempt to reconcile her two opposing faiths and refused, indeed, to see anything illogical in them.

'Madame,' I would say, 'if the war was a result of conspiracy— that is, if somebody plotted it, planned it—then it cannot have been inevitable. Don't you see? Either it happens like an earthquake, and nobody can do anything about it; or it happens like crime, is caused by human beings, and something can be done. It can't be both things at once.'

'Oh, là, là!' Maman would say. 'You talk so much! I don't understand about such things. But I have seen the villages burned down, not a stick left standing, the boys blown into pieces, and the Germans did it. They have always done it. There's nothing to be said; there'll always be war. Thank God I have no son.'

That was Maman's policy for all eternity—*y aura toujours la guerre*. Although she might have been looked upon as a good-natured simpleton who had never been outside her shop until she retired to her garden, it was curious to observe how her opinions resembled those of the prime ministers and dictators and senators, the noble lords and gentlemen, who, according to the European press, made the policies of nations. She was one kind of France, just as Papa was another.

Which, precisely, was the reason why they had never been married. To Maman marriage was a sacrament, a religious rite;

the civil ceremony was of no account whatever. Papa, who in all probability would have yielded without much argument to the suggestion of a civil marriage, was made speechless with rage at any hint of church or priest. Sometimes I came upon Maman suddenly and found her eyes red; I never knew whether she had been weeping about her dead children, the Church, Papa's incorrigible ideas, or the general melancholy confusion of existence. On such occasions she would smile brightly and ask what I wanted for dinner.

I liked Papa, Maman, their house and their food, but towards the end of the summer the attractions of the simple life grew stale, and I began to long for some view of a more peopled world. I had learned a good deal about French colloquial speech and had written the greater part of a dreadful novel that was afterwards (fortunately) lost: it had been, in these respects, a good summer. I had to have a job, but before taking up the task of finding it, I determined to spend my last money and remaining freedom on a visit to Italy—and, to begin with, Venice. I reached the incredible place one malarial day in August and made a discovery: the gondolier who received me at the railway station did not understand a word of my Italian. This was partly, as was to be shown later, his fault, but it was also partly mine, and I resolved to find a cheap place in Venice for the longest time allowed by my stock of money. Here I would learn, if I could, how to speak an easy enough version of the language of Dante to make myself understood by anybody.

I soon found the place, thanks to L'Agenzia Cook. In an old palace on the little *rio* beside the Ducal Palace, a hundred yards down from the Bridge of Sighs, there lived a gentleman who was willing to give me a vast vaulted chamber, service, three meals a day and wine, for a sum that seemed (even to me) derisory. It took me a week or two to find out the reason for such unparalleled kindness. My landlord, the Baron X, was a professional gambler. With his thin, complaining wife, the Baronessa, he ran a lively little gambling hell in his palace, and they required an American or English paying guest to make the place look respectable. I was adjudged decent enough in appearance to suit their purposes, and they made the charge small in order to be sure of me.

Respectable or not, I took the keenest interest in the Baron's business: professed to be much taken with gambling of all sorts; became a friend of the Baronessa and of her friends, the visiting Genoese. Unfortunately pickings were scant that year in the Baron's useful profession, and there were not many 'parties' at the palazzo. I attended two or three of them and found them dismal affairs, by no means up to my expectation. In the two small rooms behind the ballroom of the palace half-a-dozen gloomy Italians gathered to play baccarat. There was a roulette wheel, but it was not much favoured. Even at baccarat the customers were doubtful of the croupier and watched the cards narrowly. I never played at all. There was something altogether too shady about my amiable landlord to encourage confidence in his enterprises. And to do him justice, he never asked me to play. 'C'est bête,' he always said.

The splendours of Venice I had to enjoy alone. The Baron and Baronessa looked blank at the slightest suggestion of anything to do with art or architecture. Apart from the weather, there was no element in the spectacle of the city that appealed to them. If they asked me at lunch or dinner how I had spent the day, and I gave them an account of long hours spent in churches and museums, they sighed, said, 'Magari!' and spoke of something else. Once I persuaded the Baron to go with me to the Accademia; I wondered how that array of the glories of Venice would strike his twinkling, dishonest eyes. He was a good-natured fellow; since the foolish American wanted to look at pictures, he would humour the poor lad. The first picture to be seen on entering the Accademia at that time was the huge Titian of the Assumption (afterwards restored to the Church of the Frari, where it belonged).

'Magari!' said the Baron. 'Que c'est grand!'

He advanced towards the painting, measuring it with his eyes; walked from side to side, nodding his head.

'A fine picture,' he said at last. 'Who painted it?'

'Tiziano.'

'Tiziano? Tiziano? Ah, sì, sì, Tiziano.'

One of the beauties of the long gallery was the St. George of Mantegna. The Baron stopped in front of it, fixed it with a calculating eye.

'Now that,' he said, 'is a small picture. How much money do you suppose it is worth?'

'I don't know, Baron. It couldn't be sold anyway. There's a law against selling old pictures out of Italy. If it could be exported it would bring five or six million lire, easily.'

'Madonna! Five million lire. Santa mia Madonna! You must be joking.'

'No, Baron. It is a great picture. American millionaires pay such prices for pictures not half so good. Besides, it is by Mantegna. There are not many.'

'Cor-r-rpo di Cor-r-r-rpo di Cor-r-r-r-rpo! Five million lire.'

He walked back and forth in front of the little picture, looking at it first on one side and then on the other. Presently he returned to me, cocked his head on one side and said:

'It would not be difficult to steal a little picture like that, now, would it? There is not a living soul in this room but us. What would prevent my taking that—supposing I had an overcoat to conceal it? First it would be necessary to have something else, a copy, perhaps, to hang there instead, when nobody is looking——'

'Please, Baron,' I said, alarmed, 'don't get such an idea into your head. You wouldn't get ten feet beyond the Accademia Bridge with it. And if you did, you could never sell it without being caught. It's a very famous picture. You'd spend the rest of your life in jail.'

He broke into a shout of laughter.

'O-ho-ho!' he bellowed. 'You believe I am going to do it? O-ho-ho! *Che scherzo!*'

Then he grew quiet, looked at the picture again and sighed.

'Mind you,' he said, 'I don't for a minute think that picture is worth five million lire. Some other picture, perhaps, but not that one. Otherwise somebody would have stolen it long ago.'

As the weeks passed and my exploration of the richly unscrupulous character of my landlord continued, I made acquaintance with some of the details of his business. The first thing he did in any city was to pay a large sum to the local Fascio. The Fascisti were then little more than a national organization of hoodlums. I knew nothing about them beyond the facts that they wore black shirts, sang loudly off key, and obeyed the orders of an ex-Socialist politician named Mussolini. Every town had its Fascio, originally a sort of club of ex-soldiers, men who had fought in the war. The Fascio of Venice (like other Fascii) made a practise of smashing windows, beating up old men, and creating disturbances in the street. It was this strange new form of banditry that the Baron regarded as more important than police or municipalities.

'But why in the world should you pay money to the Fascisti?' I asked. 'What have they got to do with you?'

'They have everything to do with everything,' said the Baron. 'If I did not pay my two thousand lire every month to the Fascio di Venezia my windows would be smashed, my furniture broken up, and my roulette and baccarat tables thrown into the canal.'

'Who are these Fascisti, anyway? What right have they got to interfere?'

'All the young men who have nothing else to do are Fascisti,' said the Baron. 'There are thousands of them in every city. They think nothing of beating people up, burning their houses, killing them, if necessary. They have some kind of idea about the government, too—I don't quite know what it is. But one thing I do know: they get money from every gambling house and brothel and cabaret and bar in the country. I've paid them a lot in the past two years.'

I was diverted from my interest in the Baron's profession by this new discovery—that a band of young men in black shirts terrorized the country.

'It sounds like a form of the Ku-Klux Klan,' I said. 'That was a thing they had in America years ago. They used to murder Negroes, and they were never punished. Do the Fascisti carry arms?'

'Yes,' said the Baron. 'In Milan they have killed many people. They don't like Socialists, so they kill them. That is their own affair, but I wish they would leave me alone. *Ahimè!* Everybody is afraid of the Fascisti; the police and the magistrates are just as afraid of them as I am. But Venice is better than Milan. They don't kill people here, much. Sometimes they give them castor oil to drink. It is not pleasant, castor oil. Madonna! I pay them my two thousand lire promptly on the first of every month, I can tell you.'

The Fascisti became interesting to me after the Baron had told the story of his two thousand lire. They presented, on the whole, an unprepossessing appearance in those days. They were almost all boys, many of them dirty, ill-grown and without discipline or soldierly bearing. They were cocky and quarrelsome to the highest degree, loud of voice and eager for trouble. To see them hustling some unfortunate citizen who had displeased them out of the Piazza San Marco was not a pleasant sight. They were approaching the crisis of their existence, encouraged into hysteria by the appeals of their leaders; the March on Rome was near. Little as I knew then about their leader or his ideas, there was something ominous about a rabble army existing so boldly outside the law, terrifying the magistrates and possessing the streets. I had an idea that one fine day they would have to be suppressed by a strong government, and the suppression would not be pretty. That they would themselves—these half-grown boys from the gutters of Milan and Turin and Venice—suppress the government and the constitution, suspend the laws and abolish every principle of the democratic system, never occurred to me. I left Venice without a premonition of that not inconsiderable event, the Fascist Revolution.

3

The *tramontana* had begun to blow down upon us, and the shutters rattled sadly in the autumn air. Venice suddenly began to seem dead; a ghost; a lovely shell out of the dim past; no place for a restless young American. It is an effect that exquisite city produces on most people sooner or later. It came over me one day when I had been to the Palazzo Labia to look at the Tiepolo frescoes. It was a long jaunt from the Palazzo Labia to the Baron's house, but instead of taking the steamboat I got into a gondola and came back through the Grand Canal. The gondolier was old and not too efficient. We dawdled along past the Cà d'Oro, the Fondaco dei Tedeschi, the Palazzo Grimani, and I had plenty of time to think about the varieties of life that had been native to the place. The Palazzo Grimani, in particular—those great Renaissance windows, so gloomy now, once so filled with light—set me to squirming with discomfort at the thought of death. I was twenty-two. When I got home I told the Baron I was leaving at once. Until he asked me, I had not decided where to go, but to give an air of definition to the project I answered, 'Monte Carlo.' It was perhaps the only place the Baron would have allowed me to go to without much protest. His eyes glistened. He began to gesture and explain. He too had a system whereby anybody could get rich at the roulette tables.

I went to Monte Carlo, stayed three or four days and conscientiously experimented with the Baron's system and the system of the Baronessa's father. Neither proved to be a certain key to wealth. One evening I found myself with almost no money left. The Casino began to seem hideous to me: I had hardly noticed it before. I walked about the town and observed for the first time what a stage setting it was, how completely it had been carried out as the fulfilment of a cocotte's dream. That evening I took the train to Rome. It was my introduction to the noblest of all the cities, to the old pink walls and crumbling yellow stones, fountains and church bells and contemplative hills, which were for years afterwards to draw me back to Rome. On this occasion I stayed for about ten days, waiting for my money from America, and doing nothing but walk and stare and listen.

When the money did come I took the first train to Paris. On the night I left Rome the young men in black shirts were thronging to the railway station, singing and shouting, with banners; they were on their way to the Fascist Congress at Naples. In a week's time they would be on their way back again, moved by a collective fever, marching on Rome: the *Giovinezza* of 1922, which I had so inadequately understood or appreciated. Before I reached Paris they had already shown unmistakable signs of their intention, and I read in the newspapers at the Gare de Lyon, with surprise and unbelief, that these noisy children in their fancy dress claimed the right to control the powers of the state.

I had gone to Paris to get a job. Even if this had not been economically necessary I should probably have done it just the same, for I had no talent for leisure and wanted something definite—tasks with a beginning and an end—to fill the hours.

The only kind of work I knew anything about, or had ever been able to perform even half well, was journalism, and Paris was the centre of American journalism in Europe. When I reached Paris one day in that cold, wet October, I went to the office of the Chicago *Tribune*—drawn there by the notion that anything connected with Chicago must be vaguely all right for me—and was received by a laconic, keen-eyed, wooden-faced man who talked out of the corner of his mouth: Mr Henry Wales. By what method he arrived at his conclusions I never knew; there must have been dozens of stray newspaper men drifting into that office every week, some of them far more experienced than I was; I had no special qualification to offer, except an acquaintance with certain foreign languages. But whatever the reasons, he determined to take me on, at first as a sort of general handy-man, to be used either in his own office or in the office of the European Edition of the *Tribune*, printed in Paris; and afterwards as his assistant. Thus, in a click of time, I became what was called a 'foreign correspondent'—a rôle I was to fill, in the service of that vigorous newspaper, for the next three years.

4

My suitability for the job of foreign correspondent—as distinguished from my specific qualifications, which were dubious —must have been considerable. Little though I had known about the affairs of the world during my fox-trotting undergraduate days, in New York I had rapidly acquired a wider interest; and now, after five or six months in France and Italy, much reading of the political press in three languages, and that sharper interest in events which comes of an acquaintance with their physical scene, I was prepared (in interest and self-confidence, at least) to deal with the largest doings of the great, their words and deeds and gestures, as a journalist should—that is, without unduly yielding to their persuasions, believing in their beliefs, or crediting their enthusiasms. M. Poincaré awed me at first, it is true, as any old man of immense power and prestige must awe an insignificant youth of twenty-two; but this particular kind of awe evaporated once its instrument was removed, and when I sat down at the typewriter, an instrument even colder and more impersonal than M. Poincaré, I was already, at the outset of my experience in the trade, a 'correspondent': that is, I was able to treat M. Poincaré exactly as I might have treated any other element in the news of the day, a beggar who had been enriched by an eccentric million-aire, a film star in a motor accident, or a prize fighter who was going to America. This professional indifference to the material of journalism did not endure. As months and years passed, as I acquired a steadier, more intimate acquaintance with the struggles going on under the surface of smooth black print on white paper, the craft itself (i.e., the art of putting those struggles into the smooth-running print) lost its fascination, political interest deepened to political passion, and I came in time to 'take sides' and have opinions, feel them as deeply and express them as violently as any amateur. In so doing I only reversed the familiar procedure by which a good many of my colleagues, having begun with beliefs and enthusiasms, ended in callous indifference towards all human effort.

My job was not easy: I had to be 'on duty' from noon until two or three o'clock the next morning, an unhuman *corvée* made tolerable by the fact that for some of these hours there was little or nothing to do; but the extension of what might be called public preoccupations—politics and journalism—through the whole waking time of an inexperienced young man drove out private interests entirely, so that such figures as M. Poincaré became more consistently real to me, day in and day out, than most of my transient colleagues on the Chicago *Tribune* or my acquaintances in the bars and cafés of Paris. A good many newspaper men of the time and place could have been said to be without private lives, or to treat their private lives with indifference—to marry and be-get absent-mindedly, see their wives sometimes once a week, and live, in all the keener hours of their existence, in the 'office,' a place taken to comprise most of the other offices, bars, cafés and meeting places of the press and politicians; and this absorption in work was especially uncompromising with me, to whom it was all new and upon whom, for a long time, it exercised a fascination without precedent. I fell into political journalism as a water spaniel falls into a river, and was quickly so taken up with the new element that the days before I had made its acquaintance seemed to me dry, cramped and distant.

It was, even in the beginning, a political job. In objective fact I was an ignorant but active youth of twenty-two, earning a minuscular salary, living in a small and dirty hotel behind the offices of the Chicago *Tribune* in the Rue Lamartine; but such circumstances did not keep me from dealing magisterially with the policies and leaders of nations as they were shown in events. The power of the press, in one important aspect, was this: that its anonymity enabled such fragments of humanity as myself to exert, in spite of youth, poverty or obscurity, a kind of suffrage, at least in opinion, so that the course of events was never wholly regulated by the desires or machinations of the powerful. In the single case of M. Poincaré, the first politician I ever saw at close range, it was unquestionably people like myself who brought him to grief: he lost the friendly opinion of the world because he lost the respect of its press, and he lost our respect because we saw, with the utmost sickening clearness, week after week for two solid years, how incapable that nervous little provincial lawyer was of rising above the parochial hatreds of his native village.

I started working for the Chicago *Tribune* towards the end of 1922. The conferences of Washington, Cannes and Genoa were over; Cannes had ruined Briand for a good four years or more; Poincaré was now President of the Council in France, bent upon enforcing the letter of the Treaty of Versailles and (in such respects as the Rhineland policy) determined, actually, to go beyond it and cripple Germany forever if it could be done. The Turks had swept the Greeks from Asia Minor, incidentally sweeping Mr Lloyd George from office at the same time. Before I had been many weeks in the service of the newspaper Poincaré sent French troops into the Ruhr, and for the first two years of my experience the questions of the Ruhr, the Rhineland, and reparations, took precedence of all others in the European political struggle. The most positive single element in the struggle was the personality of M. Poincaré, and he came to dominate not only the political world in which he consciously figured, but also the minds and time of such people as myself, of whose very existence—except in the mass—he was unaware. I worked twelve or fourteen hours a day, and almost the whole of my work had to do, somehow or other, with M. Poincaré—his speeches, his doings, his decisions, his journeys and his policies. Small wonder that the squeaky little man became the Colossus of my world. I was to see scores of politicians afterwards, but nothing could obliterate the impression made in the first months of my novitiate by M. Poincaré.

He used to receive the foreign press on Monday evenings at six o'clock. On the occasions when I attended the procedure was invariable. The liveried attendants of the Foreign Office ushered us into a salon arranged like a classroom, with rows of chairs for the correspondents and a big desk at one end for the President of the Council. At exactly six o'clock, not a moment before or after, the doors of the room opened and M. Poincaré trotted in. Under his arm there was the inevitable portfolio full of papers. I never saw him without a portfolio under his arm; I used to wonder if it grew there, like a dorsal fin. A precise, pedantic little man with a high-pitched nasal voice, painfully neat clothes, a neat little walk and a trim pointed beard, he took his place, opened his portfolio and began the séance.

The questions were chiefly about the Ruhr. How long did France intend to occupy the Ruhr territory? Under what conditions would it be evacuated? What measures would be taken if the 'passive resistance' of the inhabitants continued indefinitely? These and a hundred similar questions were the staple material of the conferences. And to every question M. Poincaré had the same sort of precise, positive, but meaningless answer. To many questions he replied exactly this:

'Nous évacuerons la Ruhr au fur et à mesure des paiements de l'Allemagne.'

That phrase 'au fur et à mesure' was his shibboleth. He used it throughout his public speeches and in his private interviews. It came to have a sacred significance to him, as a declaration of faith from which he would not be budged. It was easy for us to demonstrate to our own and everybody else's satisfaction that the statement was nonsense. It was not militarily possible to equate a definite physical action in space (evacuating the Ruhr) with the bookkeeping transactions involved in reparations: you could not evacuate a valley 'au fur et à mesure': you either got in or you got out. But the magic phrase was M. Poincaré's defense against the world. His were always academic phrases. Even in those 'confidential' interviews at the Quai d'Orsay, when all the correspondents were pledged not to quote his words, he spoke a high-flown French, full of subjunctives, liaisons and involved juristic expressions. Grammatically, his language was as funny as the language of the love scenes in *La Dame aux Camélias*, in which Armand and his Marguerite address each other in formal sentences of the *si vous eussiez* variety. It was monstrous to think that this little man, whose intellectual resources were hardly more than a combination of prejudice and syntax, disposed of the destinies of many millions of people.

M. Poincaré was not only the first politician I ever observed at close range; he was also the least imposing, the least suited to his historic rôle. He had no charm of any sort, no ease of manner, little dignity; his substitute for it was a sort of stiff-necked provincial didacticism. Compared to any other political leader of the same rank known to me afterwards—Briand, MacDonald, Stresemann, Mussolini—he seemed harsh, little-minded and inhuman. I never heard him make a generous statement in political matters and did not believe he was capable of such a thing. From hearing and seeing him repeatedly throughout the momentous two years I reached the conclusion that he hated the Germans as a Jersey farmer hates a rattlesnake. In his sharp, piggish eyes and his piercing voice there came a suggestion of terror and loathing whenever he had occasion to use the words *Allemagne* and *Allemand*. He was obliged to defend his policy frequently in the Chamber, and he always seemed to me, when the Germans were in question, to be near hysteria. His voice would rise to a shriek, he would shake documents aloft in his fist, and his admirers on the right would break into loud applause. On other subjects he was exact and dictatorial. He came from Lorraine; the war had cost him dear; and he was unable to take a large view of any situation involving the Germans. He used to go about on Sundays dedicating soldiers' monuments in various villages, and in those melancholy hamlets, where sometimes every able-bodied man had been killed in the war, he did his best to keep the war hatreds alive. These speeches (which the Germans called *Dorfprediger*, village sermons) came nearly every Sunday; for months it was my duty to translate them and send them off to America; and I always considered the money spent in cabling them to be a sad loss. One model speech, sent over by mail, would have done for them all. I felt that I could have written M. Poincaré's village sermons, the 'au fur et à mesure' speeches, blindfolded. He never varied his ideas, seldom his expressions; for his whole term in 1922–24 he went on stubbornly verbigerating in the face of history. But, like anybody who resists the irresistible, he was swept away, and when he came back to power for the last time two years later the structure of 'sanctions' and 'gages,' the old reparations schedules, the impossible system he had attempted so fanatically to enforce, had gone forever.

To be introduced to politics—or at least to politicians, 'statesmen'—by M. Poincaré was to see all the unloveliest side of patriotic effort at once. True, M. Poincaré was honest as few politicians have ever been honest; he was at times almost sincere. He was amazingly industrious, capable of any number of hours or weeks of work, indefatigable of tongue and pen. Later on, when he 'saved the franc' in 1926, these qualities were of great use to French capitalism. But when I first beheld him—wondering, with all the astonishment of reluctant youth, if other 'statesmen' were as stupid and petty as this—he was a shocking example of the results of unbridled patriotism on an average bourgeois mind. Deformed, crippled and cramped by patriotic passion, he could not see straight in any question involving the immediate interests of his own country (as they were conceived to be under the patriotico-national-capitalist dispensation) or the most ordinary rights of that eternal enemy Germany. If I lived to be a thousand I could never forget the sound of his maniac shriek as he pronounced the word *Allemagne*. The whole curse of Europe was in it; and as I grew familiar with the behaviour and ideas of M. Poincaré I could see that the implacability of his hatred, the venom of his curse, was his principal—indeed, almost his only—qualification for his destiny.

Few men can have filled so great a place in human affairs with so little.

5

The death of Mme Sarah Bernhardt led to my only glimpse of Poincaré's enemy Clemenceau. Bernhardt died in the spring of 1923, giving the Parisian press and public a welcome opportunity for the display of funebrious sentiment, with street parades and tooting of trumpets, black ostrich feathers and noisy weeping. I was so carried away by the movement and trappings of grief that I wrote a rare piece of maudlin for my newspaper about the vanished divinity, and my employer, remarking that 'This oughta bring tears from a turnip,' ordered me to sign my name to it. My name was expressed in initials: J.V. Initials, it seemed, were no good for a newspaper signature, and I was ordered to use the second name, Vincent. Thus, without an effort of will on my own part, I acquired a name like a mask and have worried along behind it ever since.

Clemenceau was Bernhardt's friend, and although he had been living in retirement for months and notoriously disliked saying anything to the press, I was sent out to his house in the Rue Franklin to see him. I arrived just as M. le Président was sitting down to his early dinner. After ten or fifteen minutes, during which I waited in a stuffy little salon and looked at the furniture, the door of the cubicle opened and an old man in a skullcap catapulted in.

The effect given was that of immense energy—an effect for which he had doubtless worked many years, and achieved as the result of unwearied performance in the same rôle. He moved with a combination of bounce and drive that brought one automatically to attention. His eyes were beady, his whole expression concentrated and wary, as if both body and mind were held ever ready to spring. His skin was a deep yellow in colour, and in his silk skullcap and black velvet jacket he looked like a particularly active old Chinaman. His brisk voice was businesslike, slightly impatient, but not at all unfriendly. In his hand he carried his napkin, so as to remind me that he had left his dinner between dishes.

'Well, well, young man,' he said (in English), 'what can I do for you? You know perfectly well that I don't give interviews.'

'I've been sent to ask you for some expression about the death of Mme Sarah Bernhardt,' I said. 'Anything you want to say, Mr President, is of interest in America.'

'You think so, do you?' His yellow face was twisted in a grimace that might have passed for a smile. 'Well, what can I say about Mme Sarah Bernhardt? She was my old friend; I liked and admired her; she is dead; I'm sorry. I dined at her house ten days ago. Is that what you want to know?'

His English was excellent, clipped and briskly easy; but it was not to make this discovery that I had interrupted his dinner. I tried to get him to speak more fully about Mme Sarah Bernhardt and he did emit a few sentences of a commonplace order. But it was clear that the old man regarded the whole thing as a stupid invasion of his privacy, an *ânerie* typical of American journalism. He was right, of course. When he had yielded as much as he thought necessary to satisfy the curiosity of his American ad-mirers he bounced over to me, shook hands, wished me luck and returned to his dinner. The whole episode had taken about ten minutes in all, but it was enough to make Clemenceau a more vivid figure in my mind than many of the politicians I was to see so often thereafter. His faults were no doubt without number, but he was at any rate a man who knew his own mind and talked in comprehensible language. It was impossible not to wonder how men like Poincaré reached positions of great importance in the affairs of state, but no such speculation could arise in the youngest mind about Clemenceau. He must have been born to exercise power as a bird is born to fly or a fish to swim.

6

Along about this time I became the actual assistant to Mr Wales, our Paris correspondent. This meant that instead of being used in his office when he pleased, and loaned to the European Edition when that seemed the thing to do, I was permanently attached to the foreign news (i.e., political) service and could be sent any-where within the Paris area, which was, practically speaking, the whole continent of Europe. The first of my professional excur-sions under the new arrangement was to the Peace Conference at Lausanne in the spring of 1923.

The powers had met at Lausanne to arrange terms of peace with Turkey. There had been one peace treaty with Turkey already, and the former Ottoman Empire had been carved up with the utmost liberality by Mr Lloyd George and M. Clemenceau. But the one-sided 'agreements' of 1919 had never been accepted by the Turks of Anatolia, and when Mustapha Kemal Pasha arose to lead them westward, driving Mr Lloyd George's Greek protégés into the sea, the Western powers had either to make peace with him or fight. Mr Lloyd George, a reckless fellow, was apparently willing to fight, but British public opinion turned sharply against him, and he was driven from office; the succeeding government (under Mr Bonar Law and Lord Curzon) abandoned the Lloyd George policy altogether, flung the Greeks overboard, and made friends as rapidly as possible with Kemal. As was said at the time, Mr Lloyd George had 'backed the wrong horse,' and the mistake was not only fatal to some hundreds of thousands of Greeks who died the most horrible deaths in the campaign and the burning of Smyrna, but was also fatal to Mr Lloyd George's political career—a circumstance that aroused more interest in the West, of course, than any mere massacres accompanying it.

The Lausanne conference, in view of its origins, was bound to turn into a kind of contest between the great powers as to which could be sweetest to the once unspeakable Turk. Naturally this had to be so, since Kemal was ready to fight and nobody else was. The British and French, those loyal allies, lost no opportunity of intriguing against each other for Turkish favour, and it amused all beholders to see how, week after week, the British manœuvred the French out of their initial position of advantage, cozened and flattered and edulcorated the Turks, so that when the conference ended Britain was Turkey's friend and France was only a grudging, half-hearted acquaintance.

I went to Lausanne late in the game, when the Curzons and the Poincarés had gone, and the work of the conference was proceeding in relative obscurity. During my two months or so there the weather was perfect (it was spring); the atmosphere of the delegations was tranquil; I have seldom enjoyed myself more. There was less work to do than in Paris, and no writing at all. I telephoned to Paris every evening, but made no attempt to construct a 'story'; that was done (sometimes all too well) at the other end. There were press conferences to attend, and occasional interviews; but on the whole it was a placid and easy time, animated by the extraordinary diversity of human material spread out in the spectacle of the conference.

One of the striking figures in the scene was M. Venizelos. I had seen him before, was to see him again; but I never had a better view than on one morning when I was taken to breakfast with him by Pierre de Lacretelle. Lacretelle, who wrote for the *Journal des Débats*, was an old friend of M. Venizelos and admired him extravagantly. The Cretan entertained us throughout the meal with a wonderful flow of language. His French was excellent, his sense of humour keen, and he did not trouble to restrain himself in our presence. The general impression was one of amazing cleverness, high spirits, resiliency and malice. His personality was obviously far more complex than that of most European political leaders: you could not help thinking him capable of almost anything. Afterwards, in Athens and in Constantinople, I was to hear stories that shook my early admiration for M. Venizelos; but on that morning in Lausanne he was all brilliance and charm. His position was equivocal even in the Greek delegation. He was an exile from Greece, called from Paris to Lausanne because the new Greek government could think of nobody so clever to represent them. The Treaty of Lausanne itself was to be a failure for him. He had succeeded beyond his wildest dreams at Versailles, thanks to the way he hypnotized President Wilson and Mr Lloyd George. At Lausanne, in the urgency of the new situation created by Mustapha Kemal, he was very nearly disregarded, but it did not seem to have had much effect on his spirits. I supposed that to an old war horse like M. Venizelos one battle was much the same as another, and a success of little more account than a failure.

A somewhat different figure, but no less vivid, was that of Lili, the barmaid at the Palace Hotel. She was a sister of the celebrated Lorelei, barmaid of the Victoria at Geneva, who had attended every international conference and every League meeting since the war. Lorelei had been in Lausanne for the opening of the conference, but in the dull days that followed the departure of

Curzon and Poincaré she had returned to Geneva, leaving her sister Lili in charge. The barmaids, like the diplomats, had their hierarchy. Lili did not know quite so many people as Lorelei, but she met a good many in Lausanne. I used to ask her the names of people in the bar, even when I knew them, in order to see the air of high diplomatical importance that came over her face as she replied:

'Dot iss Mushir Bey. He iss member of Turkish Delegation, wissen-Sie? He is très important, beeg man.'

Lili was serious, pretty, dark-eyed and humourless. I liked to question her about other conferences in which she had understudied her sister Lorelei.

'Did you like it at Genoa, Lili?'

'Ach, Genova voss vonnderful, monsieur! So many beeg people —even dose Bolshevik, dey come! Moi, vous savez—je n'aime pas dose Bolshevik. But Genova so beautiful, monsieur! The sea voss nize, blue so far you can see. Mr Lloyd George, è venuto anche lui; he sign my autograph book. But I don't like Bolshevik. Die kommen nie dans le Bar; die trinken nichts. Von day somebody take me for long drife along de sea. Merveilleux, c'était! I like Genova.'

Lili and her magnificent sister were from Locarno. I wondered afterwards if that was the reason for the choice of Locarno for another palaver. At any rate, whether the dignitaries of London and Paris knew it or not, Lorelei and Lili considered international conferences to be their especial domain, an invention contrived for their benefit. Their command of languages (they could speak five, fluently and all at once) enabled them to queen it over the other Swiss barmaids of Europe. Theirs was a civilizing influence at Genoa and Cannes, Lausanne and Locarno; they embodied the pleasing characteristics of a true league of nations.

Lausanne's rank and fashion used to turn out for the dinner dances at the Hôtel Beau Rivage, and there were some odd sights to be seen there. There were a large number of camp followers whose activities were carried on chiefly at such gatherings. There were White Russians, including the Wrangels; there were Egyptian nationalists; there was a Belgian princess who had been accused of being a German spy during the war. Whether she was ever a spy or not, Lausanne gossip surrounded her with a halo of sinister repute. In an atmosphere of scent and silk and music, with champagne and flowers—or in the dark, leafy stillness of the garden outside—this lady was supposed to carry on her nefarious but interesting profession. In those days I was rather like the American Methodist lady I once met on a boat, who informed me with immense sanctimoniousness that 'our government hasn't got any secret police.' I thought spies were few and far between, always foreign, always wicked. In watching the elegant princess pursue her silken way I consequently felt all the pleasure you would expect such a sight to occasion in a young man from Illinois who finds himself for the first time on the borders of a romantically unknown world.

7

Paris, after Lausanne, was routine undistinguished by any flashes of such Châtelet melodrama. I now acted as Paris correspondent during my chief's absences at Deauville, Geneva or elsewhere. The day began with a conference at the Quai d'Orsay, in which the representatives of the English and American press attempted to get positive answers out of a polite, nervous official who was the French government's whipping boy in such matters. This official was called, in press dispatches, 'an unofficial spokesman'; he had his counterpart in every foreign office in the world; his statements had the advantage of being so anonymous that they could be officially denied whenever it was found necessary.

Our 'unofficial spokesmen' were of high rank, classed as ministers in the service, and certain to become ambassadors if they lived long enough. Often they were able to act as champions for the English-language press in the courts of the mighty. Scarcely a journalist who worked in Paris in the 1920's was without some debt of gratitude to MM. de Chambrun, Corbin or Giraudoux. Unfortunately the powers of these gentlemen did not work both ways. They were able in many matters to serve the interests of the foreign press—to represent it—vis à vis their own superiors. But they were prevented from serving their own superiors in like measure by the very ignorance and suspiciousness of those superiors. The politicians who governed at the Quai d'Orsay refused to understand that the Anglo-American press, in spite of its dislike for the Ruhr policy, was not deliberately malevolent.

But other nationalisms than that of the *grand Lorrain* kept us busy, too. The Corfu incident was the result of one of these: a beautiful example of the irate dictator stubbing his toe. Some Italians were killed in Epirus by bandits; Mussolini learned (apparently by secret communication from the Almighty, as there was no other way of knowing) that the murderers must be Greeks; Italy served an ultimatum on the unfortunate government at Athens; and when the Greeks sought to temporize, the Italians bombarded and occupied Corfu.

The astonishment of the world at large was extreme. The most militant action taken by any great power since the war had been the French occupation of the Ruhr; but it had taken place only after repeated warnings over a period of two years, and with legal justification (a 'juridical basis,' as they called it) in the letter of the treaties. Mussolini's action took place secretly, within three days, with no 'juridical basis' whatsoever and without the slightest attempt to consult with or warn the other powers. It was the sort of action that would have been called burglary or housebreaking in the life of the individual. A youth whose knowledge of international relations was imperfect could not but find the incident instructive in the extreme. Not only did it exhibit the characteristics of dictatorship and the temperature of the Fascist fever, but in the behaviour of the other powers it revealed a cynicism of motive, even in good deeds, that repelled and fascinated. The powers protested vigorously against Mussolini's action—but not, really, because it was wrong; not because it violated every decent rule of behaviour. Their protest was based simply upon the fact that if Italy annexed Corfu the Adriatic Sea would become an Italian lake, easily closed in time of war to the ships of other countries. In the press, in interviews, and in private conversations, the officials in Paris and Geneva who were engaged in attempting to get Mussolini out of Corfu expanded freely on the subject. They showed us figures to prove that guns in Corfu could rake the sea to a distance overlapping the range of the big guns on the Italian coast. Their indignation, such as it was (and it was obvious that most of them were not genuinely indignant), was based upon the danger this circumstance would represent to themselves.

The French were at the moment thrusting their bayonets into the noses of a whole German population without means of resistance; the British had, up to a year before, been busily engaged in murdering such elements of the population of Ireland as objected to the benefits of British rule; American forces were at the time in occupation of another island named Haiti. Now Mussolini, in his brutal and inexperienced way, was attempting to emulate these exploits. Perhaps the powers felt that his violence, his lack of hypocrisy, constituted a caricature of their own mealy-mouthed misdeeds. The British and Americans—even, in most cases, the more realistic French—had to find noble and high-sounding reasons for their acts of international brigandage. The fact that Mussolini did not pretend to such saintliness of character made him, for the duration of the crisis, an outlaw in the eyes of the Western world. Scurrying about from pillar to post in crowded days, I perceived for the first time the most persistent of diplomatic truths: that morality, in international relations, was measured only on the scale of interest—that one nation's heroism was another nation's crime. No doubt the Italians who bombarded Corfu felt that they were striking a blow for King and Country, defending the sacred heritage of the Latin race, etc., etc. To the parliamentarians of Paris and London they were offenders against a chimæra called 'civilization.' In such a disingenuous system of state relationships was it possible that nobody ever believed in a principle? That nobody was ever on the side of the right simply for the right's sake?

The great hope in that order of ideas was the League of Nations. But the League fell into a palsy, terrified by Italy's threat to resign if anything serious was done. The French and British then took the problem out of the League's hands altogether and gave it to the Conference of Ambassadors in Paris. The Conference consisted of the ambassadors of the great allied powers of 1914–18, and had been invented to succeed the Supreme Council of Versailles. Their excellencies met in secret, negotiated in the turpitudinous but effective style known since diplomacy began, and eventually—by a combination of bribing, coaxing and cudgelling—got the Italians out of Corfu. Mussolini, of course, was able to say that he had always intended to evacuate the island when his terms were met; the Greeks did not dare say anything; the powers had at least kept the Adriatic open. On my first visit to Geneva I was to witness the meek acceptance of the ambassadorial decisions by the League Assembly. That institution, the grave of international liberalism, should have written large upon its expensive tombstone an epitaph in one word only: Corfu.

8

I attended the League Assembly of 1923 only in its dying hours. Of the depressing congress I was to remember best two episodes: a speech by the representative of the empire of Ethiopia, and a speech by Lord Robert Cecil.[1]

Ethiopia had just been admitted to the League on a promise that it would make efforts to consider the abolition of slavery. The representative of the empire of Ethiopia (née Abyssinia) was a decorative bit of business. He wore the blue and white skirts of his country, spoke in a language nobody present understood, and was rewarded with applause. All the earnest nonsense of the League of Nations was crystallized in the episode. The gentleman spoke with fervour; his speech was afterwards pompously "translated" into French and English by persons who did not know a word of Abyssinian; and the whole thing occupied the parliament of mankind for about two hours. Meanwhile the most serious problem of war and peace then before the League—the question of Corfu—was being settled in the ornate drawing rooms of the Quai d'Orsay by a handful of tired old gentlemen who scarcely knew where Abyssinia was. The boredom and futility of Geneva were a shock to anybody who believed, as I then still tried to believe, that it might be possible to settle national differences by governmental agreement.

Lord Robert Cecil spoke at the very end of the Assembly, when the report of the Council of Ambassadors had finally been made and sent to Geneva for adoption by the League. The Assembly had been waiting for weeks to get a chance to talk about Corfu.

[1] Afterwards Viscount Cecil of Chelwood.

It had been a forbidden subject on the floor after the first week of crisis. Now, with the humiliating report of the ambassadors before them, those who believed in the League could only protest or give up altogether. Many protested. Mr Branting of Sweden— champion of lost causes—was one of those who spoke most eloquently against the methods and results of the Corfu settlement. But Lord Robert Cecil was the *preux chevalier* of Geneva. He had asserted the League's authority throughout the dispute, often in language that could scarcely have been approved by the Tory (Baldwin) government of which he was a member. He had been steadfast, a true believer, never faltering in his defence of the Covenant that Italy had so brutally violated. The question in everybody's mind was: can it be pieced together again at all? Will there be a time in the future when the Covenant can be taken seriously? Can any power in future regard the League with respect? What can Cecil say?

That he was himself sad and tired was easy enough to see. With his thin, stooped shoulders, his hooked nose and his weary, claw-like hands—that strikingly Jewish appearance which is said to be characteristic of the Cecils—he looked like a saintly rabbi, calming and solacing his people with words of resignation. One of his sentences was to come into my head again and again for years afterwards.

'We can't always have what we want in this life,' he said. 'Very often we must be satisfied with what we can get.'

Lord Robert had always suggested something steadier and more austere than was to be found elsewhere among cabinet ministers. The politicians who later cut a great figure at the League —Briand, MacDonald, Stresemann, Herriot—were what is called 'practical men'; they had their vanities and their partisan purposes; the League was useful to all of them, enhanced their reputations and solidified their support at home. They belonged to the professionally pro-League parties, the parties of the Left. Lord Robert Cecil was a different pair of sleeves: he had nothing, personally, to make out of the League; the party to which he technically belonged, the Tories, had no affection for Geneva; his own political career was near its end. Small wonder that his conduct had caused him to represent, at that time, a nobility of spirit otherwise lacking in high places. His acceptance of the Corfu bargain was more than a surrender: it was a demonstration of the impotence of idealism, however honest and brave, under the system of nationalist capitalist states. I thought of his words as the swan song of bourgeois idealism, forever dying, forever striking its flag, forever yielding sadly, regretfully, to the 'necessities of the practical world.' He said it clearly enough, the whole creed of his kind: 'We can't always have what we want in this life. Very often we must be satisfied with what we can get.'

9

By the summer of 1924—nearly a year later—the lessons of Geneva had been particularized and extended to a remarkable degree. I wondered then how the human race in its present arrangements could ever appear to be anything but despicable to its chroniclers. Older correspondents of my acquaintance had always seemed cynical, unwilling to acknowledge decent motives or behaviour in politics; but the more I saw of the materials of history the more I was forced to admit the logic of their scepticism. My elders did not seem to mind the horrors they so calmly recognized—indeed, I thought the older correspondents derived pleasure from the manipulations and treacheries of the politicians. It pleased many of them (including my employer) to know something that the public did not know; to observe, and then conceal, the degradation of governments. It was against the code to say plainly in print any of the things admitted in private conversations: that the Comité des Forges was supporting the Ruhr policy and financing the Rhineland rebellion; that the German financiers were making millions out of the deliberate inflation that ruined their poorer countrymen; that Mussolini was on the closest terms with the murderers who made away with Matteotti; that a handful of people were filching fortunes from Spain under Primo de Rivera; that the French general staff was attempting to bring about the annexation of the Palatinate and the Saar; that the press and most of the politicians of continental Europe were on sale to the highest bidder, usually the French. It amused the older correspondents to see all this, to hint at it sometimes in print;

but it never seemed a matter of personal importance to them. They were like a pack of jaded dramatic reviewers, familiar with the technique of the play but profoundly uninterested in its material. The difference, if any, between my generation (that which came to maturity in the years just after the war) and the preceding one seemed to me to lie in the domain of interest: our elders were disillusioned and rather bored, while we were—to put it strongly—avid for experience, interested in everything. Such statements ('this generation' and 'that generation') were shaky at best; they might be equally true of any two generations since the beginning of time; they might not be true at all. But events, at least, could not be altogether disregarded, and events were beginning to show that my contemporaries refused to be quiet: that they wanted a finger in every pie, that they were determined to allow no possible pleasure or power to go by default. It was they who created the extreme licentiousness that was the moral characteristic of the age. It was they who, in every country, leaped into Fascism or Communism as the democratic system glided on to lower levels of ineptitude. These phenomena undoubtedly resulted from profounder social tremors than could be indicated in the mere opposition of 'generations,' but it was in such an opposition that they first appeared on the surface.

I spent the late autumn and winter of 1923–24 in the Rhineland; January and February in Rome; March and April in Madrid. In the spring of 1924, at the time of the first Labour government, I was transferred to London for some months of comparative quiet.

But by that time I had had such an overdose of policy and politics that even MacDonald's eloquence seemed suspect to me. The Rhineland experience had shown black treachery on the part of the French, at a time when everybody pretended to be seeking a new law of peace between nations. The Roman experience—the Matteotti affair—had exhibited the cruelty and injustice of Fascism. The Spanish visit, some aspects of which were genuinely comic, had demonstrated the silliness of personal dictatorship. And when, in the summer of 1924, Mr MacDonald and M. Herriot began to proclaim their version of the new heaven and earth, I was unable to work up an enthusiasm. Even granting what was by no means proved, that they meant what they said, how could they build a new Europe out of such materials? There seemed a good deal more sense in the suggestion in the air— sometimes from Moscow, sometimes from Rome—that you had to begin by altering the composition of the material, its chemical formula.

These processes were not peculiar to me. The frame of mind was, roughly, that of a great part of the youth of Europe, of the world. It had germinated in the first resentments against the old men of Versailles, Wilson, Lloyd George, Clemenceau, Poincaré and Curzon; it was, in its maturity, to fill the Communist and Fascist camps into which Europe afterwards stood divided.

10

One evening we were told in Paris that a rebellion had broken out at Aix-la-Chapelle, directed against the German Reich authorities and not against the Belgian troops in occupation there. It was no more than half an hour after our first news of the trouble that I was sent off at the Gare du Nord. I had a hastily packed bag, into which all of the wrong things and none of the right ones had found their way. The next morning I was in the square before the town hall of Aachen, watching the siege in which a handful of German policemen defended the Rathaus against a band of 'Rhineland Separatists.' Both sides had rifles; the bullets flew about the deserted square and the streets that led into it; for the first time I had the curious sensation of being in an area where men were trying to murder each other in numbers. It was mostly sniping at Aix, neither side displaying much anxiety for a hand-to-hand fight. In the end the Separatists did storm the Rathaus and take possession of the local administration in the name of the 'Rhineland Republic.' The same thing happened on the next day, or during the next ten days, throughout the Rhineland. My job was to find the battles and report them, wherever they might be in the northern Rhineland or the Ruhr. The southern Rhineland and the Palatinate were at first set off as another correspondent's hunting ground.

The hordes of foreign correspondents who descended upon the

occupied territories during the trouble lived, generally, at the Breidenbacher Hof in Düsseldorf. It was an excellent hotel with exorbitant prices, a good kitchen, and a head waiter who bore himself like an emperor. The inflation was rising to its final height; every day the mark had a new worthlessness to record; the working people of the country had been unemployed for many months, and slow starvation was visible everywhere in the streets. Yet the foreigners who lived at the Breidenbacher Hof dined as well as if they had been in Paris, and over their cigars at night they settled calmly what was to be done with the 'buffer state' they assumed to be in the making. For some time the French, in particular, talked as if the 'Rhineland Republic' needed only the recognition of the great powers to set up business as a sovereign nation. No contrast of the same order could possibly have been more striking than that between the well-fed unreality of these foreign correspondents in the Düsseldorf hotel and the starving desperation of the Germans outside. I watched the poor being fed slops and left-overs at the back entrance of our sumptuous Breidenbacher Hof, and it was a spectacle I could have wished to show M. Poincaré.

In my two months and a half in the Rhineland, in spite of a good deal of trying, I never found an ordinary German who wanted to see the Rhineland separated from the Reich. There were recognized pro-French agents, of course, like Dorten, who busied themselves in enrolling hungry unemployed men, *à coups de francs*, to support the 'cause' of Separatism. They represented nothing, and knew it. The only explanation I was ever able to find for M. Poincaré's policy was that he believed (the wish being father, mother and drill sergeant to the thought) that such venal agitators had some section of the Rhenish people on their side. Clemenceau had refused in the treaty to hack out a buffer state along the Rhine; therefore he, Poincaré, would do so, using whatever instruments came to hand, and ensure himself the gratitude of posterity.

It was a gamble in the Rhineland whether one might hit on a battle or not; we used to go forth in the morning pretty much at random, choosing a town within three or four hours' distance to visit, and seldom coming back (during the first weeks, at least) without some new titbit of horror to relate. Once I fell upon three battles in the same day. The worst of these was at Krefeld, where the streets were barricaded and the fighting continued for a day and a half. At one of the barricades I met a man—a Separatist—who had been for eight or ten years employed in the steel mills at Gary, Indiana. He begged a cigarette, talked affably enough in the language of Gary—'Oh, boy! *Am* I glad to get a Murrican *sig*-rette! Oh, boy! *Will* we knock hell outa these goddam Prussians!"—and confided, after an intimate friendship of about five minutes, that he cared nothing about the cause for which he was risking his life; that he had, in fact, nothing else to do, having been unemployed for eighteen months; and that his wife and children were glad to have the money he was earning in these bloody affrays. It was his first real money, he said, in a long time, and Oh, boy! *was* he glad to have it! Like most of the Separatists, he was not too anxious to risk his skin—they were a furtive band of combatants on the whole—but he was willing enough to crouch behind a barricade and fire, once in a while, over it, so long as he was paid in 'real money.'

The whole thing was enough to turn the stomach. It was not made less revolting by the amenities that still, even in the Rhineland and the Ruhr, comforted those who were able to pay. As a guest at Krupp's private hotel in Essen, I had a superb luncheon one day with champagne; nothing could have been better; and the average dole of an unemployed man on the Krupp lists was then about eight cents a day. At old August Thyssen's castle above the Ruhr valley (it was called, I believe, Schloss Landenberg) I saw some beautiful erotic groups by Rodin, two marble ladies in six stages of embrace; but Thyssen's mills had been closed for a year, and the people who lived by them were starving.

One of the most disgusting of these dramas of suffering in the Rhineland was one arranged by myself. It had struck somebody in the home office of the Chicago *Tribune* that the starvation of the inhabitants of the Rhine and Ruhr valleys might be due chiefly to the refusal of farmers to take worthless paper marks in payment for food. I was asked by cable to test the theory by attempting, in company with some poor Germans, to buy food in the country districts near Düsseldorf.

I did so. A waiter at the Breidenbacher Hof helped me find my actors. They were a mixed lot; one was a boy from the bread line behind the hotel, and another was an old lady who had not had a good meal for months. They were instructed to wear their oldest clothes, but this could hardly have been necessary, as they were already threadbare. It was bitter cold. We took a closed car and set out for the country. In half an hour we were in rich farm-land, as prosperous as southern England and not unlike it in appearance. At farm after farm we stopped, leaving the car at a safe distance down the road, and approached the farmhouse for food.

Never once did we get anything in exchange for the currency of the country, although we offered many thousands of millions of marks. In one place a woman offered us some potatoes for nothing, but they were bad potatoes which, my chief aid informed me, would ordinarily have been fed to animals. In another place where we were refused food I saw a huge pile of turnips lying under a shed. When I asked why we could not have some of these my lieutenant told me that they were saved for the pigs.

In some places we tried the effect of Dutch, French or American money: it was magic. What could not be bought for marks was abundantly on sale for gulden, francs or dollars. On our cold, unpleasant tour that day we learned that no peasant was so ignorant as to mistake the relative values of foreign currencies, the scale upon which dollars, francs and gulden operated.

So there it was: the Germans themselves were no less inhuman than the French; were perhaps more so, because their cruelty was exercised upon their own people. It was difficult to understand how our old lady could fail to move the presumably good-hearted peasant women. Our old lady was just a shade or two this side of imbecility (on the more accepted side, that is); all day long she kept mumbling various things about money and getting them wrong.

'Billiarden,' she would say. Then: 'Nein, nein, ich meine, *Billionen, Billionen!* Gott! wie kann man dass verstehen!'

She had been a prosperous woman with a little shop before

the war—'*vorm Kriege*,' those words forever dropping from a German mouth—and the inflation had come too late in her life to have any meaning for her. She had forced herself to learn to count in hundreds, then in thousands, then in millions, then in milliards, each step taking months, so that she could get used to it; but now, suddenly, in the last terrifying weeks of the mark's descent, the count was in a dimension of which the old lady had never even heard the name before—*Billionen*.[1] She could never get such a fantastic computation into her head. I was giving her five dollars—a billion, or (in American) a trillion, which is to say a million millions—for her day's service, and it took her most of the day to understand what the amount was. She had been brought up to believe that *eine Mark ist eine Mark*, once the fundamental faith of all Germany; and she was too old to see why the eternal statement was no longer true.

I was to think of the old lady frequently after that, particularly at holiday time in the Rheinpfalz, where I had gone on a general tour of the occupied territory. Conditions in the Palatinate were more disgraceful than elsewhere, because that province had been less subjected to scrutiny by the Rhineland High Commission and the foreign press. The population was urged by every means at hand to go to night school and learn French, which they were freely told was going to be their language in the future. French signs had been stuck up on the street corners, alongside or above the German names. Rue Foch and Rue Joffre—what venom those names must have prepared in the feeling of the conquered! The Separatists had been installed in every city, protected openly by the French troops. Here, too, there were Senegalese, the dreaded black men, who had caused trouble the year before in the north. The people were sullen, unfriendly, rather terrifying. These same people were, soon afterwards, to revenge themselves on the Separatists at Pirmasens by a savage massacre as soon as the French protection was withdrawn (that is, when M. Poincaré was convinced that the 'Rhineland Republic' could not succeed and must be abandoned). It was at Pirmasens that the mob

[1] This figure, called a billion in European languages including English, is called a trillion in American, the word billion being applied to what other languages call a milliard, or a thousand millions.

actually tore some Separatists limb from limb and burned others alive.

The French commander-in-chief in the Rheinpfalz was one of the most detestable satraps I was ever obliged to interview: pompous, heartless, stupid, convinced of his right to force a whole German province to do his bidding. The Rheinpfalz was to join its neighbours, Alsace-Lorraine and the Saar, under French rule: that was his plan, and he said it as plainly as he dared. The German Archbishop of Speyer (Catholic), an ancient prelate, trembled with indignation at the treatment of his flock, eagerly detailing incident after incident, story after story, to show the sufferings of the vanquished. And yet, in spite of all these curses, the men still went into the woods and cut down evergreen trees to bring home for the most Germanic of festivals, and in the snowy dark night, just at curfew time, the children sang Christmas songs. There was a vitality in this people that could not be conquered; it was shown in the evergreen trees over the shoulders of the men going home, in the struggle of the mumbling old lady to skip from milliards to billions, in the voices of the children, singing 'Stille Nacht, heilige Nacht.' Why could not the French see the fact, get used to it, live with it, make it as familiar as the fact of night and day?

Why, indeed?

There was an international commission of investigation into the state of the Palatinate a few weeks later, and the rigours of the occupying force were somewhat abated. The commander-in-chief, who had been personally responsible (so they said) for some of the excesses of the régime, was given other worlds to conquer. The worst moment had passed. The French never again exceeded their powers, so far as I knew, and under the next government in Paris (Herriot's) the armies of occupation were reduced and made almost benevolent. When I went back to the Rhineland a year later for a few days the whole air and manner and feeling of the country had altered. I was surprised at the Germans for forgetting so soon, at the French for reversing everything I had thought of their ambitions and plans. A French official friend disabused me: 'Nobody has forgotten anything,' he said. 'It's the moment for fine words, that's all.' And the assistant manager of the hotel, a Bavarian: 'What the French did here won't be forgotten—not even after we've beaten them to death in the next war; no German who was here will ever forget it.' Sometimes it seems that they were both right.

22

The Matteotti affair took me straight from the Palatinate to Rome in January, 1924. Going from occupied to unoccupied Germany at that time, when passive resistance was only just coming to an end here and there, and the French bayonets still marked an uneasy frontier, was like crossing from one country to another in time of war. The train I took from Wiesbaden to Frankfurt was the first that had run for about a year; it ran with difficulty, under heavy guard on both sides, for fear of bombs or sabotage, but at least it ran. Two days later I was in Rome.

I had no special light on the Matteotti affair—no foreigner had, I believe—but it was my first straight taste of the Fascist temper and as such deserves a bow. The Socialist deputy Matteotti had been carried off and murdered by a gang of Fascists, the chief of whom was the notorious Dumini, who boasted of his nine murders and his friendship with the Duce. When the body of Matteotti was discovered and his murderers sent to Regina Coeli there was such indignation, in and out of Italy, as threatened the whole position of the Fascist government. It ended, as might have been expected, by the creation of new laws and a new system of justice, whereby the Fascist dictatorship assumed the form it afterwards attempted to grow into: that of a 'total' state consistent within itself, intolerant of dissent and constructed so as to expunge all opposition automatically the moment it appeared; a party despotism of uncertain economic basis, philosophically no more than a doubtful time-variant of Marxism, but given vigour and superficial coherency by the bold, rubbery egotism of its individual leader. Until the affair of Matteotti Fascism had governed through the 'free' institutions of democracy, with a free press, an elected parliament, and the free operation of equal justice under the Code Napoléon—all, of course, subject to intimidation, tinged with a flavour of castor oil, but ostensibly, at any rate, a government by the will of the people. After Matteotti all this changed: the 'total' state was invented and the non-Fascists put in the position of a population under tutelage. The value of the new system would obviously only be tested when its historically accidental element, that of the Duce's person, was removed. It would take years to see what force might be left, out of all this militarization of energy, when the directing genius ceased to exert itself. I suspected that there was nothing there—nothing, that is, but noise and argument, the impulses of unregulated nationalism, and a few crumbs of social and economic reality from the table of Karl Marx; out of such disparate materials it required extraordinary personal power to create a system that even appeared to hold together, stood on its own feet, and gave the observer an illusion of articulate strength and will. It was, it seemed to me, no system at all, just as a man of straw is no man at all; but it did accustom the minds of millions of people to the *idea* of a system, of systems in general; it familiarized the least thoughtful of creatures with the notion that societies might be organized on a logical basis, as the man of straw might familiarize the birds and the beasts of the field with the forms of mankind. Thus Fascism was—whatever its other merits or demerits—a kind of rehearsal in time for the truly 'total' state, an introduction to the design into which the future must probably fall.

But I did not like it: that was the difficulty. Its mood and accent were unsympathetic—harsh, acrimonious, hysterical, colossally selfish; it seemed to have almost no relation to the exquisite land in which its destiny caused it to unfold. What did these clamours of hatred and self-love have to do with the harmonious eternity of Italy? The *orgoglio e dismisura* that exiled Dante, just as he lamented them in the masterpiece that formed the Italian language, were here spread all over the place, in the streets, in the newspapers, in the courtrooms where 'justice' was administered, in the splendid salons where officials gave the foreign press an account of the New Italy and its New Ideals. The busy tumult of it confused and silenced the observer: it was only possible to take Fascism, for the moment, at its word and wonder how long that word would endure.

12

It was in Madrid that I enjoyed one of the rare comedies of these years: a farce in which I played a part in spite of myself, aided by some of the improbable trappings of spy melodrama. Only in Primo de Rivera's Spain—a régime of purely personal government, where nobody knew *why* anything happened—could such an episode have taken place.

I had gone to Madrid from Paris and consequently passed the frontier at Irun. In Madrid I spent my days trying to get some idea of the successes and failures of Primo, the extent to which he had involved the monarchy in them, the strength of the opposition (if it existed), and the progress of the campaign in Morocco; but by night I had other occupations. I was fascinated by the theatres, particularly the most popular of them: those in which an endless succession of dancers and singers stretched across all the hours, coarse, indefatigable and noisy. I was much taken with the gipsies: Pastora Imperio, the dancer Escudero, the guitarist Montoya. Pastora Imperio had been the greatest Andalusian gipsy singer of her time, and there was still left in her extraordinary throat an assortment of sounds unlike anything I had ever heard. Listening to her was like plunging far back into the past of this dark race, these incredible romantics: she evoked the veils and scimitars of Moorish Spain, the despair of centuries of slavery. I heard her first one night at the Villa Rosa, a gipsy establishment honoured by the patronage of the dictator himself; and her flamencos were more heady than yellow sherry, the common drink of such places. Montoya, who played the guitar there, became a friend of mine. He visited me when I was ill, and played the guitar (to the doctor's horror) in my bedroom at the hotel. He was a fat, yellow, slit-eyed old gipsy whose accent in Spanish was incomprehensible to me, but somehow we carried on enough conversation to fill in the few moments when he was not playing the guitar. Sometimes I visited a certain not very reputable house in the Calle O'Donnell, taking Montoya and his flamenco singer (a son or nephew or grandson) with me; Montoya would supply the rolling, measured thunder over which the girls, one after another, would lift their voices in the competitive screech of the flamenco. Such visits took place very late at night, after the theatres and restaurants were closed, and I never dreamed that they would be of interest to the government of Spain.

I had been in Madrid for some time, engaged in nothing more conspiratorial than the occupations I have named, when a sudden attack of bronchitis put me to bed for about ten days. During that time I did my work in bed; my Spanish assistant, F. G., used to come to the Palace Hotel every day with all the newspapers and with whatever else he had been able to find of interest. I wrote occasional dispatches in bed, in English, on my portable typewriter, and he took them to the post office to be telegraphed to Paris. The good man knew not a word of English, and was in consequence not responsible for what I wrote; but since our charge account at the postoffice was in his name as permanent local correspondent, it was, of course, his name that was signed at the bottom of each telegram.

One fine day F. G. did not arrive. I was a little put out but supposed his other affairs had taken up all his available time. The next day he did not come either. I telephoned to his house, but his wife was too ill to answer the telephone, and a maid (or friend or relative) was obviously unwilling to answer any question. On the third day, when he was still missing, I determined to go to the police and ask what had become of him.

It was in the morning. I had finished breakfast and was about to go out, hesitating only over what degree of muffling-up was necessary to a recent bronchitis patient. Just then a knock came at my door; I opened it to find two solemn fat men, the spit of the detective the world over. The first of these, reciting in a gloomy, nasal voice, informed me in pompous sentences that I was under arrest by order of His Majesty the King.

This seemed to me so improbable that I laughed and said so.

My friend the detective bowed; his silent partner bowed also; they shrugged their shoulders, spread their hands. The first one then showed me my name, printed on the paper he held in his hand, and followed by the words 'Palace Hotel,' with my room number. There was no doubt about it; for some reason I was to be conducted forthwith to prison. I was allowed a few minutes to put my clothes and papers in order, but not to telephone to the

American Embassy. Then, with a member of the secret police on either side of me (walking respectfully two or three steps behind), I went out of the hotel and got into a taxi and was driven off.

The prison to which I was taken was called (I believe) the San Francisco—the one beyond the Royal Palace, indistinguishable from the other barracks and gaols of the quarter. I was escorted into a dirty waiting room where a number of silent, dour characters sat gloomily on the bench that ran round the walls. I waited for perhaps an hour, divided between irritation and amusement. I had an idea that somebody would get into trouble over this, but in the meantime there was plenty of time for my own carcase to incur annoyance.

The door opened, and I was summoned inside. The room was small, almost filled by a great desk laden with papers. Behind it sat a benignant middle-aged officer in the uniform of an infantry colonel. He rose, smiled, shook hands and motioned me to a seat before him.

'You are under arrest, señor,' he said pleasantly, 'by the King's order, and will have to stand trial by court-martial.'

'But why?'

'For a dispatch you sent to the Chicago *Tribune* five days ago. That is not, of course, the exact reason for the arrest; that is the cause. The reason given is——'

And here he turned over a few sheets of paper, reflected, and read aloud:

'. . . tendencious informations with the design of bringing down the exchange value of the peseta.'

After delivering this blow he looked up, smiled with the utmost politeness, and offered me a cigarette.

'You smoke, señor? I believe you have enjoyed your stay in Madrid?'

'Yes, very much,' I said. 'But what about this dispatch? Did it do anything to bring down the exchange value of the peseta? I don't know or care anything about the exchange value of the peseta.'

'Oh,' said the Colonel, smiling gently, 'of course the dispatch was not sent out. The Censor . . . You understand . . . It is only that *if* it had been sent out, it *would* have had a bad effect on the exchange value of the peseta.'

He stopped, puffed his cigarette, allowed his eyes to rest in fatherly fashion upon me.

'We are greatly concerned about the exchange value of the peseta,' he remarked.

'Does this mean that I must stay in jail?' I asked. 'Can't I telephone to the American Embassy? And what dispatch are you talking about? I can't remember sending anything that referred in any way to the peseta. Moreover, you say I am arrested by the King's order. The King is not aware of my existence. How could he order me arrested?'

The Colonel, smoking placidly, leaning back in his chair, allowed the questions to spill out. Then he leaned forward, turned over some papers, extracted one, and pushed it towards me.

'That is His Majesty's order,' he said.

And there indeed it was: a square of paper, like a half-sheet of foolscap, across which was typewritten the instruction to 'arrest the sender of Telegram No. XX35998,' or whatever the number was. My name did not appear. This document, which consisted of two typewritten lines, was signed by Alfonso. It was a *lettre de cachet*—one of those famous military orders by which so many hundreds (and, later on, thousands) of Spaniards were thrown into prison without legal warrant and, often enough, without ever coming to trial even by court-martial. I had been told that Primo was accustomed to present these orders to the King in batches— and that the King, that docile monarch born on the throne, who had sworn fealty to the outraged constitution repeatedly since childhood, signed them all.

'And here is Telegram No. XX35998,' said the Colonel politely. 'Is it yours?'

I inspected the two sheets of paper he handed me. They gave an account, a vague and mild account, of the new disaster that had overcome the Spanish army in Morocco: an event then unknown to the world at large, which my Spaniard, F. G., had heard about from returning officers.

'I don't see anything criminal in this telegram,' I said. 'Of course I wrote it; but why not? It doesn't say a word about the peseta.'

'Señor, why does the peseta fall? I fear it is because of telegrams such as this, printed in various great newspapers in England and America. It is not possible for us to allow such things. . . . Do you want to telephone to the American Embassy?'

He rang a bell and instructed the soldier who answered to put through a call to the American Embassy, for the chargé d'affaires —*encargado de negocios*. Then he leaned back, put his fingertips together, and gazed at me again. I was getting rather uncomfortable under this persistent regard.

'So you like Spanish dancing, eh?' he remarked. 'You visit a certain house in the Calle O'Donnell. . . . Ah, señor, young men should be careful of their conduct when they are in your position. I see there is no great harm in you; I shall tell you, then. You must be very careful what you do, where you go. Everything you do is reported by the secret police. Your letters—your telegrams —you should really be more discreet.'

I was mystified into silence. The Colonel touched a great pile of papers on his desk.

'There is your dossier, señor,' he said gently. 'It is very full. . . . For instance, what did you mean by sending such a telegram as this?'

He fished out a telegraph form and showed it to me. When I read it it was impossible to keep from laughing; the whole thing had turned to farce. The telegram said: 'Vivent la France et les patates frites!' and was signed (grave, suspicious circumstance!) with my nickname instead of my professional name.

'You will perhaps find it difficult to believe, Señor Coronel,' I said, trying to speak seriously, 'that telegram is a joke—a stupid joke, but nothing more. Some American friends of mine, named Bullitt, who live in Paris, have just had a child; when I received the letter telling me about it, I sent this telegram to the mother. It means nothing at all, you see.'

The Colonel looked gravely at the telegram, read it again, and made a dutiful effort to find it funny.

'I see,' he said, 'a joke. An American joke. It was not so regarded at the Censura.'

He sighed heavily, pondering over it. The telephone beside him rang at last; communication was not quick in Spain. The American *encargado de negocios*—Hallett Johnson—was at the other end. The Colonel spoke to him and then turned the receiver over to me.

I had difficulty making Johnson understand or believe what had happened to me—for which he could scarcely be blamed; the affair did seem improbable. The Colonel was more successful. After a lengthy conversation, it appeared that Johnson gave his word to be responsible for me until such time as my trial by court-martial should come on. The Colonel put the telephone back and turned to me, politer than ever.

'On the American Embassy's undertaking to produce you,' he said, 'you may go free; but you are not to leave Madrid. I advise you to go straight to the Embassy and tell the *encargado de negocios* all about it. And remember, whatever you do, wherever you go, the secret police are following you. It is not my duty to tell you this, but hints are apparently no good to you; you have no idea . . . You should be warned. You should be more discreet in your—ah—frequentations. Some of the reports in this dossier will not sound beautiful when they are read out at your court-martial.'

'But, Señor Coronel, how can that be? I am not blind. If I had been followed by spies I should certainly have seen them.'

The Colonel smiled pityingly and rang a bell. The soldier who answered vanished and reappeared again almost at once, conducting a small, dingy, embarrassed wisp of a man with his cap in his hand.

'That is the spy who is at present attached to you,' the Colonel said.

I gazed in astonishment on the little man.

'At your service, señor,' he said ingratiatingly.

The Colonel rose, stretched his hand across the desk, said good-bye.

'I do not know when your trial will come up, señor,' he said, 'but in any case I am the military judge. . . . I advise you to keep in close touch with your embassy, which has agreed to be responsible for you. If it had not, it would have been my duty to keep you in prison. *Adiós.*'

I went out, dazed, and got into a taxicab. In a few minutes I was at the Embassy in the Castellana, telling Hallett Johnson what had happened. He seemed puzzled, amused, mildly surprised. I think that some of my story seemed to him unbelievable, although he was too polite to say so. I know, for example, that at that time he did not believe in the existence of the little spy. From the Embassy I returned, somewhat shaken, to the Palace Hotel to think things over.

There, as I entered the grillroom downstairs, I saw my little spy prowling among the hats and coats of the cloakroom. I went over to him.

'If you have to watch me all the time,' I said, 'you may as well come with me. Come and have lunch. You make me nervous standing there in the door.'

The little spy was confused, uncertain; but he did not dare refuse.

'If the señor wishes . . . The señor is very kind . . . I do not wish to disturb the señor . . .'

He came along with me. We sat at a table against the wall, and I perceived by the astonished smiles of the waiters that he and his profession were known to them. I ordered lunch after a delay caused by my attempts to translate the French names of dishes into Spanish for the spy's benefit. He ate avidly, with a knife-and-fork technique that caused the waiters to raise their eyebrows. I was burning to ask questions.

'You know my name,' I said. 'Apparently you know a great deal about me. But I don't know yours.'

He stopped eating long enough to fish a card out of his pocket with eager, grubby fingers.

'This is my name, señor,' he said. 'And I too am an American. I was born under the American flag.'

His card was a dirty little printed square that said 'Juan-María Cardenas.' But nothing under heaven ever looked or sounded less American than the good Juan-María. I was puzzled.

'Aren't you a Spaniard?'

'I am a Spaniard now, señor, but I was born under the American flag. In Cuba, that was—at Cienfuegos. The American troops were in occupation.'

He seemed delighted at this circumstance, and repeated it a

number of times: 'Yo soy norteamericano también; soy yanquí, señor!'

'Tell me something. How long have you been following me?'

'Since Irun, señor.'

Since the frontier. It was inconceivable.

'But how did you manage that? How did you conceal yourself? I never knew. . . . And why on earth did you follow me, anyway?'

'It was easy to conceal myself, señor. It is my profession. There are a number of us stationed at Irun. When you came through and they saw that you were a journalist, I was detached to follow you. I came down on the same train, mostly in the corridor. Then here, at the hotel, I stayed in the hall outside your room until you went out; when you went out, I went too.'

'Even to the theatres? Even—ah—to the Calle O'Donnell?'

'Certainly, señor. You see, with my card from the police I can take any taxi; I can get a seat in any theatre, and if the seat I want is already sold, I get it anyway; I am entitled to transportation on the motorcycles of the ordinary police if I need it.'

'When I went to the Calle O'Donnell it was late at night. There were no taxis—nothing at all, except the taxi I was in. How did you follow me there?'

'It was simple, señor. I clung on behind.'

'But you might have been killed. I don't think your profession is a safe one.'

'It is not bad work, señor. Sometimes it is quite agreeable. Now, for example, when you were sick in bed, I had nothing to do for a whole week but sit outside your room and smoke cigarettes! . . . More than a week! Ah, that was a pleasant time. . . .

'When you went so often to see Dora la Cordobesita, I used to have the seat just behind you. The management got to know about this, of course, and always saved two seats—one for you in front, one for me behind. I got tired of Dora la Cordobesita, I can tell you! I knew everything she was going to do. And then I often wanted to stay to see the next number, and it did not please me when you would get up and go away. Why did you want to see La Cordobesita so many times? *Válgame Díos!* How often I used to wish that you would take it into your head to go to the cinema instead!'

The small spy and I became friends for the moment. I owed to him my first acquaintance with that industrious, useful and under-paid profession which does so much dirty work for the governments of the world. He was the only spy I was ever to know who was not ashamed of his job; he regarded it as he might have regarded dish-washing or cobbling, as a means of livelihood.

After lunch I considered the problem of communicating to my superiors in Paris just what had happened. I knew that a telegram to my office would be stopped by the Censura. As the best way out of the difficulty, I sent a short and guarded telegram to Mr Wales at his flat in Paris—paying for it as a personal, full-rate message from the post office, which might not be sent to the Censura at all. I had returned from this errand, and was wondering what, if anything, I could do next under the somewhat bizarre conditions, when I received a visit from F. G.

In my own troubles I had almost forgotten him. Now he came storming into my room, wild eyed, agitated, thinner and more feverish than ever. As I pieced his story together out of the wreckage of his language—he talked mixed French and Spanish at a fantastic rate, in a fantastic accent, so that half one's time was taken up with wondering which tongue he favoured at the moment—I saw that what had been a rather comic episode to me had been a horrible experience for him. He had just then—an hour or so before—been released from prison, after three days of solitary confinement during which he had had nothing to eat but bread and watery soup, nobody to talk to but the great rats who swarmed in the gaol. He had been in what sounded like a genuine old-fashioned dungeon, something out of the Count of Monte Cristo. He had been arrested in the middle of the night 'by order of the King'—on that same *lettre de cachet* the military judge had shown me—and the police had given him no consideration whatever: he was a Spanish subject. For two days he had not even been examined—had been thrown, simply, into his dungeon and left there. When he was heard, he had easily convinced the military judge that he knew no English and could not have written the fatal dispatch; whereupon the military judge had asked for my name, obtained it, and sent his men out to arrest me. After my examination, and not until then, he was released. If I had denied the authorship of the dispatch in question, F. G. would have been kept in prison for weeks, months, perhaps for the whole length of the Primo dictatorship—or so he seemed to think. He was divided between anger with me for getting him into such a difficulty and gratitude to me for admitting what was, after all, the truth—that he had had nothing to do with the incriminating telegram except to take it to the post office and sign for it. He was not at all sure that the court-martial against him would be dropped; he was in deadly terror of the prison and the great rats that had visited him there at night. In his terror he would have liked to escape from Spain, but he knew it to be impossible. His little yellow face looked very old.

Such it was to be a subject of His Majesty King Alfonso XIII in the days of the dictatorship!

I dined again with my spy that night; but on the following day his attentions began to bore me. As I thought it over, it did not seem logical that any government would wish to subject the representative of a powerful foreign newspaper to such open surveillance. Perhaps if I asked the Embassy to intervene, Juan-María Cardenas would be removed to other spheres, and although no doubt a new spy would be appointed to dog my steps, at least I would be unaware of it.

I got into a taxicab and went down to the Embassy, Juan-María chugging along behind me on a police motorcycle. At the Embassy I was brought at once into the Ambassador's room, where Johnson was at the time in charge. He was apparently expecting me and was a little angry.

'What is the meaning of this?' he said. 'I have a cablegram from Washington to say you're in danger of your life. Are you in danger of your life?'

'No,' I said, 'but I'm getting bored with the way I'm treated here. Wherever I go I am followed by a spy; my letters are opened and read, and not even put back straight; I can't get a telegram sent out to my office; and my telephone doesn't work until it has been clicked into some espionage office.'

'You're romancing,' he said. 'What makes you think you're followed by spies? Such things don't happen. I think you're getting too excited.'

Johnson, a charming, intelligent man and a good diplomatist, had begun his day badly: he had had a peremptory cablegram from the Secretary of State, Mr Hughes, ordering a report on what had happened to me. He considered that he had done everything that was necessary, and somehow or other he was inclined to blame me for the tone of the State Department's dispatch.

'If you don't believe me,' I said, suddenly angry in my turn, 'I'll bring the spy in and show him to you. He's sitting outside at your gate now.'

Johnson, startled, not believing, rang a bell. The Spanish secretary who answered was given an order. In a few minutes, as we stood there glaring at each other across the majestic reaches of the ambassadorial carpet, my poor Juan-María was brought in and thrust between us. Johnson began to question him sharply. Juan-María, a pitiable figure, cringing and embarrassed, answered each question as straightforwardly as possible; the little man did not know how to lie—a grave defect in his profession. Yes, he had followed the señor from the frontier; he made a report every night; he went everywhere the señor went; he belonged to the secret police and was in the special detachment under the orders of Colonel Rico, head of the Censura.

Johnson walked up and down, getting angrier every minute. By this time he was no longer angry with me, for he saw that I had not been romancing: he was angry, rather, with the stupidity of the situation and with the necessity it put him under to take immediate steps.

'I don't think it's any good going to anybody but Primo about this,' he said to me. Then, to the secretary who answered his bell: 'Telephone to the Presidencia and ask if His Excellency will receive the American chargé d'affaires immediately.'

He frowned, considered, and suddenly showed me a decoded copy of the cablegram from Washington. It was indeed a remarkable document. Washington had been informed that I had been arrested and court-martialled and was in danger of being shot; the Embassy was to investigate immediately, report fully and take all necessary steps to protect me. The message was signed by Mr Hughes himself.

'I don't know anything about this,' said I. 'I only told my Paris office that I was going to be court-martialled and could not leave Madrid until the trial; I didn't say anything about being shot.'

'That was put in somewhere along the way, I suppose,' he said. 'You can imagine what the newspapers will make out of this! At least, your newspaper will. . . . Come on: let's go to the Presidencia.'

We went out and got into one of the Embassy's cars, with the American flag flying; Juan-María, commandeering a police motorcycle that stood at the door, came chugging along after us. At the Presidencia we went up to Primo's floor and waited, Juan-María disposing himself, meanwhile, among the other spies and guards downstairs. Primo was in a cabinet meeting, and we waited about ten minutes. Then Johnson—who, when roused, was a lion—asked a passing secretary to inform the President that the *encargado de negocios* of the United States was waiting for him.

Out came Primo, bouncing along, smiling cordially, delighted to see his dear Señor Johnson; and to what did he owe the pleasure . . . ? Johnson presented me and gave an account of what had happened, ending with Mr Hughes's request for an explanation.

Primo was dumbfounded. I never saw a man of great power so caught *in flagrante delicto*. At first he tried to say that it was all a mistake, that it could not have happened, that I must have misunderstood, that it was not possible; but I gave him the name of the military judge, told him I had seen the order of arrest signed by the King. Then, abandoning this tack, he said that perhaps a mistake had been made and that it would be rectified; everything would be all right; he would do everything the Embassy thought necessary; Señor Johnson was to assure his government that everything would be done. Johnson, smiling politely—he was indeed a lion that day—expressed his thanks, bowed and then said: 'But, Your Excellency, in the matter of the spies . . . ?'

Primo raised his eyebrows and gesticulated.

'But how can there be any spies? We don't have spies in Spain —no foreigner is subjected to——'

He lost himself in phrases, but Johnson—playing on him the relentless trick I had played half an hour before at the Embassy—

said with another smile and bow: 'The spy is downstairs now, having followed the Embassy car here, Excellency. If you care to send for him . . . ?'

Primo had to send for the spy, and in the few minutes before Juan-María arrived he played nervously with some papers in his hand, frowned, tried to make conversation. When was Mr Moore coming back? How was the health of that excellent ambassador, that admirable friend? Johnson reassured him about Mr Moore, and in came poor Juan-María with a guard on either side of him.

Juan-María had never been in such exalted company in his life. He scarcely dared to answer the questions addressed to him. His voice came in a feeble, cracked semiwhisper; he turned his cap round and round in his hands, and after one quick glance to see that he stood in the presence of the Dictator himself, he never took his eyes off the floor.

Primo was exceedingly angry—angrier, I suspected, at being put in such a ridiculous position than at anything else. He shot his questions at Juan-María and received the terrified answers.

'Stúpido, stúpido, stúpido!' he said, half to himself; it was clear that Colonel Rico of the Censura would soon receive a piece of his mind. Then, ordering Juan-María off in a voice that nearly caused the little spy to faint, he turned back to Hallett Johnson and myself and tried, not very successfully, to smile. Everything would be done; my correspondence should not be touched again; no spies should be allowed to come near me; I was to be quite tranquil; he would himself look into the matter of the court-martial and let me know when I should be free to leave Madrid; but I was not to worry about it. And with that, and more compliments and smiles to Johnson, he went back to his cabinet meeting.

A few days later Mr Moore returned from a holiday in America. He was the Ambassador, one of our more characteristic ambassadors—Mr Alexander P. Moore of Pittsburgh, a newspaper owner, a politician of the Republican party, who had been appointed to his post by the ineffable Harding. During the rest of my stay in Madrid I saw Mr Moore frequently and took a great delight in the pungent, highly seasoned flavour of his personality. I went with Johnson and the Embassy staff to the train to meet him, and from the moment he stepped down from his carriage, cigar in the corner of his mouth, glittering with diamonds and shining in the brightest of bright camel's hair coats, I knew that here was a type that would repay any amount of observation.

'Sheean, eh? Oh, so you're the young feller that got in all the trouble, are ya? I saw Hank Wales in Paris; he told me all about it. Well, y'know, these things happen. Come around and see me and we'll talk it over.'

Sometimes when he spoke his cigar would tilt 'up alarmingly, so that the furry splendour of his yellow hat seemed in danger; but he never lost control of it. Among the marvels of Mr Moore, his technique with that cigar was one of the most impressive. A subtler marvel, which only became apparent after some study of the subject, was the way in which he deliberately emphasized the crudities of his self-made Americanism—put them on, so to speak, for the entertainment of his public, like the make-up of a clown. His shrewdness consisted in exploiting this aspect of his personality to the utmost, so that he came in time to exercise the influence, and be permitted the liberties, which in centuries past might have been accorded to a court jester. As a result of such accidents, in at least two important matters (the commercial treaty and the American telephone monopoly) he got advantages in Spain that a more conventional ambassador might not have obtained.

He was passionately, blindly devoted to Spain and the monarchy. He adored the King and Queen, who seemed to him the most charming, agreeable and intelligent of human beings; he was a violent admirer of Primo de Rivera. He had come to Spain late in life—a newcomer to the diplomatic service, and not, I imagined, equipped with much social experience by his past in America. The forms and amenities of an ambassador's existence in Madrid enchanted him; nothing made him happier than a court display, unless it was a ball or reception at his own embassy. The Queen, in particular, impressed him so much that he could scarcely speak of her in an ordinary tone of voice; he referred to her (and he did it often) with reverence. It was all a childish dream-phantasm—'from news-boy to Ambassador'—and it dazzled and delighted him, just as he was dazzled and delighted by large diamonds, titles, Rolls-Royces, expensive French hair tonic, and fantastically costly cigars. He was a portentous phenomenon,

Mr Moore; here, in a word, was *the* American Ambassador, the one who most startlingly exemplified all the characteristics peculiar to the species.

I used to go to see him every afternoon at the Embassy on the Castellana. After a little conversation, he would say: 'Well, how about a walk to the barber shop?' Then off we would go, up the Castellana to my hotel, which he called the 'barber shop.' Along the way he would tell stories about the Court, reminisce, expatiate. The Queen had once broken up an official reception (on the occasion of Doña María Cristina's birthday) so that Mr Moore could leave Santander in time to keep a dinner engagement in Biarritz. . . . The King, on the occasion of the *jura de la bandera*, had ridden up to Mr Moore's Rolls-Royce and said: 'Well, how do you like it, Mr Moore?' and Mr Moore had replied: 'I think it's a fine show, Y'Majesty.' . . . The Queen had done this and that, the King had done thus and so; and Mr Moore always appeared in these stories as their jolly, funny, disconcertingly frank and colourful friend. They liked him as he was; he knew it, and aided them by making himself even more so.

'And don't you go paying any attention to all this Republican talk,' he would say, emphasizing his points with cigar and cane. 'There won't ever be any republic in this country. Not with such a fine fellow as they've got for King. That's all just hot air.'

I often wondered where he got this assurance on all questions connected with Spain, since he knew not a word of Spanish; but such things are hidden from the eyes of the humble. Only God and the State Department can tell what makes an American ambassador.

One day Mr Moore told me he had been notified by Primo that the court-martial proceedings against me had been dropped; I was at liberty to leave Spain. The 'official error' to which all these events had been due was, quite simply, a belief on the part of the Censura that the author of Telegram No. XX35998 was a Spanish subject. A Spanish subject would have had no recourse; a Spanish subject was at the mercy of the precious régime Mr Moore admired so much; and the crime to be punished was, in short, not so much the composition of the offending telegram as the graver offense of being born under the dominion of Alfonso XIII.

13

The Assembly of the League of Nations in 1924 was my second and last. It was the year of the MacDonald-Herriot 'protocol'; it was, in fact, the MacDonald-Herriot year all round. Those worthy gentlemen, shining examples of the social democracy of Europe, had made up their minds to correct all the errors of their predecessors without attacking any of the causes for those errors. The attempt was interesting to watch. Mr MacDonald, seduced and intoxicated by the footlights, was already beginning to play his 'historic rôle'; even then there could be seen the beginnings of the astonishing personal vanity and intellectual confusion that were to make him, in later years, the delight of the cameramen and the sorrow of philosophers. He had already begun to talk in sentences like 'good will between nations, upon which the relations of countries depend, is in turn dependent upon their willingness to understand each other'—the kind of harmless, meaningless iteration that permitted a whole decade in Europe to prepare for war. M. Herriot, a less ornamental figure, was at once more practical and more humane; his words were equally high-flown and round-about, but on some few points of reality he attempted to obtain settlements with the illusion of permanence. Between them, as they came to power in the spring of 1924, these two men represented for a while the hope of Europe: it was somehow expected that they, and the body of worried opinion they represented, might settle the problems of reparations and disarmament and effectively remove the causes that so obviously must lead in time to another war.

The Herriot-MacDonald régime began with the London Conference, the Dawes Plan, the evacuation of the Ruhr; it proceeded, in the memorable Assembly of 1924 at Geneva, to attempt a comprehensive system of enforcement of the peace. This system was embodied in the so-called 'protocol,' upon which the nations debated for months, and which was never ratified.

The MacDonald-Herriot 'protocol' came in the middle of the decade of wordiness, before everybody had quite lost faith in such devices. At the outset it seemed possible that the protocol might actually, by redefining the Covenant of the League, set up a peace system that could be maintained. It was hoped to fix what constituted 'war'; which side was the 'aggressor'; and what were the duties of the other powers, members of the League, in punishing the 'aggressor.' Mr. MacDonald, who lived on an island and was not in much danger, opened proceedings in fine style—supplied the organ music that brought the nations into their deliberations at Geneva: his was the grand processional. M. Herriot, who lived in a country where the enemy was at spitting distance, attempted to get some specific points of guarantee put into the document which the nations tried to draw up. But the Japanese—specifically little Baron Adatci—who seemed insensible to the blandishments of words then as always, introduced the fatal touch of reality that caused the meeting to break up in disorder: theirs was the grim recessional.

The Japanese amendment to the protocol was introduced very late in the session of 1924; I was in Geneva at the time, and witnessed the terror that one word of reality set up. Everything had been going along very nicely. Speeches galore had been made; commissions and subcommissions had met, discussed, reported. Geneva was somnolent, with the beatific, happy drowsiness the League used to know how to bestow. All was for the best in the best of all possible worlds, and before long a fine new peace promise was going to be signed by fifty-odd nations beneath the purring benediction of Mr MacDonald and M. Herriot.

At this juncture, in the midst of a warm, lazy afternoon, Baron Adatci got up in open meeting and moved an amendment to the clause of the new protocol that defined the arbitrable causes of war. His amendment provided that disputes likely to cause war should be arbitrable, even though one party to the dispute might claim that the question at issue was one of internal jurisdiction.

The phrases meant little to me at first: I was sleepy; but I could see the astonishment and agitation that suddenly broke out in the quiet corridors of the Palais des Nations. Lord Parmoor and M. Briand, who had succeeded MacDonald and Herriot at the head of the British and French delegations, went off in a hurry, beset by questions; the Prime Minister of New Zealand, Sir James Craig, was a thundercloud. I went along to the Japanese delegation, obtained a copy of the amendment, and read it over stupidly. A

Japanese correspondent—the representative of the Osaka *Asahi* —saw, apparently, that here was an example of the invincible ignorance of the Yankee. He leaned towards me gently and said one word: 'Immigration.'

Light broke; and with it something of a small thrill. Here was the first word of sense I had heard at Geneva since my arrival; here was, at last, one definite reference to a dispute that might bring on war. Moreover, here was a great 'story' for America: a warning, polite but as clear as a clap of thunder, of the storm the Japanese were not afraid to expect.

Geneva became almost hysterical for two or three days. The Australians and New Zealanders were up in arms, and even if the gentle, easy-going, absent-minded Lord Parmoor had been unable to see the dangers of the situation they would have opened his eyes. Briand—the old fox—seemed almost happy: for once the villain of the piece was not France. He would come into the room at the Beau Rivage where he received us, his head sunk in his wing collar, his marvellous, magical voice emerging gaily in the accents of a taxi-driver:

'B'en, messieurs! Ça va? Quoi de nouveau?'

And with a twinkle in his eyes, at an awkward question:

'Ah, ça——! Ah, ça——! Faut demander, vous savez, aux Japonais.'

The Japanese amendment was, of course, nothing new in history. Exactly the same thing had been proposed by Viscount Ishii at Versailles and defeated by Wilson. The Japanese had always maintained that immigration laws in any country discriminating specifically against them were an offence to their national honour. It had to be conceded by any reasonable person that they were right. The Americans (like the Australians, New Zealanders, and Canadians) were also right in wishing to prevent a flood of Japanese immigration; but the Americans, in particular, had taken the most offensive way possible to achieve their aims. Instead of continuing the quiet little agreement Lansing had made with Ishii, whereby the Japanese government itself kept its subjects from moving to America, the Congress at Washington had recently taken it into its head to pass a Japanese Exclusion Act—a wholly unnecessary insult to a susceptible people. There had been disorders in Tokio, suicides; one man had committed hara-kiri in front of the American Embassy as a protest; and here, in the calm backwaters of Geneva, we were presented with the results.

For some days the thought of war—the actual thought of a real war, not a rhetorical one—agitated the minds that had grown fat on toothsome words. The Japanese amendment, stripped bare, meant just this: some day Japan might very likely see fit to fight in defence of the national honour attacked in the Exclusion Act passed by the American Congress; when that happened the Americans would say that the question was one of their own internal jurisdiction; where, then, did the League stand? Was Japan to be judged an aggressor in that war? Or would the League compel the Americans to arbitrate the dispute?

The League, of course, driven into a corner, forced to consider such a terrible question, was paralyzed with fright. It was impossible to offend the Japanese; it was impossible to offend the Australians and New Zealanders; it would have been almost worst of all to offend the Americans, who were not members of the League and would certainly never become members if this amendment entered the constitution of Geneva. The Australians wanted the amendment rejected at once, and the Japanese wanted it accepted. The League did what the League has always done in such cases: referred the problem to committees and adjourned. The protocol was never ratified; the question was never settled.

So this poor League—broken, shattered by Corfu—was again, just a year later, despised and rejected of men; it was nerveless, without power and without will, the shadow of a dream. True, the dream had been a grandiose one. It had been the best dream of middle-class idealism in its dying years—the perfect dream flower of a culture that had always preferred to disguise ugly reality with pleasant appearance. What prettier thought had the nineteenth century, lingering on in its elder statesmen and college professors until 1919, brought forth in all its history? It wanted, that world —the world of Gladstone, Napoleon III, Mazzini; of social democracy and imperialism, antimacassars and the 'white man's burden,' Mr Asquith and Mr Wilson—to die in beauty. It hoped at the last to decorate its realities, so hideously exposed from 1914 to 1918, with something gentle, noble and persuasive. A league of nations—a Tennysonian super-parliament among the butter-cups, settling the bitter quarrels of mankind by sweet reasonable-ness . . .

That was the dream—pleasant enough, if superficial. And the shadow?

The things I was to remember best about Geneva that year were trivial, with scarcely more relation to causes than had the League itself. I remember Lord Parmoor, the gentle old Quaker who had joined the Labour party, referring to the British government, in an open meeting of the Council, as 'Her Majesty's government.' Lorelei, the smiling barmaid at the Victoria, was an optimist: 'Sie werden sehen,' she would say, 'everything s'arrangera.' The baccarat room at the Casino was open all night for delegates and accredited press correspondents, although the citizens of Switzerland were forbidden to gamble. The blue lake was particu-larly brilliant, and M. Briand's voice, that violoncello without an equal, was at its best. The whole thing was a large, pleasant, mixed house party, from which the grim suggestions of a world of struggle and death were automatically, as by the most ordinary politeness, excluded. Into this charming salon the Japanese, de-plorably blunt, obtruded their awkward question; the party broke up in a flurry and scurry of dismay.

I was not to see the League in operation again—was not, in-deed, to see any of the dispositions and arrangements of European politics again in the old way, as a working journalist every day of my life. I had been present at these arrangements in the hum-blest of capacities for more than three years. Except for a blessed month at Fiesole, in my first year, I had never had even one week away from attendance upon the pesthouse of Europe. The in-mates had been unaware of my services, even of my existence; but without meaning to do so they had considerably diminished my slender stock of belief, my narrow margin of expectancy. Three years with them had left a feeling of disgust. Possessing, in the rosiest possible view of things, nothing but an identity with sharp physical limits—a single life to be lived in a small allotment of time—I was in future to pursue the enterprise involved in that possession without any hope of their ready-made assistance. For what I wanted, such politics and such journalism were no good.

I had come to want what, I suppose, most maturing people want: to give this unique possession, this one life, somehow, a relation to the world of which it was a tiny segment—to attach it and articulate it, so that comprehension might eventually light up the darkness in which it had to be continued. There was no hope of this articulation, of this comprehension, in the politics of the time or in the journalism that was its servant. I could never again believe what I read in the newspapers, for example, because I could not believe the politicians who inspired what was printed there; and I could not believe the politicians because I had seen them squirming and dodging about, the poor powerless ferrets, trying to find a way out of the system in which they were imprisoned. In this doomed house there was no hope. If the desired sense of things was to be captured at all, it must be elsewhere. It was, quite possibly, uncapturable; but the pursuit was one of the primary conditions of life, without which its course, even in youth, would fall into emptiness.

III

The Rif

THE ROUTINE of Paris was good medicine after the Rhineland, Rome, Geneva: six or eight weeks of it had an anodyne effect, so that existence was kept from being altogether a matter of high lights and disappointments. Such an interval was particularly welcome in the autumn of 1924. I went to the Palace Theatre night after night to hear Raquel Meller sing her little *sainetes;* experimented with the varieties of French cooking under the direction of my Rumanian Communist friend Eugène Rosetti; worked as hard as was necessary; contrived, in short, to get along in spite of the general unsatisfactory state of the universe. For some reason—perhaps because I had seen the inside of a Spanish gaol—I was thought to be an expert on Spanish affairs in my office; I was given all the news from Spain to sift and pass on, and it was decided that in November I should go to Madrid again. The Spanish Republican propagandists, whose centre was in Paris, were as usual doing their best to persuade us that the hour was at hand when Alfonso XIII and Primo de Rivera would have to leave Spain.

But Madrid was calm enough when I got there. The Republican campaign did not seem to have made much impression, and everything political was said to depend upon Morocco. Primo de Rivera had come into office with promises, explicit and implicit, about the Moroccan campaign. After some twelve hundred years of conflict, the Spanish people were a little tired of fighting *los Moros*. Their eternal war, entering a new phase in the twentieth century, had been dignified by a series of international treaties under which Spain was to 'occupy' and 'protect' a zone in the northern part of the Moroccan Empire; and the reluctance of the population either to be 'occupied' or 'protected' brought about a series of advances and retreats in which thousands of Spaniards lost their lives. Primo had intended to settle all this at once. His failure to do so put him in a precarious position with respect to his clients. He went off to the front, leaving the government in the hands of the Almiral de Magaz.

Magaz was a thin, white-haired, aristocratical gentleman, who answered questions with a suavity and disingenuousness that made one think of the Renaissance. One interview with this wraithlike tyrant was as good as twenty, for it was obvious that his rule of conduct was to deny everything. No, there had been no reverses in Morocco; the situation was unchanged; the President of the Directorio had matters in hand; the rebels would be adequately punished very soon. . . .

Morocco itself was the place to go; but I had to wait for instructions from Paris. At last, in December, I was allowed to leave Madrid for Algeciras and Tetuan.

There was a brilliant sun when we passed from Algeciras to Ceuta. On the lower decks of the ship recruits for the Spanish Foreign Legion—mostly pale, discouraged Germans who looked as if they had been hungry for weeks—gazed vacantly at the walls of the two continents. Few of them would ever see Europe again. At Ceuta they were driven off like so many cattle, shuffling along, puzzled but meek, to be made into soldiers of King Alfonso. At the time I knew little of the recruiting methods for the Spanish and French Legions, and it surprised me to see that men who must, presumably, have enlisted in a foreign army out of sheer adventurousness could look so woebegone.

After a brief stop at Ceuta our boat went on around the corner of Africa to Tangier. The authorities in Madrid had not looked with a favourable eye upon my idea of visiting Morocco, and to escape their censorious attentions it seemed a good plan to make my headquarters in the international zone. There (at least in theory) an American was on the same basis as any Spaniard or Frenchman, since Tangier belonged to all nations. As we came near the city, a confusion of white, cream and yellow houses on a hill, there was firing to be heard from the black mountainous country of the Angeras at the left. The excitement of the moment came back whenever I thought of it again for years afterwards: the white city on the hill, demure and peaceful, with the long white beach beneath, and the vague thunder of Spanish guns off to the left, in mysterious mountains where no guns should have been. French and British gunboats bobbed harmlessly up and down on the sparkling water far out in front of the town. To meet our boat every turbaned rapscallion in Tangier had taken to the water: in ten minutes we were offered an infinite variety of rugs, worked leather, embroidery, beaded objects, guidance and advice. I was beset by jabbering Arabs of all colours, of whom I remember particularly a white-haired old mulatto who had a remarkable command of English. 'Me Bill Bailey,' he said loudly, grinning. 'Good guide. Take you see everyting—everyting Merican-Engleesh like to see, mosque, shop, dance, get girls, everyting. Got here cards many genmen. Bill Bailey, me.' I never had time to employ Bill Bailey's services, but the fact of his presence, his grinning preoccupation with mosques and dancing girls while the guns were murmuring unheeded in the near-by hills, gave the scene a fillip of the commonplace that increased its power of excitement. The white city, once penetrated, might prove to be a huddle of poverty and filth; the guns, close by, might be terrifying or infuriating or both; the mysterious hills might be nothing but barren and desperate rock, with no more mystery to reveal than the palm of your foot; but at the first moment they were all alive with promise.

Tangier did nothing to calm this excitement, nothing to deflect it. Rumour, rumour, rumour: the British, French and Americans were all sure that Spain had suffered a series of disastrous defeats and had been driven all the way down to the sea, but exact details were lacking. Most inexplicable of all, the guns could still be heard, day after day, in the Angera country *behind* the Spanish lines. Had the tribes, even within the tiny zone Spain still controlled, risen in revolt? Was it possible that Abd el-Krim was as near to Tangier and Tetuan as rumour said?

I went down to Tetuan to see Primo de Rivera. He looked very worried, had lost weight and wore a frown permanently on his heavy face. Through the windows of his headquarters in the little Moorish town could be heard the occasional rumble of the guns, both to the south and to the northwest. It was consequently useless for him to deny that his enemies were near. He spoke of the revolt of the Angeras (which had not yet been admitted in the outside world) and of the disastrous retreat from Sheshuan, outlining for me on a big wall map just what he meant to do. This plan of campaign was what came to be known as the Primo de Rivera Line—an arrangement of the Spanish troops intended to defend Tetuan, Ceuta and the Angera country in the north, and a thin strip of territory along the coast to Larache in the south. The rest of the Spanish Zone he was, for the moment, giving up to Abd el-Krim, with the intention of using the Primo de Rivera Line as a basis for advances in the spring. He had had no choice in the matter, since his troops had been driven out of all the positions they had held in the interior; but even so, it was an unusual experience to hear a dictator, a general-in-chief, admit defeat and make his plans accordingly. The governmental gentry as a rule had other modes of speech.

In Tetuan I began to think seriously of going into the Rif. Remaining in the Spanish or the international zones could, obviously, do nothing but whet my curiosity and make the general feeling of frustrated excitement intolerable. Except for picturesque houses, crumbling stairs under old archways, and a twisting, crowded, covered labyrinth of streets, Tetuan had nothing to show a visitor who did not know how to reach its secrets. Spanish officers, tall bearded caïds from the hills, and the miscellaneous troops of all colours who were forever pouring in and out of the town, might as well have been figures on a film. And meanwhile, as I sat there, the murmur of the guns in the south confirmed the existence of a wholly different world somewhere within easy distance—a world in which the European was not only a rarity, but an enemy: the world of the tribes of Islam. It was sheer romanticism, if you like; but it seemed to me that if I could accomplish the transition from the harassed and crowded little walled city to the freedom of the hills I might possibly understand a thing or two that would never otherwise be clear. It was difficult, but not impossible, to go into the Rif. Two foreign correspondents had landed in the country and talked to Abd el-Krim only a few months before. One was Mr Ward Price of the *Daily Mail;*

the other was Mr Paul Scott Mowrer of the Chicago *Daily News*. Both had landed at the Bay of Alhucemas from the Spanish fort there, and both had benefited by the friendliness of the Spanish authorities. This way was not open to me. I had never been wholly in favour with the Spanish authorities since our little unpleasantness in Madrid the preceding spring. It was unlikely that they would give me much aid in such an enterprise.

To settle the point, I spoke to Primo de Rivera again on the day I returned to Tangier.

'Excellency,' I said, 'I have been wondering if it would be possible for me to go into the Rif and see Abd el-Krim.'

He looked at me almost angrily.

'The idea is absurd,' he said. 'We have evacuated the whole interior. There is not a Spanish post from Melilla to Tetuan. You could not possibly do it.'

'Two correspondents have already done it, Excellency. With your approval, I believe.'

'Circumstances have changed. Up until a few weeks ago the fort at Alhucemas was in regular communication with the mainland. They used to get their water there. Now, since the Wad Lau campaign and the retreat from Sheshuan, there is no communication whatever. It cannot be done, and moreover it is against the new policy. We have established the Line. It is a blockade, and you cannot very well ask us to break our own blockade.'

I was pleased enough with this reply. If Primo had chosen to facilitate matters he might have provided me with a two hours' visit to the shore of Alhucemas and a half hour's talk with Abd el-Krim—landed me from a boat and picked me up from a boat the same day. It could have been done. But it would have been, as Tom Sawyer said, too easy. In making it difficult Primo was adding everything to the attraction of the idea, everything to its results. By approaching the Rif in some other way—from the French zone, perhaps—I could get a far better notion of the country and the people, something definite, something that might explain the rise of the tribesmen and their extraordinary success. Or so I thought, at least; and I drove off to Tangier convinced that the only way to extract the sense of events in Morocco was to go into the forbidden mountains.

On the way to Tangier my car was, for some time, lost in the waves of a dispirited Spanish regiment. In this particular section of the glorious Ejército I saw something I had often heard about and never believed in—men without shoes. It was Christmas time, cold and wet, and the road was deep with mud, but about a third of the men we passed were plodding along in makeshift sandals. They might as well have been barefoot. No doubt some good profiteering gentleman was even then buying champagne at the Palacio de Hielo in Madrid with the money that should have gone into shoes for the army. But these weary conscripts, instead of using their rifles to obtain their shoes from their natural enemies, trudged off into the unknown wastes of a foreign country to shoot at (and be shot at by) some angry villagers they had never seen before. The arrangement did not seem sensible; but (like a true American) I reflected that I at least had shoes on my feet, and passed on.

2

I arrived at Tangier determined to go into the Rif at once, but there followed a series of those delays which Providence multiplies in the path of the impatient. My office hesitated to give me the authorization to undertake such a doubtful journey and finally telegraphed that I was to 'use my own discretion.' I had none to use, but stubbornness took its place. The Christian, Jewish and Mohammedan religions between them arranged another irritating difficulty: Christmas, Sunday, Saturday and Friday, with a few other holy days and holidays of various sorts, managed to fall at about the same time, so that the banks were closed, and it was impossible to get money transferred from London or Paris for days.

The difficulties were overcome, somehow, and one brisk morning towards the end of the year I climbed into an open touring car bound for the French zone.

The only other passenger in the car was, by agreeable coincidence, an American—Miss X Y Z, a trained hospital nurse with a passion for travelling. As we rocked along towards Rabat I learned a great deal about Miss X Y Z. She had nursed various nabobs of New York through various illnesses, and most of them made a practice of giving her tips on the stock market. Her last patient had been a friend of a very rich man, a manufacturer of yeast; and in the magic manipulations to which such products were subjected, this particular man's particular yeast had become exceedingly valuable. I asked Miss X Y Z if it was good yeast, but she considered the question irrelevant.

'I don't know anything about the yeast,' she said doubtfully. 'I guess it's all right. I never tried it. But my patient said to me, "Miss X Y Z, you take every penny you've got in the world and put it into Zippo's Yeast and you'll never regret it." And I did, and more than doubled my money! So I thought I'd take a little trip somewhere, and I've never been to Morocco.'

It seemed remarkable that Zippo's Yeast should suddenly have become twice as valuable as it was before, but I obtained no light from Miss X Y Z.

'It's not the *yeast*,' she said impatiently. 'Don't you understand? It's the *market*.'

Then, looking pensively out the side of the car towards a country mosque:

'I guess you don't hear much about the market over here, but it's a wonderful thing—you can't lose. It just goes up and up. Now you take Consolidated Clips. Two months ago they were selling at . . .'

Thus, in Miss X Y Z's amiable chatter. I first encountered the Great Boom.

On the next morning in Rabat Miss X Y Z and I settled ourselves into one of the enormous motor buses of the Compagnie Générale Transatlantique. Over Marshal Lyautey's superb roads the C. G. T. operated a service primarily for tourists; but, as there were no tourists, hotels and buses were nearly empty. Meknès . . . Fez . . . Taza . . . From time to time Miss X Y Z would point out interesting details upon which her profession had given her special competence.

'That kid's got syphilis,' she would say calmly. 'Eyes, skull and bones. Look at his legs! An orthopedic specialist would go mad here. . . . Look at their eyes.'

Or again:

'Eczema. Crawling with eczema. Did you ever see such a head?'

We stopped at Taza that night; and on the next day, at Oudjda, I took leave of Miss X Y Z. She was pursuing her travels farther, to Oran and Algiers, and is no doubt travelling still if her 'market' —that magic market which bore no relation to the things it had to sell—was good to her.

The serious business of getting into the Rif began at Oudjda. My plan—such as it was—was based upon information given me by angry Spanish officials. They all said that Abd el-Krim had agents in French Morocco and Algeria; that these agents bought supplies from the French and shipped them in to the Rif in cara-vans; that the French knew all about the traffic and made only half-hearted attempts to stop it. One of the most notorious agents of Abd el-Krim, said the Spaniards, was a certain Caïd Haddu, who lived in the French zone and was busy about many things. I had no idea whether this information was correct or not, but, in the hope that it was, I intended to find the Caïd Haddu (or another Riffian agent) and propose myself as a candidate for the next caravan into the hills.

There was a biggish garage in Oudjda, to which I took my problem. The ruling opinion seemed to be that the Riffian agent lived just across the borders of Algeria, beyond Port Say. I was given a wheezy old Renault car with a French driver, and set out from Oudjda after lunch.

The Caïd Haddu appeared to live in a kind of castle over-looking the Mediterranean. The coast here was rocky, and as romantic as any Mediterranean coast would be if it were stripped of its villas and left to the sea and sun. Caïd Haddu's castle was built of stone indistinguishable in colour from the promontory on which it stood. A flight of steps carved in the rock led up to it; and in the dirty, crumbling courtyard, amid the goats and chickens, there were a few active old women and one motionless old man. Between them they succeeded in conveying to me the information that the Caïd had gone away somewhere—'Fez? Algiers? We don't know'—but that I might be able to talk to his son in another house across the fields.

Mohammed ben Haddu, the Caïd's son, was a thin, wolf-like creature of seventeen or eighteen. He wore the close-fitting snow-white turban of the Rif, which only threw into sharper relief the narrow darkness of his face and eyes. He must have been far more Arab than Riffian, for his eyes were black as truffles, and his skin was the colour of olives ripening on the tree. A sinister fellow to look upon, and the fact that he wore a grey woollen overcoat and tennis shoes made him no less sinister. His manners were as bad as his looks. He went through none of the usual gestures of Moslem hospitality.

'What do you want?' he said.

I explained my plan: to get the Caïd Haddu to send me into the Rif with a caravan. The young man said his father was already in the Rif; that the caravan routes were closed; that it was impossible to get through the Beni bu Yahi country alive. And when all this had been duly impressed upon me he added, 'But I might go into the Rif with you myself.'

I was never able to decide what Mohammed ben Haddu intended to do when he so easily declared himself willing to go with me. Certainly, as soon appeared, he had no real idea of marching all the way into that country of barren mountains, privations and danger. His plan was probably to accompany me to Oudjda, perhaps a little farther, extracting such sums as he could get along the way, and then vanish towards Oran or Algiers or some other centre of civilization where he could spend his takings on the pleasures of Christian wine and Moslem dancing girls. But that day at the Caïd's house I had no misgivings. Indeed I could not afford to be distrustful, for I had been wanting to go into the Rif for the past month, and this was the first bit of definite encouragement I had ever received. Mohammed ben Haddu went into the house to get a jellaba.[1] In less than ten minutes he was out again, having made his sketchy farewells, and we started on the long drive back to Oudjda. By the next night we were at Taourirt, the post from which caravans to the Rif usually started.

Here there was a rebellion before we had been in the village an hour.

'I have made inquiries,' Mohammed said, coming into my

---

[1]Jellaba: The loose-fitting hooded robe worn by the Riffian tribesmen and others in Morocco. In the Rif it is of rough brown homespun, slips on over the head, has loose and rather short sleeves, and falls to a little below the knee.

room at the little inn. 'It is impossible to go on. The French and Spanish have closed all the roads. They fire at night on anybody who tries to pass. Those whom they do not kill are killed by the Beni bu Yahi. It is impossible to go on.'

I suggested that this opinion was due, perhaps, to fear. He fired up at once. He was not afraid. He had killed eight 'Spanish dogs' before he was sixteen. (At the moment I thought this was just possible; afterwards I was sure he had never killed a fly.) He was willing to go anywhere anybody else could go. And so on. He was, in short, the very devil of a fellow. I was beginning to be aware, through the clouds of his abundant French, that Mohammed ben Haddu had all the braggadocio and untrustworthiness of the Arab character without any of its virtues. He had spent his short life being educated in French schools at Tlemcen and Algiers—an occupation that had given him no time to acquire the ruder but more useful qualities of his own people.

Early the next morning I took the unwilling Mohammed ben Haddu by the arm and marched him down to the post to interview M. Louis Gabrielli, the political officer of Taourirt.

Gabrielli was one of the cleverest officers in Lyautey's Arab service. He spoke Moroccan Arabic very well, was respected by the whole district, and had a number of Arab agents who regularly reported to him the news of the tribes, even from the blockaded Rif. He already knew all my business, and did not attempt to conceal the fact: Lyautey's intelligence service was a good one.

'You can't go into the Rif like this, without preparation,' Gabrielli told me. 'First you must send a courier in to Abd el-Krim, asking him to have a detachment of his own men at the border to meet you. Then you must wait for the reply. It will take two or three weeks. Or you should wait, in any case, until the Caïd Haddu returns. This son of his is worthless, even more worthless than the father.'

He had dismissed Mohammed ben Haddu at once, and was talking to me very seriously.

'You don't know this country,' he said. 'Your life isn't worth a sou once you get beyond the French outposts. You journalists are all alike. You think it is easy to go wherever you want to go. There are border tribes between here and the Rif that think nothing of robbing and killing. That's how they live.'

Gabrielli was like the American consul-general in Tangier, who had solemnly warned me against this journey and then wished me good luck. He painted a black picture, then made the best of it.

'Very well,' he said. 'If you must go, you must. But that young imp of Haddu's is no good. I'll have him in and give him a talking to.'

Mohammed was brought in and subjected to such a lecture as I have seldom heard. In the crackling, spluttering Arabic, it sounded severe enough to discourage Satan himself. I could see the sullen youth crumpling up, making protests, promises. Gabrielli finished at last, dismissed him again, and sent for somebody else.

'This is the Caïd Mimoun,' he said, 'who has a caravan going into the Rif tomorrow morning. He will arrange for you to go with it, with relations of his. Caïd Mimoun is a good man, and you can trust him.'

The newcomer in the little office was a tall, white-robed Arab with a very dark skin. For two hundred pesetas the Caïd Mimoun would give me and Mohammed ben Haddu mules, food and passage with his caravan to Midar in the Rif. The Caïd, who appeared to have a healthy respect for Gabrielli, was all courtesy; he suggested that we might seal the bargain by drinking tea with him. Gabrielli nodded; I was to accept the invitation; Mimoun and Mohammed and I departed, and I never saw Gabrielli again. In half an hour he had arranged everything I had been trying for more than a month to accomplish. He was as kindly and efficient an officer as I ever met. Some ten days later he was to come to my aid again, from a distance, and I am not at all sure that I do not owe him my life for it.[1]

We were up before dawn in the morning. Mohammed ben

---

[1] For obvious reasons Gabrielli asked me at that time not to use his name in anything I might write, and not to disclose how he had assisted me. I did as he asked; but the political situation that made this necessary ceased to exist years ago, and he can scarcely object now to being named.

Haddu, made dutiful by Gabrielli's lecture, came in and supervised the winding of my turban. I was to wear Arab clothing, not with any foolish notion of disguise, but so as to be less conspicuous in the hills. My luggage consisted of a toothbrush, some toothpaste, a small prayer rug (which I thought might be useful as a present), an old overcoat, carried along as a blanket, two passports, a French-Arabic dictionary, and a copy of M. Joseph Caillaux's book called *Agadir*. Most of my belongings I had left at Tangier; the rest I was obliged to leave at Taourirt. Mohammed ben Haddu approved my appearance after the turban had been rewound a few times; I pulled the cowl of my jellaba over my head, and we went down the dark street of the village to Mimoun's courtyard, where the caravan assembled.

'This is your mule,' said Mimoun. 'And your muleteer, Said. Cover your face with your jellaba if the French officers look at you. Trust Mohammed from Midar; he is of my family.'

The preparations for departure were as silent as was possible to a caravan of seven camels and five mules, with about twice as many men. It was still dark when we left Taourirt; dawn came half an hour later when we were on the open plain; by noon we had reached the foothills. Here, at Camp Berteaux (the last French post), Mohammed ben Haddu rebelled again; he wanted to stop for a few days or return to Taourirt. But by this time I had talked to Mimoun's relative, Mohammed from Midar, who spoke a little Spanish and was ready to go on with or without Haddu's son. If I had given the young Haddu some money he might have returned to Taourirt, and I should have been rid of him for good. A false notion of economy kept me from doing so, and after some moments of sullen, surly hesitation, he decided to follow along after me. The struggle between cupidity and cowardice made his dark face look more murderous than ever.

That journey belongs in the category of things that become incredible once they have been safely lodged in the past. I can no longer believe the day and night existed—those nineteen hours, nineteen eternities, during which I alternately rode a stinking mule on a wooden saddle or struggled along on foot. When I was no longer able to walk, I rode; and when my backside could no longer endure another minute of riding, I fell off and walked.

It was gone through, somehow. The most astonishing thing about youth (my own youth, at any rate) was its capacity for physical exertion beyond the limits of the possible.

Mohammed from Midar, who was smuggling in tea and sugar on his two mules, was in charge of our part of the caravan. We soon lost the camels; they went on ahead of us at one of our brief stops for rest, fell in with a raiding party of the Beni bu Yahi, and came to grief. Early in that cold, moon-flooded night we passed the naked body of a freshly killed man. Mohammed from Midar said it was that of a camel driver. Of the rest of the men or their camels there was no trace. After this gruesome episode we hurried on as fast as the mules could go, and as silently. In the morning the muleteers had sung raucously, told jokes, laughed and cursed. Now they were afraid even to whisper to one another. They carried their rifles ready, peered into the shadows, jumped nervously at the least sound. Towards dawn we came towards a V-shaped cleft in the hills. A little round blockhouse could be seen on either side of this pass, and men with rifles came running down towards us. Mohammed from Midar called out to them.

'The Metalsa,' he said to me cheerfully. 'We can stop here and rest.'

The Metalsa riflemen threw back the hood of my jellaba and took a good look. A clatter of argument broke out between them and my two Mohammeds. There was a flat rock conveniently near; it looked like a bed of roses to me, for I had never been so weary. I lay—or fell—upon it and went to sleep at once. At that moment nothing else seemed of consequence.

3

At some time after this, just before sunrise, I was awakened by Mohammed ben Haddu and followed him down a path made partly of steps cut into the cliff. The cold early light showed no houses, tents or other signs of human habitation. We were on a cliff above a dried-up river bed. Halfway down the cliff there was a natural ledge with a semicircular wall behind it; into this wall— the side of the hill—caves had been dug by man or nature or both. There were three openings on the shelf-like ledge. Into the middle opening Mohammed ben Haddu ducked, kicking off his shoes. The hole was scarcely three feet high, and the effort of crouching to go through it was agony to my stiffened muscles.

Inside the cave a number of bearded Arabs sat in a circle. They greeted us with the *Salaam aleikum* (pronounced much more like *S'laam wallicum* in these parts) and I could hear curious voices raised, but I was too exhausted to pay much attention to them. There was a pile of rifles in the corner, which did excellently for a pillow. I fell asleep again almost at once, and it was hours later—noon, at least—before I awoke.

The cave was now half lighted by the oblique rays of the sun, and it was possible to distinguish the individual figures in the bearded, solemn circle. It took me days to learn all their names and positions in the tribe, but from the first I could see that one of them was in command of all the rest. He was a magnificent Arab of about forty (younger than most of the other chiefs) with oxlike shoulders, a black beard, and white hands that had never done any work except to pull a trigger or wield a sword. This was the Caïd Hamid ben Dada of the Metalsa—my host or my gaoler, whichever he might be called; he changed from one rôle to the other so rapidly that I never knew my own status. Next to him sat a much older man, wrapped up in a series of woollen jellabas, who coughed into his sleeve at frequent intervals: this was Sidi Ali, a scribe, tubercular and fanatical, whom I learned to fear more than anybody else in the Metalsa. There was another, younger scribe: Sidi Mohammed, the most intelligent and the friendliest of the chiefs; and there was a sort of tribal comedian, the Caïd Absalem, a ferocious-looking fellow straight out of the Arabian Nights, who talked a great deal and made wild speeches against the Christian dogs. Caïd Absalem, for all his savage appearance, had a kindly soul, and most of his ferocity in the tribal circle was assumed to make his associates laugh.

Mohammed ben Haddu, frightened half out of his wits, whispered that I was not to speak until the Caïd asked me a question. Eventually, after six rounds of mint tea had been noisily consumed, the Caïd Hamid turned his unblinking black eyes on me. Mohammed ben Haddu, nervous and ill at ease, translated.

'Are you French? Are you Spanish? What are you?'

The word 'American' was a great difficulty for some time, until I reflected that truth was only relative and the English a mighty nation.

'Tell him,' I said, 'that the Americans are the same as the English, only in another country, like the Arabs of Algeria and the Arabs of Morocco.'

This happy lie caused a murmur of satisfaction to go round the circle. 'Glinzi,' they all said, one after the other. The Glinzi appeared to be in favour hereabouts, and for a time even Mohammed ben Haddu was encouraged.

The next step was to explain my business with Abd el-Krim; but this was more difficult. Having convinced the chiefs, by exhibiting an old copy of the *Heraldo de Madrid*, that newspapers existed, it was necessary to establish the still odder fact that some newspapers were capable of sending people like me great distances in search of news. After interminable discussion it was decided that I was a scribe; and it seemed better to let it go at that. That a newspaper could have scribes of its own appeared too incredible to insist upon, and when the Caïd Hamid—wallowing, as he did, in a marsh of unfamiliar ideas and systems—came to the conclusion that I was a scribe to the American government, which in its turn was a branch of the Glinzi government, I did not protest. For the duration of my enforced visit to the Metalsa I was a scribe to the *Maghzen el-Merikan*.

The interrogation went on, hour after hour, until the chiefs grew tired of it and began to make speeches. They spoke of the glory of Abd el-Krim, the splendour of his victories over the Spaniards, the certainty with which those who fought for Abd el-Krim would go to heaven and all others to hell. At the end of the speech-making they began to chant in unison, 'La ilaha ill' Allah,' counting off a hundred repetitions on their wooden rosaries. When the chant died there were a few minutes of prayer and meditation; then the cave suddenly emptied. This was my first opportunity to smoke a cigarette. I went up to the top of the cliff with Mohammed from Midar, and we walked up and down, smoking.

'Your muleteer was sent back to Taourirt this morning,' he told me. 'They are sending me on to Midar tomorrow morning.

It is very bad for you. I do not know what they will do. They might turn you loose on a mule in the direction of Hasi Wenzga. You would never get there, of course. They might send you on to Ait Kamara, to the Sultan. Or they might kill you themselves. I do not think they will do that, because they are afraid of the Sultan; besides, you are not rich enough.'

From the hilltop the plain looked hot and peaceful under the sun. The sound of Spanish bombs occasionally drifted our way, but otherwise the whole world seemed empty and silent. As nearly as I could tell, Melilla and the Spanish army lay to the north, the French posts from which I had come were across the plain to the southeast. According to Mohammed, at this particular point in space—known as Suk Tleta, or the Wednesday Marketing Place of the Metalsa—the main fighting strength of the tribe was concentrated. The men lay in caves all along these cliffs and issued forth when it was time to raid or to repel raids. The Metalsa were an Arab tribe related to the Beni bu Yahi, but had recently thrown in their lot with the Riffians and acknowledged Abd el-Krim as Sultan. Just how much discipline they would be willing to take, even from Abd el-Krim, was a matter of doubt.

At sunset all the fighting men emerged from their caves for the evening prayer. It was an impressive sight: some two hundred of them prostrated themselves on the hilltop, praying towards the east, while the long call of 'Allah akbar!' echoed over the plain beneath. When the prayer was over they scattered to their caves for supper, and I returned to my far corner in the cave of the chiefs.

Supper was a great disappointment to a hungry man. It began with six rounds of sickly sweet mint tea, which I was already beginning to like; but after that the menu ceased to interest me. It consisted of chunks of goat meat stewed in crude, stinking olive oil. Everybody in the cave fished for chunks of meat with thumb and forefinger; sometimes Caïd Hamid or one of the scribes would dig up a juicy bit and offer it to me, but I tried the delicacy only once. Afterwards I told Mohammed ben Haddu to tell them that in my country we never consumed any kind of meat. They accepted the information without surprise, continued their meal, and when it was all over the weary questioning began again.

That night eleven men slept in the cave of the chiefs. We were wedged tightly together, and the smell must have been like that of a congregation of mules. I do not know; for I was still so stiff and tired that I slept the moment I was given a place to lie down in. At sunrise we had more tea, and Mohammed ben Haddu— that son of all the Afrits—played his last little trick in my life.

'Today is the Fourth Day [Thursday] Market—Suk el-Arbaa —of the Metalsa,' he said agreeably. 'I can go on down there and buy some oranges and raisins, as well as some sugar and tea. You have to have food, and if you can't eat meat this is the only way to get it. The Metalsa won't want to give us food after the first day. Give me money and I'll go to the market.'

This seemed sensible enough. Shortly after sunrise I had been moved out of the cave of the chiefs to another hole in the cliff farther down the ledge—a larger hole, it is true, but without rushes or rugs, and filled with refuse. It was used by the Caïd's two little slaves and such stray beggars as there might be. Clearly I had now ceased to be a guest and had become a prisoner. Mohammed's suggestion was therefore a good one.

Some time later Mohammed returned to me in the beggar's cave, bringing the Caïd Hamid ben Dada with him. There followed a most curious conversation. Mohammed ben Haddu had us both at his mercy. He talked to me in rapid French, to the Caïd in rapid Arabic. I thought I was being asked the same old questions again ('Where do you come from? Where are you going? What do you want?') and grew a little impatient. The Caïd Hamid sighed heavily and went away after some three quarters of an hour. It was a brilliant *tour de force* on the part of Mohammed ben Haddu, for he had ably deceived us both.

'Well,' he said, 'I am going to market. Give me your money.'

I gave him a French hundred-franc note.

'You will have to have Spanish money here,' he said. 'Give me all your French money, and I can change it at the Suk el-Arbaa for Spanish duros.'

I handed it over.

'If you let me have your watch,' he said, 'I can tell better when to come back.'

This seemed unnecessary, and I refused. Mohammed was not

pleased, for which it is difficult to blame him. He had succeeded so beautifully up to this point that it seemed a pity to be baulked of such a small extra thing as a watch. But his mule was led up the hill; his face brightened; he climbed aboard the beast and made off, crying out cheerily, 'Au revoir!'

There followed two or three days of intolerable boredom. With both Mohammeds gone there was nobody in the tribe who spoke any Christian language. I got through the first day by re-reading M. Caillaux's book about Morocco (which I already knew by heart). I was hungry, but comforted myself with the thought of all the good things Mohammed ben Haddu would bring back from the Suk el-Arbaa. I would have liked to go out of the cave and walk on the hilltop, but every time I stuck my head out I was motioned back again by a rifle. Towards night I began to think that Mohammed ben Haddu had been lost. I demanded to see the Caïd Hamid.

'Where is Mohammed ben Haddu?' I asked him.

'Gone back to Taourirt,' he said in some surprise.

The conversation was carried on against great difficulties. I spoke the Arabic of my dictionary, aided by gestures; the Caïd spoke in rich, billowing phrases of which I could seize very little. I told him I had given Mohammed ben Haddu all my money to go to the market. This part of the story he appeared to understand, although he was at pains to convince me that he had had nothing to do with the affair. He spoke eloquently for some time and vanished.

I had no supper that night. The little slaves (both were named Hamid, and neither could have been more than twelve years old) took their food from the chiefs' pot after the chiefs had finished; but their tea they made themselves in our cave. They gave me tea, and I guzzled five glasses of the sweet mint mixture, but it could not have been called filling. An old beggar who appeared to be in the last stages of tuberculosis crawled into the cave and went to sleep. When he coughed too much the little slaves kicked him. The cave—all the caves—had grown silent; the whole night seemed to have been asleep for hours, when a figure appeared in the entrance to our smelly grotto. It was Sidi Mohammed, the younger of the two scribes. 'Señor,' he whispered, 'comer!'—the only two Spanish words he knew. In the folds of his jellaba he held three oranges, some walnuts and raisins. All these he dumped into my jellaba and vanished. I never knew where he found such uncommon good food in the middle of the night.

On the following day some faint hope appeared on the horizon in the shape of a Metalsa tribesman who could speak Spanish. He was beardless and ragged, might have been twenty years old, and had one eye that seemed to move without collusion with the other. He had been a servant to the Spanish officers in Tizzi Azza and knew enough of their language to get along, although I suppose our conversation would scarcely have been regarded as Spanish in the salons of Madrid. The cock-eyed one made up in resourcefulness what he lacked in grammar. It was his suggestion that I should send out to French Morocco for more money if I intended to pursue my journey. We went to the cave of the chiefs and argued the point for hours. Before the day was over I learned the full extent of Mohammed ben Haddu's treachery; he had told them that I was sending him back to Taourirt, and that I was supplied with money to pay for food and other expenses during my stay among them.

It took about two days to convince Caïd Hamid that it might be profitable to allow me to carry out my plans. Eventually, after I had presented him with every object I possessed that could interest him (my watch, the prayer rug, a tarboosh, a small metal pencil), he agreed to send a runner out to Taourirt with a message for M. Louis Gabrielli, and another to Ait Kamara with a letter for Abd el-Krim.

I had no right to call on Gabrielli for aid, but he was my only hope. I tore one of the fly leaves out of my Arab dictionary and wrote to him on it, asking for as much money as he could send and telling him to apply for repayment to the Chicago *Tribune*. To Abd el-Krim I wrote more fully, giving an account of what had happened and asking that orders be given to let me go on into the Rif.

After this the days became all alike—like hours or like years, indistinguishable units of waiting. There was nothing for me to do. I was not allowed to walk beyond the spring at the foot of the hill, where I went to drink water, guarded always by one of the boys with a rifle bigger than himself. Caïd Hamid had moved me back again into the cave of the chiefs, which, although equally verminous, was more comfortable than the cave of the servants. I was never sure how many days there were, eleven or twelve, each like the other. Anybody who has travelled among Arabs knows their passion for sitting hour after hour in desultory conversation or in silence. The habit endures even when all other habits of the desert have vanished, and European chairs have taken the place of the good Bedawin haunches; even the Arabs of New York, as I was to learn years later, can sit all day long in a circle and say little or nothing. The only accomplishment I acquired among the Metalsa was to sit on my haunches and be still. Sometimes Sidi Mohammed, my friend the scribe, endeavoured to teach me Arabic; Caïd Absalem taught me prayers. I could say, 'Ash-hadu anna la ilaha ill Allah wa anna Mohammedan rasul-Allah' as well as the next one. When the chiefs chanted, 'La ilaha ill' Allah,' I chanted with them.[1]

The Spanish air raids came over every morning and every noon, dropping a few harmless, noisy bombs. The aviators apparently had a certain number of bombs to get rid of (like boys with handbills), and they got rid of them without attempting to do any damage. The noise was a little frightening at first, but it was easy to get used to it. We sat in our caves until the planes had passed over, and then rushed out to watch their departing flight.

One evening the courier arrived from Abd el-Krim. He was a Riffian, blue-eyed and sunburned, with the features of an Irishman or a Scot. He wore the orange felt turban of a minor caïd in Abd el-Krim's army. The order he bore—a piece of crabbed Arabic writing on rice paper—was passed from hand to hand and kissed by all the chiefs before the scribes laboriously deciphered it. I was to be sent under escort to the Sultan at Ait-Kamara. And on that same night while we slept, the cock-eyed Metalsa who had gone out to Gabrielli returned with money. Most of it was taken over by the Caïd Hamid ben Dada, who knew a *duro* when he saw one. A little after sunrise the next morning, with two Metalsa as guides

[1]Such behaviour would have horrified Mr. John Galsworthy (did he not write a whole novel about the unworthiness of an Englishman who acknowledged Mohammed to save his own life?).

and escort, I boarded my mule again and started towards the mountains.

4

It took two days and a half of steady going to cross the mountains of the Rif and reach the sea. I counted three main ranges, and after the first was passed all the trails were goat tracks drawn high across the rocky hillsides, sometimes with terrifying gorges yawning two inches the other side of my mule's feet. On the third day, towards noon, I came to Ajdir, the village on Alhucemas Bay which was known as Abd el-Krim's capital. The Sultan himself (I had easily fallen into the habit of calling Abd el-Krim 'es-Sultan,' as he had no other name among his own people) dwelt in a new house at Ait Kamara, over the hill behind Ajdir.

I remained at Ajdir as Abd el-Krim's guest for about ten days before I was given an opportunity of seeing him. The whole *diwan*, his cabinet, came to visit me at one time or another; I had conversations with them lasting half a day at a time. Sidi Mohammedi bel Hadj Hitmi, brother-in-law of Abd el-Krim, saw to it that I had the best possible food and lodging. I stayed in Abd el-Krim's old house (the one in which he had lived before he moved to Ait Kamara), and the only discomfort of existence there was that it drew a disproportionate share of attention from the Spanish aviators on raids. I was so much a guest of honour at Ajdir that Sidi Mohammedi even dug up a package of Algerian cigarettes for me to smoke. This was the only tobacco I ever saw in the Rif itself, although western Morocco (the Djebala) was familiar with both tobacco and weak hashish.

I busied myself with collecting a variety of information of great interest to me at the time: how the Riffian army was organized; how big it was; where the arms and munitions came from, and how the patriarchal government of the tribes operated. I became convinced that Abd el-Krim's own Riffi troops were not more than six or seven thousand. The arms I saw were both Spanish and French—Schneider mountain cannon bought from the French; Hotchkiss guns bought or captured from the Spanish; rifles from both sources. There was no heavy artillery and there were no 'foreign advisers.' There had been two French aviators who flew an aëroplane in and attempted to teach the Riffi to fly; there were four German artillerymen at Kifane who taught gunnery; and there were a number of deserters (mostly Germans) from the French and Spanish Foreign Legions. But the deserters were usually employed at the most menial tasks, like the thousands of Spanish prisoners. It was they who built the roads that Abd el-Krim intended eventually to spread through the whole country. So far there was a road from Ajdir to Ait Kamara. On the whole, in spite of the impression of orderly administration Abd el-Krim's staff endeavoured to give, my chief feeling was one of wonder that a people so small, so ill equipped, had been able to drive the Spanish out of almost the whole of their Moroccan protectorate. You had to fall back upon more rudimentary things—the fanaticism of the Metalsa, for instance; their firm belief that they would go to heaven if they died fighting the Spaniards—to understand how such a miracle was possible.

Sidi Mohammedi sent for me one day, and I was conducted over the hill to Ait Kamara. There, in a whitewashed mud house like the one I had left behind in Ajdir, Abd el-Krim received me. He sat behind a table covered with papers: a smallish, stout, dark man in immaculate white turban. I never understood why he treated me with such formality on this occasion; months later, when I returned to the Rif, he was willing to talk for hours with me in Spanish, which he spoke very well indeed. But on this day he preferred to speak Shilluh, the language of the country, while Sidi Mohammedi translated into French; and as a result I got little idea of what he was like. My questions had all been written out many days before, and answers drawn up to them—a formality of procedure that could not have been surpassed by M. Poincaré himself. The Sultan, shrewd and impassive, waited while I wrote down almost every word of the answers as they were translated to me by Sidi Mohammedi; it took a long time, but when it was over I had a comprehensive list of the terms on which Abd el-Krim was willing to make his peace with the world.

They are strange reading now, those terms. For the conditions under which they might have been possible existed for one year only, and the leader who was so certain of his power and his mission was destined to spend the rest of his life as an exile on an island in the Indian Ocean, while the tribes he led returned to slavery. On that day he was at the highest point of his phenomenal success; it did not seem unreasonable for him to demand a total evacuation of the Spanish Protectorate, the absolute independence of the Rif, and full recognition by the powers. He was willing to allow Spain to hold the two Spanish *presidios* of Ceuta and Melilla, which Spaniards had governed for centuries; aside from that, no compromises and no concessions. He would rule his country as he saw fit, as a monarchy in the patriarchal Islamic tradition, and his brother Mohammed would succeed him when his days were ended. . . .

In that proud and rather pompous interview I got no idea of the Abd el-Krim I was to know seven months later, during the desperate days when his star was setting. The Sultan of the Rif was at his best in adversity, when bombardments by sea and land were reminding him of the power of the Christians—when he had to stand alone and fire with his rifle at a squadron of aëroplanes. Of this heroic figure, the Abd el-Krim of the last phase, my interview that day in January gave no hint.

It was Abd el-Krim's idea that I should be taken clear across the country to Tangier, so as to see how peacefully his dominion extended over the whole area marked on maps as the Spanish Protectorate. This involved a trip across the peninsula to the Beni Bufra country and down the coast by sea to Wad Lau. From Wad Lau I could visit the army's western headquarters at Targhzuit,[1] talk to the Sultan's younger brother, and then pass through the Spanish blockade and come out at Tangier.

The plan was carried out, and constituted a journey that, for all its fatigues and alarms, was full of interest. I rode to the sea on one of Abd el-Krim's horses, and at a small harbour on the Beni Bufra coast, two days later, met the charming band of cutthroats who were to run me down the coast through the Spanish fleet. The leader of this band—a gun runner by profession—was a most picturesque brigand. He wore a red kerchief on his head, great swinging gold earrings, a red jacket and flopping green breeches. He was called La Spada by all the others; whatever his Moslem name might have been, it was lost in the complications of his checkered

[1] I spell these names phonetically; for most of them no authority exists.

past. La Spada had sailed to Asia Minor and Egypt, had been a smuggler, a gun runner, a roustabout on the docks in Greece and Italy. Like the other boatmen, he spoke fluent and profane Spanish, had a wholesome reverence for the Sultan Abd-el-Krim and loved to sing ribald songs. His boat was a felucca with oars and a sail, used chiefly for gun running. In it we made a merry enough journey down the coast, dodging the Spanish gunboats and putting in at M'ter, Tgizas, and Wad Lau, which we reached in the middle of the second day.

Here I took leave of La Spada and his picturesque crew, who distinguished themselves by refusing to accept money until it was forced on them. A Riffi regular, on his way to serve under Abd-el-Krim, accompanied me on the long climb up the mountains to Targhzuit. Our way led through the valley of the river Lau, which had long been the Spanish front, and which still showed all the signs of a prolonged, savage battle. When they abandoned this front the Spaniards systematically destroyed everything they could, and the fig trees that yielded the region's chief crop were uprooted for miles.

Late that night we came to a place like the roof of the world—the high mountain village of Targhzuit, above the holy city of Sheshuan. In Targhzuit Mohammed ben Abd el-Krim, the Sultan's clever younger brother, had his headquarters—a rectangle of white tents, European style, with smart sentries goose-stepping before it. I was greeted by Sidi Hassan, Mohammed ben Abd el-Krim's secretary, who spoke perfect French. As we stood in front of the trim rectangle of tents, a voice broke in from the darkness.

"Sprechen-sie deutsch?" it inquired.

I was delighted to hear those words. For months the press in Europe had been full of stories about German "advisers" in Abd el-Krim's service; German officers in the army; German engineers; German aviators. Of all this wealth of Germanizing I had only been able to find two corroborating circumstances: the German volunteer instructors in gunnery at Kifane, and a miserable handful of German deserters from the Foreign Legion. Now I was face to face—although in the dark—with somebody who was unquestionably high in the Riffian service, since he came from the general's tent; and this somebody was a German. Sidi Hassan and the

German and I went down the village path to the house they had assigned to me—the house of the Bashaw of Targhzuit, the chief who had captured Raisuli two days before—and when Sidi Hassan had lighted candles and clapped his hands for tea, I was able to get a good look. The German would have passed anywhere for a Riffian—was, in fact, darker than most of the pure-blooded Riffi tribesmen. We talked in the formulas of politeness, and in French, until Sidi Hassan left us; then my German seemed more at ease.

'Who are you?' I asked.

'I am the *Hadj Alemán*, Caïd el-Mia,' he said.

The Hadj Alemán—the German Pilgrim! I had been hearing about him for weeks. He was the singularly reckless adventurer whose custom it was, when he raided among the French and Spanish or their subject tribes, to leave his card with the words 'El-Hadj Alemán' written on it. His card was sometimes a scrap of paper, sometimes a cactus leaf or a smooth stone, but for several years it had been known through the border country—and, I believe, feared. He professed to be a sort of Robin Hood who never took from the poor. Who he was or what, I had never found out; and I had taken to thinking of him as one of those legends which grow up in every war, a story made up around camp fires to entertain bored veterans. But here he was, sitting beside me on his haunches, sipping sweet tea.

I saw a great deal of the Hadj Alemán during my visit to Targh-zuit, and came to enjoy his boastful, wordy stories to the utmost. There was a good broad vein of the spurious in him, and many things he told me were exaggerated to emphasize his own impor-tance. For example, he said he had been a lieutenant in the French Foreign Legion, whereas the records showed (as I afterwards found) that he had been a sergeant. I might have been prepared for a good deal of misstatement by one of the first things he said to me alone, which was this:

'If you don't mind, we will talk German as much as possible when the officers are near. You see, they all think I can speak English, and I can't, but if we talk German it will sound like Eng-lish to them. It doesn't matter to you, does it?'

It did matter a good deal; the effort to speak German was al-ways a hardship to me; but I obliged the Hadj in this, in exchange for the endless stories he had to tell of his life in the desert tribes.

His name was Joseph Klems, and he came from Düsseldorf. He had run away from Germany years ago, without a passport, in pursuit of a lovely lady (or so he said), and incidentally to avoid his military service; he had wandered to Constantinople and back, had at last enlisted in the French Foreign Legion, and therein had risen to the rank of lieutenant. (Actually sergeant.) In 1920, in the course of a quarrel in garrison near Fez, he struck a superior officer, and to avoid his punishment he deserted. The first tribe into which he fell was the Beni Warrenne, who were preparing to bury him alive when he was saved by one of their old sherifs, whose daughter he afterwards married. He became a raider, and was of great use to the border tribesmen by virtue of his knowledge of the French customs and military routine. (All this part of his story was the truth, as shown in his court-martial a year and half later.) After a variety of adventures, which it took him several evenings to tell, he abandoned his lawless life and deserted again, passing over to the Rif and taking service under Abd el-Krim. His cleverness and adaptability had made him useful to the Sultan, who employed him in such delicate jobs as making a map under the nose of the Spanish guns. He had two wives in the Rif (besides his original wife in the Beni Warrenne) and was now preparing to marry a fourth wife in Sheshuan. He was in the Rif, he said, to stay, and had no desire to return to the Christians or his own country again.

By any legal or conventional standard the Hadj Alemán was, I suppose, a liar, a thief and a murderer; yet I could not help thinking him, on the whole, rather a good man. His influence in Riffian councils (such as it was—and it was by no means as great as he said it was or as the French believed it to be) was always exercised on the side of mercy and moderation. He did everything he could to prevent the tribesmen from indulging in those excesses which occasionally disgraced them in battle: he was always against torture, mutilation, or any unnecessary form of bloodshed. A large part of his fighting, in fact, was done with his camera and his mapmaking apparatus. I liked the Hadj for his bold, romantic lies as much as for his kind-heartedness and his courage. His character was so flamboyant that he attracted to himself far too much attention. In the final disaster that overwhelmed the Rif, he was captured by the French, court-martialled and condemned to death, only to be reprieved by President Doumergue's clemency and sent, instead, to Devil's Island.[1]

Mohammed ben Abd el-Krim, the Sultan's younger brother, was the main object of my visit to Targhzuit. He talked to me at length on two or three occasions, impressing me rather more, at the time, than had his famous senior. His knowledge of Spanish and, to a lesser degree, of French, opened up to him the whole field of European knowledge, and he was more accustomed to study and reading than anybody else in the Rif service. These habits of deliberation had not worked against his abilities as a commander in the field, for the two greatest victories of the Riffians had been won under his leadership—the capture of General Navarro and his twenty thousand men, with all arms and munitions, at Annual in 1921; and the capture of the holy city of Sheshuan on November 17, 1925. Like his brother, Mohammed was convinced that their victories would be permanent, and that the independence of the Rif would have to be acknowledged by the powers within a reasonably short time. Neither of them was able to foresee that the extension of their little empire would inevitably involve them in war with the French and, consequently, in ruin.

I had a glimpse of Raisuli during these days at Targhzuit, as he was carried up the mountain on his way to captivity and death in the Rif. He was accompanied by four wives (the youngest of his large harem, I was told), three black eunuchs, and seventeen pack mules laden with objects of value from his captured palace at Tazarut. It took sixteen men to carry the great wooden box in which the huge Sherif lay moaning and groaning. I was taken into his house one evening by Sidi Hassan, in an attempt to talk to him, but I got nothing out of the old gentleman save curses and lamentations. Nor did I see his face, for he kept it covered by the folds of his turban. His beard, stained with henna, had been considerably pulled about by his despairing hands. Mulay Hamid ben Absalem ber Raisul, descendant of the Prophet! He had been born

[1]A Broadway writer, reading my long account of the Hadj's career in 1925, made a musical comedy hero out of him in a work entitled *The Desert Song*. Thus, for a season or two, the Pilgrim added something to the gaiety of nations, although he certainly never knew it.

to the greatest position in western Morocco, and had used his power to carry on a career of piracy and brigandage. His final mistake had been to remain faithful to the Spanish, who had subsidized him for years; and in consequence Abd el-Krim's men had wiped him out. Every American schoolboy of my generation knew at least one thing about Raisuli: that he had kidnaped an American Greek named Perdicaris and thus brought on himself the famous blustering cablegram from Theodore Roosevelt: 'I want Perdicaris alive or Raisuli dead.' Perdicaris and Roosevelt were avenged—a little late, it is true—by Abd el-Krim.

5

My companion from Targhzuit to Tangier was the finest Riffian soldier I ever knew, Mohammed bel Hadj of the Beni Bukoya tribe, a *caïd el-hamsain*, or captain, in the Sultan's guards. Mohammed bel Hadj looked like an American Indian and rode his horse like one. In spite of his own great physical power and resistance to fatigue, he never showed a sign of impatience when I wanted to rest; he told no lies; he appeared to have no trace of treachery or greed in his character. His Spanish was fragmentary, but it served. He loved to gallop his horse like a child when he got a good stretch of level ground for it, but when the going was difficult he ambled along cheerfully, singing or telling stories that I only half understood.

On our first day's ride from Targhzuit we passed through the battlefields of the Spanish retreat, which had taken place three months before. They were a ghastly sight. We cut down into the Sheshuan-Tetuan road below Dar Koba, just above the Holy City. From this point on to where we left the military road the land was strewn with Spanish corpses. Sheshuan had been besieged for weeks and was about to surrender to Abd el-Krim, when General Castro Girona broke through on the military road from Tetuan and relieved the garrison. He then began the retreat (November 17, 1925) evacuating each Spanish post along the road as he came to it. But at each post, as the Spanish marched out, the invisible Riffians were ready for them and mowed them down by machine-gun and rifle fire. Since then no bodies had been buried.

The Spanish retreat had been such a hurried affair that there was no time; and the Moors would not touch the Spanish dead. They still lay there, putrefied and half eaten by the vultures and the pariah dogs. Our horses pranced in terror at the smell of these fields, and Mohammed motioned to me to wrap my face in my turban, as he did his. At Xeruta—a larger post, a more disastrous battle—some of the bodies had been picked clean. Others were still feeding the birds.

We visited Tazarut, Raisuli's palace, after leaving the battlefields, but there was little of interest left in it. The Bashaw of Targhzuit, who commanded there, solemnly assured me that there was gold and silver to the value of sixteen million pesetas in the cellars of the palace. At another village in the Beni M'sua country, near Tangier, a different form of wealth appeared: Spanish prisoners, more than a hundred of them, who were being marched off to the Rif to be held for ransom. They had been captured in the Angera country *behind* the Spanish lines—that line of steel, the Primo de Rivera Line—and had been marched through it the night before under ample guard. If such a large company could peacefully drift through the line of steel, I was encouraged to suppose that Mohammed bel Hadj and I might do so too.

The village of Remla, on a hill overlooking the international zone, was our last stopping place in Abd el-Krim's country. There I observed for the first time some signs of war-weariness. The young chief, Absalem, told me that war with the Christians was 'not good.' The tribes had always been used to war, he said, but to a different kind of war, among themselves, with equal weapons. This kind of war in which asphyxiating bombs, poison gas, famine blockades, and other ghastly Christian weapons obtained, did not appeal to him. His views were supported by his associates; but my friend Mohammed bel Hadj told me to ignore all this talk. 'These are only Arabs; they have been to the city too much,' he said.

We rested a day at Remla, waiting for the night appointed for passing the Spanish lines. During the day we had a particularly active air raid; but an event of greater—indeed, of unique—interest was the arrival of some Christian eggs. Mohammed bel Hadj heard that there was a woman in the village who owned a Christian hen. He bustled off to see her, and returned at last, after long bargaining, with three Christian eggs for me to eat. Christian hens and their eggs were much larger than Moslem hens and eggs, he explained. It was not clear how the village woman came by her Christian hen, but I hoped she had stolen it from a missionary. It was, anyhow, quite true that Christian eggs were bigger and better than Moslem eggs; I feasted that night.

We set out for the Spanish lines just after sunset, before it was quite dark. We had our young chief Absalem and his whole company of fifty fighting men for escort. As we came down the slope from Remla to the plain we approached a remarkable spectacle. Lines of white figures, women wrapped in woollen robes, men with chickens, goats, vegetables, all trickled out of the hills around and converged on a point about two miles away, in the plain. They were the peasants of the country, accustomed all their lives to go to market in Tangier, who persisted in the practice even now, when every trip was made under the peril of death.

There must have been about four hundred of the country people, men, women, and children. They brought the children along because it was thought unsafe to leave them at home—and besides, it was the habit of centuries for the family to go to market together. Our fighting men charged one *duro* for each man who went through, but the women and children did not have to pay unless they brought exceptionally loaded donkeys. The tribe gathered with great docility, paid their fare, and waited for instructions. The fighting men went ahead and took their places in hollows near the Spanish forts nearest to our trail, so as to engage the Spanish fire as much as possible and clear the way for us. By this time three other *hamsains*, companies of fifty, from other points in the Beni M'sua hills, had joined our contingent, so that we had an escort of two hundred in all.

Mohammed bel Hadj was taking as much care of me as if I had been a set of china. Instead of letting me take my chance on foot with the others, along with the goats and chickens, he insisted on giving me a special bodyguard of ten rifles and mounting me on a mule. When there was no mule to be found, he compromised on a donkey—a ridiculous grey-brown animal with panniers, over which my long legs dangled to the ground. Once all this was settled my ten men closed around me, and we hurried along, as silently and as swiftly as we could, towards the Spanish forts.

The first fort was to the right of the road, the second about four hundred yards farther, on the left. The moon was up; such a large party of white-clad people must certainly be visible. The hope was that their whiteness might be indistinguishable from the whiteness of the plain. As the first fort opened fire Mohammed, running along beside me, began to pray aloud. The sound of his prayer was mixed in my ears with the irritated gabble of the chickens beside me.

The second fort was harder to pass than the first, and almost everybody within earshot was praying aloud as we went through the line there. Our Beni M'sua fighting men did their best to draw the fire; no doubt the prayers were also efficacious; but our greatest help was that the Spanish fort was placed too high for the proper use of machine guns. We passed through with little loss, reached the ford of the river, and, on passing it, were safe in the international zone of Tangier. Our fighting men abandoned us here, and the marketers straggled on happily, singing their thanks in an endless repetition of La ilaha ill' Allah.

Mohammed was going to his brother's house near the central market. It was one o'clock in the morning, and the city was asleep as we rounded the curve to the shining white beach.

'If I come out in the daytime the Spanish will arrest me,' said Mohammed. 'Tomorrow night, after sunset, meet me in the market place. Adiós.'

He swung off up the street silently, and I turned to pull the night bell in the closed door of the Cecil.

IV

The Rif Again

My chief feeling, in returning to the so-called Christian world, was the fear that I had lost my job. I had vanished for two months, during which time my value to my employers had been exactly nothing. When I woke up in a bed at the Hotel Cecil on the morning after my arrival in Tangier the first urgent business was to bathe again, for an hour or so, in the hottest water there was; the second was to get rid of my stubbly red beard; and the third was to send a cablegram to my office in Paris reporting arrival. In that cablegram I boldly promised a 'good story,' hoping that the prospect might stave off the wrath that otherwise seemed to me inevitable. The rest of the day I spent writing the first parts of the story and sending it off to the telegraph office.

That night, dressed in my own clothes again, rested and restored by those remarkable inventions, the bed and the bath, I went to the market place and walked up and down. After a few minutes I saw Mohammed bel Hadj. The cowl of his jellaba was pulled well over his face, for he was not anxious to be identified by the Spanish intelligence service. He passed me without recognition. When I followed and put a hand on his arm, he whipped round suddenly like a man expecting trouble.

'Salaam wallicum,' I said, and he grinned from the shadow of his cowl.

'Come with me,' he said, 'and we will have dinner at my brother's house.'

He plunged into a courtyard leading off the *suk*, made a turning or two, and climbed a staircase. At the top of the stairs we were admitted to a small square room with cheap blue-and-white mosaics on the walls and ceiling—a room like dozens of others in

114

Tangier, but clean and comfortable. There were cushions on the floor, and the samovar was steaming on a low brass table in the middle.

'This is my brother Ali,' said Mohammed. 'And this is his wife.'

I was a little startled at being introduced to a Moslem woman, but she shook hands with me, European style, just as if she had been used to meeting Christians. She was a rather pretty little creature who had lived in Tangier for years, although she was of Riffian origin and bore the tribal marks of the Beni Bukoya. She had learned much about Western habits, it seemed, at the local cinema.

'I saw you today,' she said, 'when I walked down by the beach. I knew it must be you because your head had been shaved.'

'I didn't see you,' said I stupidly.

'Of course you didn't see me,' she said. 'All Arab women look alike in the street. But we can see, just the same, as well as anybody.'

Ali, Mohammed and I squatted around the brass table and began to drink tea. For a while Ali's wife stood talking to us, and then she went away to get the dinner. I had seen many unveiled women in the Rif, where the customs of the tribes encouraged freedom, but I had never met a Moslem woman who could talk any language I understood. Ali's wife, having been to a Spanish school in her childhood, spoke better Spanish than I did. When we finished drinking tea she brought in the food—good food, the fleshpots of Tangier. As we proceeded to enjoy it, the little wife sat beside us, watched, and occasionally talked. She did not eat with us, but in other respects she was treated as an equal by her husband and brother-in-law.

The evening had consequences for me. When I wanted to return to the Rif it was Mohammed's brother Ali—little dark-browed Ali, a servant from the Tangier Casino, who had little to say and seemed overshadowed by his brother and his wife—who made it possible. I never saw Mohammed bel Hadj el-Bukawi again, but I heard months later that he had been killed fighting the French on the Wergha front.

My employers recalled me to Paris on the day after my dinner with Mohammed's family. I stopped in Madrid to see Primo de Rivera. His unbroken record of failure in Morocco had made the whole subject a painful one to him, and it was evident that his personal happiness would be vastly increased if he could get rid of it—make peace at once, keeping for Spain only those small coast districts which Abd el-Krim would have conceded. But pride, prestige, the fatal desire to cut a figure in the world, made such solutions impossible. He had to keep on with the war and pray for better luck. I duly recorded the words, worried and disingenuous, with which he tried to conceal the necessities of his situation, and went on to Paris. There, instead of being reprimanded for my long absence, I found myself in surprisingly high favour. This was due to two circumstances: the first, that I had been given up for dead, and nobody wanted to scold a ghost; the second, that my account of the Rif was by far the most extensive that had yet appeared in the press and was consequently considered a 'good story.' My death had been purely presumptive, not actually supported by evidence. Gabrielli's agents had succeeded in tracking me all the way in to Ajdir, where they had lost me. He had reported the facts to General de Chambrun, who had reported them to the Chicago *Tribune*. But from that time on nothing further had been heard, and the last telegram from the French general had taken a gloomy view of my chances. I benefited by the accident of being alive, and was wined and dined one night at the Ritz by the owner of my paper; what more can a reporter ask of fate? But a few weeks later there arose a disagreement between my immediate superior and myself over the length of time I had stayed out to dinner, and before you could have counted ten, I was hoicked out of my job. I had been, I thought, fired, given the sack, booted out; and yet I was asked to write and sign a letter asking for 'leave of absence' in order to make everything look smooth and amicable to the home office of the paper. I wrote the letter (what were a few words more or less?) and took my departure. I was never again employed in a newspaper office, and never wanted to be.

Just the same, after some three years of relative security, it seemed odd and a little shameful to be dished in this way—to have no definite thing to do when noon came round, no salary (however minute) to collect at the end of the week. I was baffled for a few days. Being penniless was not a novelty, but there were a great many ways of being penniless, and this was the worst one—the one that suggested permanence. I met a man in a café who said: 'Why don't you write a book?' He was the second cousin of a woman whose best friend had married the assistant to a dubious publisher (since bankrupt), and his words had weight. I had always had a weakness for writing books, or at least for starting the process; I was one of those dangerous characters who will write a book at the drop of a hat; and besides, as all young reporters know, there is no surer way to get rich. I borrowed some money and went off to New York to write a book about the Rif.

It was a temerarious undertaking, that book. I had only my memory to rely upon, knew no Arabic or Shilluh, and was obliged to spell every name by ear. No good material on the subject was then available.[1] It was strange that a country so close to Europe as the Rif should have been so unknown—more unknown, in fact, than Tibet or the Sahara. I worked my way through the book somehow, undoubtedly making mistake after mistake, but protected by the fact that nobody would be likely to know the difference.

Meanwhile events in Morocco had taken a turn that aroused the interest of the whole world in Abd el-Krim's infant state. The Arab tribesmen who had been raising the Riffi flag for the past year were a lawless lot (like my friends the Metalsa), and many of them ranged over plains that lay partly in the Spanish, partly in the French protectorate. Conflict with the French was inevitable; Abd el-Krim was obliged to support his Arab allies; war broke out on the Wergha River; and by the summer of 1925 the French had entered into an alliance with Spain to destroy Abd el-Krim's power in the field. The French marked their sense of the importance of the struggle by sending Pétain himself to take command, and all the war correspondents of all the nations flocked to Morocco. They were on the outside taking their information from the French; and it seemed to me, reading their dispatches with

[1]The researches of Mr. Carleton Coon of the Peabody Institute of Anthropology of Harvard University did not begin until three years later, and, even on such elementary points as the race of the Riffians or their historic boundaries, there were no clear authorities in 1925.

rage and impatience in New York, that they misrepresented the Riffians beyond recognition.

My book was finished during the subtropical heat of the New York summer, and when it was all over I discovered that I did not know what to do with it. The only publisher I knew anything about (the one whose mother's cousin's friend's brother-in-law's janitor I had met in Paris) was deaf, unapproachable. Nobody in the whole of New York could have been more obscure, discouraged and oppressed than I: the huge, horrible town, whenever I emerged from my room and looked at it, seemed to be made of blinding heat and deafening noise, and all the people in it looked as if they were in a rage. 'Get out of my way,' they said in every movement. 'Get the hell out of my way.' Among these angry millions I had possibly a dozen acquaintances, and by one of those hazards which confound the imagination, one day, in the subway, I met somebody I knew.

I hung, dripping with sweat, from one of the straps to which a large part of the population of the city was permanently attached. Suddenly I saw a bright pink face depending from another strap in the haze of heat. . . . Coop!

Merian Cooper had been a flyer during the war, commander of the Kosciuszko squadron in the Polish army after the war, a prisoner of the Bolsheviks after the Warsaw campaign in 1920. He had escaped from his prison in Moscow alone and wandered across the snow to the Latvian frontier, under circumstances that would have made a superb story if he could have been persuaded to tell it. Just now he had been in Persia, making a film called *Grass*, which recorded the migrations of the Bakhtyiari tribesmen.

'Where the hell have you been?' he inquired.

There was an enormous difference between 'Where the hell have you been?' and 'Get the hell out of my way.' The difference did not escape me; I already felt more cheerful.

'The North American Newspaper Alliance,' said Cooper, 'has been looking for you for the past six weeks. They wanted you to go to the Rif. What have you been doing?'

Before we reached City Hall Park Cooper was in command of the situation. I suppose he saw that I did not have sense enough to command it myself; ignorance and intimidation must have been stamped all over me. At any rate, he marched me about the town: to the North American Newspaper Alliance; to the offices of *Asia* magazine; to a publisher. Things that had seemed to me mysterious and difficult were as simple to him as bread and cheese. The personages to whom he introduced me were all very polite. The editors of *Asia* (Mr. Froelick and Miss Neff) were so agreeable and gentle that I think I should have given them my book for five dollars if they had named that price; but they gave me a thousand. The North American Newspaper Alliance[1] offered me a contract for two months if I would go into the Rif and send out dispatches that could be cabled to America; I accepted the offer before Mr. Colter, the director, had finished making it. His terms seemed generous, but he told me long afterwards that he had been authorized to offer a great deal more (three or four times as much) if I had hesitated. To all these people, habituated as they were to the knowingness and assurance of New York, I must have seemed a strange kind of ninny. And yet the disposition of such things is so relative, so dependent upon the whole tangle of surrounding circumstance, that what seemed little to them was to me a stupendous plenitude of fortune, a golden shower, which I could hardly believe was meant to come in my direction. From the time I met Cooper in the subway until the time I sailed for France there were only a few days, but during their course I traversed the whole bewildering area between the illusion of failure and the illusion of success. I was back in Tangier at the end of August.

2

Tangier had changed. The careless, quiet old town had become a centre of world interest, filled with war correspondents, officers, spies, and the international strays who collect where trouble is stirring. Moreover, its neutrality had now become a polite fiction. Spain had always respected the neutrality of the international zone because it was impossible to do anything else: a violation would have brought severe reproof from the British and French. But

[1]This was a large syndicate, of which the New York *World*, the Baltimore *Sun*, the Washington *Post* and the Chicago *Daily News* were some of the leading members.

France was now a belligerent—*the* belligerent—and France was a great power. Great powers tended to do as they pleased; who was there to restrain them? Formerly fighting uniforms were not seen in the international zone; now they were everywhere. The French and Spanish had drawn up a combined scheme of blockade, and under French urging the Spanish lines had been strengthened all around the zone of Tangier. The French took a predominant part in the 'defense' of the international zone (i.e., its blockade, since nobody dreamed of attacking it). French and Spanish intelligence officers swarmed over the place, and arrests were made every day for supposed communications or conspiracies with Abd el-Krim. In brief, the international zone of Tangier had become about as international as its neighbour, the rock of Gibraltar.

All this made my task difficult, so difficult that at first I thought it might be impossible. Sidi Abd el-Krim bel Hadj Ali, the chief agent of Abd el-Krim in Tangier, had fled to the hills; the English lady who sometimes acted for the Sultan was away for the moment; my only hope was in Ali the Bukawi, brother of Mohammed bel Hadj. But even to find Ali the Bukawi was a delicate operation, as it would have done neither of us any good for me to go openly asking for him about the market place.

I began to haunt the Casino because I thought that sooner or later I must see Ali the Bukawi there. One night I ordered coffee from the waiter on the terrace, and, according to the prudent system in vogue at the Casino, an underling who did nothing but wander from table to table pouring out coffee came to fill the order. I looked up. It was Ali.

'I want to speak to you,' I said to him.

'Not now,' said Ali. 'Not here. Wait.'

He went away, his dark little face set and motionless. Presently he came to pour out coffee for somebody at the next table. When he had finished he hesitated for a bare half minute behind my chair.

'Do not look up,' he said in an undertone. 'Come to the market tomorrow morning at eleven.'

The market place next morning was crowded with white-robed women from the country, just such women as I had come through the Spanish lines with six months before, their beady little eyes peering out through the slits in their woollen wrappings. I wandered up and down, smoking a cigarette. Nothing could keep a large American in white linen clothes from looking conspicuous, so I had no doubt that sooner or later Ali would see me. As I passed a doorway I heard him say, 'Señor.' I stopped to light a cigarette without turning round.

'Don't look at me,' said Ali in an undertone. 'Go straight ahead, walk around the *suk*, and then come back to this doorway. Go through it, through the courtyard to the third door on the left.'

When my cigarette was lighted I walked on. I glanced back, as I made the turn of the *suk*, but there was nobody in the doorway now. After a leisurely stroll through the crowded market I came back to where I had heard the voice, ducked into a narrow courtyard, went along to the third door on the left and turned in. There was a hall, two steps, and then a small room filled with smoke—an Arab café. In one corner two Arabs were sitting quietly smoking, and the smell of *kif* (hashish) was in the air. In another corner Ali was installed, cross-legged, in front of a low table with coffee. I joined him.

'Don't be afraid,' I said. 'I won't get you into trouble if I can help it. I want to go to the Rif. How can I do it?'

He took off his tarboosh and scratched his head.

'Wallahi!' he said. 'It is not so easy. . . . People go in and out all the time. Arabs, that is. But it is harder than it used to be. The Spaniards have more forts, many searchlights, many *ambuscadores*. Every time people go through the line now, many are killed. Things are not the same.'

'Anyway, I have to go,' I said. 'Can you find a Riffi—a real Riffi, not an Arab—in Tangier, who is going out one of these nights soon, and who will take me with him?'

'I will talk to my mother-in-law,' said Ali. 'She has more to do with these things than I have. I am afraid just now; I have had trouble with the Spaniards. My mother-in-law is different; she can go anywhere, and they never know. You will pay her if she finds somebody for you?'

It was obvious that an Arab woman could defy the efforts of the best Spanish spies. Arab women looked all alike, bundled up and mummified, white shadows scurrying through the town. And no Spaniard would dare to take their veils off; to do so would be to provoke a riot.

'I will pay her,' I said, 'but ask her to hurry. I don't want to stay in Tangier. How will I know when it is arranged?'

'Come to the Casino café tonight,' said Ali. 'Don't look at me, but buy coffee and sit for a while. I will find a chance to speak to you, but I can only say one or two words. If I say, "No," you will know that she has not arranged anything yet. If I say "Yes," come to this café tomorrow morning at eleven. Come to the Casino every night until I say "Yes."'

I obeyed orders. In retrospect it all seems melodramatic, but it was the only way to get anything done in spy-ridden Tangier. I knew (from Floyd Gibbons and other colleagues) that the block-ade was, as they said, 'tighter than a drum,' and except for one man who had landed at Alhucemas from a boat that summer, not a foreigner had been able to get into the interior since the French war began.

For two or three nights I went to the Casino. One night Ali, passing behind my chair, whispered, 'Yes, tomorrow.' I rose in a state of high excitement, went into the Casino, threw some money on the roulette table, and won. The omens seemed to me to be good.

Next morning at the Arab café—which was a centre for Arab rebels and Riffians—Ali met me as before.

'This is Mahdani,' he said. 'He is a good man—of my family.'

'Of my family,' of course, meant a member of the same clan, a Bukawi.

Mahdani was a broad-faced, simple creature, a very ordinary type of the Riffian countryman. He spoke little Spanish and had never been in Tangier before. I gave him the money agreed on for his share, and he grinned happily.

'Muy bien,' he said, 'muy bien. Vamos en el Rif!'

'Yes,' said I, 'but when? I can't stay any longer in Tangier. I may be expelled at any time.'

'We must wait until some others are going,' said Ali. 'This is the plan my mother-in-law has made. Mahdani here will pass in front of the Hotel Cecil, walking down the beach, on the day of the start. He will walk along slowly, not looking at the hotel. He will do this after the noon hour, probably between half-past one and three o'clock; when you see him, you must get up and follow him, at a distance. Be sure not to speak to him or to let any Spaniards or French see you are following him. You must follow him all the way to the end of the beach and across the sand dunes. When you are there he will wait for you in a convenient place with a long jellaba to put over you. He will then take you to Zaina's—my mother-in-law's house—where you will wait. She will tell you the rest. But do exactly as I say, for if the Spaniards get us they will shoot us all.'

I agreed without argument.

Mahdani broke in, grinning.

'Bring nothing,' he said, nodding his head. 'Bring nothing. Must run very fast, no good bring anything.'

('No tomar nada'—and so on. His Spanish, like that of most of the Arabs, was made up of a few words and a few infinitives.)

'All right,' I said. 'Anything you tell me I will do. Only hurry. I have no time.'

I shook hands with them. Ali's solemn dark face broke into a smile as he refused the money I offered.

'I do this for my brother Mohammed,' he said, 'and for Abd el-Krim. I hope you go through safely. If you see me again, do not speak to me—it is very dangerous for me. I have been in trouble. Tomorrow or the next day you will go, *Inshallah!* Remember me to my family. *Adiós. Emshi besselema.*'

I went out of the courtyard and turned down the street towards the British telegraph office. Here I asked to see the manager and showed him my cards from the N. A. N. A.

'I have to ask you a peculiar thing,' I said, 'but I hope you will be able to oblige me. I am going away from here, but some telegrams will come from me. They will be written in pen and ink, or in pencil, on any kind of paper I may happen to have. They will be delivered to you by stray Arabs, country people, perhaps sometimes by women. I will give you my signature now, and any telegram that comes in, in whatever form, signed with that signature, I want you to send off to London to the registered address of the N. A. N. A., receiver to pay.'

The British manager smiled and stroked his chin.

'I believe I know what you mean,' he said. 'I believe you sent a number of dispatches through this office six months ago. I remember them. I will give instructions to accept anything that comes from you.'

'The people who bring these messages,' I said, 'will undoubtedly be very frightened. They will probably drop the messages in front of you and run. But don't say anything to them or ask them any questions. They're all afraid of their lives nowadays anyway.'

'Very well,' he said, 'everything will go through and no questions asked.'

It was weeks before I knew what the consequences of this conversation had been. When I came to Tangier again I heard the full story of the messages—how they had popped up unexpectedly, two or three at a time, without anybody in the office knowing where they had come from. Usually they were found lying on the counter in front of the telegraph clerks; sometimes they were stuck under the door in the morning. The bearers of the papers were never seen at all; but every message I sent out reached that office, and every one was sent at once to London. Among the curiosities of communication in my experience, this was the oddest and the luckiest. Every one of those messages had to be carried for several days' journey, across mountain and plain, under almost constant bombardment, through the Spanish lines and probably through the hands of a number of agents; so that it seemed to me, miles away in the Rif, that it would be a miracle if any got through. That they all did was due partly to luck and partly to the fanatical devotion with which Abd el-Krim's agents did his bidding.

3

I had nothing to do now but wait; and only two or three days, at that. They seemed unending. The Hotel Cecil was full of Spanish and French officers; I suspected every one of them of itching to arrest me or deport me to Europe. (Nonsense, probably; but the atmosphere of the place had infected me.) While I was waiting a German journalist or adventurer was arrested by the Spanish as he tried to pass through their lines, and was put in jail in Tetuan. I grew as nervous as a cat. Every day I sat through the afternoon on the terrace of the Cecil under the blinding sun, watching the beach.

I bought a little notebook and a metal pencil. This, with my passport and a toothbrush, was all I could allow myself to take along into the interior. In the notebook I began to keep a kind of diary, for I had been much handicapped on my previous journey by having no notes of any kind and no way of knowing exact dates. This diary was kept up, intermittently, for years afterwards; its entries are too obscure to be of use without explanation, but they are like stones thrown into the pool of memory: they set up a movement. The first entry reads:

Sept. 3rd. Delay. Mahdani did not appear, although I was ready at 1:30.

The second entry in the book was written under far different conditions—early in the morning of September 5th, in a ditch on the other side of the Spanish lines. It reads:

Sept. 4th. Just after lunch, at 2:30, Mahdani appeared. I followed to a deserted place in the dunes, where I changed into Arab clothes. He walked ahead to Zaina's, I followed, hiding my face with the hood. At five we started across the frontier, over the fields towards the lines. Crossing very difficult—many searchlights, much firing. None of us killed. Sleep in a ditch on the safe side of Spanish lines.

Between these two entries were crowded many hours of anxiety, excitement, terror and relief. Floyd Gibbons was lunching with me that day. As we came out into the hall of the Cecil for coffee and a brandy I made a hasty reconnaissance on the terrace. No Mahdani. I came back in and we ordered the coffee. At this point Floyd saw a French naval officer to whom he wanted to speak. As a matter of fact he was busy arranging a visit to the French and Spanish fleets bombarding the Rif, although I didn't know it; such was the hide-and-seek game of the correspondents.

'I'll be back in a minute,' he said, and vanished into one of the sitting rooms after the Frenchman.

I seized this opportunity to go out on the terrace again, and on the beach directly in front of the hotel I saw Mahdani. He was loitering along slowly, looking at the sea, but there was no mistaking him. In his short Riffi jellaba he looked very unlike a native of Tangier.

I had no hat, but the passport, notebook and toothbrush were in my pocket, where they had been for three days. I glanced back at the hotel; Floyd was still invisible, and the terrace was unobserved. I walked down the steps to the beach and, allowing a good free space between myself and Mahdani, began to follow him. He saw that I had picked up the trail; he quickened his step and in ten minutes had reached the end of the beach and turned off into the deserted dunes. The beach was empty under the boiling sun. I went on into the dunes, wondering what had become of Mahdani; at the sound of a hiss I found him in a hollow surrounded by drifts of sand. He pulled out from under his jellaba a bundle of clothing: brown jellaba, sandals. I changed as rapidly as possible while he kept an eye out over the barrier of sand. He rolled up my European clothes and stuck them under his jellaba, pulled my hood as far as possible over my face, and started out.

The next fifteen minutes were the most anxious of the day. I was acutely conscious of my shanks sticking out at the bottom of that jellaba. However much I stooped, the jellaba did not hide those white shanks with the red hair on them. I followed along after Mahdani, cursing quietly to myself. It seemed asinine for me to wear Arab clothes through even the back alleys of Tangier, since anybody who looked closely enough could tell by my legs that I was not an Arab. However, Zaina had made the rules, and presumably Zaina knew her business.

Mahdani went as fast as he could without running. We passed few people, all Arabs, and none of them—to my surprise—appeared to notice anything strange about us. Zaina lived in one of the poorest Arab quarters of the town, in a network of alleys at the foot of the hill. Finally Mahdani ducked into a low doorway, and I followed him.

The room was dark, but I could see a woman sitting on some mats against the wall. This was Zaina, a middle-aged Riffi woman with the orange tribe-marks of the Beni Bukoya on her cheek and forehead. She put her hands to her forehead, lips and breast, made a place for me to sit, and addressed me at length in Arabic. I understood practically nothing of what she said, except that

she wanted her money. We counted it out. Mahdani, after bringing me into the house, had vanished. Zaina brought me some tea
and then went away. The two hours I spent lying on a mat and
waiting seemed interminable.

Towards five o'clock Mahdani returned, and we had a little
food. He brought another jellaba, long enough to hide my legs
down to the ankles. My European clothes were rolled up and
given to Zaina, who chuckled with a kind of hoarse, whispering
laughter as she examined them. When Mahdani was ready we got
up; there were the usual invocations to Allah, the usual 'go in
peace'; and we started out.

The walk across the fields was easy enough. By avoiding all
roads we escaped the notice of the Sherifian troops and the foreign
gendarmes. Occasionally we passed an Arab, said, 'Salaam
aleikum' and went on. By eight o'clock we were near the edges of
the international zone and had a brief rest while other dark-robed
figures gathered around us—all bound for the same destination as
ourselves. There were fewer women than I had expected from my
previous experience, fewer donkeys and mules, and no children
at all. The whole enterprise had a much grimmer air about it, and
I was soon to see why.

Towards nine o'clock we started moving, strung out in a thin
column across the plain. We had no fighting men this time, and
no exact plan. Apparently we were to run for it and take our
chance. The trail was the same as that of six months before (the
Beni M'sua road) with some new detours necessitated by the positions of the new Spanish forts. Mahdani had attached himself
(and me) to a small group of Riffians, all men, to whom we stuck
until we got across to safety. Sometimes we seemed to lose the
main body of the blockade runners and sometimes they were all
around us again, scores of darker forms in the darkness.

The elements that made the blockade so much more efficient
than before were new searchlights and more machine guns. The
biggest searchlight remained on the Djebel Habib road, but there
were now others, almost as big, guarding the other roads. Our
technique with both searchlights and machine guns was simple
enough: the minute the light came near us or the guns sounded
ominous we were to drop down flat on the ground and lie there,

crawling along without raising our heads. Mahdani had explained this to me again and again in his broken Spanish during the evening as we approached the lines.

Well, we got through; and of our particular Riffian group nobody was either killed or wounded. I know nothing about the rest of the people, for before the night was over we had left them far behind. Probably some of them were killed, as happened on such occasions. I was terrified by the machine-gun fire; I had never been under it before, and the mechanical precision of the sound made it seem far worse than ordinary guns or rifles. But even beneath a searchlight it was not easy for the Spanish to get their range on those wide, deceptive plains, and the rat-a-tat-tat passed over us harmlessly. When the lights were on us we lay on our bellies, crawling along; and as soon as they switched off somewhere else we rose and ran. From first to last we were under fire more than four hours—not constantly, of course; but with enough persistence to discourage a naturally lazy and rather cowardly young man of sedentary habits. As soon as we passed beyond the lines of fire I called for a halt to rest. Our companions were not in favour of this, as sometimes Spanish raiding parties—*ambuscadores*, native troops—swept the plains outside their own lines. But Mahdani, against his better judgment, allowed himself to be overruled. We found a good, comfortable ditch, arranged some stones for bed and pillows, turned our jellabas upside down with our feet tucked in the hoods, and slept there. Our companions went on to the Beni M'sua; but I doubt if I could have walked another step that night, even if the *ambuscadores* had been after us. I was asleep as soon as I stretched out on those providential stones.

Mahdani was up before sunrise—a habit of his—and by noon had succeeded in dragging me along to the house of a sherif in one of the Beni M'sua villages. Here we had a meal, a rest, and the opportunity of observing a Spanish air raid. The sherif supplied me with a mule, upon which I reached Bohrabish, a large village, one of the principal posts of Abd el-Krim's army in the direction of Tangier. We stopped there to rest all that night and the next day (September 6th) while the Spanish planes buzzed over us and the guns roared on the plain below.

By this time I had already become aware that the character of the Rif war had changed. The Spaniards had been discouraged, defeated; they had scarcely fought at all when I was in the country the preceding winter. Now, with the mighty aid of the French, they were putting up a fight. Their aëroplanes seemed to be in the sky all day long, raining bombs. They did not do a great deal of damage, it is true, but the noise was terrific, the effect on the spirit of the Arabs profound. Nobody at Bohrabish seemed to have much enthusiasm for the war. When the planes came everybody cursed or prayed, but between raids the fighting men sat about moodily, seldom speaking. The era of wild enthusiasm, of fierce shouting and singing, was over, and every day of this second journey emphasized the fact.

From Bohrabish we set out at six in the evening for Dar ben Karish, another important post in the Tetuan zone. This was one of the main fronts, under bombardment throughout the day, and to avoid trouble we thought it best to travel at night. We were accompanied by a smuggler named Abdullah, from Sheshuan, whose villainous face and loud voice had aroused my dislike from the first. Mahdani, a good-natured soul, did not want to insult the Sheshuani by telling him to go on alone, and we were obliged to put up with his company all through the night. Towards morning we lost our way in the darkness, wandered for a time without knowing where we were, and stopped to rest in a village mosque until daylight.

4

When I consider the problem of courage—what it is, or whether it exists in a pure state, cut off from necessity and circumstance—I am obliged to think, somewhat wryly, of the events of the next day, September 7th. I always knew that courage, in the sense in which it was generally understood, was not a quality to which I could lay any claim. The sound of bombs falling on the inoffensive earth, the whistle of shell, the bitter crackling of machine guns, were noises that I loathed and feared. The happenings that were supposed to have demonstrated my courage had demonstrated exactly the opposite: in the Rif, even on my relatively peaceful first journey, I had experienced for the first time all the agonized anxieties of cowardice, the plain fear that chokes the heart at the approach of death. That this cowardice was complicated by a willingness to do anything, to undertake anything, was one of the accidents we all owe to circumstances beyond our control—to ancestry, to blood pressure, to the chemistry of our glands or the shape of our heads; to the course, an astrologer might say, of our stars. The egotism and recklessness of the wild Irish were in it; they led me into positions from which it was impossible to escape without acquiring some kind of credit for being brave, no matter how firmly fear had sat in the saddle during the crisis. I did see bravery in the Rif, as is to be told hereafter; but it was not my own, and may have gone by another name in the minds of other people. On the whole it is easier to believe in these fine individual qualities, the historic food of mankind's vanity, under conditions that do not require them to be shown.

The episode of September 7th is recorded in my diary, by an entry written the next day in Targhzuit, as follows:

Sept. 7th. Early start. Mahdani, Abdullah, the owner of the mule and I. Many meals of cactus fruit, melons, figs, roasted corn. In the Beni M'sua we came on the village where, six months ago, I saw the Spanish prisoners from El-Ksar Sghir. At about one o'clock in the high mountains we lost Mahdani. I went on with Abdullah (who was very insulting—always called me 'kelb') and with the owner of the mule, a young boy. By night we had arrived at the Suk el-Arbaa of the Beni Hassen, where we had directed ourselves because the other way—to the north, to Dar ben Karish—was too fully covered by the Spanish aëroplanes. The mule and its owner turned back here, and Abdullah led me across the Sheshuan-Tetuan road to the flat plain, where he presently got out his big knife and indicated a willingness to carve me up. I ran away. When I got across the river I found a cornfield where I slept for the night.

The bare notes thus scribbled in my little red book give no notion of the terrors of that afternoon and night. Perhaps I was too vain to write them down, once I had arrived in the safety of Targhzuit; but they were not so easily forgotten. My distrust of Abdullah, the Sheshuani, had the best of foundations. He was a bad egg, and the accident by which we were separated from Mahdani was mostly his doing. Mahdani, happy to be returning to his wife and child in the Rif, went ahead along the mountain trail, singing. Shortly after midday he drew far ahead of us and was lost to sight. I did not relish being left with the glowering Abdullah, but no matter how loud I shouted for Mahdani, no shout came back. There was nothing to do but go on. Abdullah seized the opportunity to take another trail, still more to the south, and we pushed ahead at a speed guaranteeing that we should never meet Mahdani again that day. The smuggler growled and snarled and beat my mule across the rump. When he had occasion to speak of me or to me, he called me the 'Christian dog' (*kelb rumi*). All through the afternoon he behaved like a slave driver, except that he never actually touched me. He took great delight in showing me the huge knife he carried at his belt. This was good, he said, for cutting Christian throats. The boy who owned the mule I rode did not approve of such tactics and said so. At the fourth marketing place of the Beni Hassen, near the Sheshuan-Tetuan road, the boy and the mule were sent away. I knew that they had been engaged to take me all the way to Targhzuit, but in my ignorance of the language I was helpless. The boy was terrified of Abdullah and did not dare stay with us. He went off down the road towards Sheshuan, and we walked towards the east, on the road to Targhzuit.

Now, actually, there was not one chance in a thousand that Abdullah would have cut my throat. He could never have escaped punishment if he had done so, for he was a well-known smuggler of Sheshuan and could have been tracked down within an hour or two by Abd el-Krim's men. In all probability he was enjoying himself, exercising a genuine hatred of the Christian dogs, by threatening me; particularly as he may have hoped to extract some money by doing so. I was determined to give him no money and, if possible, to cheat him of his pleasure by hiding my alarm. The way to do this was to walk along and pay no attention to his grotesque antics. After the muleteer had left us we were quite alone in the dusk of the empty plain; Abdullah talked without ceasing, fingered his knife, made motions indicating the cutting of a throat, snarled and snapped. Even then, anxious as I was, I reflected that he probably never would go to the lengths indicated by his preposterous gestures. And yet there were suspicious circumstances. Why did he insist on taking me beyond the Suk el-Arbaa of the Beni Hassen, for example? There we could have camped for the night in the company of half a dozen other travellers. There were other villages, houses, mosques, somewhere in this plateau, and he must have known them well. Why did he want to stop in the most deserted place we had seen for hours?

I resolved to run away from him at the first opportunity. Supposing that he did intend to murder me, he could scarcely do so until it got quite dark. If his intentions were a little less drastic (robbery, for instance) he might even wait until he supposed me to be asleep. If he intended no harm at all, he was still the most disagreeable and disquieting of companions, whom it would be well to quit as soon as possible.

We came to a field in which there was a stream of water. In the profound stillness of that plain, over which the stars were just beginning to emerge, the world seemed to consist of Abdullah and me. He gave me a tin bucket, extracted from his donkey's panniers, and ordered me to go down to the stream for water. As I went, he sat down and began to sharpen his knife on a rock—probably so that it would serve better for the cutting of food. But the sound sent a spasm of fear through me. I went along to the stream and put the bucket down. Glancing back, I could see that Abdullah was too deeply interested in the sharpening of his knife to notice me. Besides, the plain was large: it would not occur to him for some time that I had actually run away. I crept towards the river bed, crossed it in shallow water, and reached the cornfield on the other side before he even noticed my absence. When his shout arose, I was in the corn, and he could not see me. Cautiously I poked my way deeper into the field and lay down. I could hear him shouting up and down the river bank, cursing mightily. After a long time—perhaps half an hour—he crossed the river and began to search the cornfield for me, beating the stalks of grain with a stick. His voice never stopped grumbling, cursing, shouting, complaining. Once he came very near to me, and as I held my breath in sheer terror I wished, for the first and last time in my life, for a revolver. I had always refused to have any traffic with firearms, even on the urgent advice of men like Gabrielli, who knew their usefulness. On this occasion a revolver might have preserved me from some of the agonies of fear. But I had no weapon more deadly than my small metal pencil, and it was certainly outdone in efficiency by Abdullah's long knife. I waited, motionless. The flailing stick went past, and after a while Abdullah gave up the search. I could hear his slow steps retreating, his raucous voice subsiding into the last curses of anger and bewilderment. Above me, where the corn was opened to the sky, the stars had come out by the million, and the upper air looked dangerously bright. I lay for a long time without moving, straining my ears for any slight sound from the other side of the river. When the silence had been prolonged enough to convince even me, I removed my jellaba with infinite care, turned it upside down, put my feet in the hood, and went to sleep.

In the morning I did not move until the sun had risen. By this time, certainly, Abdullah would be on his way to Sheshuan. Still I waited, peering out through the corn at the road on the other side of the river. Once in a great while a traveller passed that way, some countryman with a donkey or a mule, sometimes groups of three or four people. When I saw a particularly large group approaching from the west I rose out of my cornfield and made for them across river and field. There was no sign of Abdullah, or even of his camp for the night. The strangers waited for me, staring with considerable curiosity. There were seven or eight of them, young Arabs of the Djebala in ordinary countrymen's clothes. In the usual mixture of Spanish and Arabic I asked for a mule and a guide to Sidi Mohammed ben Abd el-Krim, at Targhzuit. There was some haggling, after which I acquired the necessary mule and muleteer for the remainder of the journey. At half-past eleven that morning we ended our climb to Targhzuit, and my old friend Sidi Hassan, secretary to the general, came out to meet me.

My immediate anxieties were over. Mahdani had arrived at Targhzuit that morning, had been severely taken to task for losing me, and was now confined in the barracks that served as prison, awaiting developments. If I had not turned up during the day there would have been a search of the countryside, and the belligerent Abdullah would have found himself in serious difficulties. Now that the danger (real or imagined) was over, I could afford to assume that he had meant no harm. But ever afterwards, when friends or acquaintances made a point of the courage that is supposed to be shown in such journeys as this, I remembered my night in the cornfield.

5

I remained at Targhzuit for a week, installed in one of the best of Sidi Mohammed's immaculate European tents, with a camp bed and a chair and a table in it—luxuries unusual even at head-quarters. On the first day Sidi Hassan came to lunch with me and told me the news of the day, neither very good nor altogether dis-heartening for the defenders of the Rif. There were heavy bom-bardments at Wezzan (I could hear them) and at Dar ben Karish, and in general the entry of France into the war had made the conditions of battle more unfavourable for the Riffians, the out-come more doubtful. Still, Sidi Hassan was cheerful enough. A long experience of almost uninterrupted victory had made the Rif leaders confident beyond the limits that seemed to me reason-able. I asked Sidi Hassan if he really believed it was possible to win such a war against the immense power of France. He smiled politely.

'The country, the ground and the climate are on our side,' he said. 'They have money, men, and big guns, but what good are they here? We shall win. Only, it will take a little longer. It is a pity this war had to be fought at all, but in any case we must win in the end. Their superiority lies in things that do not count in this country—aëroplanes, big guns, tanks, all useless.'

This stiff-lipped and stubborn belief in an ultimate victory was what made the war possible at all. It was the characteristic faith of a small, devout nation fighting on its own soil (the faith of the Boers, of the Irish), and the idea of a partisan God had a great deal to do with it. A people that had learned how God was on the side of the big battalions—the primary lesson of modern Chris-tendom—could never have fought at all.

The week in Targhzuit passed with mortal slowness. In that peaceful village on the roof of the world we seldom had even an air raid to break the monotony. Sidi Mohammed ben Abd el-

Krim sat all day at the telephone; couriers came and went; by one of them Sidi Hassan sent my first dispatches out to Tangier. I had a long talk with Sidi Mohammed one day, and briefer interviews afterwards. The entries in my diary for that week emphasize the inactivity into which I had sunk, as into a feather bed—and the boredom.

I said my farewell to Sidi Mohammed on the sixteenth, and did not see him again, for the next morning I started towards the Rif.

A week later, after a journey that wore my feet to wounds, I woke up one morning at Mahdani's house near the bay of Alhucemas. The guns had started their infernal din before we finished eating breakfast. From Mahdani's house we could see a huge silver egg floating in the sky: a Spanish (I believe *the* Spanish) dirigible balloon, which neither cruised nor bombarded, but hung suspended there like a shimmering menace to all good Riffi. Mahdani's wife, smiling with pleasure at the thought of her husband's return, but growing sombre again when she thought of sending him down to the guns, gave us an excellent breakfast, beginning with cactus fruit (prickly pears), which I had learned to depend upon as food and drink, morning after morning. I had learned all about prickly pears: how they must be picked before the sun has risen, and held carefully by the beam-ends in the left hand while the right slits them open. I demonstrated this accomplishment, to the delight of Mahdani's wife and little boy, before the bombardment began.

We started off at eight o'clock, riding straight into the Moro Nuevo Peninsula. We had now reached the point at which it was no longer any use trying to dodge bombardments. Consequently, although we tried to find shelter when the aëroplanes came directly over us, at other times we kept a direct course and made the best of it. By noon we had reached the front—that is, the area known to the Spanish and French to be held by Abd el-Krim's fighting men. Here there was an outrageous din all the time, and no respite from the circling of the aëroplanes.

We approached Abd el-Krim's headquarters by a long gorge that offered some shelter, at its sides, from the bombs. As Mahdani and I came along it, joining with such other country people or soldiers as we could meet on the way, it was well covered by the

Spanish aëroplanes. I had never seen Spanish aviators fly so low or return to the charge so often. That infernal road seemed to have a permanent ceiling of Spanish aëroplanes, flying in small circles, swift, low and deadly. People and mules were squashed; it was not a pleasant sight. We took refuge, when we could, in ledges along the side of the gorge, but this seemed to me almost as dangerous as the open road, since the ledges were easily commanded by the machine guns of a tilting plane. It took us an hour to get through the zone of noise and terror, and an hour under such conditions (at least to me) seemed an eternity.

Abd el-Krim's headquarters had been temporarily established in a house on the slope of a hill in the curve of the Moro Nuevo Peninsula. It had the unmistakable look of a centre of activity; it was in an exposed position; the flag of the Rif was flying over it; and yet it was not under bombardment as we came up to it. After the miseries of the past hour, it had almost a look of peace. We marched boldly up to the gate of the main house, and Mahdani told the sentry that I wanted to see the Sultan. In a moment out came a spruce young man in starched shirt and turban: Sidi Mohammed Motassarif. His elegance made me ashamed of my ragged old jellaba and my dirt, just as his perfect Spanish put mine to shame. He vanished, to return again with a broad smile, asked me to come into the courtyard, and then ushered me (as if we had been in the Royal Palace at Madrid instead of a mud hut in the hills) into one of the low doors of the house.

I stood there for a moment, blinking. The room was bare and dark; I could see nobody in it.

'Quiero ver el-Sultan,' I said into the dark. 'Está aquí?'

A low voice came almost from my knees.

'Sí,' it said. 'Abd el-Krim está aquí.'

I looked down. He was sitting cross-legged on the floor, just beside me. His irregular teeth showed in a friendly smile; he reached his hand up to me. I dropped down to my haunches, and we talked, exactly as if we had been old friends who had parted only a week before. The formality of my previous visit was forgotten.

'I got your letters,' he said, 'both of them. My brother answered one of them and Sidi Hassan the other. You never received them? Strange. . . . But there is no use talking peace terms until Primo de Rivera and the rest of them will recognize our independence. That is the one condition we cannot give up. That's all we said in our letters to you. . . . Why have you no shoes? It must hurt to walk barefoot over these hills; you can't go on like that.'

'I am getting used to it, Sidna,' I said. 'I lost my sandals coming out from Tangier. We had to run so fast. The blockade . . .'

'I know,' he said. 'But come on out here in the courtyard. Let us see if we can get you some shoes. We have hundreds of Spanish shoes—captured ones. Most of our men won't wear them. Maybe we can find some to fit.'

'I have very large feet, Sidna.'

He looked at my feet and laughed. By this time we were in the courtyard, in one corner of which there was a great pile of yellow-brown leather shoes.

'Por Diós!' he said. 'You have feet as big as those fine ships out there in the bay. I don't believe any Spanish shoes are so big. Let's see.'

We poked about in the pile of shoes. Occasionally Abd el-Krim found a pair that he thought might do, but they always turned out to be about half the size of my feet.

'Wallahi!' he said, laughing. 'With feet like that, it is perhaps better to go barefoot! Less trouble. . . . If I find some big shoes I shall remember you. In the meanwhile, let us talk. What does America think of our war? Who are these American aviators in the service of the French? Are they officers of the American army?'

'I don't know anything about them, Sidna,' I said truthfully. 'They may be officers of the American reserve, but that doesn't mean much: there are a great many reserve officers, from the last war. I think they are only young men in search of adventure.'

'They might find it in some other manner, it seems to me,' he said. 'If they want to fight, why do they fight for the French? . . . A French aëroplane, a Bréguet bombing plane, fell in the Branès the other day. We think it may still be in good enough shape to fly.'

He was off, talking about the war—the events in the south,

where his Arab allies were fighting the French; the events here at Alhucemas, where I learned that the Spanish fleet had been reinforced by the French. A Spanish force of infantry and artillery had been landed on Moro Nuevo Peninsula, where they held a bare and deadly shelf of rocky land, subjected to constant fire from the superior positions of the Riffi. It sounded like a miniature Gallipoli. As he was describing the course of the fighting here one of his officers suddenly popped through the doorway, breathless, and interrupted with a sentence in Shilluh. Abd el-Krim got up and made his way out, taking me by the arm. His limp—which dated from five or six years before, when he had broken his leg escaping from a Spanish prison in Melilla—became noticeable when he walked fast.

'A squadron of aëroplanes,' he said cheerfully, 'seems to be coming directly over this house. We shall carry on our conversation in the cave.'

We entered the cave, and the raid was on. The planes flew very low indeed, rained bombs and used their machine guns. The bombs made a particularly thunderous noise in this cave, which was not very deep. I squatted inside the door. The figures of a number of Abd el-Krim's spruce young officers could be seen farther in. The Sultan himself stood in the entrance. As the aëroplanes swooped just over the slope in front of us he reached for a rifle and stood half in, half out of the cave, aiming carefully. He continued a sentence he had already begun (something about the irreducible minimum of his conditions for peace) and punctuated it thus:

'. . . la independencia [BANG!] . . . absoluta [BANG!] . . . del Rif [BANG!]'

In spite of the discomfort that always came over me during these raids, I was thrilled at the spectacle. He was in plain view of the bombers, and why they did not get him with their machine guns was a mystery. The sight of such intrepidity against such odds might have served as a figure for the whole war: one man (and lame at that) firing with a rifle at a squadron of aëroplanes.

His officers protested, whispered, even put hands on his jellaba. 'Sidna, Sidna!' Sidi Mohammed Motassarif was muttering. In view of the nearness of these aëroplanes (the nearest I ever saw) Abd el-Krim was taking a terrible risk. But he remained in the entrance of the cave throughout the raid and only put the rifle back when the aviators had decided to drop their hot cakes elsewhere.

'Does it do much good to fire at planes with rifles?' I asked when we came out.

'You can never tell,' he said. 'We have brought down planes with rifles before this. Usually they fly very high to avoid it. ... Will you have some tea?'

It developed that he was going on a tour of the front positions on Moro Nuevo that night after sunset. I asked to go with him. He replied to this suggestion with his characteristic grin—friendly, tolerant, humorous, with slightly crooked teeth that parted company in the middle.

'I don't think you'd better go,' he said. 'It is very dangerous. You are the press, you know—the only press we have here. The press must not be exterminated."

Of the various things I heard Abd el-Krim say this was, for some inexplicable reason, one of the most characteristic, one of the most haunting. It is one of a trio of trifles, which it seems to me nobody else in the same position would have said in quite the same way. The first was 'Abd el-Krim está aquí.' The second was 'La prensa no debe ser exterminado.' The third was (two days later) 'Faltan muchas cosas a Alhucemas.' When I search for a common quality in these remarks, so simple, so commonplace in their appearance, the only thing that occurs to me is good-humour. They were all three remarks of a calm, easy, almost Olympian good-humour. I can still hear his voice saying 'abd el-Krim está aquí' when I have long since forgotten exactly how he talked of war and peace, government, religion and politics. There was in his voice and manner, his turn of phrase, his way of saying such inconsiderable things, just that quality of being in but above the battle which is, it seems to me, the mark of greatness.

I went with him, in spite of the risk of exterminating the press, but I was not allowed to stay long. The front lines on Moro Nuevo were the realm of the hand grenade; the Riffian hand grenade was a tin can filled with any kind of explosive that happened to be available, but the Spanish grenade was a more serious matter. A little taste of this medicine made me moderate my protests when Abd el-Krim sent me off, on a fine white horse of his own, to one of his houses in Ajdir.

In my notebook that night I scribbled:

. . . His courage is magnificent. His ideas have not changed, have even been reinforced by the present danger. From what I saw of him today I know that I had no idea of him before. He has a grandeur, added to by the circumstances of horror and great danger. But in spite of this he is humorous, funny: makes me laugh, especially when he assumes a schoolmasterish air and corrects my Spanish.

On the next day, at Ajdir, I was left to pursue my avocations as *la prensa*. I wrote in the notebook that afternoon:

Thursday, Sept. 24th. The bombardment is heavy. The Spanish fleet is half-mooned across the bay, firing. (Looks very pretty.) The island of Alhucemas, the fort, is bombarding, and the Spanish and French aëroplanes are dropping bombs all the time. There is a dirigible over above Moro Nuevo—the same one—but it hardly moves, and never bombards. Scouting? It is a beautiful silver object in the blue sky. I suppose it must be French.[1] I have written two articles today—one what my contract calls a 'colour story' and the other an interview with Abd el-Krim. He telephoned me today to say that I can return to the front line tomorrow if I come early, before the aëroplanes are out—at about 4 A.M., probably.

The following day was, for reasons known only to the Spanish, a very quiet one, with neither air raids nor bombardment of any severity. My mule and muleteer did not turn up at the crack of dawn, as I expected, but at ten o'clock, an hour that was normally a busy one for the bombers. I rode peacefully over the hill to field headquarters on Moro Nuevo, where I joined Abd el-Krim. After lunch he took me up to the top of the mountain; we lay on our stomachs and surveyed the scene in the bay below. He had excellent field glasses, through which the ships of the fleet were picked out in every detail. It was a cloudless day, and in the silence, the sunlight, the shimmer and gleam of this interval, ships and balloon floated harmless as children's toys, mere decorations across the lovely landscape in which a people of shepherds and

[1]It was Spanish.

peasants lived out their long, calm lives. Surely, some day, they might be permitted to do so undisturbed?

I had had an unusually good lunch; there were charm and variety in Abd el-Krim's conversation; an air of smiling peace, almost of gaiety, had crept into the past two or three hours. I began to talk at random. Alhucemas reminded me of the curving bay at Monte Carlo, I said; none of the celebrated resorts along the Riviera had a more striking confrontation of sea and land; when the war was over, the Sultan could make a kind of African Côte d'Azur out of it. I ended this discourse by a singularly imbecile remark, intended partly as a joke, partly as a suggestion of what the scene might be under other circumstances—a remark that made me go hot with shame a minute later.

'Falta un Casino a Alhucemas,' I said.

Abd el-Krim had been listening to my babble with a kindly, absent-minded smile. When I made my brilliant suggestion about the Casino his face darkened and saddened for a moment. He looked clear across the bay, as if he were seeing through the Spanish ships, through the sparkle of the water to its cold secret depths. In a silence that lasted long enough for me to appreciate the complex silliness of what I had said, his gaze traversed the sea and the hills, went through them and came back to me.

'Faltan muchas cosas a Alhucemas,' he said; and I understood that nobody had ever felt more deeply than this man how far our hopes and dreams outrun us all.

6

If I had had only my own wishes to consult I might have stayed on with Abd el-Krim almost indefinitely. He personified his people in the best of their qualities, expressed and defined them, more than it is possible for any one man to do in more complicated societies. His genius was his people's raised to a higher power. In spite of his considerable acquaintance with the culture and ideas of Europe, he never for one moment saw the world or his particular problems in it from the point of view of an European. He saw them as any Riffian might see them; his superiority consisted in the fact that he could see them more clearly.

attack them with greater courage and a more masterful intelligence. His ruling ideas, his purposes in life, were very few; they might all have been reduced to one, the 'absolute independence' of the Rif. He could have defended this apparent narrowness of vision in the words of Savonarola: *Le mie cose erano poche e grandi.* In a country like his, where the organization of society has scarcely passed the pastoral stage, the first aspiration of men must always be towards freedom, and the highest duty of a leader among them must be to secure it. The singleness of Abd el-Krim's purpose was not, in the hills and valleys of his own people at that particular moment in their history, a proof of limitation; it was a proof of greatness.

He can never have appeared a more heroic figure than he did to me during those days. Against his quality, the best of the pettifogging politicians of Europe looked like so many puppets. It would have refreshed my belief in the capacity of mankind to rise above itself—its ability to reach, on occasions however rare, the summits indicated as possible by so much of its own literature and tradition—if I had been permitted to stay on at Ajdir and contemplate the phenomenon for a little longer. But I had a contract to fulfil, and its terms required me to make a tour of the beleaguered country and come out, after another three weeks or so, at Tangier. I had to leave Alhucemas as soon as possible if I was to see anything of the fighting on the southern front. I said my *Adiós* to Abd el-Krim, and on September 28th—three days after our afternoon on the hill—set out for the tribe of the Branès.

Fate, luck, the hazards of the road, whatever the accidental element in these matters may be called, had been steadily on my side since the day I left Tangier. From now on it turned as steadily against me, so that it seemed at times that I could never get out of the country alive. Later on, under the accumulation of misfortunes, I even lost interest in the outcome, and surrendered to accident as a drowning man surrenders to the waves. The disaster that was overwhelming the Rif seemed about to take me along with the rest.

I never reached the country of the Branès. The remaining entries in my notebook were made at Targheest. Since I was very nearly a prisoner there—or at least a guest whose movements were sharply restricted—I scribbled a good deal in that book for some days.

Sept. 29th. At 10:30 A.M. yesterday, a man named Mohammed Abdullah arrived with a mule and we started for Targheest. Exhausting day: Beni Warriaghel, Beni Bukoya, Beni Ytofft; at the end of which it was impossible to find a house where we could sleep. All the men away at the wars, and the women afraid to admit us. We had to sleep under a tree. I nearly froze to death, didn't expect to sleep at all, but did. The automobile road from Ajdir to Targheest looks good, but I observe that as between a good road and a bad most Riffi will choose the bad one. We spent the day on trails a goat would have scorned.

Today we started at 6 A.M., frozen stiff. Stopped to eat prickly pears— only food since yesterday morning. Arrived at the Macama of Targheest (Targuist, it is, on French maps) at 11:30 A.M. Waiting now for food. There have been no instructions given here—nothing. I was not expected. A German called Allal—tall, pale, disgusted-looking—came to see me.

4 P.M. Food was produced at noon—barley bread and six boiled eggs, with salt (very dirty, like the bread). Afterwards, after an interminable wait, tea. It all had a grudging look. Then I, perhaps impolitely, made myself a bed out of my jellaba and went to sleep. I have just now wakened and don't know whether they have succeeded in getting Ajdir on the telephone. If they don't get instructions before tomorrow morning I may be unable to go on to the Branès. French planes, three of them—Goliaths, which make a noise like the end of the world and a hole in the ground the size of a house— bombed here yesterday.

There were no entries made in the useful little notebook after October 1st, for I was at the outset of a journey of pure nightmare from beginning to end. On the second of October a brilliant cavalcade arrived at Targheest in a cloud of dust: Sidi Hassan and the German Pilgrim, bringing with them Sidi Said er-Riffi and the three sons of old Mohammed Tazi, the ex-viceroy of the Sherifian sultan at Tangier. I spent the day with them. The garrulous, luxury-loving Sherifian princes had run away from home to join Abd el-Krim, and had evidently no idea, in all their silks and satins, of what was in store for them. One of them (he was an albino with a shining pink face) lectured me for an hour or so on the inner significance of the Riffian movement. Dirty, ragged and barefoot as I was, crawling with lice and weak with hunger, I could only sit and look at him. He wore so many fine clothes of varied colours, was so pink and well-fed and comfortable in his brocaded velvet *bedaya* and silk shirt and satin pantaloons, that I did not have the cruelty to tell him what I thought would be the inevitable result of his escapade. Sidi Hassan, at any rate, understood my predicament. He told me the southern Arab tribes were wavering in their allegiance, and advised me strongly against going among them; by his advice I decided to return to Sheshuan and Tangier.

On the next day (October 3d) I started out, equipped, by Sidi Hassan's orders, with a guide and a mule for the day—but for the day only. It should have taken four days to reach Sheshuan. It took nearly three weeks—weeks of such long-drawn-out misery that time ceased to have any value whatever, and I was only able to establish the length of the ordeal afterwards by subtracting the date of my departure from Targheest from the date of my arrival in Sheshuan.

On October fourth, when I woke up in a mosque in the mountains, I had malaria. At first I had no idea what it was, although I had seen enough of it in other people by this time. In my case it may have been complicated by some other form of fever, for I was certainly verminous enough to have acquired everything from typhus to cholera and back again. At any rate, I was ill; soon I was very ill. The fever would burn me like a blast furnace, so that I could not bear to keep my clothes on; and then the chills swept down, shuddering and icy. I must have been delirious for at least part of the time, for whole days vanished from my memory. I had neither mule nor guide (my first day's man and beast had returned to Targheest); I had money, but was not anxious to show any more of it than was strictly necessary among a particularly treacherous people, the border Arabs. At first it proved difficult even to hire a mule or a guide. When I could get no such help, I went on alone in the general direction of the west, for the one idea I had firmly fixed in my otherwise feverish head was that I must get to Sheshuan. I slept in ditches, sheds, or among the rocks when I could not find a house to take me in. If I had been in the Rif I might have found a hospitable house or mosque and stayed there until I was better able to travel. But among these Moroccan Arab tribes, so changeable, treacherous and bloodthirsty, I trusted nobody. I was protected by two things only: the word of Abd el-Krim (which seemed to fade in power as I went onward) and the natural reluctance of any human being, however violent, to suppress another without reason. If some of my hosts in those hungry southern tribes, exasperated, as they were, by poverty and war and the exactions of their chiefs, had known just how much money I carried on me, they might have stuck a knife into me for the sake of the few duros. But I did not look rich: my homespun jellaba, old when I acquired it, was now in tatters, and looked as if it could hide nothing but my lousy and flea-bitten skeleton. They let me pass; and if I had my difficulties with some of them, there were others who obeyed the law of the Prophet and showed me kindness.

One evening—it must have been after I had journeyed in this desperate fashion for about two weeks—I came to a village in the Beni Dherkoun, which I remembered. I was pleased, excited; for a long time I had not seen anything that looked in the least familiar, and for all I knew I might have been going in circles. This village was one I had passed with Mahdani a month or so before. There was a hut there, near a stream, whose owner sold tea and coffee to wayfarers. There were some mats and rags thrown on the ground in this place, and the owner of the café told me I could use them. The captious Baedeker would not have given his establishment a star, but I was glad to find it, crawled under the mats and rags on the floor, and lay there, dulled with fever. I was trying to count the time so as to know exactly what date it was, and thinking, too, that I could not be far from Sheshuan, when a most extraordinary thing occurred: I heard an American voice.

It was a rather soft voice, speaking in broken French—*petit nègre*, the pidgin-French of Morocco.

'Vous—vendre—thé?' the voice said.

I looked up and squinted hard. It occurred to me at once that the fever might be playing tricks with me. But there was certainly a new form there, in the open entrance of the hut, bending over to talk to the squatting Arabs. The new form was dressed in a ragged khaki uniform, a French uniform. I still could not trust my first notion; no American could possibly be here, in this place.

'Vous êtes Français?' I asked.

He looked down at the pile of rags from which I had half emerged.

'Je suis Américain,' he said, with—even in French—the blessed furry voice of an American Negro.

'Then come over here, for God's sake,' I said, 'and sit on me. I've got another chill coming.'

He did not dispute the point, but calmly removed his coat and put it on top of the rags I already had on top of me. Then, looking about him, he caught sight of another bit of old carpet that served to support the hams of an elderly Arab; he pulled it away, with a polite 'Pardon' and put it also on top of me. When he had done all this he sat down on top of me. I had discovered that this was the best treatment for the chill, as it not only gave warmth, but prevented me from twitching all over the place and throwing off the covers.

'How did you get here?' he asked, without undue surprise. 'You've got *paludisme*, haven't you?'

'A v-v-very b-b-bad case,' I said. 'Oh, Lord, oh, Lord, why the hell don't I die?'

'You won't die,' he said, sitting harder. 'In ten minutes this'll be over, and I'll rustle up something for you to eat. There must be something in this dump to eat. Let yourself go. Yell if you want to. Maybe it'll help. Yell hard. Don't take your arms out; keep 'em covered. Yell harder.'

Ten or fifteen minutes of this sensible treatment and the chill had passed; I lay quiet again, sweating. The Arabs in the hut, sipping their coffee noisily, regarded the performance with the utmost stolidity.

'You lie quiet,' said the heaven-sent American Negro, 'and sleep a little if you can, for a few minutes. That always helps. I'll go and see what I can buy to eat in this dump.'

I tried to find some money.

'Don't bother about that,' said the American Negro. 'I've got some money.'

(He may have had a few pieces of Spanish silver, but no more.)

When he came back, twenty minutes or so later, he brought eggs and milk. Eggs I was used to, but I had never seen any milk in these mountains. I gulped it hungrily and left little enough for the ambassador of the Almighty. The fever was gone, now, and I had a good look at him. He was very young, and his kind brown face looked worried.

'I don't know what to do with you,' he said. 'Where are you going? Are you able to travel?'

'I've got to,' I said. 'If I can talk the local sheikh into finding a guide for me, I'm going to Sheshuan. Then to Tangier.'

'Me too,' he said.

His name was Wesley Williams, and he was twenty years old. He lived in Oakland, California, across the bay from San Francisco. Why anybody who has the luck to live in such a place should have joined the French Foreign Legion was mysterious enough, but no more mysterious than the accident that had sent him into the Beni Dherkoun that night. He had wandered away from California to France, in a spasm of adolescent romanticism, and over a café table in Bordeaux had met the inevitable recruiting agent for the Legion. The Legion seemed to him, before he joined it, a dashing sort of affair. Sidi Bel Abbès and the desert corrected this notion, and he deserted one moonlight night, with a number of his companions, to join Abd el-Krim. In the Rif he had been employed on roads and in making gun emplacements. Now, with the permission of Abd el-Krim and some money for his labour, he was on his way out to Tangier and home.

Williams wanted to stay and see me through the rest of my journey, but I was against the idea; it was important for him to get out quickly, and I might have held him back for weeks. Besides, my fever was gone for the moment, and the events of that evening had filled me with encouragement: I had recognized my whereabouts; I had seen an American; I had eaten a meal. After these miracles the rest seemed easy.

Williams went on in the morning, and I had my debate with the local sheikh. For arguments of silver he supplied me with a mule and a man. But the journey to Sheshuan (which should have taken six or seven hours from here) was strung out over the next three days, as the fever had weakened me so that I could not keep going. On the fourth morning we crept into Sheshuan; and in front of the local Macama, which had been the house of a sherif and wore a look of opulence, I collapsed. My clock had been wound to run only so far and no farther.

Fortunately, there was somebody there to pick up the wreck—Sidi Mustafa Akhamlich, a clever young man from Tangier who belonged to the secretariat of the Riffian government. He installed my filthy, aching bones, with their burden of subsidiary animal life, in a comfortable room where there were plenty of rugs to pile on during the chills. He brought food, tea, cigarettes, soap, water, quinine and all sorts of beneficent drugs, and in a day or so I was able to view the prospect of continued existence without disgust. When I had reached this point in convalescence Si Mustafa also brought me visitors—Mario Magri and Alfredo Morea.

Magri and Morea were exactly what I needed just then. They were an extraordinary pair, who would have found something to laugh at in the gates of hell. Alfredo Morea, the younger of the two, was then twenty-eight; he was a deputy in the Italian Parliament, the youngest *onorevole* in Italy, a Nationalist Republican, and represented the traditional Republican fastness of Fabbriano. Mario Magri was a Fascist, and had been vice-prefect of Sardinia; it was he who had arranged Mussolini's exceedingly successful tour in Sardinia the year before, for which he had been made a knight of the Corona d'Italia. But these definitions did not begin to define them. They had fought throughout the war, and had each a string of decorations as long as your arm; not content with this, they had gone off to Fiume with Gabriele d'Annunzio and remained there when the whole enterprise was officially condemned by their own government. Alfredo said he had come to the Rif to write about it for his newspaper, the *Voce Repubblicana* in Rome; Mario had no such ready-made explanation, but I suspected that his journey had something to do with aëroplanes.

When next I heard of these two, they were confined as political prisoners on the volcanic islands—Mussolini's friend Mario and his enemy Alfredo alike.

Their careers, however fantastic, did not interest me in Sheshuan as much as their other accomplishments. They could both talk; and the delight of talking a familiar language with people of my own general breed was better than quinine. They could also sing, laugh, tell stories, and cook—a variety of talents so singularly apposite that they, like the American Negro, might have been ambassadors of the Almighty. Mario's special dish was a sugar omelette, in the concoction of which he equalled the most dazzling achievements of the great Escoffier. True, there were not many things to cook with at Sheshuan, but he did wonders with what he could find; and when I had stuffed myself so full that I could eat no more, he would set up a doleful chant out of *La Boheme* or *La Tosca*. His favourite morsel was Mimi's death scene, in which he sang both parts with melancholy and abandon. 'Sono andati! Fingevo di dormire,' he intoned, rolling his little black eyes. As I grew better I was determined not to be left out of this, and Alfredo and I would come in strong on the part of Rodolfo. 'Ah, mia Mimi, mia bella amante!' we bellowed, all three at once.

The Arabs thought we had been touched by the fever, and except for Mustafa Akhamlich, none came near us.

7

I was anxious to get through to Tangier as soon as I was strong enough for the journey. My contract with the N. A. N. A. had expired, and I did not even know whether the dispatches I had sent them had ever arrived—whether, in fact, this whole enterprise had not been, from the point of view of my employers, a failure. Mario Magri was staying on in the country for reasons of his own (I still suspected aëroplanes, but it was none of my business). Alfredo Morea had come to the Rif for excitement, had found it, and was now getting bored; he decided to make the run to Tangier with me. It was a piece of transcendent good fortune for me that he did.

Mario and Mustafa Akhamlich rode with us as far as Bohrabish, and there we left them—Mario shouting 'Ciao!' and grinning over the parapet of the sherif's roof. As Alfredo and I, with three men assigned to us by Akhamlich, rode off on a detour to the south of Tangier, we could hear Mario's voice bellowing after us in our eternal tune from the last act of the *Boheme:* 'Sono andati! Fingevo di dormire . . .'

We crossed through the lines to Tangier, on the Djebel Habib road, on the night of October 29th to October 30th. Until then I had regarded myself as, in a small way, rather a veteran. At least I had already had a good deal of experience with the various arguments used by France and Spain in their laudable effort to win the inhabitants of this country to Christian civilization: machine guns, rifles, guns big and little, bombs, hand grenades. Nearly every day in the past two months I had been under some kind of fire, sometimes for hours at a stretch, and although I had never acquired that longing for the smell of powder which is said to distinguish the brave, I did believe I was getting used to it. The passage to Tangier disabused me of the notion.

We were under fire for five hours that night—five mortal hours, with the searchlights ploughing the sky and the plain, and a few score miserable, frightened Arabs scuttling along as best they could, running or crawling or lying hidden while the fire passed over them. The numbers of those willing to risk their lives to go to market had notably diminished since I had first gone to Tangier. There were still some, and we still had the guard of sturdy riflemen from the Beni M'sua. But the enterprise, on a bright moonlight night made brighter by the powerful Spanish lights, was hardly a sensible one for people who had only a few chickens or eggs to sell. It seemed, after an hour or so, of no particular interest even to a malarial newspaper correspondent from New York.

At intervals when the attention of the Spaniards seemed to be directed elsewhere we talked a little, in whispers. Alfredo Morea, in the account he afterwards published of this night, declared that my conversation consisted of remarks addressed in all the wrong languages to our companions of the road—that I spoke to the Arabs in English, the Germans in Italian, the Italian (himself) in German, and the American in Spanish. This may be so, for I was too tired to know one from the other. At one moment I found myself suddenly walking along beside Wesley Williams, my American Negro friend, who had been waiting all this time for a chance to go out to Tangier. With him were two or three Germans, also deserters from the Legion. A searchlight swept over us; we scattered; I did not see them again for many hours.

The machine guns on this occasion were really bad, and by the time we got through the last of them I had no energy left. It seemed, by the whisper that swept through the company, that this was the end—there were no more Spanish posts or block-houses, and in a moment we should be safe in the international zone. To reach it we passed through a sort of ravine—a dried-up river bed—and already one or two of the Arabs had begun softly to chant their 'La ilaha ill'Allah.' I was picking my way with some care through the stones, as my bare feet would have to last a good many more hours before I could drag them into the para-dise of the hotel in Tangier. And just then, when the worst of the night seemed over, its worst moment arrived.

On both sides of us, at not more than fifteen or twenty feet, a line of rifles opened fire. Two or three of our men shouted, '*Am-buscadores!*' Our own riflemen returned the fire, but into blank darkness. There were some shouts and shrieks, a sudden hell of noise.

It was an ambush. The *ambuscadores*, native troops in Spanish service, had no doubt been waiting in this spot all night long for us. The technique in such cases was to stoop down as low as possible and run forward in a kind of loping crawl. I did so, al-though without spirit. I could distinguish nothing in this hollow. There were only a number of agitated forms, darker shadows in the dark. Farther along, on a hill with a peaceable mud hut on it, the scurrying figures of our vanguard could be seen running towards the other side. The sky was already growing light, and they were outlined against it. If I could reach that hill and get on the other side, all would be well.

Suddenly my foot came down on a particularly pointed stone, and the little jab of pain made me stumble. I fell down, cracking knee and elbow, and found it difficult to get up again. Then the idea came to me: why get up? Why not just lie here? Either I am killed or I am not killed, and I don't particularly care which it is, but I can't get up when every bone in my body aches, and I have not strength enough to put one foot in front of the other.

These cheerful reflections may have occupied a minute, per-haps. They were interrupted by a hullabaloo from the top of the hill. I heard my own name and looked up. It was lighter there, and I could distinctly see Morea's European figure, the only one on that whole plain in riding boots and breeches.

'Vincenzo! Vincenzo!' he was bawling in a voice that seemed to drown out the rifle fire. 'Dove sei?'

I was seized with a feeling of shame. Morea, with his yards and yards of decorations, his whole past of fearlessness, must not be allowed to see me lying there like a sheep, waiting to be slaughtered. I made a determined effort and got to my feet. But before I was up he had seen me, and, letting out a bellow of sheer rage, plunged back into the line of fire. He reached me in the middle of it, grasped me by the arm with a firmness that almost broke the bone, and dragged me out to rising ground. As he did so he released flood after flood of the most lurid language known to the forty million sons of Italy, who, in this matter, are not to be outdone by the profanest people on the earth. He cursed me, my malaria, the Arabs, the rifles, the moon, the country, the ravine, the hill, the United States of America and its inhabitants, the profession of journalism and the pastime of war. I think he was cursing as some people laugh, out of sheer excitement. But as he cursed he ran, and as he ran he dragged me along with him, until we had gone over the hill and the shallow plain beyond and reached the stream that was the frontier of the international zone of Tangier. When we passed it I succeeded in getting his attention.

'For the love of God,' I said, 'let me lie down here and rest for five minutes. I'm dead.'

He released me, and I stretched out on the ground.

'You should not have stopped like that in that place,' he said in a tone of mild reproof. 'You might have been killed.'

Even though I was dead, my ghost had to laugh at this.

'Your rest is over,' said Morea, looking at his watch. 'Su! Coraggio!'

He kept me going as long as he could. Having preserved my life at the risk of his own, he was apparently determined to deliver me by hand to the hotel in Tangier. After an hour's march I could stand no more and picked out a comfortable ditch to lie in.

'You go on to Tangier,' I said. 'I've got to rest. I'll be all right.'

He sat down on the edge of the ditch and frowned at me.

When I woke up, two hours or so later, he was still sitting there. He had apparently slept sitting up.

'Avanti, Savoia!' he said, and off we went again, but not at a pace that would have won us many prizes. I was dragging along, casting covetous glances at the ditches beside the road, when we came to two Sherifian sentries stationed to catch blockade runners. They arrested us; our troubles were over; for the officer in charge at the post was Captain Panabières of the French Intelligence Service, who knew all about us and had been expecting his net to bring us in almost any morning. We sat in his office, drank coffee, smoked cigarettes, and talked, or at least Alfredo did. I was too drowsy to take much part in the conversation.

'I have sent for my car,' said Panabières, rising. 'It should be here now, and you can go on to Tangier in it.'

Thus, in pampered luxury, we came back to our own world.

As we left the Sherifian post a figure started up from among those crowded to one side of the door. It was Wesley Williams.

'Ah, so they caught you!'

'They did. And—' he looked round him anxiously—'I'm a deserter. I may be shot.'

'Probably not,' I said. 'I don't think anybody shoots Americans, much.'

'Will you speak to the consul?'

'Yes. But I'll write something in the papers about it—that's the best way. Cheer up. You'll be in California soon.'

I never saw him again. He was held by the French for a while, but they wisely decided that his youth and his nationality made it inadvisable to punish him further, and in a few weeks he was released and sent home. He wrote to me once afterwards from a boat that carried tourists up and down the Pacific Coast. His *Wanderjahr* over, he had taken a job as steward on a steamer and thought of his days in the Legion as of something strange and improbable that had happened to somebody else. Almost, it seemed from his letter, he regretted them.

Alfredo and I went on to Tangier. Twenty-four hours' rest, food, quinine and the general operation of cleansing did wonders for me. On the second night after our tumultuous passage through the lines he came to dinner at my hotel. He was exactly as he had been before: spirited, profane, light-hearted, quizzical, a very gallant figure. Even his clothes were the same, for he had come to Morocco in campaign kit and had no others. He had shaved faithfully every day in the Djebala, so that his face looked no different now. He had been eyeing me strangely from time to time; towards the end of the meal he broke out.

'*Cristo Madonna!*' he said. 'Are you two people, or are you one? I don't recognize you, or anything you do . . . Champagne, Egyptian cigarettes, all this fuss about food—so clean that you shine—white, fine clothes! Which is the masquerade?'

'There isn't any masquerade,' I said, feeling that the cause needed a good deal of defence. 'The lice and fleas, the beard and the rags didn't look like my permanent condition, did they? Or maybe they did. . . . Anyhow, they weren't. Neither is this. Why must anybody have a permanent condition? If there is a masquerader, it is you, because you insist upon remaining the same under circumstances that vary enormously. You are true to yourself, as they say—true to something that probably exists only in your mind or against a background known only to you. You went into the Rif just as if it had been Fiume. And you were a foreigner there every minute. This is the moment for luxury and Egyptian cigarettes and champagne, but you don't really like them either. You have adopted the worst of masquerades, the masquerade of consistency.'

'I deny it,' he said. 'I don't try to take on the colour of my surroundings, because I don't see any sense in it. I was a foreigner in the Rif, but I admitted it by wearing foreign clothes and insisting on foreign food if I had to cook it myself. This restricted me to the big places, of course, but do you believe you learned any more by going into the jungle and growing a mat of hair on your face and supplying sustenance to millions of lice? You were just as much a foreigner as I, but you wanted to give yourself the illusion of being a part of your surroundings—the last refuge of romanticism. I am a twentieth-century Italian, and to imagine myself anything else would be moonshine. At least, in this way, I am a fixed point. My surroundings may change, but I know where I am.'

'The advantage,' I said, 'is dubious. Champagne is better after two months of rags and lice; its taste comes out. . . . You preserved your fixed point, your beloved identity, so completely in the Djebala that you never acquired the slightest idea of how the people there really live. You . . .'

And so on, into the latest hours allowed by the night in Tangier, we argued. The problem was not one that could be solved, and we left it as we found it. Alfredo took his 'fixed point'—a notably movable one—to Italy the next day. He sent me what he wrote in the *Voce Repubblicana* about our passage to Tangier, and although I figured largely in the account as a form of comic relief, with my bare feet, my malaria and my hopeless mixture of languages, there was not a word in it about how he had gone back into the ambuscade to lug me out. Some two years later, hearing that he was confined on the island of Lipari for having annoyed the Duce del Fascismo, I went from Berlin to Sicily to see him, no doubt with a lunatic notion at the back of my head that I might be able to help him escape from those silver volcanoes in the Tyrrhenian sea. Reaching Lipari, after some inconvenience, on the night before Christmas, I found myself securely guarded by two carabinieri who had no intention of letting me land. I stood on the deck of the little ship for a long time trying to decide if one of the figures on the shore of the prison island was Alfredo. Presently a nervous stranger thrust a letter and two bottles of wine into my hand. 'You will have to go back,' the letter said, 'but the Governor allows me to send you these two bottles of Malvasia, the *specialità* of this island, to celebrate Christmas Eve. I am here for years yet. Drink the Malvasia with a sugar omelette. Sorry. *Tante belle cose! Ciao.'*

8

Hot baths, clean clothes and champagne were not the only gratifications of my return to Tangier. Professionally considered, the trip had been a success: all my dispatches had gone through, all had been printed in Europe and America. My employers professed themselves satisfied and gave me more money than they were obliged to give under their contract. Again, as on the first journey, I experienced the pleasures of resurrection. This time I had been shot as a spy by Sidi Mohammed (of all people), and duly interred in the columns of the *Daily Telegraph* in London. The fact that the rest of the correspondents had been on the side of the French and Spanish, all sending necessarily the same material, had given my dispatches a fortuitous, momentary importance, the signs of which I thoroughly enjoyed. For a few days, in Tangier, Rabat and Paris, I was able to delude myself into the belief that I was a Personage—which was soothing to the vanity of youth, even though it did make me think of amateur theatricals as played in a certain barn in Illinois.

The rôle was that of War Correspondent. This character, for the ten days or two weeks of his supposed existence, received visits from persons who shared his delusion, and paid visits to persons who had to pretend that they shared it.

In the first category came an improbable collection of people in Tangier, hangers-on of the Rif war, who streamed in and out of my room of the Hotel Cecil for a day or two. There were the wife of a Norwegian engineer in the Rif service, who was in great straits and wanted her husband; Captain Mundy, who had hospital supplies from the Indian Red Crescent (Ameer Ali and Lord Lamington in London), and wanted to send them in to the Rif; an officer of the Grenadier Guards, who wanted to know how long Abd el-Krim could continue the war; the local Turkish spy, employed just then by the Italians, who wanted to know anything I would tell him; Lieutenant-Colonel Otto Zeltins, once of the Imperial Guard at Potsdam, now of the Lettish cavalry (or so he said), who wanted to go into the Rif; an English mining engineer from Melilla, who wanted to know whether the mines were being worked in the Beni Tuzin; and my old friend the woman Zaina of the Beni Bukoya, who appeared one day wrapped in veils and mystery, and wanted—money. I looked wise and thoughtful, tapped on my desk with a pencil, gazed out through the window, frowning, and occasionally dropped a few significant remarks, just as I had seen real personages do under such circumstances, but I can hardly believe that any of my clients went away satisfied. For, as is the way of clients, they all (except Zaina) wanted something I did not have to give.

The second category included the French Résident-Général at Rabat (M. Steeg) and the cabinet ministers in Paris. I had little nope of getting anything out of them, but my contract obliged me to interview them on the subject of the war and the peace, if there was to be a peace. Some of the American aviators who formed the Sherifian Escadrille in the French service turned up at Tangier just as I was ready to pay my round of visits. We found, by comparing dates, that I had been bombarded by them a week before in Sheshuan, which obviously constituted one of the best known bases for a firm friendship; when they returned to Rabat I went along as a passenger in one of the Bréguet bombers. This was, apparently, against the Ten Commandments, the rules of war, and the traditions of the French army. My American aviator had forgotten to fill his tank with gasoline that morning, and we settled gently down into a cornfield near Rabat when he observed his omission, which no doubt added to the heinousness of his offence in taking me along. I continued to Rabat in a car, interviewed the statuesque and stupid Résident-Général, who did not even know the geography of the campaign accurately, and a day or so later I was off in a Latécoère postal plane for Paris.

The Prime Minister and Minister of War, that week, happened to be M. Paul Painlevé. It might easily have been M. Briand, M. Caillaux, M. Herriot, or any other leader of the Left, for they juggled the presidency of the council about among themselves all during the Moroccan War with consummate dexterity. They disliked the responsibility of the war, and for the best of reasons, for they had built their careers upon Pacifism, Anti-Imperialism, and a variety of other high-sounding principles, which they were obliged to violate repeatedly when they were in office. It was characteristic of French politics that the unpopular war against Abd el-Krim, which took place mainly outside the French Protectorate and was therefore justifiable only from the point of view of the strictest Imperialism, should have been carried on by Anti-Imperialists of the Left. The whole business illustrated a favourite political principle of the Third Republic: faire de la politique de Droite avec des hommes de Gauche.

M. Painlevé received me with evident distrust. There was a screen beside the desk in his colossal office at the Ministry of War, and I acquired the impression that it concealed a stenographer. When I left the Ministry I was followed, and for the next three or four days—while I remained in Paris—my progress from night club to night club was duly observed by a bored detective. This was stupid; most unlike M. Painlevé; but he had (as I discovered in time) no alternative. I enjoyed a small but baleful reputation in Paris just then. Some of the newspapers, quoting my dispatches as they had appeared in Berlin or Vienna newspapers, had tried to suggest that I was a German. The *Journal des Débats* called me '*le press-agent attitré d'Abd el-Krim*.' *Le Temps* had given me a harsh word or two, and nearly every paper in Paris, taking up the challenge thus presented to the journalistic imagination, had contributed some detail to the general inaccuracy. I was an agent of the Communists, of the Germans, of God knows what. All in a small way, of course—there were no great, splashing accusations —but the general impression was that this M. Schéan (or Schauen or Schérén or however the printer's fantasy happened to spell it) was a pretty shady character. Most suspicious of all, I was in high favour with the French Communists. M. Jacques Doriot, one of the leaders of parliamentary Communism, had tried to read a dispatch of mine into the minutes of the Chamber, desisting only after the angry deputies had drowned out his voice with their protests. Such scenes of disorder are a special and endearing characteristic of the French legislature, but they do not appeal to anxious old gentlemen who, like MM. Painlevé, Briand and Caillaux, spend their lives trying to keep a government in equilibrium.

I knew nothing of all this when I went to see M. Painlevé, but you may be sure that he did. He frowned, pursed his lips, blew out his cheeks—which were already blown out a good deal more than symmetry required—and gazed anxiously towards the window. He kept a metal pencil in his hand, with which he occasionally tapped his desk or made a mark on a piece of paper. The papers all had an official look, and the marks M. Painlevé made on them were most extraordinary: cubes, crosses, circles and plain lines. I was convinced he did not know what he was doing, and that various documents of the highest importance were being irreparably defaced, but I could hardly take the pencil away from him. Another peculiarity that distracted the attention was his hair. There was an uncommon amount of it, luxuriant but suspiciously neat, and all jet black. At his age it did not seem possible.

If I could remove his pencil and pull off his hair, I thought, this conversation might become a little more natural. As it is, it is a ghastly failure; I can't find out what he is thinking at all. . . .[1]

It went on for two solid hours, that interview, and came to nothing. He asked me innumerable questions: questions of fact, questions of opinion, questions of personality. I had told him that I intended to write to Abd el-Krim, and asked if he had anything new to say—if there were any conditions under which he would consider a peace. He kept coming back to the question of frontier: what tribes belonged to the Rif, what tribes belonged to French Morocco? I knew Abd el-Krim believed (as was no more than reasonable) that such questions should be left to an actual peace negotiation, and not imposed beforehand—a contention that Painlevé either honestly distrusted, or pretended to distrust in order to avoid entering a negotiation.

The truth was that he could do nothing. Painlevé could not struggle against the inevitable course of history. The French had either to destroy Abd el-Krim or, in the long run, to give up their imperial position. But the disingenuous thing about Painlevé and all the politicians of the Left was that they pretended, in public, to be anxious for peace. Perhaps they even believed that they wanted peace. It is just possible, in view of the limitless capacity of politicians for deceiving themselves. But to my knowledge they could have had peace at any time in the winter of 1925–26 on almost any terms they liked, providing the independence of the actual Rif itself (a territory over which they had no claim) was recognized.

They did not want peace: that was the clear impression I took away from M. Painlevé. All their fine Pacifist speeches in public were devised to conciliate the opposition and disarm criticism until Abd el-Krim could be crushed forever.

With this unpleasant certainty in mind I had no further taste for the game of playing War Correspondent in Paris drawing rooms and night clubs. A few days after my interview with M.

[1]Years later I met the amiable, absent-minded M. Painlevé under other circumstances. His black hair was, as it happened, real. So were his pacific and liberal intentions. It was he who ordered the aviators in Morocco not to use bombing sights. This minor concession to humanity encouraged him to pursue the war.

Painlevé I went to Corsica for the winter. On the red rocks above the Gulf of Piana, an energetic Breton persisted in keeping a hotel in spite of the paucity of travellers and the high price of meat; I sat down there to write a novel.

The winter rains always imposed a truce on Moroccan warfare. On the other side of the Mediterranean, above the Bay of Alhucemas, Abd el-Krim was waiting for the spring. He must have known that it would be his last at Ajdir.

9

That Imperialism was murderous and hypocritical was no discovery. The Imperialists themselves recognized the character of the undertaking by the vociferation of their denials—denying, always, before they were accused. You could not be immersed for years in political journalism without getting to know the nature of the beast. But until these journeys to the Rif I had not realized its awful stupidity—the ghastly wrong-headedness with which it sacrificed the time and the lives of its best men for the enrichment of its worst. A few Frenchmen were richer for the possession of Morocco, and many were dead. Those who died in such disreputable enterprises were for the most part the young, the honest, the unsuspicious—men who had been fed on patriotic lies until they thought they were accomplishing something for their native country by murdering the inhabitants of another. Populations that had shown, in their own defence, the very qualities Europeans called heroic under other circumstances, were rewarded by economic enslavement. The Banque de Paris et des Pays-Bas and the Schneider-Creusot company could declare dividends; MM. Painlevé, Briand and Herriot could make speeches about the *œuvre civilisatrice de la France;* the big battalions were still on their side.

So, as all know, the French empire in Africa was preserved from danger, and the Spaniards returned to that strip of land out of which Abd el-Krim had driven them. When the spring arrived, the Arabs of the border had reconsidered their position—aided, no doubt, by the persuasive words and bank notes of the French. The Riffian had only a remnant of his own tribes to count upon;

he surrendered and was exiled to Reunion Island, in the Indian Ocean, where a number of other resistants to empire had preceded him. The Spanish flag was raised again over those little clumps of tin-roofed general stores and drinking saloons which indicate the presence of a superior Christian culture. And the bones of my friend Mohammed bel Hadj, after so many summers' suns, must long ago have added their pinch of dust to the dust that whirls and sifts across the Moroccan plain. The traveller in such regions, riding through it, does well to wrap his turban around his face to keep it out of eyes and throat; it will sting no less for being the dust of an honest man.

V

Desert Gardens

In the spring the Corsican maquis smelled of the seven herbs of heaven. Young trout leaped recklessly in the cold mountain streams near Evisa, the punctual birds came back, and the sea regained its sparkle of blue. This was, of all times, the time to be in Corsica, and yet the season only made me want to go away. There was a special curiosity that became irksome to me in spring: a feeling that I must hurry, that the world might perish very soon and I with it before I could find out what it was like. I raged up and down the hills, trying to think of a plan—a place to go to, a way to get there, and something to do when I got there.

A copy of a Marseilles newspaper appeared one day at Piana. When my turn came to read it I was struck by some paragraphs about Persia. That country had, it appeared, a new monarch— Reza Khan, the soldier of fortune, had deposed the Shah Ahmad and was to take his place on the Peacock Throne at the end of April. I knew nothing about Persia, but the ready-made sentences of the Marseilles newspaper suggested what I needed: a destination. In a day or two all the wavering impulses that had been looking for an object settled upon Persia, just as if that country corresponded to some need of mind or body. I knew enough to realize that no newspaper could be interested in events so far away, but there was always the possibility that my publisher or a magazine editor might take a different view. My enthusiasm mounted to the level of my ignorance; I made for Paris and New York, and before many days there I had arranged the necessary contracts and was ready to sail again.

This was more accidental than it sounds. By a coincidence unknown to me until I arrived in New York, the president of my publishing company had once been financial adviser to the Persian government and retained a lively interest in Persian affairs. The editors of *Asia* had (also by coincidence) an idea that they ought to publish something about the new Shah and his régime. Neither publishers nor editors wished to carry their interest to the point of extravagance, and my special qualification was a willingness to undertake almost any journey on tuppence. The interaction of these circumstances made it possible for me to go to Persia and stay there for a little more than two months, and it was not until I had done so that I understood the brazen effrontery of the proceeding. For a half-educated American twenty-six years old, knowing nothing about the Persian language, literature, religion, history, art, economy or social structure, to write a whole book about any aspect of that complex civilization after two months' acquaintance with it was an undertaking rash enough to bring the blush of shame to the cheek of impudence.

The journey to Persia turned into a kind of game, a race to get there before Reza Shah formally installed his unroyal posterior on the Peacock Throne. The event was set for April 25th, and I had precisely twenty-one days in which to travel from New York to Tehran. Nowadays it would be easy; it was possible even then, but the cards were not running my way. I encountered the first obstacle in Paris when I asked for a visa to cross Syria. The French were still engaged in repressing the Syrian national rebellion, and they retained the impressions they had formed of me during the Rif campaigns. My visa was not refused outright, but delays and difficulties multiplied. In short, the answer was no; but it could not have been more politely disguised.

I went on to Marseilles and Alexandria. The boat, a fragile relic called the *Chili*, pursued its precarious way through a Mediterranean storm, carrying numerous French officers who were going to fight the Druse. These amiable fellow passengers did not seem to know exactly who the Druse were, or why there was a war with them, except that they had 'rebelled.' Against what? 'La France, quoi!' The simplicity of the military character was one constant in the midst of variables.

I had letters to Ahmed Bey Hassanein in Cairo. He was the King's chamberlain, a desert explorer of great distinction: a dignified figure, a cultivated mind. He was kind to me, took me to Gezireh and to the Mehemet Ali Club, and set his mind to my problem. I had to get to Baghdad, and Syria was much in the way. A word from him made it possible for me to take a British military aëroplane across the intervening deserts, but for a sum of money (fixed by Air Force rules) that I could not pay. I spent a week in Cairo, corroded with impatience, filling in the time by visits to museums, to the Pyramids, to the Arab citadel. At the end of that time Hassanein Bey made the suggestion that swept the difficulties away.

'You might,' he pointed out in his still, calm voice, which seemed to me the result of desert plus Oxford, 'you might simply send your passport to the French consulate by a dragoman from your hotel. He might get you a transit visa for Syria. The ordinary way sometimes works when no other will.'

He was right. The visa over which higher dignitaries had made such a fuss was granted by an ordinary French vice-consul in five minutes without question.

I took the Jerusalem express that night, reached Haifa in the morning, and continued to Beirut in one of the cars of the energetic Nairn brothers. These gentlemen, New Zealanders who had come to Europe to fight and remained to make money, operated regular caravans of motorcars across the Syrian and Mesopotamian deserts to Baghdad. Sometimes they were attacked by Bedawin; only a week before they had had one of their recurring disasters, and in the battle the wife of the French consul at Baghdad had been killed. They continued rather grimly, in the face of extraordinary difficulties, trusting to their own skill and courage and the protection of the Royal Air Force.

We made the journey in ordinary Cadillac touring cars. There were two of them, one with passengers and one that also took luggage and food. The passengers were assorted: a young Baghdadi Arab returning from school in Paris, a British colonel in the Indian Army, the sister of a British diplomat, on her way from Abyssinia to Baghdad; a shy, faint-voiced American woman whom the rest of us took to be a missionary; and an elderly English pair on their way to visit the grave of their son, killed in Mesopotamia during the war. There were few stops, all brief—

lunch, dinner, and an hour for sleep in the darkest part of the night, just before daylight. Day and night we kept on going at a forced speed, never falling below fifty miles an hour, and sometimes, on very level ground well known to the driver, reaching seventy-five. We avoided Damascus and the zone of the rebellion altogether; we saw no human beings from Palmyra to the first post of the Royal Air Force near the Euphrates. How our drivers kept to their road in this void was a puzzle, but they did. I remember the yellow-pink ruin of Palmyra in the yellow sun, the whirling dust devils that chased each other across the flat plain, and the derisive cackle of a hyena that greeted us when we stopped early the next morning for an hour's sleep on the ground. At Ramadi the brown, naked airmen gave us beer, and when we reached the Euphrates and stopped for food the diplomat's sister taught me the trick of cooling it in the river. We reached Baghdad that night, some thirty-six hours after the start of the trip. And in Baghdad, grimy, sleepless and red-eyed from the dust of the desert, I had the pleasure of hearing that I had lost my race: Reza Shah was to be crowned King of Kings the next day at Tehran.

There was no hurry, therefore, about going on from Baghdad. Even if there had been, I could not have gone until the invaluable Nairn brothers had a car to send over the passes of Kurdistan. I spent the time as tourists do, gaping about the town, staring at the Tigris and wondering what had become of splendid mediæval Baghdad. The place was now as dismal a collection of mud huts as you would see anywhere in the east, dignified—if at all—only by being near the great, bland, treacherous river.

Perceiving me to be ignorant of the ways of empire, my friend the Indian army colonel took me in hand. I was not to talk to Wogs, he told me, and particularly not to sit at table with them in public, as I valued the future of my race. I asked what Wogs were, and was told that they were the inhabitants of countries enjoying the protection of the British.

'The word was first used in India,' my colonel said, pleased with the rôle of educator, 'but since the war it's spread to Mespot and Palestine. I saw you having a drink with that young Wog that crossed the desert with us. It's all right, of course—nothing downright wrong about it; but it just isn't done. Leave them alone.'

I pointed out to my friend that I was not British and therefore did not feel obliged to maintain a pose of superiority to the inhabitants of other countries.

'That doesn't make any difference,' said my colonel. 'These people don't know what you are. You should not be seen having a drink on the terrace of the Carlton Hotel, sitting down at a table with a Wog. It lets us all down. So long as our race is in a position to govern theirs, every one of us must be superior to every one of them.'

'In Morocco and Syria,' I pointed out, 'the French don't have any such idea. You've seen Frenchmen and Arabs together, haven't you? And French women dancing with Arabs in the cafés?'

'Exactly,' said the Colonel. 'And that is why the French are a failure at empire. They don't understand it. They are fine soldiers, and they may be fine administrators as well, although I doubt it. But they don't know the first thing about maintaining the prestige of their race. It makes my blood boil to see the French tarts in Damascus and Beirut dancing with Arabs. Why, do you know, there's not a British tart allowed anywhere in our Empire? If one blows in at Bombay or Calcutta she's shipped home again before she knows where she is.'

The Colonel was a cheery soul, remarkably intelligent for a soldier, and possessed of a rare capacity for candid, unshrinking cynicism. He had no high-minded pretences. Like other soldiers, he left that kind of eyewash to the politicians at home. He said frankly that he intended to serve the Empire as long as it survived, and when it was destroyed, as he expected it to be, he would take service under one of the Indian princes for the rest of his life and get rich. The Indian princes would be engaged in unending wars, he seemed to think, as soon as the British withdrew, and a good *condottiero* would be much in demand.

To enlarge my acquaintance with the benefits of Imperialism the Colonel took me to the Club, where small frightened flowers from England were wet-nursed through their uncertain infancy in a dry, inhospitable soil. Most of them died soon after they were entrusted to the ground, but the Club was indomitable and kept on trying. Here there were dances, shade, drinks, and even a little plot of carefully nourished grass—perhaps the only grass in the whole kingdom of Iraq. He took me to the races, where Arab horses performed for the benefit of the pari-mutuel, and I lost a few of my few dollars. He took me to the army mess, a small one, kept up by cheerful souls of his own kind. When the Colonel entrained for Basra to rejoin his regiment I am sure he believed he had done his best to convert me to his gospel of empire. He would have regarded it as irrelevant that the only Arabs we saw on these pleasant excursions were in the rôle of servants.

When my instruction in these matters had been attended to I set out with a Cockney chauffeur for Kurdistan. The car (one of the Nairns') was carrying goods to Persia; I was the only passenger. We entered Persia at Khozrovi and slept that night at Kermanshah. The next morning for breakfast we had tea and caviar, to my delight, but the Cockney driver satisfied himself with bread alone.

'Why don't you eat caviar?' I asked. 'It's good stuff, even this black kind.'

'I can't touch caviar,' he said mournfully. 'I was at the siege of Baku.'

It took questioning to find out what this meant. He had served under Dunsterville, fighting Turks and Russians (they scarcely knew who the enemy was, he said) in the mad expedition across Persia. He was in the force besieged by the Bolsheviks at Baku, and when the food supply ran out there was nothing to eat but caviar, morning, noon and night. The Tommies had never been fond of caviar, it seems ('foreign stuff—nasty'), and they had to eat so much of it during the siege that they all grew to regard it with a queasy loathing. This particular Tommy had remained in Persia after the peace and was now married to a native Christian girl, but he had never been able to overcome his feeling of disgust at the sight of caviar.

Kermanshah, Hamadan, Kazvin, crowded oases in the baking plateau, were cities with mosques and bazaars, but little else to reward an uninformed curiosity. One of the mosques at Hamadan, I remember, had a dome shining brilliantly, if patchily, in the sun. I thought it might be covered with something strange and precious, and inquired.

'A. P. O. C. tins,' I was told.

The Anglo-Persian Oil Company's square tins of petrol were to become most familiar to me in Persia. Emptied of their original cargoes, they served every purpose a receptacle can be adapted to, and when their usefulness grew less with age they were battered out into sheets of tin for ornament. The letters A. P. O. C., stamped on each square of tin, were visible all over the dome of that Hamadan mosque as we came nearer to it. It was a suggestive circumstance.

At four o'clock on the morning of May 4th—our fifth day out from Baghdad—we entered Tehran. The Tommy-chauffeur took me to a caravanserai with the ambitious name of Hôtel de Paris, where, after a scandalous amount of pounding and shouting, we succeeded in arousing somebody. That afternoon, rested, bathed and shaved, I felt equal to presenting my letters of introduction to the American Administrator-General of the Finances of Persia.

Dr A. C. Millspaugh, a modest and tactful man, once an economic adviser in the State Department, had exercised the powers of Financial Administrator in Tehran for four years. He was not an 'adviser': his contract had given him complete control over the collection and expenditure of the Persian state revenues, and little could be done in the country without his approval. He had centralized the financial control and the whole civil service in his own office, exerting himself to balance the budget, defeat tax frauds, and get rid of the more systematic embezzlers in the government service. He had made many enemies, as I was to learn, and the combination of their efforts was bound, in time, to bring his career in Persia to an end. He lasted another year after my visit; of all his accomplishments, that of remaining five whole years in Persia was probably the most remarkable.

Millspaugh's mild manners, his slow, almost pedantic speech, his trick of glancing down over his eyeglasses, suggested colleges and libraries. Actually he was a kind of dictator, and his gentle, deprecating style of talk was no clue to his character. He was capable of extreme stubbornness, sometimes of extreme severity, and his tenacious control of every branch of government expenditure made him one of the two central powers of the state—the other, of course, being the Shah. To these the devout Persians added still another, making a trinity addressed in one petition published in Tehran as: 'O God! O Shah! O Dr Millspaugh!'

The potentate from Baltimore received me agreeably; he was to show me much kindness during my stay in Persia. It was his belief that I could not be comfortable at an inn, and his first good deed was to arrange for me to stay at Tom Pearson's house. I had some compunctions about being wished off on a total stranger, but Dr Millspaugh quietly ignored them. Pearson was the head of the Civil Service section of the Financial Administration and lived in a comfortable 'garden' (i.e., house) on the western edge of Tehran. On that first day, therefore, I was shifted from the inn to a pleasant Persian establishment, where I remained for a month.

That month took unexpected forms. I had come to Persia with one small bag and a typewriter as my only luggage. In the bag were not many clothes. My plans had been vague, but they had all tended towards a kind of life and work in which a tweed suit and an odd pair of grey flannels would be enough to see me through. By sheer accident the bag also contained a dinner jacket and a couple of stiff shirts, stuck in for possible use in Paris or Cairo. No set of circumstances that could demand more than this had seemed likely to me in New York. I was to wander about, look at things, talk to people, ask questions, perhaps learn a little Persian, find out what I could, and go away again—the ordinary pursuits of a tramp journalist. This was a notion that showed deplorable ignorance of the country I had set out to visit.

Life in Tehran was as elaborate as a requiem high mass. Neither the Persians nor the foreigners believed in relaxing any of the minute details by which rank, dignity, and the relations between people of importance are said to be maintained. This was no doubt always so—as it is in other Eastern capitals—but it was particularly the case at the time of my visit, when the Shah's coronation had instigated a series of pompous ceremonies to celebrate the event. Pearson, my amiable and intelligent host, pointed out on the first day that it would be nonsense to visit Tehran at this time without seeing what went on; and what went on involved an amount of calling, card dropping, bowing, scraping and partying unique in my experience. The life was rather like that of a Victorian society novel—something between Disraeli and Mrs Humphry Ward—with mixed international characters against a Persian background. A string of camels against the horizon, a flight of coloured birds into the sky, or the dark noises of the narrow bazaars, might suggest a different Persia: the immense life of the land and the people. But how was I to go, in such a limited time, beyond the surface at hand? To know anything about the Persian people would have taken years, a knowledge of the language, a great deal of hard work. I still hoped that the subjects of immediate interest to me—the career of the new Shah, his régime and that of the American financial administrators— might be comprehensible upon a superficial acquaintance.

And, too, the surface was agreeable. As Tom Pearson's guest I was bidden to all the festivities of the time, enjoying the spectacle no less because my lamentable wardrobe made a blot upon it. Pearson took me to a review of the Amnieh on the second day, where we saw the Shah and the Crown Prince; Dr Millspaugh took me to call on the Prime Minister, Zoka el-Molk (Forughi); in the afternoon we went to a garden party at the Belgian Legation, where we met the corps diplomatique and the cabinet ministers; that night we dined at the Millspaughs' to meet Sir John Cadman, the active head of the Anglo-Persian Oil Company. Other days were not unlike this: there were huge evening receptions, with music, dancing, cards and fireworks; there were quieter expeditions to the palaces and gardens of the Persian princes; there were diplomatic dinners. It was not a programme that provided knowledge of the ordinary existence of ordinary Persians. For this I had to depend on books and hearsay, as foreigners usually do, and on such casual observations as an uninformed visitor might be expected to make in the streets and bazaars.

But even the life of the Persian aristocrats, Europeanized though they were, was not without some of the peculiar qualities of national character. Splendour, formality and an inherited regard for careful arrangement were combined, in these great houses, with an almost patriarchal attitude towards family connections and servants. Wealth and taste had declined. The houses depended for their best effects upon arrangement of space, and the gardens upon arrangement of trees and water. The great works of Persian art were, for the most part, no longer in Persia, and the treasures that remained were guarded in mosques to which no infidel was admitted. Thus it was not until some years later, when Persian works in carpet and miniature were gathered together for the great show at the Royal Academy in London, that I had a really comprehensive view of the splendours of the Persian past in these matters. Most of the princes and grandees were fond of European objects, which they mixed with work of their own artists in their Tehran houses. Their carpets were modern, their furniture from France or England, and their manners—except in one particular—were those of any formal superior caste. The one particular was their rigid maintenance of the old rules for seclusion of women. The women were black shadows in the streets, muffled in the silk *chadar;* and in the palaces and gardens they were never seen at all. Some of them had been educated in Europe and delighted in receiving the visits of European and American women friends. It was impossible to see one of the great establishments without wondering how many women of all ages dwelt—like the *Désenchantées* of Loti—in eternal seclusion there. They were mentioned seldom, and the sudden reference to 'my mother' or 'my sister' in this world where women were invisible struck oddly on a foreign ear. I never heard anybody say 'my wife,' and supposed that the custom of the country did not encourage it.

The festivities that followed the coronation of Reza Shah thus differed in one important respect from similar festivities anywhere else: the men outnumbered the women twenty or thirty to one. The only women who appeared were the Americans and Europeans, wives and daughters of the diplomatic body, the Financial Administration, the Anglo-Persian Oil Company. In the midst of black throngs of frock-coated Persian dignitaries they gave a sprinkling of lighter colour, a tinge of Europe. Even more brilliant colour (the colour of Asia, this time) was added by two of the potentates who awaited Reza's pleasure in Tehran—the Emir of Bokhara with his suite, bright as rainbows; and the melancholy Sheikh of Mohammerah with his attendant Arabs, silent and thick-robed against the Persian walls that kept them prisoners. On rare occasions another sort of variety was added to the scene by the correct, silent, impassive Bolsheviks, who put on bourgeois clothes and sallied forth from their immense legation only when it was diplomatically necessary to do so.

One of these fiestas was much like another. The one I remember best was that given at the Club Iran by the Shokert el-Molk. The garden walls and walks, the staircases and walls of the palace, were hung and strewn with rugs; the whole garden was illuminated; the band of the Imperial Guard played; there were dancing, card-playing, food and drink in lavish quantities, a general air of extravagant celebration. The Shokert el-Molk was a feudal prince from southern Persia, very rich, who took this method of demonstrating his loyalty to the new Shah. The fireworks that always started off such evening parties were particularly magnificent on this occasion. After displays of various sorts, fountains and starry rockets that dazzled the whole city, a complicated framework of fire began to blaze across the sky. In French and in Persian its flaming legend proclaimed: Long Live His Imperial Majesty Reza Shah Pahlavi! His Imperial Majesty was not at the party, but even from his balcony at the Rose Garden (Gulistan) he could have had no difficulty seeing the pious wish.

The Imperial band, a novelty in Persia, played whatever music happened to be available. I went to the Shokert el-Molk's party with Harold Nicolson, the first secretary of the British Legation. As we came into the illuminated gardens we heard the brassy strains of something that sounded like the Hallelujah Chorus from *The Messiah*. Nicolson found it hard to make his entrance with the gravity becoming to a British diplomatist, for after the first bars the music turned incontinently into the celebrated American work, 'Yes, We Have No Bananas.'

It had been a pleasant surprise to find Harold Nicolson in Tehran. He had been at Lausanne, and, as I already knew, his witty and irreverent spirit was capable of adding some kind of spice to any scene. His guest at the Legation was Raymond Mortimer: clever, dark, inquisitive, interested in everything. That Legation was also graced by an absent-minded second secretary, Gladwyn Jebb, whose capacity for forgetting things was a delight to behold. The next time I saw him, in London, he had just left his car for a week in St. James's Square without knowing what had become of it. Nicolson and Jebb, with a military attaché and one or two other British officials, had the assistance of a large number of Persians in their labours, and the huge shaded garden where they lived and worked was like a city within the city. I came to know that garden well, and had a number of illuminating conversations with its presiding genius, Sir Percy Loraine. The British Legation was not so much a legation as a residency, and the British Minister was more like a viceroy than a diplomatist. These differences, supported by a judicious display of power and majesty, were supposed to impress the populace (and others) with the might of Persia's friend.

Persia's other friend—and between the two of them it was sheer luck that Persia still existed—was Russia. Tsarist Russia had claimed a sphere of influence in northern Persia, England in the south. The Bolsheviks, carrying out the Asiatic policy of Lenin after 1921, had abandoned all the Tsarist claims and based their subsequent attitude upon a profession of friendship for Persia's 'national aspirations.' The exact degree of friendliness depended a good deal upon the changes of Persian politics; for all parties and leaders in Persia had to choose between one or the other of the country's patrons, the British or the Russians. War and revolution had changed the forms of this necessity, but it remained the central dilemma in Persian affairs, just as it had been before 1914. As an almost invariable rule, England's friends were Russia's enemies.

I went to see the Bolsheviks in their sumptuous legation, the largest in Tehran. Yurenev, the Ambassador,[1] gave me tea and a lecture. The tea was good, and the lecture was one of the most sensible that came my way. Yurenev, a small, careful, slightly pedantic but good-humoured man, was the first Bolshevik of any consequence I had ever met. His trick of disregarding detail to get at the essentials of a subject impressed me at the time; I was afterwards to learn that it was a necessary intellectual qualification of any good Bolshevik. His question, upon a given situation or

[1]Afterwards Soviet Ambassador to Japan.

process in Persia, was not 'How does it work?' but 'On what is it based?' Once this had been cleared up he was willing to discuss temporary details as long as anybody liked, but always in relation to the basic fact.

With little trouble some of the members of that large Legation could have taught me a lot. They did not do so; I was a bourgeois, probably an enemy, living too close to the American financial administrators and the British to be trusted; and besides, they had other fish to fry. It was no part of their duty in Persia to take care of the instruction of stray Americans who happened to need it.

In June I went to the south. Raymond Mortimer was also bound for there, and we made the trip together. Nicolson gave us his car, chauffeur and a servant; the British Consul was our host in Isfahan; Major Hall took us in at Shiraz. This method of travelling *à l' œil* was pleasant for my flattened pocketbook, but at first it seemed to me rather hard on the other people. I was told, however, that it was the system all foreigners used in Persia, where inns were bad and hosts willing. Bristow, the British Consul in Isfahan, was particularly experienced in the rôle. It seemed that for the past twenty years no English people, and few Americans, had passed through Isfahan without resting for days or weeks in his cool, spacious garden. Bristow's hospitable soul converted his garden into an oasis within an oasis, doubly grateful after long days of dust, heat and mirage in the desert.

The journey to the south revealed the secret of the Persian cult for gardens. In Persia nobody spoke of his house, but always of his garden; the house was an adjunct, not worth mentioning; and the foreigners in Persia had taken over the expression into their own languages, so that the word 'house' almost disappeared from conversation. 'You can rent a nice garden for such-and-such a sum a year,' they would say; and only a rank newcomer would inquire if the garden included a house. The two material objects that seemed to signify most to Persians and foreigners alike were gardens and rugs. This preoccupation had seemed strange to me for the first few weeks, since neither the rugs nor the gardens were very beautiful. It was easy enough to explain the emphasis on carpets. Here tradition, history, the whole psychological persuasion of the Persian idea, worked to magnify the importance of the things. But gardens? You could not spend many hours a day buying and selling gardens, or even talking about buying and selling them. They did not constitute a special science, in Persia, at least, for they were almost all alike; you could not get credit for intelligence by pointing out the differences between them. The only thing you could do to a garden, unless you were a gardener, was to look at it. And this pursuit was robbed of its keener pleasures by the fact that almost all the gardens were the same, few were well kept, few seemed genuinely beautiful as an Italian or French or English garden is beautiful. Many of the great Persian gardens were entirely without flowers, for instance; and what, the Westerner would ask, is a garden without flowers? In fact, Mrs Nicolson, herself a gardener of ability, settled the whole question by saying that Persian gardens were not gardens at all.

The journey over the desert taught me what they were and how they had come to take such an enormous place in Persian literature and life. They were oases. The idea of the oasis must have dominated the minds of Persians for centuries. Every city was an oasis in the desert; every house (i.e., garden) became an oasis in the city. The first characteristics of an oasis were water and shade. Consequently the Persian gardens were built originally for water and shade, arranged to give rest, coolness, tranquillity. And it was marvellous how perfectly they fulfilled their intention—how beautiful they became once they were understood. The pattern upon which all the larger Persian gardens were built was the same: a stream of water running over successive terraces, between trees, to a pool at the lowest terrace of all. There might be flowers, or there might not, but in no case did the flowers become an end in themselves, as they did in European gardens. The Persian garden took its peculiar form by natural process: it was one instrument (to Persians a precious one) in man's battle with the earth. My Persian friends in Tehran had never been able to explain to me why the peculiar pattern of their gardens seemed to them more beautiful than the botanical displays of the Europeans. The inheritors of a style cannot easily explain why it seems right to them, for its origins have been forgotten with those obscure combats between nature and necessity that once governed the experiments of mankind. It is easiest for a foreigner to understand, not by intellectual effort in front of the *fait accompli*—which is asking a good deal of the imagination—but by reproducing, at least in part, the experience that first made one design above all others the inevitable, the right one.

From Tehran to Isfahan, and from Isfahan to Shiraz, the dusty desert edged with hills becomes, nowadays, little more than an exotic picture through which the traveller can pass almost as swiftly as one of its own small, bright-coloured birds. It took two days for my journey from Tehran to Isfahan, and three from Isfahan to Shiraz. They were relatively pleasant days, too, for the heat and dust were easily enough withstood, and the mirage, instead of acting as a form of torture, became a delight—far-off fountains and palaces constantly dissolving, re-forming, deepening and fading from moment to moment in a shifting, luminous variety unknown to the real world. But the Persians of old, those who invented all the restricted, formal patterns that enclosed the best of their life and art for succeeding generations, were obliged to make such journeys under far different conditions. In camel caravan it took them eight or nine days to get from Tehran to Isfahan, more from Isfahan to Shiraz. They were baked by day and frozen by night, struggling against dust, thirst, fatigue and the dangers of the desert, wild beasts and wild men. They were not Arabs, not desert people, and must have gone to sleep every night thinking of the rest that would come at the end of the journey. What, then, must have been the exaltation of such people when, after ten days or two weeks in the desert, they came to the hills that surrounded Shiraz and, at the great cleft called Allah-Akbar Pass, looked down upon the city lying like a deep green carpet in the plain beneath, soft and shaded and waiting for them? Even nowadays it is customary for devout Moslems to pause at this place and pray. Their forefathers regarded every oasis as an evidence of the providence of their creator, to be treasured more jealously than anything else in their system of life.

From this profound feeling must have sprung the whole design of the Persian existence—the small, compact, enclosed forms taken by Persian life, literature and art, between high walls in the shade. The Persian inherited a passion for privacy and tranquillity. To understand this was to understand some, at least, of the symbols that ancient passion had left. Progressing—as I did, though not at once—from the garden to the general shape and mood of Persian art, it could be seen that the most beautiful works of the fifteenth and sixteenth centuries, such as the great rug in the Poldi-Pezzoli Museum in Milan, were expressions in finer form, by finer artists, of the racial genius that had seen Paradise as a small, exact garden with running water and singing birds, and restful, limited carpets spread under the private trees.

The ruins of Persepolis, in the midst of the desert between Shiraz and Sivand, had nothing in common with anything Persia had evolved since. You turned off the main desert road, and, in half an hour of bumping along a smaller trail, came to a tremendous, assertive mass of ancient grey stone. This was the palace of Darius the Great, in whose day the desert was sedulously irrigated and the city was not an oasis at all, but the concentration of a prince's power and wealth. These massive columns and steps, bolder and grander than any ruin I had ever seen, were monuments to the egotism of a rich, cruel and successful empire. The mood that produced such pomp in architecture was not unlike the moods of triumphant empire in Egypt and Rome, perhaps in modern America; it had no relation to the refuge-seeking, peace-finding mood that expressed itself in the styles of Persia. Darius must have felt himself equal to the gods when he complacently surveyed the majestic gateway to his palace platform, the great Propylæa. Europeans who had visited the neglected ruins of his splendour carved their names on the stone of the Propylæa: Malcolm and his officers (the first of the British) in 1800, George Curzon and others in later years. Legends in Pahlavi, Arabic and modern Persian recorded the visits of successive centuries to the remains of Darius in the desert; and these idle carvings, the grandeur and desolation of the ruins, the emptiness of the surrounding plain, must combine to force a shudder of mortality upon the most insensitive traveller. 'My name is Ozymandias, King of Kings.'

I returned to Tehran in July; it was half deserted. The Shah, the Court, the corps diplomatique, most of the Americans, and in a general way all Persians who could afford it, had gone to the hills for the summer. I spent a good deal of time in fruitless visits to those palaces, trying to arrange my long-postponed audience with the Shah. The little Crown Prince was very ill at Gulistan (the Rose Garden) in the town, and every morning at seven o'clock the Shah's Rolls-Royce went tearing down the hill to visit him. Teymortash, the suave and clever Minister of the Court, then high in favour with His Majesty—since disgraced and dead—gave me a good deal of his time, but the Shah himself was a wary bird. If I had waited until the Crown Prince's illness was over perhaps I might have had my conversation in complete formality through interpreters, but the possible results scarcely seemed worth so much time and money. I already knew much about Reza Shah and his improbable career, the rise of an illiterate soldier from Mazanderan to the dictatorship and finally to the throne; you could not be in Persia a week without hearing an immense amount about him. Direct conversation might have added something to these impressions, but I was already beginning to think that all I knew—the very subjects that constituted my knowledge of Persia: the American Administration, the Shah's career, the details of the régime—would be pitifully superficial and misleading in print. To know even one thing about Persia thoroughly it was necessary to know a great many other things, and Reza Shah would always be incomprehensible so long as I did not know the people and their languages, their ways of thought and familiar manners. Under the circumstances the only sensible thing was to go away quick, while I had enough fresh, detailed and various information to take the place of a more solid understanding, and could thus fulfil, to some extent, the contracts that had sent me there. The Bolsheviks made no difficulty about my visa, but gave it at once; and before dawn one morning in July I climbed into an aëroplane bound for Russia.

Years later, in London, I went to Burlington House to see the unique collection of Persian works assembled there from all over the world. Until then, if I had been brusquely asked what good it had done me to make the expensive, time-consuming journey to such a far country, I should have been puzzled what to answer. True, I had acquired some friends among the foreigners in Tehran; I had amassed a lot of immediate political information, forgotten a few months after I left the place; and I remembered a number of trivial things that would probably always stick in my head. There was a little Anglo-Indian lady, the wife of a doctor, who did not like Persia. Pressed for reasons, she had said: 'For one thing, they don't have punkahs here—at least, not pukka punkahs.' . . . There was the man who gave me a horse; I had rashly admired it, and he said, '*Pishkash*' (It is yours), in best Persian style, until I understood enough to refuse it. . . . Then there was the small *anderun* garden where Josephine Hall had lived in Tehran. It was unlike any other: full of lilacs, sweet, unkempt, shaded, inhabited day and night by nightingales. . . . Oddities of this kind would always stick in the memory from any scene, any experience, but they seemed to have little to do with Persia. On the whole, in answer to the hypothetical question, I should have been inclined to say that the long business of going to Tehran and Isfahan had been so much waste motion; that aside from the political and social details I had collected, written about and forgotten, I had learned nothing there; that Persia itself *sub specie æternitatis*, the lasting special spirit of the place, was still totally unknown to me.

The Persian Exhibition at Burlington House corrected the worst inaccuracies of such a view of experience. It might still be true that I knew nothing of Persia, but it was not true that the visit to that country had been waste motion.

And, of course, it had to be so. No experience vanishes without leaving some trace, somewhere, of the power it once exercised upon its particular present moment. Every present moment is, in this sense, extended through subsequent time for the duration of our tenure, overlaid by successive experience or clouded by the vagaries of memory, but subsisting always, like its parallel accretions or modifications in nerves, glands, arteries, to form in our final sum of time (i.e., a life) that possession peculiar to each of us, a view of the world. We can't, in short, *really* forget anything, and 'waste motion' does not exist for human beings. The soft brightness of the great Persian works shown at Burlington House brought back confused recollections with the vividness of a kind of sense film, mixing the smell of lilacs with the sting of desert dust, the sound of running water with the shape of cypress trees above a tomb. Such agitations in the rubbish of memory can be stirred up by an ordinary postal card. But in the Persian treasures at Burlington House, with their sudden, powerful appeal to sleeping memory, there was a particular truth for me, of almost unlimited application—a truth learned by other people in other ways, learned by me (or so I thought) by effort alone, and never, until that moment, related to the journey of five years before.

It seemed to me that I understood these works of Persian art. I did not *know* them, as an expert knows such things, with an instant recognition of the details of excellence, a comprehension that went from type to individual and back again. In fact I knew nothing about them. But their form and colour, I believed, spoke clearly to me. I knew why the artists of the great centuries on the plateau of Iran worked in this way and no other: I understood their dialect. It was the gentle dialect of the desert garden, the speech of privacy and repose. The soft, glowing splendour of the golden carpet from the mosque at Qum, the lovely light that came out of the great rose carpet from Rome, must have been put there by artists whose essential nature did not differ from that of (say) Pollaiuolo or Poussin or Renoir or Sir Christopher Wren. The impulse to create in beautiful form would have been in all cases the same, but the specific shape in each was determined by a set of circumstances the artist could not control, against which, as often as not, he spent his life protesting. The conditions of daily life produced the conditions of the art that undertook (at least in the great centuries) to embellish or enhance it. The life of the oasis, when it was lived by sensitive, sedentary, indolent and passionate people of the Irani race, compelled its art works to assume the mood of refuge, of rest, under forms predetermined by the oasis itself, the actual instrument of man's struggle with surrounding nature—so that the garden determined both the architecture and the carpet, and the works produced by artists under such conditions of life coalesced, when they were assembled together, to give the impression of a style.

If this was true—and it seemed to me incontestable—then the problems of style and form in general in the whole range of creation had to take a secondary place, like the elaborate considerations of scholarship, which could never rise to greater dignity than that of the footnote. These works were something more than the toys of rich men, the objects of a dilettante's fascination, or the themes chosen by bourgeois intellectuals to display the cultivated subtleties of their minds. These were actual instruments in the long battle of mankind to make life more tolerable, and were in their consequent shapes and styles determined by race, climate, the forms of society, the economic shape and style of the world in which the artists lived.

Perhaps I already knew all this, but the spectacle of a thousand great works of Persian art assembled together cleared the conviction I already possessed, related it directly to the half-forgotten journey of five years before, and strengthened the light by revealing its source.

So, if I had now to answer the hypothetical question about what good the Persian journey had been to me, I might reasonably say that although I have forgotten the details that once seemed important, the experience did establish an apprehension of the right relation between any given society, understood as a race of people living under characteristic systems of climate, manners and economy, and its works of art. The journey had made possible in time, after a good many second thoughts, and in spite of powerful dilettante influences, a view of the transaction by which such wonders as the Dome of St. Peter's, the Sposalizio of Raphael and the Golden Carpet of Qum, had been deposited by the artists' minds and hands upon the visible course of history. The whole weight of what Cézanne called *l'art des musées* came to life with a bound when it was seen, not as an accumulation of certain beautiful tricks that some men had been able to do better than others, but as an organic part of the life of man, a supremely useful instrument in the adaptation of nature and control of society for his greater happiness.

VI

Revolution

BAKU SURVEYED the Caspian Sea with an air of brash, complacent wealth. There was so much oil that it stood ankle-deep in the fields, and the whole landscape outside the city looked like a marsh across which an army of Don Quixote's giants waded impassively as far as the eye could reach. The aëroplane (a Junker, with two German pilots) came down efficiently at the appointed place, where a customs inspector, a political inspector, and a representative of Junkers were waiting for it. I had no more luggage on leaving Persia than on arriving, and the customs inspector wasted little time on me. The political officer, a solemn young man, was more careful. When he found a pad of that excellent toilet paper upon which the health and greatness of the British Empire depend, he examined it sheet by sheet, holding the first few sheets to the light to see if they had been written on. Even this admirably conscientious examination did not take long, and within ten minutes of landing I was released to the immensities of Russia.

Those immensities were less striking to me than they are said to be to European travellers. Baku, in spite of its great Mosque and its visible mixture of Oriental peoples, seemed violently Western and almost familiar after the sleepy dignity of Persia. The only thing difficult to understand was the direction taken by the wealth you could smell in the air. In the American West there were just such bustling oily encampments as this, but for a different purpose: to enrich everybody who could get rich, particularly the shrewd or lucky entrepreneur upon whose land the gush of wealth had chanced to come. It took an effort to realize how different was the canalization of wealth here, where busy men supposedly bestirred themselves all day long for the benefit of the Soviet state. The analogy with America—in spite of such differences of purpose—grew stronger after the train moved out of Baku. On the next morning we were running through plains that might have been those of Nebraska or Kansas. The train was European, with wagon-lit and wagon-restaurant, but the landscape seemed to me American. Hot, flat fields of wheat, vast spaces, few people, and a general barbaric sharpness of sun and air, cast my mind back to one of my earliest journeys, at the age of five or six, from Illinois to Colorado. Only when we came into Great Russia, in the neighbourhood of Moscow itself, did the country become definitely European, with villages and copses that might have been almost anywhere in northern France or southern England.

Moscow excited me, at first view, more than any city I had seen. Its original savage splendour, slightly down-at-heel, set off by a variety of contrasting styles of architecture, was enhanced by the vitality of its inhabitants. Perhaps that vitality was more noticeable by contrast with the passive indolence I had seen in Persia, but in any case it could not have failed to impress a newcomer. The city had retained a few of its Muscovite glories—the Kremlin, the Cathedral of St. Basil, the Kitai Gorod—and a short distance away, at the convent of the Trinity (Troitzkaya Lavra) were the carefully preserved treasures of Russian ecclesiastical art and architecture, but for the most part it was a city of the nineteenth and twentieth centuries, no older than (say) Brooklyn. Much of its nineteenth-century architecture was ugly. It abounded in museums of every description, for the Bolsheviks had an exalted idea of the value of historical study; and in the museums of painting, particularly in the great collection called the State Museum of Modern Western Art, it afforded delights almost wholly new to me.

My acquaintance with painting, by the time I got to Moscow, was an oddity of the oddest sort: I knew a good deal about Venetian art, was aware of almost every picture in Venice, and had seen no others at all, save on hasty visits to the Vatican and the Louvre. The magnificent collections of modern painting in Moscow therefore made their impression upon a mind unprepared for them. Renoir, Cézanne, Van Gogh, Gauguin, Signac, Seurat, Bonnard,

Vuillard, Matisse, Picasso—all were new to me. It is extraordinary that anybody could have lived in Europe during the closing years of such an era of painting without having taken the trouble to notice it. I knew the names of these artists, of course (what names does not a journalist know?), and had even occasionally read a book in which they figured, but as for the works in which they cast their brilliant and revolutionary view of the world, I had missed them all. The fine collections in Chicago and New York, the Camondo at the Louvre, the current shows at galleries—I had seen none of them.

The misfortune was more than compensated for in Russia. Indeed, the Shchukin and Morosov collections in Moscow, with some additions from other sources, formed, in their united impression as a 'museum of modern Western art,' the most dramatic introduction the world at large could offer to the vigorous genius of late nineteenth- and twentieth-century painting. Anybody must be accounted lucky who makes his first acquaintance with the sombre green slope of the Mont Ste Victoire, or the amiable figure of Madame Cézanne, from the examples of these subjects in Moscow. Jungle pictures by the Douanier Rousseau, lush and dank with imagination; the cool green lawns of Pierre Bonnard, the golden Café de Nuit of Van Gogh; Matisse's lovely Moroccan pictures and his celebrated *ronde des danseurs* on the staircase of the Shchukin house; and a huge collection of pictures of all periods and styles by the restless Picasso, combined with scores, even hundreds, of pictures only a little less brilliant, to give a sudden, wonderful view of the genius of modern art in all its range. It was the discovery of a new world.

Moscow itself fascinated me from the beginning by its bizarre and violent contrasts. I had not then read Trotzky, and had never heard of the 'law of combined development,' according to which extremely backward countries are said to be able to skip whole centuries of economic development, their backwardness producing a higher degree of revolutionary readiness than can be found in more advanced countries. But although the phrase was unknown to me, Moscow appeared even then, as I can see by the notes I kept, as a concrete example of 'combined development.' Inside the ancient Kitai Gorod, one of the Oriental roots of the semi-Oriental city, I saw a detailed public exhibition of plaster casts and anatomical models to demonstrate every variety and stage of venereal disease. The chapel of Catherine II in St Basil's Cathedral, one day when I was there, was the scene of a Communist lecture to visiting peasants, who made no secret of their feelings. The red flag draped the arch where once all Russia had revered the shrine of the Iberian Virgin; and the new tomb of Lenin stood foursquare against the glowering Kremlin wall. The whole spectacle suggested a compression of time, a hasty, vaulting vigour, too concentrated to be understood at first by a visitor from the more timid world outside. My eyes and mind registered these phenomena and many more (I even recorded them carefully in the daybook), but I was not yet prepared to examine the fundamental ideas of which they were the direct or indirect results. Indeed, I shied off political implications on that first visit to Moscow with the nervousness of a suspicious colt. Aside from a general disillusionment with Europe, a dislike of Imperialism, and a half-conscious emotional sympathy for the Bolshevik effort (as distinguished from its methods or results), I had no preparation to receive political theory of any kind, and no hospitality to it. I believed, as the valuable daybook shows, that I could keep on my way as a perpetual spectator, so far as the historic movements of mankind were concerned, without any pronounced inclination towards any of them, and without personal interest in their consequences. In this state of suspended development, lasting through the year and a half between my departure from the Rif and my arrival in China, I appear to have believed that books and music, to which I was becoming more and more addicted, and works of art, which I had discovered in Persia and Russia, combined with the satisfaction of physical needs, would have to be (for me) the whole material of life. The desire to find some relationship between this one life and the millions of others into which it was cast—that search for sense, vividly pursued and sharply disappointed during my first adult years—could fall off and cease to be; it could come, in time, to seem as foolish as a desire to tell the future by tea leaves. Accepting the fact that there was no sense in things, that it was a solipsist's world, books, music, friends and the changes of seasons could then take up the whole of it, and life pass as pleasantly as a good play. I might be able to say, in the end, as Lady Mary Wortley Montagu is supposed to have said on her deathbed, 'It has all been very interesting.' This was the frame of mind of the dilettante, into which the first disappointments of a more vigorous attitude had partly precipitated me. In that frame of mind I was naturally not susceptible to any but the spectacular aspect of Russia, and denied, as much as I could, any other interest. It was also a frame of mind in which the State Museum of Modern Western Painting would inevitably exert more fascination, leave a more permanent impression, than anything else in Moscow.

We take what we are ready for. I might have seen hundreds of modern paintings in Chicago or Paris without discovering any intimate response to their vision. It so happened in Moscow that a phenomenal collection of those pictures was open to me at the moment when my belated awareness of the power of art had put me into a state of capacity to see them. Some of the keenest pleasures of the next few years were due to the discovery thus made, and although it may appear on the surface to be purely accidental that these pictures were seen in Bolshevik Moscow, I am persuaded that a relationship exists between the revolt of the artists— their expression, the most perfect in its results, of the general revolt against middle-class ideas—and the conflicts that accompanied that rebellion on the plane of exterior events. Instead of being, as one Bolshevik told me, 'bourgeois and decadent,' the works in the State Museum of Modern Western Painting were as revolutionary as the Communist Manifesto. When Picasso threw the left side of his grey-pink dancing boy out of drawing to give it lightness and animation, in the beautiful early picture in the Morosov collection, he was beginning a career as disruptive to the received prejudices in painting as Lenin's became to academic politics and economics. The artist's revolution was the only one that engaged my sympathies then, but it was not without significance that I had encountered it in Moscow.

2

I returned to Paris by way of Riga and Berlin. My immediate problem was to get the journalistic results of the Persian journey

down on paper as quickly as possible, in fulfilment of various engagements; and to do so without undue interruption I found a
village on the Normandy coast, Les Petites Dalles, where, for a
minute monthly payment, a family of fisher people gave me their
house. I remained there through the late summer and autumn; but
once the information gathered in Persia had been duly set down,
sent off, and (happily) paid for, I left Normandy for Paris and
London. I was already hankering after China, where the armies of
the Kuomintang were making their belated advance towards the
north. This time, I determined, there would be no book-writing
about it. Journalism of the most immediate variety (temporary
information) had no place within book covers, as the Persian
experience had shown. Not only was it presumptuous to write
anything about a country on such scant acquaintance, but the
skin-deep phenomena, those I still felt qualified to observe,
changed so rapidly that the only place for them was the convenient, perishable newspaper. True, I already knew a great deal more
about China than I ever had known about Persia. I had been reading books about China all my life, and if much (even most) of
what I knew was wrong, out of date, inadequate or distorted by
the prejudices of various worthy authors, it still constituted some
kind of familiarity with the subject, enough to keep me from being
at the mercy of the first talkative person I might meet after getting
off the boat at Shanghai. In fact I thought, reading the contradictory and sketchy reports in the London and Paris papers, that the
Chinese Revolution in its present stage was an event—a whole
school of events—that I could hardly bear to miss. Certain kinds
of events to which newspapers gave their attention had this effect on me for years, and had to be explained (when I thought of
it) by the antique fancy that newspaper men, like fire horses,
could never outgrow their instinct for the 'game.' It seems to me
now that this was no explanation, for the events that aroused my
fire-horse instinct were not, actually, the ones the newspapers
found most interesting. I cared nothing about such events as
earthquakes, murders, political elections in the United States,
divorces, or transatlantic flights (except Lindbergh's, which captured every imagination). The events that aroused in me the desire to attend, to witness, were invariably those in which large

numbers of men were engaged in some difficult enterprise involving a fundamental idea—an idea of race, class or even of nation. In what looked like the impending triumph of the Chinese Revolution there was an event of the kind that excited my imagination to the utmost. Without regard to what kind of job I might do in China, I wanted above all to get there.

I wrote from Paris to my friends on the North American Newspaper Alliance in New York. They hesitated. By this time I had a set of ready-made characteristics in my profession and was not regarded as fit for any kind of newspaper work that did not involve crawling through barbed wire or galloping across deserts in Arab disguise. The injustice of this legend was obvious, for a newspaper man who could only work in Arab clothes and on a horse would soon starve to death. But my last bits of newspaper work had been the two journeys to the Rif, of which the second had been (from the employers' point of view) eminently successful; consequently I was expected to repeat that experience or do nothing. China was regarded as too large, too complicated, too political, and in a general way too unexciting to justify the employment of a young man whose only gift, it seemed, was for running through blockades.

I wrote again, waited, and wrote again. In the meanwhile the wolf had long since passed the door, and to support him adequately I worked for two months on the Paris *Times*, where a number of my old friends from the Chicago *Tribune* had migrated.[1] Thus the winter passed, and in February the armies of the Kuomingtang captured Shanghai. This event instantly endowed China with all the attributes of suitability and excitement that had been lacking before, and a cable from the N. A. N. A. summoned me to New York. I could have reached China much more quickly by way of Russia, but it was believed that instructions delivered viva voce were more efficacious than instructions by letter, and to New York I went.

I spent several days in New York receiving instructions and collecting (whether I wanted them or not) letters to people in China. Most of these letters were never presented, but one among

[1] The Paris *Times*, an amiable curiosity among newspapers, belongs to the next chapter, where, if the print holds out, it will be found.

them was to prove a document almost as valuable as my passport. It was an open letter ('To Whom It May Concern') written by the senior Senator from Idaho. Mr Borah's fame throughout the world was at its height during the reactionary era of Harding and Coolidge, and his reputation for liberalism and anti-imperialism was nowhere greater than in China; his letter was to constitute my best introduction to the leaders of the national revolution.

From New York to Shanghai by way of Seattle, Yokohama and Kobe seemed to me an unnecessarily lengthy journey, but at last, on the fourteenth of April, my ship pushed through the swarming Whangpu River to the dock at Shanghai.

The International Settlement and the French Concession, the two foreign enclaves that constituted the original city of Shanghai, around which a colossal Chinese city has grown up, gave an instant impression of pompous and rather purse-proud arrogance. The confrontation of European power and the swarming, fluid, antlike life of the poverty-stricken Chinese was more obvious here than anywhere else in China, as I was to learn; the great banks towered above streets where the Chinese appeared chiefly in the guise of coolies, beasts of burden: a physical contrast as vivid as that between the foreign cruisers and gunboats in the river and the innumerable Chinese junks and sampans that clustered noisy and impotent about them. The arrogance of the European city was, just now, tempered by a certain amount of apprehension, for the Cantonese armies had occupied the surrounding Chinese city a month before and were held to be 'threatening' the existence of the foreign settlement. The frontiers of the Anglo-American-French city were guarded by sailors and bluejackets, and one of my earliest impressions in China was that of the glint of bayonets above barricades of sacks filled with dirt. It was strange and not very pleasant to see slovenly Spanish sailors, representatives of a nation that had never had any real interest in China, searching Chinese men and women as they attempted to pass the boundary. I took myself and my belongings off to the Majestic Hotel, a luxurious establishment in the midst of a parklike garden some distance out the Bubbling Well Road. This splendid empty château was then the only alternative to the celebrated Astor House, which was filled with newspaper correspondents and 'old China hands' expounding their philosophy of *Gott strafe China* all day long. At the Majestic I was slightly irritated by too much grandeur, too many servants, too much obsequiousness, but at least the place was quiet, insulated from the two kinds of noise that made Shanghai difficult—the actual physical noise of the streets and the no less positive uproar of hatred and recrimination in which the Shanghai foreigners habitually lived.

If I had to find an example of a place and time in which calm reflection was apparently prohibited by the conditions of life, I think I should name Shanghai in 1927. Even Jerusalem, that home of hatred and despair, during the worst moments of 1929, was not without forms of refuge. It had its architecture and its religions. Shanghai had nothing—nothing but its money and its ghastly fear of losing it. Cowering angrily behind its barricades, it exhibited human nature without dignity or generosity, denying any fact that might sooner or later threaten its hold over wealth and the sources of wealth. As a portal of China, it was at least characteristic of the conflicts within.

3

I arrived in China at the most fateful moment of the national revolution, that in which the victors surveyed the field and took stock of themselves. It was not a good moment for a journalist: from the professional point of view, I was too late. The capture of Shanghai and the sack of Nanking had been the high points of interest for the newspapers in America, and by the time I got to Shanghai the 'story,' as we say in the language of the trade, was already fading into obscurity. After a few more weeks it vanished altogether, for Colonel Lindbergh's flight to Paris drove all other news out of the American newspapers and the American mind for most of the summer. If China had been swallowed up by an earthquake and tidal wave it could scarcely have excited much attention in the United States just then. Moreover, the particular kind of personal exploit that my employers wanted of me—what they called, in their cabled instructions, 'personal adventures'—proved impossible in a country where, so far as I could discover, all the inhabitants when treated with courtesy were invariably courteous and kind. I made various attempts to encounter these 'personal adventures' in parts of China from which all foreigners had fled, and never got so much as a harsh word out of any Chinese. Consequently the whole result of my experience in China was, so far as my newspapers were concerned, flat failure.

But from another point of view, the one adopted in this history, the experience was richer in consequences than any other I have to record. Here, for the first time, I began to approach the fundamental meaning of those vast disturbances that had fascinated me (in part unconsciously) for years—began to be able to discern the general under the particular, to take what Borodin called 'the long view.' In my first direct meeting with the Bolshevik philosophy in action (even in rather circumscribed action), I was disturbed by the precision with which it answered the questions I had begun to think unanswerable—the questions of a sensible relationship between one life and the many. Whether the Bolshevik solutions were the correct ones was another matter, which might take a long time to determine, but they were at least solutions, and represented the effort of human thought to bring order into the chaos that on every side oppressed and appalled the imagination.

I do not mean to say, of course, that I had known nothing about the Communist view of life before I went to China. I had as much acquaintance with it as most people have—perhaps more—and had even read a certain amount of its literature, including huge indigestible lumps of Karl Marx. But the difference between an academic acquaintance with Communism and an actual perception of its spirit is very great. The step required to pass from the first state to the second is so easy that it may be accomplished in a moment, and so difficult that it may involve the effort of a lifetime. It may be compared, I think, to the step by which, at an equally momentous frontier in literature, we pass into the world created by the *Divina Commedia*. Every schoolboy knows about the *Divina Commedia:* how Dante, having lost his way in a dark wood, was found by Virgil and conducted into the depths of hell, rising from there to Purgatory and to the circles of Paradise through which he was led by the blessed Beatrice. But this knowledge of the vast, perfect poem is no knowledge at all; it is like being told in the schoolroom that Paris is the capital of France, a bald statement that can only become a living fact when we have smelled the acacias and eaten the food and investigated the literature that make it true. With Dante the difficulty of the language supplies another barrier (even for Italians); but when the step has at last been taken, the barrier passed, we enter a world in which all parts of the structure of existence are so related and harmonized, so subjugated to a sovereign system, that its ordered beauty and majesty give us the sensation of a new form of life, as if we had actually moved off into space and taken up our abode, for a time, on another star. Such miraculous translations are rare and difficult; it took me thirty-four years to set foot inside the world of Dante. The world of Lenin (which is, after all, all around us) can be entered in a moment, but only if the disposition of circumstances, persons, influences, can conquer the laziness of a bourgeois mind. The required combinations occurred for me at Hankow, and were given force and form, particularly, by Michael Borodin and Rayna Prohme.

But before I went up the river to Hankow I had to make the acquaintance of the parts of the Chinese revolutionary movement that had already begun to be corrupted by power—the counter-revolutionary group of Shanghai and Nanking. Its position was interesting and typical; some such position is always assumed by middle-class revolutionaries at the moment of triumph, and Chiang Kai-shek, the shrewd young man, was even then engaged in the Kerensky-like manœuvres that were to make him President (so to speak) of China. It might be useful to recall, just here, what the course of the Chinese national revolution had been up to 1927. It was a long, slow, cumulative movement, the awakening of a giant; it had been going on for thirty-odd years. Its original organization was the work of the great revolutionary Sun Yat-sen, whose power to move and convince throngs of people had made him the natural leader of the whole south, and, for a time, of all China. In 1911, with the overthrow of the Manchu dynasty, Sun Yat-sen had been proclaimed President of China at Nanking, but, robbed of the actual power by the clever reactionary, Yuan Shih-kai, had retired to Canton to establish there the central point, the focus, for all revolutionary activity. Even in Canton Sun Yat-sen's career was checkered; he was always being driven out and returning in triumph. In 1923, pursuing their announced policy of friendliness to all Asiatic national movements, the Bolsheviks (through Joffe, their ambassador at Peking) made an agreement with Sun Yat-sen by which they were to supply him with military and political advisers, money and munitions. From this point onward the development of the Cantonese revolutionary movement was rapid and overwhelmingly successful. The Bolsheviks had given Sun Yat-sen what he needed: an army. They also moulded, to some extent, the ideas of the movement, although Sun Yat-sen himself never became a Communist, and always, apparently, believed that it would be possible for China to assume the forms of an organized industrial society without going through any kind of class warfare. Sun Yat-sen himself died in 1924, but the movement, becoming increasingly social and economic, with an intensive labour propaganda, became harder to resist after his death than it had been before. The various war lords who governed China on the feudal system dreaded it, and with reason, for it was by its nature inimical to them, even when it made use of their services.

Finally, in 1927, the armies of Canton had swept all the way up to the Yangtze-kiang, had taken Hankow, Shanghai and Nanking, and with them the revenues of the richest part of China. The capture of Nanking, about two weeks before I arrived in Shanghai, had been marked by a collapse of discipline; certain of the Cantonese troops had run wild in the city, looting, raping and killing. These incidents—'the Nanking outrages'—had been promptly avenged by an Anglo-American bombardment of the city, in which numerous noncombatants were killed. Anti-foreign feeling, always strong among the Chinese revolutionaries, was at a high pitch, and all foreigners had been ordered by their own government to leave the interior of China and concentrate at Shanghai and Tientsin. The Cantonese movement had, practically speaking, won its victory, for it was only a question of time until the remaining war lords (the chief of whom was old Chang Tso-lin, supported by the Japanese) would be swept out of the way by the better trained and equipped soldiers, and by persuasive propaganda, from the south.

This moment of triumph was inevitably the one in which the two elements among the Cantonese victors would separate. Genuine revolutionaries—those who wished to change the conditions of life in China, and not simply the forms or names of government—found themselves obliged to cling to the Left Wing of the Kuomintang, in which Russian influence was paramount. The others—those who took part in the revolution for their own advantage, or were prevented by the tenacity of middle-class ideas from wishing to disturb the established arrangement of wealth—collected around the treasuries of Shanghai and Nanking, under the patronage of the Chinese bankers of those cities and their new ally, Chiang Kai-shek. The Left Wing had its capital at Hankow, and the Right Wing at Nanking. The division was not yet open and public, and the Kuomintang (People's party—Sun Yat-sen's old organization) kept up a pretence of unity for some time, but the opposition of the two tendencies was too glaring to be denied in private talk, and constituted, in fact, the chief immediate problem of the revolution.

I went, first, to see Mr T. V. Soong. He was a young man of about my own age, trained at Harvard, intelligent, competent and honest, and had been Minister of Finance for the Cantonese government. The same post had been assigned to him at Hankow and also at Nanking, but at the precise moment of my arrival he had resigned it. He continued resigning it for years, only to take it up again, until he was to become a kind of permanent Minister of Finance in all the Kuomintang governments. His usefulness came not only from the confidence inspired by his known capacity and honesty, but from his relationship to the semi-divine figure of Sun Yat-sen; he was a brother of the great man's widow. When I arrived in Shanghai he was living in Sun Yat-sen's house in the French Concession, the house given the old hero by the city for a permanent refuge in his turbulent career.

Mr Soong—'T. V.,' as he was always called—received me well, thanks to the Borah letter. He spent some time explaining to me the difficulties of his own position, a problem that always worried him a good deal. As I came to know T.V. rather better in the following months, I grew to regard him as the most typical Liberal I had ever known—honest, worried, puzzled, unable to make up his mind between the horrors of capitalist imperialism and the horrors of Communist revolution. If China had only been America his happiness would have been complete, for he could have pretended not to know about the horrors. But in China it was impossible to step out of doors without seeing evidence, on every hand, of the brutal and inhuman exploitation of human labour by both Chinese and foreigners. T. V. was too sensitive not to be moved by such spectacles. And yet he had an equally nervous dread of any genuine revolution; crowds frightened him, labour agitation and strikes made him ill, and the idea that the rich might ever be despoiled filled him with alarm. During a demonstration in Hankow one day his motorcar was engulfed by a mob and one of its windows was broken. He was, of course, promptly rescued by his guards and removed to safety, but the experience had a permanent effect on him—gave him the nervous dislike for mass action that controlled most of his political career and threw him at last, in spite of the sincerity of his idealism, into the camp of the reactionaries. He was an amiable, cultivated and charming young man, but he had no fitness for an important rôle in a great revolution. On the whole, I believe he realized it perfectly, and was made more miserable by that fact than by any other.

T. V. gave me a note to Chiang Kai-shek, who was then at Nanking, and another to Mme Sun Yat-sen in Hankow. He intimated that I might find some difference of opinion between these two dignitaries, but at the time he was still trying hard to pretend that no split between the elements of the Kuomintang had taken place. As I knew later on, the pretence was hollow, for actually the split had taken place in the exact middle—the very place where T. V. wished to stand—and had probably been more painful to him than to anybody else. So far as I was able to determine, he was the only real Liberal among the revolutionary leaders, and as the others moved freely, almost happily, towards their natural positions to Left or Right, he went through all the agonies of mind and spirit to which, on a larger scale, world liberalism had been subjected since 1918.

The idea of going to Nanking was regarded as foolhardy by the foreigners in Shanghai, and particularly by my colleagues; nevertheless, I went. It was an illuminating little journey. The foreigners had withdrawn from the railroad and from the Chinese city of Shanghai as well as from Nanking and the whole interior. The train, therefore, was about two hours late in starting and four hours late in arriving. It was crowded with Cantonese soldiers, but instead of tossing me about on their bayonets, as my Shanghai friends wished me to believe was their habit, they made way for me and actually gave me a seat in one of the best compartments. I was accompanied by an interpreter obtained through one of the missionary groups. This young man had studied in the United States and talked the 'Oh, boy!' and 'Geez! You said it!' kind of English. His ideas were as shallow and chaotic as his language. He had a great enthusiasm for the Revolution and the Kuomintang, but knew remarkably little about either. I spent an hour or so explaining to him what the party organization was (its rôle in the 'era of tutelage' as outlined by Sun Yat-sen), as I wanted to be sure that my questions to Chiang Kai-shek would be correctly understood in transit. As we carried on this conversation, packed tight into a corner of the carriage with soldiers all over us, I noticed that a long-gowned Chinese (i.e., a member of the middle or educated class) was listening. Presently he joined in the talk, but in the accents of Oxford, with such a command of literary English that my interpreter was abashed. The long-gowned Chinese was one of the secretaries to Quo Tai-chi in the Ministry of Foreign Affairs, and had just the kind of fluid, voluble intelligence that the Shanghai foreigners most disliked. He spent an hour or so airing the grievances of the Shanghai Chinese, their constant humiliations in the foreign city, the insults their pride suffered in not being allowed to go into parks or clubs, etc., etc. It was not a sympathetic character or a sympathetic complaint, but I listened with interest. When I ventured to say that there seemed to me to be more valid subjects of grievance in Shanghai, and mentioned, as an example, the dreadful conditions I had glimpsed only the day before in certain textile mills where men, women and children worked twelve hours a day for a wage barely sufficient to buy rice, my long-gowned friend shut up like a clam. The Revolution, for him, apparently meant that educated Chinese ought to be admitted to social equality with the half-educated foreign merchants in their clubs and parks and houses—a strange ambition, but one I was to meet with fairly often among the heirs of the Mandarinate.

In Nanking I repaired to a Chinese inn with my interpreter and sent a note to headquarters with T. V. Soong's line of introduction. An hour or so later I was summoned to see the general, Chiang Kai-shek.

This remarkable young man, who was then about thirty[1] and looked less, had been born a poor Cantonese and was, to begin with, a common soldier. He was without education even in Chinese, and spoke only the dialect of his native city. (His name, too, was always pronounced in Cantonese—Chiang Kai-shek, whereas in Chinese it would have been Ch'ang Kai-shih.) He had been singled out for advancement by Sun Yat-sen, and showed enough ability to be pushed ahead through all ranks until he became, in 1927, commander-in-chief of the armies and, so far as the public was concerned, the military hero of the Revolution. Having arrived at his present eminence in great part by the aid of the Russians, he had now decided—under the persuasion of the Shanghai bankers and the immense revenues of the maritime provinces—to break with them and establish himself as a war lord, modern style, with all the slogans and propaganda of the Kuomintang to cover his personal aggrandizement and give it a patriotico-revolutionary colour.

Chiang seemed (rather to my surprise) sensitive and alert. He was at pains to explain that he intended to carry out the whole programme of Sun Yat-sen, the Three People's Principles (*San Min Chu I*) and all the rest of it, but without falling into 'excesses.' I was unable to bring him to any clear statement of his disagreement with the Russians or the Left Wing, and his thin brown face worked anxiously as he talked round the subject, avoiding its pitfalls. I cursed the necessity for an interpreter—particularly one whose command of both languages was obviously so limited—and wished, not for the first time, that the Esperantists had been more successful in their efforts. But even through the clouds of misapprehension set up by my friend the returned student from the United States I could discern the eager, ambitious nature of Chiang Kai-shek's mind, his anxiety to be thought well of, his desire to give his personal ambitions the protective coloration of a

[1] The general was, or believed himself to be, some ten years older than this, as I did not know until long afterwards.

revolutionary doctrine and vocabulary. The phrases adopted by all members of the Kuomintang, from Right to Left, were used by him over and over again: 'wicked gentry' (i. e., reactionary land-lords), 'foreign imperialism' and 'unequal treaties,' the traditional enemies of the Cantonese movement. But upon the methods he intended to use to combat his enemies he was vague. It was im-possible to avoid the conclusion that with this young man, in spite of his remarkable opportunities, the phrases of the move-ment had not sunk beyond the top layer of consciousness. He remained a shrewd, ambitious, energetic Cantonese with his way to make in the world, and I fully believed that he would make it. I thought I detected, about his mouth and eyes, one of the rarest of human expressions, the look of cruelty. It may, indeed, have been only the characteristic look of a nervous, short-tempered man, but in later weeks, when his counter-revolution reached its height and the Communists were being tortured and butchered at his command, I was to remember the flickering mouth and anx-ious eyes of Chiang Kai-shek.

The remarkable thing about my visit to Nanking—where I remained three days—was that everybody in the streets, in the inn, at headquarters and wherever I went, treated me with cour-tesy. I was a citizen of a country whose ships, only a few days be-fore, had bombarded the city, killing scores of people and setting fire to many houses. I was, I believe, the only foreigner in the area; I was neither armed nor guarded; the guns of the American and British ships were still trained on the city from the middle of the Yangtze River, and an informal state of war was felt to exist between the Chinese of the river towns and the hostile foreign navies that frowned upon them. From Hankow to Shanghai there was no communication between the foreign warships and the shore: for another five or six weeks the tension remained acute. And yet nothing whatever happened to me—not a shout, not a stone, not a gesture—to indicate that my presence was a reminder of the miseries and humiliations of China. Perhaps the inhabitants of Nanking were ashamed of the disorders of a fortnight before, and perhaps they were afraid of the gray ships in the river. But, on the whole, I took the experience as another confirmation of a principle in which I had always firmly believed: that human beings of whatever complexion or nation were 'safe' enough if one clearly wished them no harm. The excited troops had disproved this principle, you might say, in Nanking itself only a short time before; but had they? In the frenzy of victory, drunk with success and mob anger, they had attacked the houses and persons of the 'foreign imperialists'—those foreigners who lived in conspicuous luxury among them by means of the exploitation of their labour and their markets, supported visibly at all times by foreign war-ships in the Chinese river. The Nanking outrages, however deplorable, were easy to understand; they were an inevitable consequence of the conditions under which the foreign colonies were imposed upon China. Such things might happen anywhere when an oppressed population gets out of hand. They have, indeed, happened in most countries at one time or another. But it seemed to me that the lone foreigner, unarmed and friendly, with no wealth to excite envy and no power to excite fear, would certainly be safe enough among any people, and particularly among the courteous Chinese, if the pretences of superiority could be abandoned.

I returned to Shanghai, the atmosphere of which had already begun to seem fantastically artificial. Its inhabitants considered that they had built Shanghai out of nothing, and, in the most obvious sense, they had; the site of the city had been a worthless mudbank, given to the British, Americans and French because the Chinese did not want it. The British, Americans and French had reclaimed the land, built upon it with increasing pompousness, and now regarded it as an exhibition of their own superiority to the despised natives of China. It never seemed to cross their minds that every penny spent upon Shanghai had been wrung from the Chinese in one way or another, either by the exorbitant profits of foreign trade—the exploitation of what is called an 'undeveloped market,' which is to say a market made up of people who do not know when they are being cheated—or by the direct exploitation of Chinese labour. The second source of wealth was more recent, and its profits had been enormous. The British, Americans and Japanese were able to employ Chinese people of all ages in their factories for any number of hours a day, for wages so small that they barely supported a half-starved and ever-threatened life.

The coolie population, which never had enough to eat and often no place to sleep, was easy prey for manufacturers who wished to make the modest profit of a thousand per cent. Against any mention of these unpleasant facts the Shanghai foreigner, sipping his cocktail reflectively in the cool recesses of one of his clubs, would reply with a number of statements that seemed to him irrefutable. He would say that many Chinese of the middle class, compradores,[1] had grown rich with the foreigners; that conditions in the British and American factories were not so bad as in the Japanese, and conditions in the Japanese factories not so bad as in the occasional Chinese establishments; that the prosperity of Shanghai benefited all China; and that, in any case, the Chinese were an inferior race, had never been used to anything but starvation and overwork, misery and oppression, and consequently 'don't feel anything—not, at least, as we do.' I never met anybody in Shanghai who revealed the slightest feeling of shame, the slightest consciousness of degradation, in thus taking advantage of human misery in its most appalling forms. On the contrary, the Shanghai foreigners felt virtuous because they gave their coolies a slightly better chance of survival than did the worst of the Chinese employers. Shanghai saw itself as the benefactor of all China, and was horrified at the rising Chinese demand for better conditions of life and a recognized share in the spoils.

A different attitude was, perforce, adopted by the missionaries, whose religion compelled them to concede in theory the fraternity of all creatures. They were, on the whole, better educated and temperamentally more civilized than the other foreigners, those who had come to China simply to make all the money they could out of the country. But the missionaries had as their supreme objective the conversion of the Chinese to Christianity. Such an objective, so contrary to common sense, good manners, and the genius of Chinese civilization, was pursued by the best of the missionaries for the best of reasons—that they firmly believed in a future life eternal, to which only those who adhered to their particular sect could be admitted. To bring the Chinese into the fold

---

[1]Compradores were interpreting middlemen, always Chinese, who worked on a kind of double-commission basis with foreigners from the earliest days of foreign trade in China.

was thus an act of Christian charity. Their effort brought about a considerable incidental benefit in the form of education and good works—for which they were detested by the other foreigners— but the supreme objective was still religious conversion, and the American missionaries, in particular, tended to count their harvest of souls in much the same way as the merchants counted their profits, with a similar convenient disregard of motives and methods. This organized attempt to impose a foreign god and an alien system of supernatural beliefs on the rationalistic character of the Chinese was not likely to be successful no matter how many hundreds of years it was continued; it was essentially an incongruous and presumptuous enterprise, which the Chinese could scarcely take seriously even when they made use of it; but it created a large class of especially privileged foreigners in the country, enjoying the protection of foreign armies and navies, presenting a strange religion of mystery and dogma in a mixture of free rice, machine guns, schools, gunboats, and unintelligibility. The finest of the missionaries—and there were admirable, even noble, characters among them, however unsympathetic their purposes— often bewailed the conditions under which Christianity had to be presented to the Chinese, when a sermon about brotherly love might be interrupted by a murderous bombardment from the loving Christian navies.

Like the merchants of the treaty ports, the missionaries had grown to think of themselves as an integral part of China; not at all as visitors to be tolerated so long as they behaved themselves, but as benefactors without whom the country could scarcely continue to exist. The difference between the merchants and the missionaries, then, it seemed to me in Shanghai and afterwards, was that the first group frankly asserted themselves a superior race, designed by nature to make money out of the Chinese, while the second group, denying racial superiority but acting upon the assumption that it existed, felt themselves appointed by the same mysterious nature to bring light, charity and faith to the heathen. It was the old, jerky rhythm of capitalism and philanthropy: the system of profit was accustomed to take all it could get, and then throw off a little of the unneeded surplus on its victims. There should be no surprise if such a muddled relationship appeared, at times, wholly incomprehensible to the rationalistic Chinese. One had to belong to the great, dominant, all-wonderful races of western Europe and the United States to appreciate how greed and sanctimoniousness could inhabit the same house, speak the same language, fight with the same weapons.

4

Hankow, Wuchang, Hanchang, the three great cities called, together, Wuhan, blackened the flat shores of the river early on our fifth day from Shanghai. Of the three cities, Hankow was the most important, although not the largest. It was the one in which the foreigners had built their own city, in concessions taken from the Chinese in the nineteenth century. The Germans, Russians and Americans having been counted out for assorted reasons, the foreign city consisted, in 1927, of the British, French and Japanese Concessions—or, practically, of the first two, since the Japanese Concession was almost indistinguishable from the surrounding Chinese town. Foreign women and children had left Hankow when the Cantonese captured the city the preceding winter; many of the men had followed them; the city was consequently regarded as 'evacuated,' although a handful of Americans, British and French remained in charge of their various properties. The British Concession had been (by the Chen-O'Malley Agreement a few months before) entrusted to the Chinese to administer under a régime of transition—a conciliatory move that infuriated most of the British in China. But the French still guarded their streets with small Annamite soldiers, and the British and American navies, represented in great strength at Hankow, filled the town from morning to night with sailors on leave and the naval police sent out to guard them. In spite of this excessive protection, the foreigners persisted in regarding Hankow as dangerous. Mr Lockhart, the American Consul, offered me a bed. He already had a number of fortuitous guests, and it was his duty to warn all Americans, I believe, that they could be protected only if they lived in the consulate under guard. But the large, comfortable Hôtel des Wagons-Lits in the French Concession was almost empty, and as I could see no immediate likelihood of its being stormed by an angry Chinese mob, I installed myself there. Its only 'protection' was a stolid little brown Annamite who stood wearily with rifle and bayonet under the arc light on the corner, and even his presence was, so far as I ever saw, quite unnecessary. For in Hankow, as in Nanking, I saw no real disorder. I remained there two months or more, and the nearest thing to an international incident that came under my observation was the effort of a drunken American sailor to pick flowers in Mr Eugene Chen's garden. This occurrence had no dire results, and on the whole Hankow, in spite of its hysterical atmosphere and its baleful reputation, was an abode of peace.

My first interviews were with Borodin and Chen, whose names were best known in the world at large as representatives of the point of view of Hankow, of the Left Kuomintang. Borodin had never sought public attention and disliked giving interviews, but by this time it was no longer possible for him to avoid them. Eugene Chen loved public attention as a cat loves milk, and was at his best in an interview, rolling forth his grand, oratorical sentences with long pauses so that they might be written down in detail. Both Borodin and Chen used English, not only with representatives of the press, but in their communications with each other and with most of the other members of the Hankow government; for neither had a good command of Chinese. Chen was Foreign Minister, the spokesman for all his colleagues, and so could freely exercise his gifts as a proclamation-monger; Borodin, chief of the Russian advisers, tried to avoid speaking for the Hankow government, and restricted himself as much as he could, with interviewers whom he did not know, to discussions of principle.

My first impressions of both Borodin and Chen were overlaid by a mass of later impressions, by a whole tangle of experience in China and Russia in which they figured, and yet that first view of them in Hankow still seems to me clear and substantially correct. Borodin, a large, calm man with the natural dignity of a lion or a panther, had the special quality of being in, but above, the battle, to which I have already referred in speaking of Abd el-Krim—the particular quality that seems to me to deserve, in itself and without regard to the judgment of the world, the name of greatness. His slow, resolute way of talking, his refusal to be hurried or to get excited, his insistence upon the fundamental lines of action that determined detailed events, gave a spacious, deliberate character to his conversation, lifting it far above the shallowness of journalism and the hysteria of politics. He seemed to take 'the long view' by nature, by an almost physical superiority of vision. As I knew him better I perceived—or, rather, he showed me—how his political philosophy made breadth and elevation inevitable in the mind that understood it. He was an Old Bolshevik; that is, he had been a member of the Leninist school since its underground days before the war. His exile had been spent in the United States, where he acquired a better first-hand knowledge of the industrial system than was common among Bolshevik intellectuals. He had returned to Russia in 1917, to 'party work,' and had been entrusted with the Chinese mission in 1924. His whole adult life had been lived by a system of thought in which the immediate event was regarded as meaningless unless related to other events on both sides in time; in which the individual was valued by his relationship to his fellow beings; in which the most important of processes was held to be the comprehension, however disagreeable, of cause and effect. Disregarding the economic structure (Marxian economics) with which the Bolshevik mind was preoccupied, it could be seen that the method of thought in itself was 'good'—produced, as in the case of Borodin, a clear, calm view of life. Borodin himself would have attributed the quality I have called greatness (the quality of being in, but above, the battle) to the political philosophy and to nothing else. He would have said that the philosophy gave 'historical perspective,' and that historical perspective, once thoroughly understood, enabled the mind to inhabit a clearer air. But as, during the succeeding months, I came to know a number of other Communists more or less well, I was obliged to conclude that this was not so. However adequately they may have learned their political philosophy, it did not always lift them above the mud in which we flounder, and a Communist could be just as stupid, petty, and egotistical as any bourgeois. Borodin would have said that such a Communist was not a good Communist—which, although probably true, demolished the idea that an acquired political philosophy was alone enough to raise human beings to the highest power of which they were capable in the sense of life. The political philosophy had to be thoroughly understood, articulated and applied, made into a constant medium in which the good Communist could live as the saints lived in God, as the fish live in the sea. Something like this must have happened before 'the long view' and the reasoned plan of existence came to be Borodin's native element, from which he could look calmly upon the chaos of immediate events; but since it worked for him and not for others, there must also have been in his nature, from the beginning, an aptitude for reflection, a capacity for detached thought, superior to the aptitudes and capacities of other men who professed the same beliefs without thereby coming a shade nearer the stars.

Eugene Chen was, in some ways, a relief after Borodin. Borodin's large calm, his preternatural certainty, although they made an instant impression upon me, did, at first, leave me puzzled and a little humiliated—made me feel, as I used to tell Rayna Prohme, insignificant. Borodin was too big to be absorbed all at once. Mr. Chen, a small but concentrated dose, could be absorbed thoroughly in fifteen minutes, and although subsequent events did reveal fact upon fact in his complex character, no single fact about him ever surprised me after our first meeting. He was all of a piece, a small, clever, venomous, faintly reptilian man, adroit and slippery in the movements of his mind, combative in temper, with a kind of lethal elegance in appearance, voice and gesture. His talent for grand, bad phrases had made him famous throughout the world. He was English secretary to Dr Sun Yat-sen, and some of the documents to which the great revolutionary's name was attached in his declining years, in particular the Farewell to Soviet Russia, bear the unmistakable marks of Chen's style, florid, grandiloquent and theatrical. After Sun Yat-sen's death the clever secretary became Foreign Minister, a post in which he remained until the collapse of the revolutionary government at Hankow. In 1927 he was probably the best known of all Chinese political leaders to the world outside, and one of the least known among the Chinese.

I went from Borodin's great barracks straight across the road to the elegant Foreign Office where Chen dwelt and gave audience. In less than half an hour I had been stuffed with sharp, crackling phrases until neither my notebook nor my head could contain any more. The Foreign Minister was a remarkable man; but although remarkable, the type was not new to me. Wherever partisan political life offered a congenial career to clever and ambitious men with an axe to grind, there would naturally be Eugene Chens. Physically and in some of his ways of speech Mr Chen reminded me of the French politician Malvy; his complacency was like that of Austen Chamberlain; his delight in his own language, and the care he took to see that it was written down in all its baroque magnificence, suggested Mussolini. He was as theatrical as Briand, without any of the old fox's charm; he was as ingratiating as Stresemann, as bitter as Poincaré. In short, Mr Chen was a politician. Within a few minutes after my arrival in his spacious office —to which I had come with my head still a trifle confused from the unexpected nobility of the Bolshevik across the road—I knew exactly where I was: I was a journalist interviewing a clever politician, engaged in the old game of trying to pick out the truth from the lies, the sense from the welter of phrases.

When he began on his favourite subject, the inconceivable selfishness and brutality of the white foreigners in China, particularly of the British, I attended not so much to the immoderate language of the man as to the accents in which it was delivered, the quickened pulse and rhythm of the sentences, the added sharpness of eye and voice. For in spite of my youth—which probably encouraged Mr Chen to believe that I was a suitable subject for his eloquence—I was, by this time, experienced to the point of satiety in the art of interviewing gentlemen who had an axe to grind. The interesting thing in that process, which remained interesting after all the other tricks and devices of the art had palled, was to locate the axe.

In the case of Mr Chen I hesitated for a long time to believe that his axe was where my instinct and experience told me it was. The influence of Borodin's unquestionable selflessness, the spectacle of so many single-minded and devoted Chinese in the service of the Kuomintang at Hankow, and the general atmosphere of the place, suggestive of the gallantry of a lost cause, inclined me to think that Chen, too, must be sincere. If he had wanted personal aggrandizement only, he could have found it better on the other side, the side of Nanking. And yet I never met him without realizing that here was an intense egoist, for whose revolutionary impulses there must be intensely personal reasons. His every phrase and act displayed the character of the careerist politician. Months passed before I was willing to recognize what my instinct had told me at our first interview: that Mr Chen was indeed a careerist politician, but that his particular motive power—the axe he had to grind—was a hatred. As a pure careerist politician he would normally have gone over to the side of the money and the big battalions. He was prevented from doing so by the hatred that was the original spring of all his action—a hatred of the pretentious white race, particularly of the British. His hatred made and kept him a revolutionary.

Mr Chen had been born a British subject, at Trinidad in the West Indies. His name as a British subject was not Chen. He was of mixed race, part Chinese, part Negro; he received the education of an Englishman, studied at London University, and elected to become Chinese after the Revolution of 1911 had made a career there possible for him. These were the bare facts; but behind them it was easy to discern a tale of thwarted ambition, offended sensibilities, and dreams that turned to nightmare. Without unduly romancing about a character and situation common among us, we may suppose Mr Chen to have suffered greatly from the injustices to which persons of the coloured races are subjected in the Anglo-Saxon world. His hatred of that world was too intense and personal not to have been produced by intense and personal injuries. He had chosen his wife from the Negro race, and in his four charming children the Chinese strain seemed almost to have vanished. In him it was very strong—strong enough to bring him back to China from the other side of the world, and to engage his considerable talent, his hate-driven energy, his huge vituperative vocabulary, in the service of the Chinese Revolution.

Three years before, in a series of conversations with Blasco Ibáñez, I had obtained my first view of the romantico-literary and poseur revolutionist. Mr Chen provided me with a view of a more interesting pseudo-revolutionary type, that of the careerist with powerful personal motives. He was on the right side (if I may be allowed to call it that) for the wrong reasons.

The door at the end of the darkened reception room on the second floor of the Ministry of Finance opened, and in came a small, shy Chinese lady in a black silk dress. In one of her delicate, nervous hands she held a lace handkerchief, in the other my note of introduction from T. V. Soong. When she spoke her voice almost made me jump: it was so soft, so gentle, so unexpectedly sweet. The shutters had been closed to keep out the heat, and I could not see her until she had come quite near me. Then, looking down in bewilderment, I wondered who on earth she could be. Did Mme Sun Yat-sen have a daughter of whom I had never heard? It did not occur to me that this exquisite apparition, so fragile and timorous, could be the lady herself, the most celebrated woman revolutionary in the world.

'You saw my brother in Shanghai,' she said hesitantly. 'Tell me, how is he?'

It was Mme Sun.

For a good ten minutes we were at sea. I had heard an enormous number of things about her, most of them lies. The American newspapers had surpassed themselves on the subject. According to them, Mme Sun was 'China's Joan of Arc'; she was the leader of a Chinese 'woman's battalion'; she was this, that and the other thing, depending on the fantasies of the headline writers. The notion that she had actually led troops in battle was so widespread that even in China some of the foreigners believed it. In Shanghai this grotesque legend was complicated by more offensive lies, in which her personal character and motives were attacked—a favourite method of political argument in the treaty ports. Although I had sense enough not to believe most of the stories about her, they must have made, collectively, an impression; for I had certainly expected to meet something formidable. And instead, here I was face to face with a childlike figure of the most enchanting delicacy, only too plainly trembling with terror at the sight of me. Never had I felt so big and clumsy, so hopelessly barbarian.

But Mme Sun was aided by a number of characteristics that always enabled her, with an effort, to conquer her own timorousness —not only with me, that is, but in the general conduct of life. She had a dignity so natural and certain that it deserved the name of stateliness. The same quality can occasionally be observed in royal princes or princesses of Europe, especially in the older ones; but with them it is a clear result of lifelong training. Mme Sun's stateliness was of a different, a more intrinsic quality; it came from the inside out, instead of being put on like a harness. She also possessed moral courage to a rare degree, which could keep her steadfast in grave peril. Her loyalty to the name of Sun Yat-sen, to the duty she felt she owed it, was able to withstand trials without end. These qualities—dignity, loyalty, moral courage—gave her character an underlying strength that could, at times, overcome the impressions of fragility and shyness created by her physical appearance and endow her figure with the sternest aspect of heroism. I shall have occasion, in the course of this narrative, to show that death could not intimidate her; that poverty and exile, the fury of her own family and the calumnies of the world were unable to bend her will towards courses she felt to be wrong. She was, in a truer sense than the merely physical one intended by the headline writers, 'China's Joan of Arc,' but you had to know her for a good while before you realized the power of the spirit beneath that exquisite, tremulous envelope.

Mme Sun was born Rosalind Soong (Soong Ching-ling), of a family of rich Shanghai merchants. The Soongs belonged to the very compradore class attacked by the Chinese Revolution— the class that had grown rich in traffic with the foreigners, and had strong economic interests in the maintenance of the old régime. Soong Ching-ling was educated in the United States (in the Wesleyan college for women at Macon, in Georgia) and returned to China when she was nineteen. It was then that the Tsung Li met, fell in love with and married her. He was a great deal older than she was, but he had all the magic of a name that had already assumed symbolic significance in China; and whatever his other qualities may have been, Sun Yat-sen must have possessed a rare and wonderful power of personal influence. Few men in history have had his gift of commanding devotion. In his long, adventurous life, which reads like the invention of a romantic writer, he was constantly being saved from disaster by the fidelity of his friends. The last of his faithful followers was his second wife, his present widow, who was to carry her loyalty to his person and his ideals (quixotically, perhaps) far beyond the grave.

Mme Sun's friends used sometimes to discuss a question suggested by the contrast between her natural shyness, her love of privacy, and the public rôle she was obliged to play. It was this: what might have been the development of her life if she had never met Sun Yat-sen? A theory advanced was that, left to herself, she would have married 'well' and spent her time in all the private dignity and family self-sufficiency of a rich Chinese lady in Shanghai. It is possible. But no character can be studied in this way after the events that shaped it have taken their place in the ordered memory of the past. A fusion has occurred; single strands of character no longer mean anything; the nexus alone can be made to yield some of the secrets of a human personality. The nexus in this case was the marriage, which subjected Soong Ching-ling in her first youth to the most powerful influence of revolutionary idealism China has ever known. She travelled with Sun Yat-sen, acted as his secretary, participated with him in mass meetings and party councils, public triumphs and secret flights. She learned to share his passion against injustice of every kind, his determination to organize and prolong the revolt of the masses until the whole country had been brought under a national party dictatorship for the three objectives of his revolution—the San Min Chu I: Democracy, Nationalism, Social Welfare. When Sun Yat-sen died she took her place in the Central Executive Committee and the other governing bodies of the Kuomintang, and in spite of her dislike for debate, public speaking or public appearances, she performed her duties to the party without complaint. At the time of my arrival in China, in the open schism in the party, she had already resolutely taken her place with the faction of the Left Kuomintang and its Communist minority.

That was Mme Sun when I first saw her. The events of the following months, the massacre of the Communists, the crushing of the labour movement in blood, were to arouse her indignation to such a pitch that she seemed, before one's eyes, to take on stature. Without physical or intellectual power, by sheer force of character, purity of motive, sovereign honesty, she became heroic. In the wreck of the Chinese Revolution this phenomenon was one of the most extraordinary: generals and orators fell to pieces, yielded, fled, or were silent, but the one revolutionary who could not be crushed and would not be still was the fragile little widow of Sun Yat-sen. A 'doll,' they used to call her sometimes in the treaty ports. The world would be a less painful object of contemplation if it contained a few more such 'dolls.'

6

I was not, to begin with, a 'sympathizer' in Hankow. It was part of the middle-class dilettante view of life that I had half adopted, to accept experience of this kind much as the translated experiences of art (a play or a poem) are accepted, and to value them, what is more, as separate parts of a continuous process of education. To the dilettante the Chinese Revolution might have been of interest as an exciting spectacle, like a new ballet of Diaghilev's, and of value as a contribution to his own education, like the acquirement of a new language. By 1927, after constant exposure to the atmosphere of London and Paris, such ways of receiving experience, although not natural to me, had ceased to be altogether alien, and it was in some such frame of mind as that of your plain seeker-after-curiosity that I first went to Hankow.

To Hankow, then, I brought the mind and character of an American bourgeois, twenty-seven years old, who had divided his adult years between the subjects to which this book has been chiefly devoted—the living history of the time—and the preoccupations of personal taste. In these preoccupations, which had assumed greater importance in the last two years, influences of a powerful order had deflected what must originally have been a nature of considerable vigour and simplicity into channels where it was not wholly at ease. The character of the American bourgeois —let us call him Mr X—had been tinged with the colour of his surroundings, had taken on some of the flavour of Paris and London, and disengaged, no doubt, a light aroma of decay. The American character is not made to withstand, over long periods of time, the influence of older cultures in their most self-conscious forms. Our Mr X was almost—and could in time have become—a dilettante. That is, he already possessed by nature, and had fertilized by experience, those tastes by which a man could live through sensation alone. Books, pictures, music and the satisfaction of physical appetites constituted this world of sensation, and although it had always existed in some degree for our Mr X —as it exists for everybody—it had only recently shown signs of taking over the whole of his life.

He was preserved, then and afterwards, from this fate. Aside from any possible reasons that might be sought in deeper regions of the personality, he was preserved by two rather obvious circumstances. The first was that he had no money at all except what he could earn. The second was that, independently of the first, he wanted (why, God knows) to 'write'—that is, to put into words whatever he could learn about the mysterious transaction of living. His attitude towards work was neither consistent nor serious; he was capable of writing the most undisguised piffle to make money when he needed it; but he did possess, at the core, a determination to do some little work of which he need not be ashamed before he was finished. These two circumstances fought against the world of sensation at every point. A man who has to earn his living cannot spend his whole time, or even much of it, in pursuit of the experiences in art and life that might yield sensation; and a man who wants to do good work at some time or other can only learn how to do it by working.

The second circumstance was the really powerful combatant. Money, in the world in which Mr X lived, could be come by in various ways. For instance, it was not wholly impossible (however unlikely) that somebody might die and leave him a million dollars. But even with a million dollars in pocket and all the pleasures of the world at hand for the taking, he would still have been harassed by the thought that his time, the most precious and the most precarious of his possessions, evaporated with terrifying speed; that he had done nothing with it, was doing nothing with it; and that he must learn how to light the light before darkness descended.

Mr X was thus, through no effort of his own, and indeed almost automatically, protected against the worst results of his own laziness and self-indulgence. But he was lazy and self-indulgent, just the same. He preferred the line of least resistance, avoided conclusions that might be troublesome to himself, and was tending, more and more, to treat the whole of the visible universe as a catering firm employed in his service. The mind he directed upon people and things in China, and upon the whole drama of revolution, had been originally a good one, acquisitive, perceptive, and retentive, but it was softened and discoloured beneath later influences, which constantly suggested that fundamental questions were not worth bothering about. The shock of general reality was what he needed, and he was about to receive it —a seismic disturbance of greater intensity and duration than he would have believed possible a few months before.

So much for Mr X.

7

Misselwitz of the New York *Times* was staying at the American Consulate.

'One thing you ought to do right away,' he said, 'is to go and see Mrs Prohme.'

'Who's that?'

'You know—you must have heard something about her. Red-headed gal, spitfire, mad as a hatter, complete Bolshevik. Works for Borodin.'

'Oh, yes, I remember. Somebody told me about her. American.'

'Yeah—American. But I don't know if she still has a passport. There was some talk about her giving up her nationality. You can't pay any attention to what she says—she's the wildest Bolshevik in town—but she's a nice girl, anyway, and you'll enjoy talking to her. I kid her along all the time, but she doesn't seem to mind. She can laugh, anyway, and that's more than most of these people can do.'

'O.K., let's go see her now.'

This conversation must have taken place early in May, soon after my arrival in Hankow; but it was so casual, and led to an event of such seeming inconsequence, that it was not even mentioned in my daybook. I remember it, however, far better than I do many of the circumstances that seemed worthy of careful recording. Misselwitz—Missi—led the way down a shaded side street in the Concession to a low building that served as the editorial office of the *People's Tribune*, the propaganda newspaper of the Hankow government. It appeared in two daily editions, one in Chinese and one in English, and I had already had the pleasure of reading some copies of it.

'Bill Prohme, her husband,' Missi went on, 'is another wild one—gets excited and shouts at you. He's in Shanghai now, I think. Fine Bolshevik pair. You ought to hear the way the navy people talk about 'em!'

'Are they Communists, do you mean?'

'Oh, sure—must be. Of course, they say they're not, but you can tell. Everybody that's got anything to do with this government is a Red, whether they admit it or not.'

We reached the office just as Mrs Prohme was coming out, and she stopped to talk to us on the step.

'Hello, Missi,' she said, laughing at him, 'what's the matter now? More outrages to report?'

'Oh, no,' he said. 'We just came round to get a little dose of propaganda. Any news?'

He introduced me, and we walked down the street with her. She was on her way home to dinner, and it was neither the time nor the place for any kind of serious conversation. She was slight, not very tall, with short red-gold hair and a frivolous turned-up nose. Her eyes were of the kind the anthropologists call 'mixed,' and could actually change colour with the changes of light, or even with changes of mood. Her voice, fresh, cool and very American, sounded as if it had secret rivulets of laughter running underneath it all the time, ready to come to the surface without warning. All in all, she was most unlike my idea of a 'wild Bolshevik,' and I told her so. She laughed. I had never heard anybody laugh as she did—it was the gayest, most unselfconscious sound in the world. You might have thought that it did not come from a person at all, but from some impulse of gaiety in the air.

'You've been listening to Missi,' she said. 'Don't believe anything Missi says about us. He thinks everybody in Hankow eats bourgeois babies for breakfast. As a matter of fact, I'm not sure what people mean when they say Bolshevik in this place. It seems to me a Bolshevik is anybody that doesn't want to make coolies out of the Chinese.'

'That's true enough,' said I. 'In Shanghai they all thought I was a Bolshevik because I talked to some Chinese and went to Nanking.'

She inspected me for the first time with sudden gravity—the kind of gravity in which there lurks a suggestion of suppressed laughter. I was shaved within an inch of my life, and was dressed in the white uniform of the foreigner in China.

'No,' she said soberly, 'you flatter yourself. I don't believe anybody could possibly think that you were a Bolshevik.'

'You ought to be glad I'm not,' said I. 'If I were I couldn't get anything printed in an American paper about your Revolution, and as it is, I do.'

'I know,' she said reflectively. 'You're what they call "fair to both sides." You sit on the fence and say, "On the other hand." How's the weather up there? Is it a nice fence?'

'It's comfortable,' I said, 'and I get a good view. How do you like it down there where you are? You don't see much, do you?'

'Oh, I'm all right,' she said. 'I can see over the fence if I try hard. But it's more interesting down here where the stuff is growing. I don't care about the view, anyway; I've seen it.'

This kind of sparring was not uncharacteristic of our talk even when I knew her much better. In the beginning of our acquaintance it was inevitable, for she could see at a glance all that I have been at such pains to explain in the preceding section—the character of Mr X, the American bourgeois as modified by Paris and London, with a goodish but lazy mind. She could see it at once, not only because it was to some degree apparent to anybody, but because her acquaintance with the original material of the character was so exact and complete that its discolorations and the subsequent shapes to which it had conformed became immediately obvious. She could easily, perhaps too easily, consign me to the pigeonhole where many of her own friends and relations belonged. She was from Chicago, had been educated at the University of Illinois, and must have known hundreds of our contemporaries of the same general social, economic and intellectual stamp as myself. Her instinctive attack or defence took the form of a quizzical flippancy, as it might with a contemporary (a brother or friend) known years ago in Illinois, who had, since the

days of remembered acquaintance, gone off in an opposing direction and acquired a set of ideas that she could not regard as
idiosyncratic.

Exactly the same thing was true, of course, on my side of the
argument. She was the kind of girl I had known all my life, but
she had, by the direction she had taken, acquired a purpose and
point of view that did not seem to me to belong to her. From the
first I was conscious of a great puzzle, the puzzle of why she was
doing this particular thing at this particular point of the world's
compass. The easiest suggestion for a solution was that she was a
romantic idealist, to whom a 'cause' was a necessity—any 'cause.'
Nobody, after one glance at her, could have supposed her to be
animated by ordinary selfish reasons. Her sincerity floated over
her like a banner. The hunger for a 'cause'—that was it: the kind
of thing that made so many nice American girls go out and get
themselves cracked over the head by policemen during the suf-
fragist campaigns. Some of these same nice girls, now that they
had the vote, were busy with other 'causes,' getting prohibition
either repealed or enforced, getting prisons reformed, or organizing the local ball for charity in their own home town. It must have
taken a peculiarly insatiable cause-hunger to bring a girl like this
into the exact middle of the Chinese Revolution, but except for
the difference in degree, it was the same motive as that which
caused ladies to spend a day or two in the suffrage jail in Washington and then come out and write books with titles like *Jailed for
Freedom*. Perhaps Mrs Prohme, too, would write a book about
her work in China—an excited volume in large print, with pictures, called *Up from Canton* or *China in Travail*.

These assumptions, however frivolous—and nobody knows
better than I how grotesquely frivolous they were—controlled my
mind in the earlier stages of our acquaintance and had their com-
plement in similar assumptions on her part. She had, in a sort of
way, 'known me all her life'; not only that, but I was an American
newspaper man from Paris (i.e., the worst kind), and she could
not take me seriously. She was obliged to assume, from what experience had taught her, that it was useless to expect a rational
and unshrinking examination of any subject from such a person as
myself. Neither of us was willing, therefore, to risk an attempt at

discussion of the central reality towards which we were both un-escapably magnetized—she because she already knew, or thought she knew, where it was, and did not believe me capable of the drastic enterprise of reaching it; I because I was profoundly uncertain and did not realize that the obscure necessity was felt in the same way by anybody else. There was a basis of perfect misunderstanding, with a superstructure of familiarity (sameness of culture, social and economic identity, Illinois, Illinois!); and as a result we could only throw our whole relationship into a key of sustained flippancy. Sometimes the flippancy wore thin, but it seldom broke down altogether. The most important conversation in my life—in the true sense, the only conversation I have ever had—began, and for months continued, as a kind of joke.

8

For a few months in 1927, a little more than half of the year, Hankow concentrated, symbolized and upheld the hope for a revolution of the world. Delegations came there from all over Europe, Asia and America to see for themselves what constituted Hankow's success, the surprise and delight of a generation of thwarted Communists. The great expectations of 1917 had come to nothing. Social revolution had failed in Europe, partly (as in Germany) because of the repressive power of the upper classes, partly (as in Austria) by the treachery of socialist leaders, and partly (as in Hungary) through isolation in the midst of reaction-ary forces. Revolutions in Asia, towards which some elements of organized Communism had directed their highest hope after Lenin's great speech in 1921, had either failed to materialize or had turned (as in Turkey) into purely nationalist-republican movements. Even in Russia it was no longer possible to conceal the life-and-death struggle of opposing elements in the Com-munist party: one that wished to fight for the world revolution and one that wished to advance it by concentration on the existing Soviet State. Communists everywhere regarded Hankow as not only the most conspicuous success of revolutionary technique since 1917, but as the test case: if its success could be extended and made permanent, the victory of the international (Trotzkyist) tendency was assured; but if Hankow failed, the militant world-revolutionists failed as well, and even in Russia the future became obscure.

You could not be in Hankow a week without being aware of all this. French Communists, German Communists, Hindoo Communists, British I. L. P. people, and numerous agitators responsible to the Komintern[1] gave the place a fine mixed flavour of international revolt. The fact that many of these revolutionists preferred not to appear in public, and liked to conceal their comings and goings as much as possible, made the phenomenon more significant. The beautiful carved-oak head of Manabendra Nath Roy, head of the Far Eastern section of the Komintern, could be seen across a restaurant table in effective contrast to the dishevelled pate of Jacques Doriot (the Doriot who had once caused a rumpus by trying to read a piece of my prose into the minutes of the Chamber of Deputies). Russians with ill-defined functions appeared and disappeared. One of them, who said he had been employed by the Komintern but was probably employed by a very different organization, aroused the treaty ports at about this time by publishing some 'revelations' and 'confessions' that represented the life of the agitators in China to be as full of adventures as a story by the Baroness Orczy. When I saw agitators they were not adventuring but talking—talking, talking, talking, as only theoretical Communists can talk when they see under their eyes the materials for a manipulation of history. The impression given by much of their conversation was like that of a modern composer's —too much theory and not enough music. For the music, the thing itself, I always had to go either to the Chinese or to Borodin.

Nobody could be blamed for assuming, after one glance round Hankow, that the government there and the movement that supported it were Red. The numerous foreign revolutionists were only the froth of the brew, but they caught the eye. Other immediately visible phenomena: frequent strikes, mass meetings and demonstrations; the workmen's place (the New World, it was called, a centre in the Russian and Italian style), and the conduct of

---

[1] The Third or Communist International, abbreviated to Komintern in the revolutionary vocabulary, will have to be mentioned rather frequently, and for the sake of brevity I shall call it by the name ordinarily used among its adherents.

students or trades unionists, gave the illusion of a highly organized social-revolutionary movement that might, at any moment, seize the machinery of production and proclaim the dictatorship of the proletariat.

But it didn't happen. Month after month passed and it didn't happen. Far away in Moscow Trotzky and Radek and others, consumed with impatience, were writing and speaking as if the Chinese Soviets already existed and had only been prevented from asserting themselves by the fatal short-sightedness of Borodin and the Kuomintang. In England, France, and the United States the opposite fallacy was held, and a Chinese Communist government was supposed to have been created by Borodin and the Kuomintang with Russian support. The European press referred to 'the Communist government at Hankow' as soberly as if the thing had been recognized by all parties and powers. Even now, seven years afterwards, it is not unusual to run across a reference to the 'Communist experiment at Hankow,' although the supreme characteristic of the Hankow experiment was that it was not Communist at all.

It is impossible to imagine a Communist state, or even a Communist experiment, in which private capital would be at liberty to maintain and fortify the domination of the employing classes over the workers. And yet this is exactly what happened at Hankow throughout the time of the so-called 'Communist' experiment. Private capital was at liberty to move where it liked, to lock out strikers, to emigrate, to shift and to re-invest. Neat little fortunes could be made in those days by buying depreciated property, and the entrepreneur who was tired of labour troubles had only to lock up his establishment and try his money on the New York stock market. The operations of exchange, credit and transfer were at all times free in Hankow—had to be, as will be shown hereafter. The processes of production were hampered, it is true, by strikes, and the labour committees did make some demands that foreshadowed a possible share in the control of industry, but it was all the kind of thing that could happen in a capitalistic country. What made it ominous to the entrepreneur and raised the terrified cry of 'Communism!' round the world, was the fact that it took place at the instigation of known Communists, supported by the Left Kuomintang and the Chinese Communist party, to the accompaniment of all the shouting and hallooing of revolutionary propaganda.

If the capitalist press of Europe thought Hankow 'a Communist experiment,' the Communists themselves did not. They hoped it might become a Communist experiment, sputtered with rage because it did not, exerted themselves in every way to push it in the desired direction, and, finally, when nothing seemed to be of any use, looked about them for somebody to blame. It was only natural that they, like the press of Europe and America, should have blamed the most conspicuous figure for everything that happened; and Borodin quietly slipped into the rôle of universal scapegoat for the Chinese Revolution. The Europeans held him responsible for its success, the Russians for its failure, the Chinese for its division into two parts. By the beginning of June he was not only the most famous, but the most execrated person in China, and the official representatives of the Komintern had no more love for him than had the official representatives of the Standard Oil Company.

'There is only one thing to do,' the Komintern people would say, 'and it should have been done in April. That is: Proclaim the Soviet!'

The fact that there were no Soviets in China made no difference to a full-fledged Komintern delegate from Moscow.

'There's just one thing to do,' the Standard Oil representative would say, 'and that's to call off all these strikes and patch it up with Chiang Kai-shek. It should have been done long ago.'

The fact that 'to call off all these strikes and patch it up with Chiang Kai-shek' would have meant abandonment of the Revolution was not the sort of fact a Standard Oil man could regard as relevant.

Between the unrealistic demands of the theoretical Communists and the reactionary demands of foreign capital Borodin was bound to become the scapegoat, not because he attempted to keep a middle course or believed in compromises, but because the situation did not permit a daring experiment in Communism. At first I, like most of my journalistic colleagues, assumed that Hankow was Red; then, seeing that the endless strikes led no-

where, that capital was as firmly entrenched as ever, and that the
proclamation of proletarian dictatorship was apparently never
going to be made, I assumed that Hankow was not Red—that its
character was that of a Left national revolution with no subversive
aims. It took a considerable acquaintance with the mood and
temper of the revolutionaries, as well as with their current literature and specific manifestations (speeches, mass meetings, party
and union decisions) to reveal the truth: that Hankow represented
the *desire* to create a Red China, frustrated at all important points
by the coalition of the great Western powers, which (in fact if not
in theory) occupied China with their armies and navies and protected all capital in the foreign banks. Hankow was as Red as
possible, but the limits of the possible were reached much too soon
to satisfy any thorough-going Communist. To put it into other
terms, the movement was subjectively but not objectively Leninist.[1]

The Red desire and the Red machinery were there. I could support these statements by details that no longer have much interest, but they need no such proof, for the facts are not contested.
In four years Borodin had transformed the whole Left (i.e., active)
part of the Kuomintang into a social-revolutionary movement,
with Chinese and Russian agitators indefatigably at work among
the workers and peasants. Why, then, did he hesitate to take the
final step in April or May and proclaim the Communist formula of

---

[1]A question of nomenclature arises in writing of these subjects. It should be explained that I call revolutionary quantities by the names they bear in revolutionary
literature. Many such names come from the Russian, but they may as well be
adopted into English when our language has no exact equivalents. Red, for instance, is the colour symbol used by partisans of the social revolution of the world,
whether they are party Communists or not. In Russian the word Red (*krassny*)
has overtones that it does not possess in English, and for this reason it has always
been popularly extended far beyond the mere meaning of colour. The Red Square
in Moscow was so named centuries before the birth of Lenin. A bright, charming
or attractive girl can be called 'red' in Russian no matter what her complexion.
The word is almost an equivalent of 'bright' and suggests the general mood of hope
as well as the particular hope for a proletarian revolution. I use it not only because
it is a commonly accepted word in revolutionary literature, but because it includes
ideas and shades of meaning that are excluded from the rigid word Communist.
The word Communist, as I use it, refers only to members of the international
Communist party and their system of thought and action. Having served warning,
I shall proceed on this principle without further explanation.

All Power to the Soviets'? Why, having gone so far and threatened so much, did he not take his revolutionary machine (the Chinese Communists and the Left Kuomintang of which they were minority members) and with it defy the world? The question was being asked by exasperated Communists everywhere, most of all in Moscow, and, as it turned out, the fate of the Communist party in every country hung upon the answer. It was a question that was asked even in the most bitterly anti-revolutionary circles, and I well remember a pause in a poker game one night in Hankow, when a local magnate (American) turned to me and said: 'When is Borodin going to go the whole hog? I wish he'd hurry up and get it over.'

All these people, Communist or reactionary, in every shade of thought from Trotzky to Rockefeller and back again, seemed to think that Borodin could make exactly what he pleased out of the Chinese Revolution, or at least with the more advanced wing represented by the Hankow government. And Borodin himself?

He had no such illusions. Calm, slow and thoughtful, without a trace of personal ambition or egotism, he examined his problem as if it had been one in his favourite game, chess. He could do certain things, and certain results would ensue; he could do certain other things, and certain other results would ensue; but there remained a large class of things that he could not do at all. Two things that he unquestionably could not do—that Trotzky himself could not have done—were: first, abolish the navies of America, England, Japan and France; and, second, make flexible and resolute revolutionary instruments overnight out of the mass of half-awakened Chinese workers and peasants (the '*Lumpumproletariat*'). He knew better than anybody else exactly how far the process of political education had gone even in the most advanced labour unions, and just how much sacrifice it was possible to ask of people who had only begun to understand the principles of revolutionary action. And as for the navies—! He had only to look out of his window to see the river choked with them, their guns trained on the shore, their officers and men openly, boastfully anxious for a chance to 'clean up the mess,' as they put it, with machine gun, rifle and bayonet.

These were the realities with which Borodin lived every day

of his life in China—with which he had lived for three years. Trotzky, the most brilliant technician of the Russian Revolution, its hero and its historian, was a long way from China; and although he undoubtedly knew everything there was to know about the subject on paper (as did Radek, Bukharin and the rest), he was betrayed into absurdities by the fact that he had no practical acquaintance with the material. Borodin should have proclaimed a Soviet Republic at Hankow in April, should he? Well, exactly, how?

Let us develop the hypothesis. A proclamation of power to the Soviets is made, the bourgeoisie disenfranchised, the machinery of production, credit and commerce taken over. What happens then is that Chinese capital flies to the foreign banks—such Chinese capital as is not already there—and half the productive property raises foreign flags. (This is not guesswork, for the thing has happened, is constantly happening whenever political events make Chinese capital slightly nervous.) Then, to give effect to your proletarian dictatorship, you *must* confiscate properties belonging in whole or in part to foreigners. Not to do so would be to make Communism impossible. But the moment you confiscate or seriously interfere with any property belonging to foreigners you are desperately, irretrievably in the soup; the foreign navies fill the river, the foreign governments are irate, the foreign marines are in your streets, and within twenty-four hours your Communist government, your dictatorship of the proletariat, has been drowned in blood.

Men who have not actually seen the Chinese river cities can scarcely believe how easy it is for the British, Japanese, French and American navies to overawe them. All these cities are built along the river, depend upon the river, exist for and through the river. And the river is no more Chinese than I am. Its waters are navigable even for large cruisers up to Hankow, and for gunboats up to Chungking and Ichang. The parts of China bordering the Yangtze-kiang, therefore, cannot be considered independent except in theory, and if maps were made according to realities instead of according to political fiction, the map of China would show a country impaled upon its terrible foreign river.

Borodin saw the facts as clearly as if they had been diagrammed on a blackboard. He knew that riparian China was at the mercy of the foreign ships, and that genuine independence for China could only be hoped for when the navies of Europe could be kept out of the Yangtze-kiang. He had intended to pass over Hankow and reach Peking: that was his plan in the autumn of 1926, and if Chiang Kai-shek had carried out the decisions of the Central Executive Committee (decisions made upon Borodin's advice) no attack would have been made on Nanking and Shanghai until the whole of China had been conquered and united. But Chiang Kai-shek, to whom Nanking and Shanghai had long been a tempting plum, disobeyed his instructions, took the ripe plum when he could get it, and satisfied himself, afterwards, by declaring his independence of the central organization and Borodin. The Yangtze-kiang, which has always defeated every popular revolutionary movement in China, triumphed again in 1927, and in April and May—the very months when, according to the Trotzky school of thought, Borodin should have forced or persuaded his Chinese clients to proclaim a proletarian dictatorship —the Chinese Revolution already lay in ruins.

I saw Borodin frequently. As I knew him better, and overcame the feelings of insignificance and frivolity that had originally oppressed me in his presence, I was able to discuss anything with him. Later on, when he was sick in bed with a serious attack of malaria, I used to go to see him every day; and although the conversation during these visits ranged over a wide field, involving many subjects that had nothing to do with the Chinese Revolution, the intellectual resources he displayed were at all times those of a trained Bolshevik—his cast of mind was Leninist. Whether he was discussing a new book (*Elmer Gantry* was one that aroused his interest just then) or an old political theory, reminiscing or analyzing, telling a story or advancing a hypothesis, he took 'the long view.' I had never before examined such a mind at close quarters, and there is no doubt that I was profoundly impressed by its clarity and consistency. But I do not believe that the influence of Borodin shaped any of my opinions; I was too old and too independent to accept other people's ideas about phenomena that I could easily observe for myself. What did happen was something a little more complicated. In Borodin I found an older, better

-disciplined, better trained and more experienced intelligence than my own: it had already traversed regions that still lay before me. Sometimes Borodin was able to disentangle a principle from the confusion of external events and show it to me; sometimes he was able to point out a historical direction or a prevailing tendency. He never made the slightest attempt to impose his opinions—often, indeed, he talked as if I were not in the room. He was concerned with the truth, and his object in conversation was to extract and demonstrate it. If, therefore, I found every conversation with him illuminating, and approached, in the end, more nearly to his view of the Chinese Revolution than to any other, it was not because of any personal influence he exercised, but because the truth, for me, lay on his side.

There were plenty of other influences in Hankow, and I was subjected at one time or another to most of them, but they missed their target in me. Eugene Chen used to address me in long, hifalutin sentences, even when we were quite alone and I knew him a good deal better: they left me cold. The American and British business men, the naval officers, the foreigners in general, harangued me on the subject of their grievances, and many Chinese revolutionists did likewise. But among the foreigners the personal motives were so obvious that it was impossible to treat their statements with respect. No one of them could see beyond the end of his own nose. I enjoyed playing poker with the business men and hearing their opinions leak out as they dealt the cards, or drinking whisky with the navy people and sampling the ferocity of their desire to murder the Chinese population; but such diversions were, after all, only diversions.

The Chinese revolutionists impressed me often by their self-abnegation, their willingness to endure and to persevere, their loyalty to ideas that meant life to China even though they might mean death to the individual. But no single Chinese revolutionist ever set my mind on new paths, as I believe Borodin did. One reason was that I never met the intellectual leaders of the Chinese Revolution. Sun Yat-sen died three years before I went to China, and his written works seemed to me to lack logic—to lack, above all, a genuinely long view. The other great revolutionist of modern China, Li Ta-chao, founder and head of the Chinese

Communist party, was strangled to death by the reactionaries in Peking before I had been in China a month. The leaders I did know all professed to follow the teachings either of Sun Yat-sen or of Li Ta-chao, with, occasionally, a Confucian or Christian coloration. Some of them were admirable in character, like Mme Sun Yat-sen; others were striking or picturesque, like Wang Ching-wei, the type of the fiery, romantic revolutionary; still others engaged my personal liking and respect, like T. V. Soong; but it happened that I never met a Chinese intellectual who could put his view of history into terms of absolute truth as Borodin did.

Even so, it was not Borodin alone, but the Chinese Revolution with Borodin as its interpreter, that gave me my first perception of the spirit of revolution in general. Borodin alone, talking in a vacuum, would have been merely a Communist intellectual. It was in his relation to the whole mass movement in China, the immense and complicated disturbance of which he was temporarily both the directing genius and the interpreter, that he acquired grandeur. His calm may have been a native characteristic, but it seemed singularly noble in the midst of confusion and danger; his political theory may have been as simple as geometry (they taught it, after all, at the Lenin Institute in Moscow) but it seemed profound and irrefragable when it was seen to support the weight of otherwise meaningless events. He exemplified in his own person, and pointed out in the phenomena around him, the peculiar qualities of intellectual consistency, social philosophy, selflessness and determination that combine to form something I have called (for lack of a more exact term) the revolutionary spirit.

That spirit was abroad in Hankow from the time the Cantonese armies entered the city until the collapse of the revolutionary government on July 5th. It was to be seen in Chinese and Russians, Left Kuomintang organizers and Communists, workmen, students and agitators—not in all of them, of course, but in a large enough number to confirm the existence of something new in the confusion of China. There were Communist students, sometimes of rich families, who became coolies so as to be able to organize the coolies for revolution. There were educated Chinese girls who risked death in the effort to tell the workers and peasants who their real enemies were. One of these girls—we all knew her in Hankow—was disembowelled by Chiang Kai-shek's soldiers on June 21st in Hangchow for saying that the Nanking war lord did not represent the party or principles of Sun Yat-sen. Her intestines were taken out and wrapped around her body while she was still alive. Girls and boys were beheaded for saying what they believed; men were hung up in wooden cages to die of hunger and thirst or were broken on the rack. Little Phyllis Li, the seventeen-year-old daughter of the hero Li Ta-chao, was tortured by Chang Tso-lin's men for three days and three nights before they mercifully strangled her, and in the whole time she told them nothing. The horrors of the counter-revolution were not unexpected: these young Chinese knew what awaited them and went ahead just the same. The impulse that made them offer their lives for the cause was not a suicidal, neurotic yearning for Nirvana, as it might have been in similar crises in India or Japan. Such varieties of mystic ardour were, so far as I ever saw or heard, unknown to China. The Chinese operated on a colder and purer conviction, the belief that courageous sacrifice in the service of an idea was the best means of propagating that idea. The individual was, as so often in China, sacrificed to the race, and the young men and girls died for generations unborn.

The Chinese surpassed all others in such extreme forms of heroic devotion, and for every case of treachery and cowardice in the dark days of their Revolution there was at least one case of loyal courage. But the other agitators, in particular the Russians, could produce evidences of the same spirit in their own way. It was a less obviously heroic way, as the Russians believed it to be a revolutionist's duty to save his life for the cause if he could. A Russian agitator was supposed to live for the Revolution, not to die for it. Consequently he had to change his name and appearance, his passport and his ostensible business, and evade danger even on occasions when he might have preferred to stay and face it. There were Russian agitators in China whose lives had been as adventurous as those described in the 'revelations' printed in the British-Chinese press, although not quite in the same penny-dreadful style.

Borodin showed iron control of the personal motive during the weeks in which his wife, Fanny Borodin, was imprisoned by the northern reactionaries. Mme Borodin was on her way to Vladivostok to join him when she was arrested by soldiers of Chang Chung-chang, the Shantung war lord. Chang kept her in prison for some weeks and then turned her over to his feudal superior, the Manchurian bandit Chang Tso-lin, who governed at Peking with Japanese support. Chang Tso-lin was as bloodthirsty a tyrant as any modern China has seen, and his first decision was to strangle Mme Borodin without ceremony. He was dissuaded from this course by some of the foreigners in Peking, who suggested that it would make a better impression on the outside world if the lady had a trial.[1] I shall come to the end of Fanny Borodin's story later on, but the part that here concerns us is the effect of these events on Borodin in Hankow during April and May. He betrayed no anger and no excitement, in spite of the personal nature of the attack. He pointed out simply that Mme Borodin had never been engaged in Communist party work in China, that she took no part in politics, and that Chang Tso-lin's vengeance was vicarious—the old *hung-hutze*[2] was unable to get at the real object of his ire, and took it out on an innocent hostage; that she was in prison and in danger of death for one reason only: that her name was Borodin.

The ardent but impersonal devotion to which I have applied the name 'revolutionary spirit' was apparent in many characters and incidents in Hankow, and I have named only a few of them. There was one other, more important to me, as it turned out, than all the rest, a more significant and memorable example of that spirit than any in my experience. I mean Rayna Prohme. The flippancy in which our acquaintance had begun continued for weeks, but before long I began to have an uneasy feeling that my judgment of her character had been ludicrously inaccurate. I made a number of small discoveries that shook my first ideas. She had no enthusiasm for 'causes' in general, had never been the kind of romantical busybody I had at first assumed her to be. She

[1]The American Senator Bingham, from Connecticut, was one of those who were said to have influenced the old marshal in favour of a form of trial.

[2]A *hung-hutze* ('red beard') is a robber chief on the Manchurian plains. Chang Tso-lin had been a *hung-hutze* before the Japanese discovered his usefulness.

had had a sound education in economics and sociology; her interest in social revolution had been aroused at an age when I was still learning new steps in the fox trot. She had already acquired a remarkable revolutionary past in the service of the Kuomintang, and she enjoyed, in the spring of 1927, the confidence of many Chinese Left leaders. She not only edited the official newspaper, but had a general consultative usefulness to the Hankow régime in matters of propaganda designed to appeal to foreigners. Borodin, Mme Sun Yat-sen, Eugene Chen and Sun Fo treated her opinions with respect. I still could not take her seriously as a revolutionist—it was like expecting me to believe my cousin Cecilia, with whom I grew up, had suddenly turned into a Red—but I had to concede that this revolutionary phase, however temporary it might be, was an interesting and unexpected development in the character of a charming American girl. I fell into the habit of going to see her every day, and as I knew her better I came to depend heavily on that daily visit for many things—not only, that is, for the pleasure of conversation with somebody who so thoroughly spoke my own language, and not only for the delight of her high spirits, the refreshment of her laughter, but also for the daily necessities of my job as a journalist, to learn the news and to learn, so far as possible, what the news meant. For a peculiarity of Rayna Prohme's, I found out, was her ingrained dislike of lying. She was a very bad liar indeed, and although it was often a part of her duty to make things appear under a somewhat artificial light, her candour was such that she did not succeed in doing so, at least with me. I could always tell when she was saying something she did not herself believe: her looks gave her away. She took her instructions from Borodin and Chen; and although Borodin had a high respect for the truth and avoided deviations from it as scrupulously as anybody I have ever known in public life, the same could not have been said of Mr Chen. Consequently, for propaganda purposes, Rayna Prohme was often obliged to write and say things her own candour resented. The official newspaper contained these statements, but she could never make them convincingly enough in conversation. After a bit she gave up attempting to give me official versions of anything, and either told the plain truth or else confessed, with a wry smile, that she could not speak. It was no small thing, in a place like Hankow and a profession like mine, to know somebody in whom I could believe without reserve.

Bill Prohme, her husband, returned to Hankow after I had been there a week or so, but we did not hit it off as well as might have been expected. His violent revolutionary enthusiasm resented my bourgeois lethargy, my innumerable changes of white silk clothes, my Scotch whisky and Egyptian cigarettes. In turn I disliked his excitability, his refusal to argue a subject through in a calm and logical manner; I suspected that his revolutionary convictions were not sufficiently grounded in economic and social science—that he was an emotional Red, if a Red at all; and that his presence in China in his present rôle was due to the accident of his marriage to Rayna Prohme. Partly for these reasons, and partly because his absences and illnesses made our meetings infrequent, I never knew him well in Hankow. It was only long after I had left China and Russia that I learned to respect his intelligence and value his friendship. During the period with which this chapter deals, he was a rather shadowy figure to me, and his name does not appear in the notes I put into my useful daybook.

Rayna's assistant was an American woman journalist who regarded every moment I spent in the office of the *People's Tribune* as a calamity. Under these circumstances a more sensitive subject might have stayed away, but I didn't. The daily conversations with Rayna Prohme had become such a necessity that when a day passed without my seeing her at all (as happened twice when she was ill) it left an extraordinary feeling of blankness and malaise. This being so, it is strange to remember, and stranger still to record, that I never understood her importance to me until months later. I was as stupid as M. Jourdain with his prose; I had already passed under the most powerful and significant personal influence to which I have ever been subjected, but I did not know it.

Hankow, then—to sum up—was a marvellous revolutionary spectacle, in which the courage and devotion of the Chinese agitators, the skill of the Russians, the high hope and frenzied determination of the workers, and the individual splendour of characters like those of Mme Sun Yat-sen, Borodin and Rayna Prohme, combined to give me a glimpse into a new world. In its spirit, at least, if not in its accomplishment, it was the world of Lenin. That the dead bones of economics and sociology could be animated with such irresistible life was something I would never have believed six months before in Paris, when the principal event of the century had seemed to be the anniversary performances of *Pelléas et Mélisande* at the Opéra Comique. But although this glimpse into the world of Lenin did supply an electrical thrill, and the characters of the spectacle aroused my sincerest admiration, I still did not surrender to the logic of their being. It seemed to me that the whole revolutionary system of thought reposed upon a number of assumptions that defied proof. This became apparent when the fundamental question of revolution was put into the form of a simple syllogism, like this:

A controlled egalitarian economy is desirable;
Revolution is the only way to obtain a controlled egalitarian economy;
Therefore Revolution is desirable.

The only part of such a syllogism that needed no defence was the major term *desirable*. The major premise, although probable enough, could not possibly be proved because models for a controlled egalitarian economy did not exist, even in Russia. The minor premise was equally shaky; it might be true or not, but it was not susceptible of proof. The conclusion, therefore, had to be taken on faith, or (at best) as the result of two probabilities.

The logic of revolution can be put into other and more persuasive syllogisms than this; indeed, at a later time, Rayna Prohme and I used to spend hours trying to get the fundamental question into its barest and simplest terms; but during the Hankow period the syllogism I have given seemed to me the correct one, and no matter how much my sympathy and admiration were engaged on the side of the revolutionaries, I could not share their conviction. As I have said, the one indisputable thing was that something was desirable in a world of misrule; something that could bring order out of chaos had to be found if the human race was to justify its pretence of intelligence. But whether or no the desirable something was revolution did not seem to me susceptible of proof, and the revolutionary spectacles that moved me most deeply were still only that and nothing more.

9

I went down to Shanghai in June. The purpose of the trip was, of course, to see what was going on, and from that point of view it was uninteresting; not only did I see little, but whatever I had seen would have been of no value to my newspapers, engrossed, as they were, with the affairs of Colonel Lindbergh. But there were incidental results of the Shanghai journey, and two incidents of the week amuse me still when I think of them.

One was a luncheon given by the proprietor of the *North China Daily News*. The guest of honour was the colonel of the Grenadier Guards, Lord Gort, a pleasant and modest soldier with a brilliant war record. (He had won the V. C., the rarest of military distinctions, seldom given to persons of his rank.) To meet the distinguished guest came the cream of the Shanghai merchants, a prosperous and important company.

I had scarcely been inside that hospitable house for ten minutes before I realized a number of things. One was that I had changed a good deal since my last visit to Shanghai; another was that I could never again take the Shanghai *taipans*—big merchants—seriously. Their strange remoteness from the country on whose edge they perched had never struck me so forcibly; when they talked about China (as, of course, they constantly did) they revealed a point of view that now seemed to me fantastic. Many of them had been born in Shanghai, and they all knew the Chinese very well in the rôle of servants; but as for any other knowledge or sympathy, they might as well have been people from a distant planet. I had never been sympathetic to the Shanghai point of view, but at least it had been arguable before. Now it was only funny.

In the middle of lunch Lord Gort started to ask me questions about Hankow, and particularly about Borodin, who was always the centre of curiosity for foreigners. I answered that I knew Borodin rather well and both liked and admired him. If I had taken off all my clothes and jumped on the table I could not have shocked the company more. (Not Gort, of course—he was a soldier, fresh from England, and had none of the Shanghai prejudices.) One of the *taipans*, looking rather as if he thought he had not heard correctly, asked: 'But what sort of fellow *is* Borodin, then?'

I answered this at some length, and then returned to my food with a feeling that the subject had been disposed of. But the *taipan* was still puzzled. I had spoken of Borodin's mind, which was not at all the sort of thing the *taipan* wanted to hear.

'But that's not what I mean,' he said, leaning forward from the other side of the table, 'I mean, what sort of fellow *is* he? I mean, is he a *gentleman?*'

I was afraid to laugh for fear that I might not be able to stop.

The other incident of my Shanghai visit—not so much comic as tragi-comic—was my effort to bring T. V. Soong back to Hankow with me.

Hankow needed T. V. badly. The ability of that young man to inspire confidence, to make the books balance, to coax money out of hiding places, was an ability nobody at Hankow possessed. Nanking needed him for exactly the same reasons. In Hankow the financial situation was beginning to be desperate. The bank notes of the Central Bank of China (to which T. V. nostalgically referred as 'my bank notes') had been falling in value so rapidly that the point of worthlessness would certainly be reached before long. When I was ready to go to Shanghai I asked Rayna Prohme if I could do anything for her there.

'You can bring T. V. back,' she said.

'All right,' said I confidently, 'I will.'

Borodin did not ask me to do this, but as I was taking my leave of him he remarked that it would be an excellent thing if T. V. returned. And T. V.'s lovely sister, Mme Sun Yat-sen, gave me a note to give to him; she too remarked that she wished he would return to his post in Hankow.

I thought the enterprise would be easy—all I had to do was to bring T. V. along with me under some kind of assumed name, as my interpreter. Travelling in my cabin on a British boat he would have been safe enough, for the boldest of Chiang Kai-shek's soldiers would never have dared break in. But in taking the idea so lightly I reckoned without T. V.

When I went to see him in Shanghai he seemed ready to fall in with the plan. He was living in Sun Yat-sen's house in the Rue Molière, and after his years of work for the Kuomintang he was miserable in idleness. He could see—or said he could see—that the true inheritor of the Kuomintang ideal was the Hankow government, and not Chiang Kai-shek's military dictatorship. He had steadily refused to join Chiang Kai-shek's government in spite of persuasion and threats. The house was constantly watched by spies (it is one of the houses that are under observation at every hour of the day and night, as it has always been since it was built); and T. V. was very nervous. He did not dare go outside the French Concession and the International Settlement, for Chiang Kai-shek's soldiers were everywhere in the Chinese city, and they would have seized upon him in a moment. His alternatives, if Chiang Kai-shek ever caught him, were simple: the Ministry of Finance or the gaol. I do not believe he would have been put to death, but he was not at all sure of it. He was, in fact, in a rare state of funk, and the suggestion I brought from Hankow seemed to offer him a way out of all his troubles. He agreed almost at once, asked me to take a ticket for him in my cabin in the name of Mr Wong of Canton, and displayed a lively curiosity about the course of events at Hankow.

On the next day he had changed his mind. In the interim he had talked to his mother, his sisters, his brother-in-law, and they were a fundamentally reactionary family.

'There's no point in my going to Hankow,' he said, worried and nervous. 'You see the truth is that I'm not a social revolutionary. I don't like revolution, and I don't believe in it. How can I balance a budget or keep a currency going if the labour policy frightens every merchant or factory owner into shutting up shop? I can't make the Central Executive Committee understand. . . . Look at what they've done with my bank notes, my beautiful bank notes! . . . They've been inflated out of existence. . . .'

'Your sister said——'

'Oh, my sister . . . ! My sister doesn't understand. Nobody understands how difficult it is. How do I know I won't be dragged out of the Ministry of Finance and torn to pieces by the mob the day after I get to Hankow? How do I know I can stop the currency from falling? Nothing can be done if they keep on encouraging strikes and mass meetings. They get the people into a state of excitement in which they expect everything, and they're bound to be disappointed. . . . And I'm not popular, mind you. I've never been popular. The mob doesn't like me. They would have killed me last winter if the soldiers hadn't come in time. . . . They all know I don't like strikes and mass meetings. . . . What could *I* do at Hankow?'

On that day he was definitely anti-revolutionary. But on the next he had switched again—took a more hopeful view of the possibility of persuading the Central Executive Committee to modify the labour policy; yearned over his beautiful bank notes; agreed that the Nanking régime was only a disguised form of personal dictatorship, and that Hankow still represented, in spite of the Communists, the pure party tradition of the Kuomintang.

These fluctuations of sentiment ruled his mind throughout the week. It was the most vivid illustration of the typical Liberal hesitancy I had ever seen, or have seen since. T. V. wanted to work for China; he proved it afterwards in illogical fashion by entering the government of Chiang Kai-shek, of which he could not have approved. But at this time he was unable to reach a decision that remained stable for as much as an hour. I had always liked him, and liked him even more as I watched his painful struggle to make up his mind, but I could hardly regard him as a statesmanlike figure. Nothing but accident—the accident that made him a brother of Mme Sun Yat-sen—could explain his connection with a militant revolutionary movement. He was one of those politicians who might have been happy and useful in private life, but could only, in the uncongenial surroundings of a 'career,' be forever harassed and afraid.

When the day on which I was to sail for Hankow came round, T. V. happened to be in one of his pro-Hankow states of mind. We made all our arrangements with great care. I was to leave the Majestic Hotel at midnight in a Rolls-Royce car as big as a house, which I sometimes rented in Shanghai. I was to draw all the blinds on leaving the hotel. (I assured T. V. that I was not under observation, but he saw spies everywhere.) The car was to take me to the Rue Molière, drop me at the corner some distance from the

Sun Yat-sen house, and then, after circling about in the French Concession for a few minutes, was to creep quietly into the Sun Yat-sen garden, as if to call for me. When I got into it again I was to be accompanied by Mr Wong of Canton, my interpreter, but in the darkness the spies would presumably not see him.

The first part of the programme went off well enough. I saw no watchers in the Rue Molière, but no doubt they were on duty. The rest of the events of that night must have given the spies a queer puzzle and a good deal of leg work; for T. V. had changed his mind again.

'I can't go,' he said the moment he came down the stairs. 'I can't do it. I'm sorry I've caused you all this trouble, but I simply cannot do it.'

He was excited and very jumpy. I sat down on a stair step in the hall and gaped with surprise. That very afternoon his mind had been conclusively made up, and now—!

'What am I to say to your sister?' I asked.

We must have talked for an hour round and about the subject while T. V. paced the floor and I sat wearily on the stairs. Suddenly he reached for his hat.

'Let's go talk to my family,' he said.

We clambered into the Rolls-Royce and made a round of visits at about one o'clock in the morning. I took no part in the conversations with the Soong family, and can only imagine how they all urged T. V. not to cross the Rubicon. One of the persons to whom he spoke was his hyper-Americanized sister Mei-ling, who afterwards incomprehensibly married Chiang Kai-shek. Another was Dr H. H. Kung, his brother-in-law. After some hours of argument T. V. came out of the recesses of the Kung house and spoke —dejectedly, gloomily.

'It's all settled,' he said. 'I'm not going. Tell my sister I shall write to her. I'm sorry you were troubled for nothing.'

I drove him home in the immense, hearse-like car, and neither of us said a word. I was exhausted from the sheer indecision of the proceedings, and he was very gloomy. I have never seen him since, and the events of that night were to give my final impression of Soong Tse-vung both as an individual and as a type, the honest Liberal at sea between opposing shores.

Perhaps T. V. will think it inexcusable of me to have told this story. I have never told it before, and only tell it now because it belongs in the record of these events as a significant detail that was not without its influence on history. The line of journalistic license rightly excluded such a private happening as this from the light of print; but history is a different matter, and this book is, or sets out to be, a history. And besides, if T. V. dislikes the story enough he has only to deny it. There are still a great many people who believe official denials.

10

The idea of smuggling T. V. Soong through Chiang Kai-shek's blockade and restoring him to his place in Hankow may seem a strangely partisan one for an American newspaper correspondent to entertain, but at the time I was, or believed I was, animated by the desire to 'get a good story.' Yet when I returned to Hankow without T. V., and reported the circumstances to Borodin, Mme Sun Yat-sen and Rayna Prohme, I perceived, rather abruptly, that my feelings in the matter had been partisan all along. There was no harm in this, so long as nothing but my individual feelings were concerned, but I began to be conscience-stricken about my New York office. There was a danger that I might get so interested in the fate of Hankow that the purposes for which I had been sent to China at considerable expense would be forgotten. I cast about for some definite enterprise that might yield material of interest for my newspapers, and decided that I ought to go to Changsha and see the first Chinese Soviet in operation.

The Chinese Communists were in control in Changsha and had proclaimed the dictatorship of the proletariat some weeks before. The movement was premature and badly organized; reports from Hunan were confused, but the embryo Soviet was clearly not doing very well; the Hankow government was unable to support or patronize too openly a movement with which it was actually in sympathy. All this made the position of Hunan obscure, and I had wanted some weeks before to go and investigate it for myself. I have ever since regretted that I did not do so while there was still time, for that Changsha Soviet was the beginning of a Chinese Communist state that was to endure, against innumerable difficulties and with many territorial changes, for years.

But I had not been back in Hankow long before the approaching catastrophe became evident; and with the fall of the government in sight—the end of the Kuomintang-Communist alliance, the end of the worldwide hope for an immediate social revolution in China—it would have been foolish to go away. My superiors in New York had repeatedly asked me to ignore the news and write my personal impressions, but it seemed to me that the collapse of the Hankow government, with all it represented to the world at large, was an event too significant to miss. And I knew it was coming long before it happened—so long before that I did not dare put it into my cables to America. A piece of news that is one month early is as worthless as a piece of news one month late.

My daybook records, on June 21st: 'Situation very serious. Borodin ill, Feng Yü-hsiang cutting capers. The end is in sight.'

And on July 2d: 'The Government here is doomed. It will fall very soon, any day. God knows what will happen to Rayna.'

This is, by the way, the first time Rayna Prohme's name appears in my notes.

The fall of Hankow was to determine the conduct of the Communist International for years afterwards; it was to turn the mind of the Russian Soviet government away from the militant internationalism of Trotzky to the national socialism of Stalin; it was to drive the genuinely subversive or revolutionary forces in China underground for a desperate struggle that has not yet fully come to the surface; it was to chasten the impatience of Communists all over the world more than any single event since 1917. In view of these proved results, most of which I could obscurely foresee (with the help of Borodin) before the event had taken place, I was determined to cling to Hankow to the last possible moment, to see the drama played out, to be in at the death. In doing so I got myself into an awkward position vis à vis my New York office, for I was unable to explain such complicated affairs in cablegrams at a dollar a word, especially as nothing had yet happened. In the end, as shall be told, I was peremptorily ordered off to find 'personal adventures' and missed the actual catastrophe at Hankow by ten days.

The Hankow government lasted approximately three months after the rebellion of Chiang Kai-shek. It had retained the loyalty of twenty-one out of the thirty-three members of the Central Executive Committee of the Kuomintang. It was supported by the greater part of the civilian Kuomintang and clearly represented the later tradition of Sun Yat-sen; but in military force it was weak. Its generals were not trustworthy, and the best of them could not compare in ability or popularity to Chiang Kai-shek. A series of rebellions against the civilian authority of Hankow took place in April and May. General Li Chi-sen revolted at Canton, the home of the Kuomintang, and proclaimed a government of his own; Hunan, half Communist and half reactionary, was almost detached from Hankow's control; the armies of Szechuan began to move down from the west.

A god from the machine was badly needed, and the Russians undertook to provide one in the person of Feng Yü-hsiang. Feng, the 'Christian General' (save the mark!), had been driven out of Peking in March, 1926, by Chang Tso-lin, and had gone to Moscow for a year. Now he suddenly appeared in Mongolia with an army, marched across Shansi without encountering resistance, and entered Honan as the saviour of the Kuomintang. Everything he possessed, from his army to the shirt on his back, he owed to the Russians, and it never seems to have occurred to them that he would forget it. The news of his progress across Honan was received with rejoicing in Hankow. The *People's Tribune* called his forces the 'new revolutionary army,' and the labour unions and Communists celebrated his every 'victory' with a mass meeting.

As a matter of fact he had no victories. He marched across Honan without difficulty; the elegant Fengtien troops of Chang Tso-lin, of which so much had been written in the foreign press, retired before him. His Mohammedan cavalry entered Chengchow, the capital of the province, just as the last of the northerners vanished up the railway towards Peking. He was now in control of the central province of China, and from Chengchow, on the Peking–Hankow railway, he could strike either at his friends in Hankow or his enemies in Peking.

He did neither. To the consternation of the Russians and even some of the Chinese (who should have known their 'Christian General' by this time), he went into a conference with Chiang Kai-shek and declared himself opposed to the whole policy of the Left Kuomintang. His game was, as it always had been, to carve out a principality for himself and exploit it. He really supported neither Hankow nor Nanking, but his performance removed the last hope for an assertion of Hankow's authority and the survival of the revolutionary government.

The 'Christian General' started to bombard Hankow at about this time (early June) with an extraordinary series of telegrams in which the utmost cynicism was combined with the formulas of old-fashioned Chinese 'face-saving' and political politeness. He suggested, for example, that 'Mr Borodin, who has already resigned, should return to his own country.' Borodin had never resigned, but these forms of speech are usual when one war lord drives out another, and Feng Yü-hsiang was a war lord through and through. He pointed out, with exquisite courtesy, that 'those members of the Wuhan government who may wish to go abroad for their health should be allowed to do so.'

The episode of Feng Yü-hsiang seemed to me a piece of mediæval buffoonery that might have discouraged the most ardent believer in the Chinese Revolution. What was to be done in a civilization harmonized to such extremes that an illiterate coolie with an army at his back could dominate the relationships of capital and labour, of men and government, of parties and programmes?

Borodin retained his calm. Sick in bed and stuffed with quinine as he was, he kept his emotionless objectivity and his faith in the cause he served.

'I shall remain until the last possible minute,' he told me one day. 'When I am forced to go, I shall go. But do not suppose that the Chinese Revolution is ending, or that it has failed in any but the most temporary sense. It will go back underground. It will become an illegal movement, suppressed by counter-revolution and beaten down by reaction and imperialism; but it has learned how to organize, how to struggle. Sooner or later, a year, two years, five years from now, it will rise to the surface again. It may be defeated a dozen times, but in the end it must conquer. The revolutionary impulse is profound in China, and the country is filled with wonderful revolutionary instruments. For every one of those instruments destroyed by the war lords two or three new ones will arise. What has happened here will not be forgotten.'

He seldom discussed specific dangers until they were past, but on that particular day it was known that the city was almost defenceless. An army from the west (a Szechuan force to which Ho Chien and a Kuomintang army had 'gone over') was very near, and it was currently believed that Hankow would be captured that night. I told Borodin what I had heard and asked him what he was going to do. He smiled, looked out the window, and replied without any evidence of feeling.

'We have asked all or part of the "Iron army" to return to defend the city,' he said, 'but if it does not come, the city will be captured. After that, who knows?'

He turned back to me.

'A few heads will come off,' he said mildly.

That one of the first heads to come off would be his own was understood, but he appeared to face the possibility without excitement.

On that same day (it was July 1st) an extraordinary conversation took place in Rayna Prohme's office. I had gone in there to talk to her and had found Mme Sun Yat-sen. We sat in the back office and drank tea. Mme Sun had resisted persuasion and pressure for the last three months from her own family. It was no light thing for any Chinese woman to defy the influence of mother, brothers, sisters; it had been particularly difficult for Mme Sun, so sensitive and so modest; it had been an ordeal from which she emerged ready for any contingency. The conversation on that day was restricted to the immediate situation, which was canvassed in all its aspects. I had already urged Rayna Prohme to take refuge in the American Consulate, and asked Mme Sun if she did not think this wise. Rayna said—half laughing, as usual—that she was not at all sure the American Consulate would take her in or that she wanted such protection even if it were available. Mme Sun, speaking with sudden gravity, said that she agreed with me:

that the capture of Hankow would be a terrible event, in which only those under the protection of the foreign guns would be safe; and that Mrs Prohme had already done enough for the Chinese Revolution without dying for it.

Then, suddenly, the conversation took a gruesome turn. It would have been gruesome under any conditions, but on that particular day, in the presence of two women who stood in such awful peril, it made my blood run cold. Mme Sun began it by speaking of the tortures to which the twenty Communists (including little Phyllis Li, the daughter of Li Ta-chao) had been subjected in Peking. She explained the difference between garrotting and plain strangling, named a number of the more agonizing torments in use among the Chinese reactionaries, and discussed the relative merits of the various forms of execution from the point of view of the person to be executed. Although she seemed a little nervous, and was conscious that the dangers she discussed were only a few hours away, I do not believe she was primarily thinking of herself; she was indirectly attempting to persuade Rayna Prohme to go to the American Consulate for the night.

When Mme Sun went home and Rayna returned to her work I went to see Lockhart, the American Consul. He was as slow and impassive as Borodin, reluctant to express himself clearly on any political matter, but his inner satisfaction at the approaching defeat of the Reds shone unmistakably in his face. I asked him flatly if the consulate would protect the three Americans who worked for the Hankow government, the Prohmes and Mrs Mitchell.

Lockhart answered with immense deliberation. I felt sure that he was enjoying the moment, for the Prohmes had been something of a thorn in his flesh for many months.

'You tell Mrs Prohme for me,' he said, 'that I will protect every American citizen who takes refuge in this consulate. I can do nothing for anybody outside it.'

I was a little annoyed at his assumption that Mrs Prohme had sent me to see him.

'I don't know that the Prohmes want to be protected,' I said. 'I was only asking on my own hook, because I think they are in serious danger. If Mrs Prohme is tortured to death in the streets of

Hankow while half the American navy looks on, it won't make a very pleasant impression at home.'

This was a stupid and flighty remark, but Lockhart did not take it up.

'I cannot protect Americans in Borodin's office,' he said, still smiling. 'I can protect this consulate, and shall do so. If the Prohmes and Mrs Mitchell come here they will be protected. That is all I can say.'

He was quite right, of course. I record the incident merely to show what contradictions can arise in a mind under stress. I disliked the whole principle of extraterritoriality, and regarded the presence of American warships in the Yangtsze-kiang as an unwarrantable invasion of China; and yet here I was asking Lockhart to extend his consular protection to absurd lengths. The only thing that can be said to justify such a request is that American business men and missionaries had often been protected at equally absurd lengths, and (in the case of the missionaries) even against their own will.

But Rayna Prohme dismissed the whole subject with a plain no. Her husband was at home, seriously ill; she had no desire to make a contrite pilgrimage to the consulate; she very nearly agreed with the navy people, who used to say that people who worked for the Chinese Revolution had no right to expect American protection. She thanked me for speaking to Lockhart, but was sorry I had done so. And that was that.

I made up my mind to a course of action that would force her to be rescued if the city fell. These were the counsels of alarm, of course, and as it happened they were useless; but sometimes what might have happened has a curiously revealing light to shed on what did happen. I was going to wait until the army from the west had taken the city. Then, at the first shot—all the western army had to do was fire a few rounds, as the city was without defenders —I was going to ask the Prohmes to go to the consulate. If they refused, I intended to demand of Lockhart a naval detachment to remove them to the consulate—to 'evacuate' them, as the strange diplomatic language puts it. Lockhart then would have been obliged to march them to the consulate under escort, or to take the responsibility before American opinion and his own superiors for whatever happened to them. It may be seen that in my excitement I was ungenerous to Lockhart, who would have been put in an awkward position in either case. It is even possible that the navy would have refused him the detachment necessary to rescue three people from a house some distance from the Bund; for the naval officers were unanimous in their dislike of the 'American Reds,' and would have loathed the necessity for helping them. But in the high temperature to which I had been brought by Mme Sun's description of the tortures and death that might be expected that night, I was ready to go to any extremity.

The necessity did not arise, and in a few days I was ashamed of my truculence. Fortunately neither Lockhart nor Rayna knew just how extreme had been my intentions, and all I had to my discredit was a hot-headed remark or so. But the might-have-been of this incident not only reveals the strength of sympathy that already attached me to the red-haired revolutionist from Illinois, but does, also, involve a principle. I was too excited to state the principle clearly at the time, but I felt it, however obscurely. It was this: that extraterritoriality either should be abolished altogether or enforced altogether. The tendency of the American authorities to protect such Americans as they thought worthy of protection and to let the others take their chance had been shown clearly enough in the Mitchell-Burton incident in Peking. On that occasion two Americans working for a partisan Chinese newspaper had been jailed by Chang Tso-lin and treated with considerable indignity. Until American public opinion had been aroused by the press, and the State Department had sent formal instructions, the American Legation in Peking had done nothing for these two. The general idea in the consular and diplomatic services, and above all in the navy, was that Americans who sympathized openly with the Chinese Revolution or associated themselves with it were not entitled to American protection. On the surface this was a reasonable contention, but it did not survive the second look. Any stray missionary, engaged in the futile and unnecessary effort to convert the Chinese to an alien religion, was considered worthy of having his life saved no matter how many other people might be killed in the process. Still more, any employee of the Standard Oil Company, engaged for the most part in the effort to sell low-grade petroleum for the best possible price to a population that didn't know the difference, was to be protected by navy and marines against every accident of the Chinese civil war. But persons who (like Rayna Prohme) were in China neither to squeeze money out of the Chinese nor to mystify them with religion, but to work for and with them, belonged to a small, special category, excluded from the benefits of the pernicious treaties. Lockhart would have protected her only if she had come to the consulate; but he would have sent the whole navy, if necessary, to rescue the vaguest missionary or the most insignificant little trader. This was the potential situation that aroused me to such a fury on the night of July 1st, and that it remained potential does not diminish its significance as a landmark in this story.

In the morning the immediate danger had passed. The western army (troops of Yang Sen and Ho Chien) had unaccountably failed to press onward in time, and during the night a large part of the 'Iron army' of Canton, which had been camped along the railway in Honan, poured into Hankow in crowded trains. The 'Iron army' was the one army out of the Cantonese hosts that remained faithful to the civilian Kuomintang and obeyed the orders of the committees. It was commanded by Chang Fa-kwei, who was credited with being a Communist. But however dependable this one army might be, it was alone, encompassed on every side by superior enemy forces. The tradition of Chinese warfare was overwhelmingly against fighting under such conditions. Battles took place in China only when the contending forces were of equal or nearly equal strength; when one side obviously outnumbered the other, it was customary for the smaller force to surrender or to join the larger. These customs, which the cheap humour of foreign newspapers found very comic, were in fact a proof of the profoundly civilized nature of the Chinese even in such barbaric enterprises as warfare; and without some such convention the loss of human life in the constant but meaningless civil wars of 1911–26 would have been frightful. By 1927 civil warfare had come to be genuinely significant, it is true, and there were plenty of Chinese who had the courage to die for their convictions; but the professional soldiery—however much affected by revolutionary propaganda—could not shake off the whole tradition of war as China had known it for thousands of years. This being true, it was obvious that the Hankow government, having lost its provinces and all but one of its armies, could not survive for many more days.

I knew that Borodin intended to make his escape, when the collapse came, by way of Mongolia. It was my intention to go with him if possible, and he was quite willing. The flight from Hankow, the journey across the interior to the desert and across the desert to Siberia, would make the kind of story my newspapers wanted, I thought—an 'exclusive' story, a 'personal' story, of exactly the genre stipulated in my contract. But I was not allowed to wait for the fall of Hankow. At this precise moment, when the climax was at hand, my New York office cabled me the last and most peremptory of a strange series of instructions.

The idea behind all my instructions had been, in brief, this: that I had not been sent to China to write about politics or the Chinese Revolution, but to engage in some kind of personal enterprise, capers or high jinks, that would carry on the tradition of romantic adventure (the 'Richard Harding Davis tradition,' it was called) to which my various employers insisted on assigning me. I have already explained that this legend corresponded to no reality whatever. My two Rif journeys had been adventurous, it is true, but only incidentally: I had not gone to the Rif in pursuit of adventure, but to learn what I could about the Riffians and their country. Adventure for the sake of adventure seemed to me dull and silly, of no value to the adventurer or to anybody else. I disliked the assumption that I was incapable of doing anything except gallop about foreign fields on a horse; and although I made attempts in China to satisfy this strange requirement of an unfortunate reputation, all my real interests were in the revolutionary movement itself, its meaning, progress and failure. The misunderstanding between my employers and myself was therefore complete.

The last of my instructions came on July 2d. It was a longish cablegram, and I cannot quote it exactly, but the gist was this: You are sending us entirely too much about politics; this kind of news is adequately provided by all the established news agencies; what we expect of you is something quite different, and we want you now to 'have personal adventures.'

Even in the desperate anxiety and tension of Hankow that lovely phrase 'have personal adventures' made an instant success. Borodin laughed out loud when I told him about it, and Rayna Prohme—even though she realized what a predicament it put me in—thought the wonderful cablegram should be framed and kept as a monument to American journalism.

But there it was, just the same, and no amount of laughing would get rid of the necessity: I had to find a Rosinante and go off in some direction to tilt at windmills. The Changsha trip was now out of the question, and would in any case have been far too political in interest to satisfy the requirements. I consulted Borodin, hoping that his escape to Mongolia might be near enough to justify me in waiting for it; but he could fix no date. He was, as always, determined to hang on until the last possible moment in the hope that the accidents of Chinese politics might turn in his favour. He believed the end might come 'any day, any night,' but he was not going to anticipate it.

I waited two or three days more, and then, when an opportunity came to visit Feng Yü-hsiang at his camp in Honan, I took it. The journey across China from Hankow to Peking at this particular time represented at least the possibility of 'personal adventure,' as the whole interior was beset by the confusion of rival armies and robber bands, peasant volunteers and individual outlaws. All foreigners had left the interior three months before, and, by and large, the proposed trip looked dangerous enough to satisfy even the most captious employer.

'If you get your throat cut,' Rayna said helpfully, 'just telegraph us and we'll send off the story. You might write it in advance, and then there won't be anything lost if you're killed.'

I said good-bye to my Hankow friends and their remnant of a revolutionary government on July 5th. Ten days later Tang Sengchi, one of their generals, proclaimed the expected counterrevolution; Borodin, Mme Sun Yat-sen, Chen, the Prohmes and the rest scattered in flight, escaping in various disguises and under various names from the vengeance of the war lords. I did not see them again for many weeks, and not the least of my troubles was the constant speculation as to what had become of them. The last entry made in my notebook in Hankow was a line of Shakespeare: 'So foul a sky clears not without a storm.' I no longer remember why it was written in the book on that particular day, but it is not a bad description of the point of view of those who had, in the tremendous effort of 1926 and 1927, attempted to raise the storm.

22

The journey from Hankow to Peking took three weeks. It was an interesting journey, but no more perilous than an ordinary trip from London to Paris. It was uncanny how the Chinese forestalled my every effort to 'have personal adventures.' They got up and gave me their seats in trains or inns; they treated me with the utmost consideration; they made me presents of fans; sometimes they even refused to let me pay for my board and lodging. I was surrounded by courtesy from the time I left Hankow until I arrived in Peking; and although the journey involved incidental hardships, they were invariably lessened as much as possible by the anxious politeness of the inhabitants of the country. I am at a loss to explain this, except by luck. The fact is that the country was very disturbed, and my friend Basil Lang, correspondent of the London *Times*, who followed me to Honan ten days later, was certainly murdered; he vanished in the middle of Chengchow and has never been heard of since. But the day I spent in Chengchow was—except for the heat—no more dangerous than a day in any provincial town. I wandered about the streets and shops, accompanied only by my interpreter, and never a rude word or gesture disturbed the general impression of smiling calm. On the next morning we went on across Honan to Loyang at the other end of the province, where Feng Yü-hsiang had his headquarters.

My visit to the Christian war lord was pretty much what I had expected. He turned out to be a big, slow brute with a highly developed sense of his own power. He was ignorant, violent, and authoritative, but probably sincere; his staff and his armies in general had the most salutary fear of him. In his speeches, his public prayers, and the little booklet printed to distribute to his armies, he exhibited a system of thought based partly upon

Christianity and partly upon Confucianism—an ethical system, not a religious one. Except in the matter of prayer, he did not pay much attention to the supernatural element in religion, but his prayers were wonderful. He used to issue his requests to the Almighty regularly, and they ranged all the way from a demand for rain to a modest petition that his enemies be exterminated. Most of the ethical notions put forward in his book of the Kuominchun (People's army—the name he called his own bands) could be found in the Confucian Analects, but they were simplified to skeleton form by Feng's primitive mind, and lost all the lofty philosophical quality of the ancient Chinese. Such qualities as Modesty, Magnanimity, Meekness, Liberality, Love, Humility and Purity were as highly prized by Feng as by Confucius, but whereas they came naturally from the meditative nature of the old philosopher, they struck me as being inappropriate to the character of the treacherous coolie war lord.

The train from Hankow went back on July 9th, and I left its relative luxury and safety for a Chinese inn at Loyang. There (July 10th) my interpreter and I climbed aboard a troop train bound for Hwei-hsin-chen, the last point on the Lung-hai railway in the western end of Honan. The train was slow, filthy, crammed with soldiers, indescribably hot, and yet the innumerable belching, spitting, stinking passengers were most polite to the stray foreigner. I sat in a corner of a box car stuffed to overflowing with coolies in uniform, and the heat and smells were the worst I can remember; but in the midst of the journey, to my astonishment, one of the soldiers took off his jacket, rolled it up and gave it to me for a cushion.

My daybook has only this to say of Hwei-hsin-chen: 'Arrived at night and stayed in Chinese inn (bugs).'

On the next morning we crossed the Yellow River in the ferry to Mao-chin-tu in Shansi, the territory of the 'model war lord' Yen Hsi-shan. From Maochintu to Taiyuanfu, the capital of the province, was a long, uneventful journey in mule carts, on foot, and at times in a ricksha. Sometimes I slept in the abandoned houses of the missionaries who had fled the country three months before, but oftener the only refuge was a roadside inn. The inns were invariably verminous, and sometimes the heat and vermin made it impossible to sleep inside at all; on such occasions I moved out into the courtyard and slept on the ground with the coolies. My interpreter, Peng Ta-mu, was a jewel. At night, when the vermin retarded sleep, Peng Ta-mu told me old Chinese stories or answered, with admirable tolerance and restraint, my questions about life in his native province. He wanted to be a doctor, but the revolution had played ducks and drakes with his family, his money and his plans. Peng had almost no interest in politics, but he was fascinated by rocks or plants, geological specimens or the leaves of a tree. It gave me no small satisfaction to think that I might be able, through the Rockefeller Foundation or in some other way, to start Peng off in his medical career and leave a good doctor in China as a trace of my passing.

We reached Taiyuanfu nine days after the start of our journey. The old city seemed restful and charming after the rigours of the road, and the railway hotel (French) could not have delighted me more if it had been run by César Ritz himself. Yen Hsi-shan, the 'model governor' of the province, received me with the gentle, old-fashioned courtesy of an educated Chinese. He had governed Shansi in uninterrupted peace and prosperity ever since the night in 1911 when he, as the head of the Kuomintang faction in the garrison, had expelled the imperial authorities and raised the flag of the Republic. Yen's record was unique in China. His province, although large and rich, was remote enough to guarantee him immunity from the hazards of the civil wars that agitated the rest of the country. It was not directly in contact with any of the great powers and had no fatal river to open it up to foreign gunboats. Yen himself, intelligent and benevolent, had known how to take advantage of his geographical advantages; he had welcomed French and German technical advisers, who were always less dangerous than Japanese, Russian or British; with their help he had built roads, sunk artesian wells, widened and lighted his streets, encouraged commerce and maintained public order. But in the past two years the Kuomintang and Communist oganizers had been at work, and Shansi was no longer the sleepy, prosperous backwater Yen had tried to make it. He professed to be a follower of Sun Yat-sen, but of the Sun Yat-sen of 1911—not of the Socialist Sun Yat-sen of 1924. The idea that coolies might

be organized to demand better wages and better conditions of life
shocked him, and he was even then engaged in the effort to suppress the labour and peasants' unions.

The philosopher king gave me a motorcar to go to Kalgan in,
and there, at the point where Shansi, Mongolia and the China of
Chang Tso-lin came together, Peng and I took a troop train for
Peking. My contract with the North American Newspaper Alliance had expired, and for the rest of my stay in China I was released from the necessity of finding something to put into cablegrams. My employers had had no reason to be satisfied with me,
but to my surprise they did not complain. They had done well
enough with my Rif articles to counterbalance the failure of the
Chinese journey, and philosophers, it seemed, could exist as well
in a New York office as in a Chinese garden.

12

Peking in the summer of 1927 was a nervous capital. Old
Chang Tso-lin still governed there with the help of the Japanese,
and my Hankow friends were regarded with horror by most of the
foreigners and the Peking Chinese. Foreign women had been
ordered to leave the city three months before, and many had
obeyed. I spent a week in Peking and felt that I knew it well. It
was not hard to know the Peking of the foreigners: it consisted
of the legations and hotels, a few shops, a club, some dance halls
and a great deal of whisky. I enjoyed these amenities as well as
anybody could, but to get a little reading and writing done I
moved up into the Imperial Hunting Park in the Western Hills,
and thereafter went in to Peking only when I felt the need of conversation or a drink.

I could learn nothing about the fate of Hankow except that
the government there had collapsed. The most contradictory reports were printed in the English and American newspapers about
Borodin, Mme Sun Yat-sen, the Prohmes and Eugene Chen. It
was clear that nobody really knew where they were; they had all
vanished. One report about Rayna, published in a Shanghai reactionary newspaper, made me curse with rage. It said that she and
Borodin had gone to Kuling, where they had given gay parties

every night, using up most of the hotel's supplies of champagne. I had never seen Borodin drink anything but water, and Rayna's limit was a glass of beer; the story in the newspaper was ridiculous, but the sheer malice of it infuriated me. The same kind of invention was exercised at the expense of Mme Sun Yat-sen, and worse: China was filled with rumours about her, one of the principal ones being that she had married or was about to marry Eugene Chen. The poor lady herself was the last to hear this absurd story, and when she did hear it, months later in Moscow, it gave her a nervous breakdown.

Randall Gould, the correspondent of the United Press, introduced me to the Soviet Embassy, where there was some likelihood of getting news of the Hankow people; but even the Bolsheviks were without information.

I found friends among the Bolsheviks, and two of them, Grinievich and Kantorovich, were ready to argue with me on any subject for any number of consecutive hours. Perhaps for this reason, perhaps because I had grown to dislike the bourgeois point of view in China too intensely to enjoy the company of my own people, I spent more time with the Bolsheviks than with any other foreigners. Roy Chapman Andrews gave me a dinner or two in his beautiful old Chinese house; the American Minister fed me at lunch one day; the club was always hospitable and my colleagues of the press friendly; but I actually felt more at ease with the Bolsheviks than with anybody in Peking. Their way of searching for the sense of events had been made familiar to me by Borodin, and although Borodin's luminous intelligence was not a common quality even among Bolsheviks, I could at least *talk* to Kantorovich, Yurishkevich, Grinievich and the rest. Communication with Americans and British was more difficult, oddly enough, for the fact that we used the same language only made more obvious the fundamental opposition of ideas. Except for Randall Gould and his wife, there was not an American of my acquaintance in Peking who had any tolerance for the spirit of Hankow. One American lady gave me an excellent dinner in her fine Chinese house and said to me afterwards:

'Will you tell me what's the good of organizing coolies into labour unions? What good have labour unions ever done to anybody? They've ruined America, so that you can't get a decent servant in the whole country. Why can't Mme Sun and all those people leave the coolies alone? They're quite happy as they are.'

I had reached the point where conversation with anybody like this good lady was impossible. I might have said that her feelings would be different if she were a coolie, but this would have seemed to her irrelevant and rude. She represented the Peking point of view, and while it was being expounded I could only smile politely and try not to be bored.

The Peking point of view showed remarkably little acquaintance with the laws of historic development, but it was at least more civilized than the point of view of Shanghai and the treaty ports. The characteristic of the Peking foreigners was, in a word, civility. In Peking there had always been an equal association of foreigners and upper-class Chinese in society, and every foreigner there had a few Chinese friends. Some had many. Peking foreigners were kind to their servants, interested in Chinese art and literature, fond of jade, embroideries, the theatre of Mei Lan-fang and the inventions of Chinese cookery. They really did establish some kind of relationship to the country they lived in; they were interested in China in a dilettante way; they liked, admired and sometimes even understood the culture of the Chinese, and the simple savagery of the treaty-port foreigners seemed as bad to them as it did to me. But it seemed bad to them for social reasons —because it was bad taste, or vulgar, or characteristic of uneducated persons. They were all very cultivated, polite and upper-class in Peking, and their lovely Chinese houses, filled with soft silken embroideries and beautiful carvings, were among the most charming I have ever seen. What made their point of view alien to me was their perfect contentment with the state of things around them. The world seemed a good world to them; the coolies of China, human creatures ground into equality with the beasts, seemed to them 'perfectly happy as they are'; and anybody who wished to change this state, particularly any active revolutionary, was a weird monster. If one lived long enough in Peking drawing rooms almost any kind of activity involving exposure to the heat, dust, smells and rude behaviour of the poor might come to seem ridiculous.

The Bolsheviks, I strongly suspect, knew little about jade and embroideries. Certainly the Soviet Embassy would have caused shudders to course up and down the back of any interior decorator. But the remnants of the Embassy staff kept up a lively interest in everything that went on in China, and my friend A. I. Kantorovich, in particular, had a passion for thought and discussion. You could throw any idea at him, and he would pursue it until he had run it to ground and thoroughly examined or rejected it. On one occasion, when he came to lunch with me at the Imperial Hunting Park, I remarked (I forget why) that Queen Victoria seemed to me to have left her impress all over the age in which she lived—that the age would have been different if the Queen's character had been different. Kantorovich pounced upon this notion and proceeded to destroy it. The Queen had not made the Victorian Age; the Victorian Age had made the Queen. He knew a great deal about the subject, and the argument grew vigorous. Napoleon had not remade Europe; Europe had called for, had in truth created, the necessary Napoleon. The stumbling block in his ultra-Bolshevik argument seemed to be, for a long time, Alexander Makedonsky, who was the one example of a pure personal accident with immense historical results. I was puzzled about this gentleman until the turn of the conversation revealed that he was only, after all, our old friend Alexander the Great in Russian guise. The argument continued for many hours; and Kantorovich, who had come to lunch, did not return to Peking until midnight.

I lived in a temple in the Hunting Park—a temple that had turned into a hotel. My part of the temple was a separate little house in the silver birch trees, isolated from the sights and sounds of the main buildings. There it was possible to spend days without seeing anybody but the silent Chinese who brought my food, and without hearing a sound but the slither of a scorpion across the terrace, or the chatter of a bird in the silver trees.

From the Hunting Park I went down to Peking once a week and saw either the gay world or the Bolsheviks or both. The Peking expeditions were liquorous affairs, for the only diversion offered a rather bored and worried visitor on the hot summer nights was whisky—unless, indeed, it was champagne or beer. There was a dinner or banquet given to a departing journalist by the Anglo-

American press one evening, and somebody rashly invited me to it. Whoever my host was, he probably saw his error before the evening was over. I consumed so much beer that I was puffed with eloquence, made a speech to the assembled Fourth Estate, quarrelled with an American marine captain, and ended up by sleeping on the Tatar Wall to prove that I could evade the vigilance of the marine sentries.

When you feel as foolish as I did the next day it is small consolation to have won a silly bet. I made up my mind to leave Peking at once, drove out to the Hunting Park before lunch, packed, and was ready to go. I had no destination in particular, but as a general principle I intended to end up in Moscow; for there, sooner or later, Rayna Prohme and the rest of my Hankow friends would be sure to come if they were still alive. The last thing Rayna had said to me, as the train started to move out of Hankow, had been: 'We'll probably meet in Moscow.' This 'probably' was the nearest thing to information on the subject that I had been able to obtain from anybody.

But a delay occurred at this point—a very special delay. I had recently acquired a new relative, whom I had never seen, and I could not leave Peking until I was sure whether or not she would be able to accompany me.

There can be no harm, at this late date, in telling the true story of Fanny Borodin. Chang Tso-lin is dead; the whole state of affairs in China and Russia has changed; the circumstances of the Borodin case are unlikely to be repeated in our time. What was a secret of state in 1927 is only an amusing anecdote in 1935. It differs from many amusing anecdotes in that it really happened.

It will be remembered that Borodin's wife was captured by the Shantung war lord in May and turned over by him to his feudal superior, Chang Tso-lin. The old bandit was dissuaded from strangling her, and after a great many delays and legal quarrels she was brought to trial in July. The person in charge of her defence was my friend A. I. Kantorovich, whose work in the Soviet Foreign Office was supposed to be that of an economic jurist (or juridical economist). Actually he had been obliged to spend most of his time for three months attempting to defend the fifteen or sixteen Soviet citizens who had been imprisoned by Chang Tso-lin, and the chief of these, at least in the judgment of public opinion, was Mme Borodin. To save her from torture and death was Kantorovich's job, and in view of the importance of the case and the innocence of the prisoner his methods need not be questioned too closely; they were the methods of Peking in 1927.

As a matter of fact, I never knew exactly what the method was, but the results were as follows: the judge before whom the case was to be tried suddenly called it one morning before Chang Tso-lin was up. Mme Borodin was heard and immediately acquitted. When Chang Tso-lin got out of bed Mme Borodin had vanished, and so had the judge. He was next heard of in Japan, a pleasant country to which his peaceful habit of mind had urgently invited him as soon as the hearing in the Borodin case was over.

Chang Tso-lin flew into a terrible rage. He had counted on being able to strangle Mme Borodin, but to have lost the principal victim and also the judge in one morning was too much for any war lord. Peking was turned upside down, the trains were watched, suspected houses were raided. The Soviet Embassy suavely invited Chang's men to search the premises, in which Mme Borodin was not to be found. Chang Tso-lin believed—and rightly—that it would be difficult for a Russian woman with Mme Borodin's known appearance to travel far in China. Photographs of the lady were circulated, and the ships at Tientsin were watched. Chang announced in the newspapers that he was determined to catch her at whatever cost; the foreign press displayed the liveliest interest; and all in all there was a fine to-do about it.

Then, some ten days after the acquittal and disappearance, a dispatch from Vladivostok reached the Chinese and foreign press. It had been sent out by the Rengo News Agency (Japanese), which exchanges news dispatches with other agencies. It described the arrival of Mme Borodin from China and Japan on a Soviet steamer and quoted in detail the things she had to say about her imprisonment and trial in Peking. Eight days later Mme Borodin arrived in Moscow on the Trans-Siberian Express and was interviewed again, this time by the Tass (Soviet) news agency. There was no doubt about it, for it had been printed in every newspaper in the world: Fanny Borodin had escaped from Chang Tso-lin and was now safe in Moscow. Chang Tso-lin, suspicious and bitter, had to confess himself beaten and call off the search.

Mme Borodin's odyssey had taken place at about the time of my arrival in Peking, and by the end of August it was no longer a burning subject. Lunching with Kantorovich one day at the Grand Hôtel de Pékin, I was struck by the unwonted earnestness of his manner when he spoke of this faded episode. After a good deal of preamble he asked me if I would do something for him and for Borodin—something required by the iniquities of the Peking régime, something to save a human life. I agreed to do so if I could. And only then did I learn that Fanny Borodin had never left Peking at all—that she had been under Chang Tso-lin's nose the whole time that his cutthroats were ransacking the town for her; that she was still in hiding, in only slightly diminished peril, in the house of a Chinese friend.

The proposal was that I might take Mme Borodin with me to Japan as a relative (sister, cousin, aunt) and there, at Shimonoseki, get her aboard a Soviet steamer that would be warned of our coming. The dangerous part of the trip would be that from Peking to Tientsin, on trains watched by Chang Tso-lin's soldiers, with officials and fellow passengers who had all seen photographs of Mme Borodin at some time or other. The hope was that if my sister, cousin or aunt pretended to be ill, and only my extremely un-Bolshevik appearance was presented to the view of ticket takers and soldiers, no questions would be asked.

I agreed to this proposal at once; it delighted me. Nothing could have pleased me more than to smuggle a victim away from the irate war lord, and the mere notion of that trip from Peking to Tientsin made me feel cheerful. That the victim was Borodin's wife and Kantorovich's client added to the rosy aspect of the whole enterprise. I made only one stipulation: that my American passport must not be touched or in any way involved in the business. I had a healthy respect for my passport, and life would have been nearly insupportable without it. Kantorovich laughed at this.

'What do you think we are?' he asked. 'We can't do anything about American passports. Our only hope is to borrow one.'

So for some days I had a new relative. But in the end the American lady who had at first intended to supply the all-important passport changed her mind; I could not very well travel with a sick female relative who had no papers; the most blatantly un-Bolshevik appearance would not have guaranteed safety under such conditions, and the whole plan fell through. I was disappointed. I should have enjoyed that trip.

On the day when Kantorovich's plan was given up for lack of a passport, the newspapers carried a dispatch from Vladivostok that aroused my impatience to be off. Mme Sun Yat-sen, the Chens 'and their party' had arrived in Vladivostok on a Soviet steamer from Shanghai and were taking a special train to Moscow. Mme Sun had said only a few words, but Eugene Chen had talked at length, and I recognized the characteristic turns of his phrases. I might have had my suspicions of the Vladivostok dispatch, so strangely like the one announcing Mme Borodin's arrival a month before; but no Vladivostok correspondent was likely to be able to parody Mr Chen's style as well as he parodied it himself. I took my leave of 'that Mongolian encampment known as Peking,' went down to Tientsin to collect my belongings from various parts of China, and crossed to the other side of the Great Wall early in September.

Manchuria unfolded like a dusty carpet, one half of it infested by Japanese, and the other half crowded with Russians. I had never known quite how obvious the Japanese control of their zone was until I reached Mukden and found the Japanese currency, stamps, police and language everywhere. Harbin was even stranger—an almost purely Russian city, with street after street in which the Chinese were outnumbered by foreigners. The architecture and complexion of Harbin were the most foreign I had seen anywhere in China, and here even the lowliest kinds of labour—those reserved in other cities for Chinese coolies alone —were performed by white men. I never heard a word of Chinese spoken in my hotel or in the restaurants I frequented during my three days there. These were fleeting and trivial impressions, to which no undue importance should be attached, but I did certainly feel when I reached Harbin that I had left China behind. I recorded the feeling in my journal with a sweeping comment:

'Five months in China and everything I thought worth a damn has gone to pot: depressing experience.'

The Trans-Siberian journey is at best monotonous and exhausting. It takes the traveller over a country so flat, limitless and dreary that one day seems exactly like another, and by the time we reached Moscow I felt that I had been on the train most of my life. There had been floods on part of the line, and the train could not keep up to its schedule; we arrived in Moscow twenty-four hours late. The journey from Harbin had taken nine full days.

23

I went to the Savoy Hotel and sat down to reflect. How was I to go about finding Mme Sun Yat-sen, the Chens 'and their party'? I did not know anybody in Moscow, and the atmosphere of Soviet rule was still strange. It never occurred to me, for example, that I might go to the telephone, ring up the Third International, ask for Manabendra Nath Roy, and find out where the Chinese were staying. That kind of behaviour would have been natural in London or New York, but it seemed inadequate to the difficulties that obstructed (according to the general impression) movements of life in the land of the Soviets.

The hall porter at the Savoy suggested that I might try the Associated Press of America and gave me its telephone number. After an unsuccessful attempt to make myself understood on the telephone I repaired to the office of the agency and found myself in the presence of an agreeable, expansive Russian, Mr Kotov. I told him what I wanted, and he suggested that we might have tea and talk it over. We had tea, and chicken, and vodka, and tea, and bread, and vodka, and chicken, and after I had been there an hour or so I asked Mr Kotov if he could do anything to find out what I wanted to know. He said he could, but that he would have to think about it. So we had more tea and vodka and chicken, and the afternoon rapidly turned into evening.

Among other things Mr Kotov told me a distressing story about his predecessor, an American correspondent who had died in Moscow some weeks before. On instructions from the family in America the gentleman had been cremated, and it was thought fitting that his ashes should be scattered over Moscow, in which he had spent his last years. Mr Kotov had endeavoured to carry out these wishes to the letter, but ashes cannot be scattered—truly scattered, diffused and disseminated—except from a relatively high altitude, such as may be reached in an aëroplane. And it had proved impossible to obtain an aëroplane from the Soviet authorities for this purpose.

'They do not understand,' said Mr Kotov hopelessly. 'I have explained to them all, in all the offices and all the bureaus, but they cannot understand why we want to scatter the ashes. It is dreadful.'

I was, I hope, sympathetic.

'And in the meanwhile,' I added, 'what have you done with the ashes?'

'There they are,' said Mr Kotov sadly, pointing across the table.

And there they were, in a square mahogany box, very trim and neat.

On top of all the chicken and tea and bread and vodka this was a shade too Russian for me. I asked my amiable host if he had thought over the matter of finding the Chinese revolutionaries, and after a sip or two of tea he was able to reply in the affirmative. He went to the telephone, chanted a few melodious phrases in Russian, and turned back to me.

'They are at the Metropol Hotel,' he said. 'That's in the square in front of the Great Theatre, to the left. They are not all living there, but that is where they have their office.'

I thanked Mr Kotov for his kindness, wished him better luck with his predecessor's ashes in future, and took my leave. It was by this time eight o'clock in the evening, and I had not much hope of finding anybody in an office, but I found a droshky and went to the Metropol. There, just as I reached the top of the marble steps and was about to ask the hall porter for information, I saw Rayna Prohme coming towards me.

For six weeks I had imagined her dead, torn into pieces by a mob, broken and sunk in the mud of the Yangtze-kiang or buried obscurely, after days of torture, in some dreary and forgotten Chinese field. These morbid fancies had alternated with others in which I imagined meeting her again, but it had never been wholly credible to me that I might find her, alive and well, by the mere effort of going to Moscow. And yet here she was, coming swiftly across the hall, laughing, hands stretched out, her eyes alight beneath the conflagration of her hair.

Here I must state, as clearly as possible, the nature of our relationship then and afterwards. It was not a sexual relationship—at least, not as the phrase is currently understood. Neither in words nor in gestures did it take the forms of intimacy known to the readers of a thousand erotic novels. I shall not attempt to explain the mystery of an all-pervading, all-controlling emotion that had no physical basis, but it existed. If these words fall under the eyes of a reader who cannot believe such a thing possible, he had better stop reading at once, for it will be assumed from here onward that the fact is plain.

I had left Rayna Prohme in Hankow on July 5th without agitation. It was an amicable, offhand farewell: a shout, a laugh, a sign and a nod as the train began to move. This may not have been natural behaviour, for the future was obscure, the tension of the place and time extreme; I had no idea whether I was ever to see her again. But we behaved like that because that was the way we behaved. The contingencies were too terrible to be considered in Hankow, and the defence provided in such cases by the manners of our contemporaries was flippancy. As a defence against excessive seriousness or depth of feeling the weapon was useful, but it went beyond its first purposes: it affected the impulses it was meant to protect and dulled them into insensibility.

Between July 5th and September 18th, when I went up the steps of the Metropol in Moscow, a profound change had taken place in the texture and organization of my mind with respect to all the subjects brought together in this chapter, and, in a wider sense, to the subjects considered in this book. As nearly as I can define it, the change had consisted in a steady, orderly concentration of thought and feeling within this cycle of experience—to which I have given the name 'Revolution'—and, concurrently but less precisely, within the subsidiary or preparatory cycles outside it, upon a single phenomenon containing the principles of energy diffused (but neither organized nor put to work) throughout the system. The central phenomenon—the sun of this solar system—was Rayna Prohme. During those weeks in the Hunting Park, when her fate as a human creature (as Human-Being-Number-Eight-Trillion-or-so) was seriously disturbing my molecular activity as another member of the same series, her essential principle was taking its place at the centre of my world of ideas; the first process was minute, demands the microscope and has no place in a narrative not concerned with private matters; but the second process, for which the telescope is the appropriate instrument, involved every fragment of material within my experience of life or view of the world.

When I turned from the hall porter's desk at the Metropol and saw her coming towards me the process was already completed, but it needed that moment of blinding significance to become irrevocable. From then on it was impossible to seek the relationships that seemed necessary to life (a relation of one to many, a place in the chain of cause and effect) without reference to this solar phenomenon, this sun perceived, lost and found again, a focus of reality for which the only solid expression was a slip of a girl with red hair. The issues that converged for me upon her fiery head were the most serious any human being has to face, and they converged there, most of all, because she had faced them first. When I said, in the account of our meeting in Hankow, that we were unescapably magnetized toward the same pole of reality, I was describing a state of things that had now ceased to exist; for now, as we met in the hall of the Metropol, she had already moved so far towards that pole as to become part of its immediate radiation. The problems of minor movement no longer counted for her; they had been solved; she had reached her centre. If we define this central reality as the meaning (or conviction of meaning) in the existence of an individual, his sense of exact position with respect to the multitudinous life of his species in its physical environment, it may be seen that, for persons like ourselves, it had to be the whole thing, the sum of good. I say 'for persons like ourselves,' because there existed other kinds of persons unmagnetized to any central reality—willing to expend their allotment of time without attempting to relate it to the time of which it was a segment—and still other kinds contented in this necessity by the easy promises of supernatural religion and the immortality of the soul. A settled polarity was harder to establish for persons like ourselves because we sought it in the natural world of men and things; but once reached (as she had reached it), it gave the only satisfaction that could inform a life and last it out.

These were the processes that had supervened upon the separation in Hankow for the two of us. She had reached her central reality (which was also mine) and become part of it. As she came across the hall of the Metropol I knew that my world revolved about her. If this sounds like the language of sexual or romantic attachment it is the fault of the words, so hard to dig out pure from their tangle of associations; but in simple fact it was not so. The feeble, perfumed sentiments, the romantic illusions, the limited personal desires and disappointments of boudoir 'love' had no part in the moment; nor did they afterwards influence the course of our related systems of thought and feeling in the spiral plunge to catastrophe. This tragedy may have contained love, but if so it was love resolved into the largest terms of which such personal emotions are capable, related to the whole life of mankind and the eternal effort of the human spirit to find its own place in the universe.

She came across the hall, I turned and met her, and we both laughed.

'I knew you'd turn up,' she said. 'I expected you any day.'

14

We went out into the square and walked up and down. The Great Theatre was lighted for a performance of *Boris Godunov*, for which I had bought seats as soon as I arrived that day; but we had so much to talk about that it seemed a waste of time even to hear *Boris*. We crossed to the gate of the Iberian Virgin and went into the Red Square, huge and empty, walked it up and down and across, talking, talking, talking. Presently Rayna decided that it was foolish to have tickets to *Boris* and not use them; we went to the Great Theatre for one act (the third) and then, as the reserve of things to say had piled up unbearably during the interruption caused by Moussorgsky's music, we took a droshky to the Filipov Café in the Tverskaya. This was a huge crowded place where innumerable Muscovites sat for hours every evening over their tea or coffee, and nobody minded if we talked while the gipsies sang. When the café closed we walked again, and by the time I had deposited Rayna at the door of the Sugar Palace on the Sofyskaya Naberezhnaya, opposite the Kremlin, I had acquired a fairly good idea of some of the things that had happened since July 5th.

At the collapse of the government in Hankow Borodin had gone to Mongolia, taking with him his Russians, the two Chen boys, and our friend the American correspondent Anna Louise Strong. Of this section of the Hankow fugitives nothing was yet known. Rayna and Bill Prohme had gone down to Shanghai, where they were safe enough, as Americans; Eugene Chen had escaped in the disguise of a Japanese merchant; Mme Sun Yat-sen had returned to her own house in the French Concession at Shanghai. Most of the Chinese leaders had been obliged to assume various disguises in their flight, and their destinations were unknown; it was thought that Wang Chin-wei had reached France safely, and some of the others had gone to Japan. A few (mostly Communists) had retired to Hunan in the hope of keeping up the movement there.

In Shanghai Mme Sun Yat-sen had been exposed to the merciless pressure of her entire family but had steadily refused to abandon her position in any particular. She not only refused to give Chiang Kai-shek's victorious reaction the cloak of her name: she publicly denounced it in terms that would have meant, for any less sacred character than the widow of Sun Yat-sen, a certain and terrible death. Even for her the situation was not without danger. She was almost a prisoner in her house; there was a possibility that her name might be used, while she was helpless there, to sanction the massacres that were taking place by order of the triumphant reactionaries all over South and Central China. A decided action was required to express her dissent from the opinions of the victors, her loyalty to the defeated principles of the Revolution. It had been Borodin's idea (and Rayna's as well) that this could be accomplished best by a public visit to Moscow, and after a week or ten days in Shanghai Mme Sun came to share that opinion. But her movements were so circumscribed, so carefully watched, that the journey had to be prepared for with the secrecy of a flight.

The Prohmes separated in Shanghai, and Bill went to Manila to await developments. Mme Sun and Rayna escaped one night from the house in the Rue Molière and reached the river in safety. There a sampan awaited them, and they were rowed down the Whangpu to a Soviet steamer that sailed at dawn. Mr Chen and his daughters, with one secretary, joined them with the same elaborate but necessary precautions. They reached Vladivostok without trouble; the Soviet government had a special train there for them, and they had been in Moscow for a week.

In the story of this flight the part that struck me as most remarkable was the courage and decision shown by Mme Sun Yat-sen. I should never have believed her capable of the sheer physical daring involved in a flight at three o'clock in the morning by sampan down that crowded, murderous enemy river. Fragile though she was, she had some reserve of power unknown to lesser spirits, for she deliberately chose the hard, uncertain way of exile in preference to the luxury and consideration that might have been hers for the asking. She could have had anything in China, except one; but it was the only thing she wanted. Power, wealth, the satisfactions of high position—the things her own family pursued and had attained through their relationship to her—had no importance in her eyes. What she wanted was to prolong the social, economic and political revolution of Sun Yat-sen until it had attained its ends; and this was the only thing the generals and cabinet ministers who made up the Soong family circle would not consider.

I spent the week in the company of Rayna and the Hankow fugitives. They were a worried, anxious group. Not only was reaction in the saddle everywhere in China, but the future attitude of the Soviet government was uncertain in the extreme. The conflicting tendencies of Trotzky and Stalin had clashed so often in the weeks immediately past that the crisis drew visibly near, and such a crisis—partly brought about by the collapse of Hankow—could not fail to determine the friendship or indifference of the Russian Communist organizations toward the Chinese Revo-

lution. In the absence of Borodin, who was still somewhere in the desert making his way towards Siberia, the Chinese revolutionists felt rather at sea in Moscow. The Russians who had shown most interest in China were Trotzky, Radek, Bukharin and a few of their friends, all, at the moment, under a cloud; while the official (Stalinist) Russians, although uniformly courteous to their visitors, could not help giving the impression that China was only one of their many problems, and not one of the most important.

Mme Sun Yat-sen and Rayna were lodged in the Sugar Palace, a huge house built out of the profits of the sugar trade before the war. After 1917 it had been taken over as a Soviet house, and served a variety of purposes. Several high officials had rooms there; other rooms were assigned to guests of the Soviet government; and the great ballroom served the Soviet Foreign Office for its occasional diplomatic receptions, the nearest thing to a bourgeois entertainment provided by the official life of Moscow.

On the day after my arrival I went to the Sugar Palace for the first time, and the experience was bewildering. In that colossal establishment, with its uncarpeted marble stairs, its signs of vanished wealth and splendour, I could find nobody to tell me where to go. It seemed to me that the Soviet dignitaries who lived in it were badly guarded. I found two sentries at the foot of the staircase, said 'Soong Ching-ling' in a loud voice, and was told with a grin and a movement of the hand to go on upwards. But once I got to the first floor there was not a soul to be seen, not a lamp lighted, not a sound heard. I stood in the cold, dark, empty place and debated. Should I shout? If I did, what would happen? Should I pound on doors, walk straight ahead into the darkness, or simply sit down on the floor and wait for somebody to come?

After five minutes I walked straight ahead and came to a door. A knock brought no answer; I pushed the door open and walked into absolute blackness. As nearly as I could tell I was in an immense room, for only one wall was discovered by my anxious fingers in a great deal of groping. But as I did not intend to stay in the dark forever, I kept on going, and eventually found myself falling over a concert grand piano of the largest size.

This gave me an idea. Perhaps if I sat down and played the piano loudly for a few minutes somebody would come to find out who was making such a disgusting noise. I found the chair by falling over it, sat down, opened the piano, and thumped away. I had been playing for perhaps ten minutes and was about to give up hope when all the lights in the room suddenly went on.

There, directly in front of me, was the least predictable of phenomena: a large, handsome Englishwoman with her arms full of sheet music. I should have known her for an Englishwoman anywhere, but what an Englishwoman was doing in this labyrinthine official palace in Moscow I could not imagine. She looked at me and spoke (after some act of divination) in English.

'I say,' she said, 'do you play duets?'

'I wish I could,' I said, 'but I can't read well enough.'

'Oh, these are very simple ones,' she said. 'Surely you can try.'

'Honestly, I can't,' I said. 'You can tell by the way I play that I'm no good.'

She came a few steps forward into the room, started to put the music down and picked it up again.

'They're really awfully simple,' she said. 'I'm sorry you won't try them. I like to pay duets.'

Without saying another word she went out of the room again by the way she had entered it, and I was left wondering. But at least the lights were on, and I felt less like a burglar. I kept on playing for another ten or fifteen minutes, and eventually Rayna appeared in the doorway at the other end of the long room.

'I've been waiting for you for an hour,' she said. 'What in God's name are you doing in here?'

'Playing the piano,' I said. 'An English lady has just sprung out of the floor and asked me to play duets with her, or else I dreamt it. Do you think it can be one of the effects of vodka?'

'No,' said Rayna. 'It must have been Litvinova you saw. She lives in there, and she probably thought it was less painful to play with you than to listen to you. Come along.'

I was led down a passage to another carved door, which admitted us to the room assigned to Mme Sun Yat-sen. Like the rest of the overgrown house, it was on the grandest scale, and Soong Ching-ling looked like a child in the middle of it. She was dressed in European style for the first time in many years, and felt rather embarrassed in her short skirts; they did, actually, make her look about fifteen years old. The contrast between her appearance and her destiny was forcible at all times, but never more than on that evening. The room itself, so huge and gloomy that I could scarcely discern its opposite wall, might have been chosen to figure forth the scale of events against which this exquisite fragment of humanity was obliged to pit its hour of time.

The week passed. Rayna and I went to the theatre on two or three of these evenings; one night Mme Sun had a box at the Great Theatre for a ballet performance; one afternoon we went to the Petrovsky Park to see some military manœuvres.

Our night at the Great Theatre was the Chinese Revolution's night. A ballet called *Krassny Mak* (*The Red Poppy*) had just been produced with music by Glière and a choreography by (and with) Gellzer; it was the most ambitious 'revolutionary ballet' yet attempted, with a plot in which all the forces of the Chinese revolutionary and counter-revolutionary struggle were supposed to be shown in choreographic form. I did not like it; the crude simplicities of Russian ballet style did not seem to me to bear any relation to the Chinese Revolution, or to indicate, except in the most childish way, its awful seriousness; but the evening was like a genre painting, full of character and difficult to forget. Mme Sun, the Chens, Mr Wu (Chen's secretary), Rayna and I sat in one of the boxes that had once accommodated the bejewelled figures of the Muscovite aristocracy. In other boxes were soldiers, functionaries or workmen; the audience as a whole had the peculiar quality found only in Moscow—the quality of an audience that takes its drama and music as it takes its food, as one of the necessities of life, for which no dressing up and no social excitement are necessary.

One afternoon Rayna and I took Mme Sun to a cinema to see the films of her own arrival in Moscow. The expedition made her nervous, for she had a dread of being recognized in the streets. This had happened several times, and on each occasion there had been a certain amount of staring. The Foreign Office had given her a motorcar for the length of her stay, and she used to pull down all the blinds the moment she got into it, so as to move about Moscow as invisibly as possible. We reached the cinema in this darkened car, and when it had drawn up at the curb Rayna stood guard over it while I got the tickets. Then, the way being clear, Mme Sun made her dash from the car to the darkened interior of the theatre.

There was an ordinary film to be shown first, and it was indeed ordinary—a dismal affair in which Miss Mary Pickford (or Miss Norma Talmadge or Miss Somebody Else) made faces at two or three calf-faced young men for an hour or so. We none of us ever knew what the film was about, for Mme Sun was getting more and more nervous, and her appearance had already been noticed by two or three of the people sitting near us. Eventually the news films began, and the first of them was the arrival of Soong Ching-ling in Moscow.

It did not last long—six or seven minutes, perhaps—but during that time Mme Sun tore one of her minute handkerchiefs into bits. The film showed Litvinov and others arriving at the railway station; soldiers, Chinese Communists, youth organizations and other groups lined up, with their banners; a military band; and finally, the special train pulling in from Siberia. When it had come to a stop the camera moved nearer, and we saw the small figure of Mme Sun, hesitant and bewildered, appear on the steps to be greeted by Litvinov. At this Mme Sun, sitting beside me, gasped and whispered that she could not stand it any more. We got out as quickly as we could, which was a good thing, for a good many people in our neighbourhood had already made up their minds as to her identity.

The painful shyness from which Mme Sun suffered was not unknown to me; I had seen it in English people, for instance, particularly among artists or writers; but she was the only person so afflicted who ever, in my experience, deliberately faced it out. When she felt it her duty to do something that involved a public appearance she did it, although the agony was such that she might be obliged to take to her bed for days afterwards. In Moscow she tore all her handkerchiefs to ribbons and had to get new ones. Public attention was such torture to her that for this reason alone I never believed she was or could become an active revolutionary leader. In the hurly-burly passions of a street insurrection she would have been like a white rose in a furnace.

But theatres, the military spectacle, the picture of Moscow it-self, and even the rare and wonderful figure of Soong Ching-ling, took their place in that week (for me) as subsidiary parts of the continuous conversation with Rayna Prohme. It was a conversation in which no debate was possible. Fresh from China, imbued with the feelings and ideas of Hankow as they had been strength-ened by the opposition of Peking, I had no desire to attack the de-cisions she had made. They seemed to me the best decisions. She was going to continue her work for the Chinese revolutionary movement as long as it was required, but when—as she foresaw clearly—the parts of that movement would disintegrate, sending its vital element underground and leaving its bourgeois remnant stranded on the surface, she wanted to take a direct part in the work of the forbidden and secret organization. She had decided that life was not possible for her on any other terms; that she could not bear the spectacle of the world under its present arrange-ments, and that her place was within the organisms struggling to upset and rearrange it. This necessity was not wholly the result of social or economic theory, although she had a solid basis of training in the social sciences and was convinced of her solutions (the Leninist solutions); a deeper necessity had driven her on-ward. She felt a genuine relationship to all forms of human life. That was the essence of it. To her the Chinese coolie was another part of the whole life, rich, various, cruel and immense, that she shared to the extent of her limits in space and time. She could not see a Chinese coolie beaten and half starved, reduced to the level of the beasts, without feeling herself also beaten and half starved, degraded and oppressed; and the part of her that rebelled against this horror (her mind and spirit) was inflexibly resolved, by now, never to lie down under the monstrous system of the world. She was—to use Gerald Heard's word—'co-conscious' with all other parts of the human race. Man's inhumanity to man seemed to her a great deal more than that; it was an inhumanity of one part of the same body to another. The Shanghai entrepreneurs who em-ployed thousands of Chinese men, women and children at starva-tion wages for twelve and fourteen hours a day were, to her, like the hands of a body cutting off its legs. Capitalism, imperialism, individualism, were more abhorrent than cannibalism, but had the same inner character. They differed from cannibalism in being more universal and more difficult to correct.

I had not her purity or courage and could not feel these things with her deep sureness. But I did feel them. As I have said, she had now reached her centre and was sure; I was only magnetized towards it. I was at once more complex and less integrated than she. Often my first feelings had to be chastened; hers were clear at once. I may illustrate the point—which is not without importance—by a little incident of the road near Peking. One day I was driving in from the Hunting Park to lunch in Peking. The taxi sent out to me that day was, by chance, a particularly large and sumptuous Packard limousine. As we rolled along in to the capital we passed, somewhere near the Summer Palace, a gang of coolies working on the road. It was noon, and they had been eating their scraps of dinner. My car had to go a little slower as it passed them. Nothing happened until we had gone beyond the main gang; then one of the coolies suddenly reached for a bucket half full of water and dashed its contents at the open window of the car. Not much water came in, of course, but it was enough to wet one shoulder of my white silk coat.

Now, if anything like this had happened to Rayna, she would certainly have laughed—that laugh peculiar to her, a gaiety with tears behind it. She would have felt instantly what I felt only ten or fifteen minutes later: that to these miserable coolies, obliged to work out their days under the most appalling conditions, with never enough to eat and seldom a place to sleep, digging and fetching and carrying like beasts for the advantage of those who happened to be born elsewhere, the passage of such an insolently shining great motorcar with an insolent white-clad foreigner in it was intolerable provocation.

I felt exactly this, but not at once. My first impulse was one of unreasoning fury—just as if I had been a Shanghai merchant or an employee of the Standard Oil Company. I wanted to go back and 'give them hell.' Fortunately, my Chinese chauffeur had a better sense of reality than I had: he stepped on the accelerator with a heavy foot, and we shot down the road at sixty miles an hour, while I shouted vainly at him and beat on the glass in front of me. Ten minutes later I was ashamed of myself, ashamed of the shining car and the white silk clothes, ashamed of belonging to a race stupid and cruel enough to permit such wide variations in the development of its material. I would willingly have apologized to the coolie for having obliged him to throw a bucket of water at me—for taking advantage of my better grasp of the odious arrangements of which we were both parts—but the unfortunate thing is that if I had been able to do so I might have broken his head open first. Either because my impulses were strong and my intellect weak, or because the vanity, pride, selfishness and frivolity of middle-class surroundings had encouraged and indurated my individualist character, I could seldom trust to instinct in any such matter. My intelligence, such as it was, had to combat a set of thoroughly unruly impulses, and only succeeded in doing so by means of time and afterthoughts.

Rayna's individual impulses had been, by now, so subjugated and harmonized by her intelligence that the conflict was over: she was unified, integrated, and burned with a pure white flame. She was prepared for any sacrifice, up to and including death itself; petty questions (among which she included her personal destiny) could not disturb her any more. It was a marvellously pure flame, and even though I clearly could not hope to share its incandescence, it seemed to me that I must hover as near it as possible. Nothing else I had ever seen gave the same light and heat.

I decided to spend the winter in Moscow. The immediate problem was (of course) one of money: I had earned large sums and spent them in the past year, and the only way of getting through a winter in Moscow was to find editors or publishers who would pay for it. The matter was not easily arranged in Moscow itself, where cablegrams were expensive and letters slow. It was possible (if at all) by going to London. Towards the end of September I left Moscow for London, on the understanding that I was to return in about two weeks.

15

How can I characterize the clash of influences that filled every minute of the next three weeks in England? I was like a fish that had learned to walk on dry land for six months and now was plunged back into the ocean again; I was like a valley farmer inured to life on the top of a mountain, only to be thrown back into his lush native field when he could no longer till it. I found all my English friends unchanged; the pleasures of the mind and body, the agreeable diversions and preoccupations of modern Western life in the educated classes, had not undergone the slightest modification in all this time; these people were so sure of themselves, so accustomed to viewing the spectacle of the world without a direct interest in it, that they could discuss even the terrible alternatives of revolution with cool intellectual curiosity, neither feeling nor attempting to feel the need to choose between them. England—in spite of the General Strike of the year before— seemed as far from a genuine revolutionary situation as ever. Revolution was a melodramatic word without significance in these green fields and spacious houses, where any subject could be discussed and all subjects were of equal interest. The crippling thing—the really disastrous thing—was that my friends in England were more intelligent and better educated than myself; I might *feel* that I was right, that the moment in which we all lived presented a breathless intensity of meaning, that a decision was necessary if we were not to perish, but I could never *prove* it. They all knew too much for me, were too cool and logical and altogether superior to such alternatives.

I seemed more than a little eccentric to my English acquaintances just then, for their intellectual frigidity only drove me by reaction into excesses of statement and feeling. For a good part of the time I must have behaved (by any bourgeois standard) insufferably badly. I remember once when I went so far that a glazed look came into every English eye in the neighbourhood. I was staying with the Nicolsons at Long Barn, and another of their guests was Mrs. Nicolson's cousin, Eddy Sackville-West, the heir of Knole. The devotion of all members of the Sackville family to that monumental house, which sits in the midst of its lovely park like a visible history of the race that made it, was as well known to me as to anybody present, but I forgot the fact when Harold Nicolson (prompted by his familiar imp) propounded this question:

'What would a revolutionary government, or a Soviet government, or a proletarian dictatorship, do with a house like Knole? Specifically, let's take Knole and leave the others out. What would a revolution do to it?'

The question seemed very interesting, and I answered it at length. The special value of Knole was architectural and historical, I said, and would be so recognized by any revolutionary government. It had no value as a health resort or home for workmen, for it was neither healthy nor properly arranged for such purposes; it would not, therefore, be converted to other uses, but would almost certainly become what it was, in fact, today: a museum of the history and taste of the English aristocracy from the sixteenth to the nineteenth centuries. Such a museum would find its best guardians and interpreters in the people who knew it best—in fact, in Eddy Sackville-West and Vita Nicolson, who could usefully become its curators.

Only when this speech had come to an end did I observe the faces of the two 'curators.' Mrs. Nicolson recovered first and joined in the sudden laugh that turned the subject off, but I thought for a moment that her cousin was going to have a *crise*. I knew him only slightly then, and ought to have refrained from disposing of his house (not to speak of his own future) so cavalierly; but I had got into the habit, in the past six or seven months, of stating any idea as clearly as I knew how, with no nonsense about good taste or the behaviour of 'gentlemen.' It seemed to me that the whole trouble with the upper classes, in so far as I knew anything about them, was that they were afflicted by too much good taste and too many superstitions about being 'ladies and gentlemen' to form a correct idea of the materials of life. My temper of mind was—after six months of China and a week in Moscow—so different from theirs that their conventions and training, which obviously helped to make their company agreeable, nevertheless aroused the instinct of rebellion.

Incidents of the kind were numerous during those weeks. They testified to my own immaturity and instability of character more than to anything else, for a convinced revolutionary would either have stayed away from bourgeois and aristocratic influences or would have kept from affronting them with his ideas. I could do neither. When Captain Gordon Canning—my friend of the Rif—took me to lunch at Buck's Club I delivered a lecture to him, in those incongruous surroundings, on the necessity of world revolution as the only solution to the problems of oppressed nationalities (all this because he was going to Egypt). At Sir Horace Plunkett's house, when the kind old man was trying to tell me about some scheme of agrarian reform in India, I made a similar speech that left him bewildered. Hankow and Moscow had filled me so full of Leninist ardour that, although I did not know one member of the working classes in England, and seldom met anybody who was even partly sympathetic to the Communist idea, I was prepared to carry on a conversational class war all by myself.

The reason can be guessed by anybody who has endured to the present point in this book: it was a defence. I was angry and alarmed, on arriving in London, to discover that the old world of comfort, pleasure, taste, diversion and amusement still powerfully appealed to me; that the misery of nine tenths of the human race could seem dim and distant when considered from the midst of a well-supplied bourgeois dining room; that the things a Bolshevik—a working Bolshevik, like Rayna or Borodin—had to give up were things I valued. The material seductiveness of the bourgeois world was strengthened by an attack on the revolutionary idea itself: I was always having J. M. Keynes quoted at me, and being told that the waste of life and wealth (i.e., productive machinery) incidental to revolutions was uneconomic. My English friends, who were not themselves doing a thing to bring about the social rearrangement, always assured me that the rearrangement would take place; only, they said, it would take place in an orderly democratic fashion under the parliamentary tradition. They pointed to their advanced social legislation—unemployment insurance; death duties and income taxes scaled up to attack accumulations of capital; their pension system and the rest—as a proof of the capacity of a capitalist state to submit to orderly, progressive reformation. That these arrangements were, after all, at the mercy of political accident, and that the so-called 'social legislation' of bourgeois governments could not possibly protect the workers against the results of such crises as war, overproduction and speculation (the characteristic crises of capitalism according to the Marxist view), were objections ruled out by the Englishmen I knew with a succinct phrase: 'You want too much.'

Another aspect of English life that warred successfully against the enthusiasm I had brought from Moscow was, to put it in the most general terms, its poetry. By this I mean the exquisite prettiness of the English countryside; the fresh faces and cheerful voices; the lovely land that calls up, moment by moment, innumerable haunting echoes in the language of its innumerable poets. 'How sweet the moonlight sleeps upon this bank'—such things could be written only in England. It is hard to pin down this influence and label it exactly, but most people born into the races that speak English must have felt it in visiting the mother of the language. I had almost no English blood (one of my great-grandmothers was English, but so far as I know this was the only stain on a simon-pure Irish ancestry), and yet I could not help being stirred by a kind of home-coming of the imagination in the sights and sounds of the English country. On this particular visit the influence I am attempting to isolate, to which I have given the general name of 'poetry,' was most powerfully exercised at Cambridge. I went there one week-end, and I doubt if Borodin himself could have felt any urgent need of revolutionary activity in such a place.[1]

Cambridge, with its lovely stillness, its graceful, reflective innocence, made the melodramas of China and Russia fade out of my mind altogether for two days. I felt, face to face with the pure beauty of Clare or the nobility of King's, that the upper classes had not altogether abused their long tenure of wealth and power. Lytton Strachey took us to a pool in the garden of Christ's College one afternoon, and the scene is stamped on my memory more vividly than many more important scenes. The pool was stagnant, dark and ancient; in the days when Milton was an undergraduate at Christ's it probably was no different; it was surrounded by trees. In one vast solid tree there was an owl. Lytton stood under the tree and peered curiously up at the beast, which re-

---

[1]The undergraduates at Cambridge are said to be for the most part Communists or Socialists now, but they are English; I am talking about the influence of these poetic haunts upon the foreign visitor.

turned the compliment in kind. Nobody spoke except a gardener, who pointed out, in mild, respectful reproof, that the animal was dangerous. I cannot explain why this scene seemed to me so infinitely English, but there was something in it that caught at my breath. At all such moments I forgot about British imperialism, the warships in the Yangtze-kiang, the students slain on Shanghai's May Day, or the brutal egotism of so many Englishmen I had met in other countries; I could only think of what was before me: the peace and gentleness of England. If I had met just one rip-snorting British imperialist, or made just one visit to the coal-mining hells in Wales or Lancashire, the enchantment of England might have been dissipated easily enough, but no such salutary reminders came my way.

The sum of all my impressions on that visit to England would have meant nothing at all to Rayna or to Borodin. They were certain; their political philosophy never deserted them; they knew the economic bases of English upper-class life too well ever to be charmed by its graces. But I was (intellectually, at least) far from certain. The process by which my desire for integration had become involved with, and centred upon, Rayna Prohme was not a purely intellectual process, or it could never have been affected by any amount of bourgeois charm. I felt convinced that the issue of revolution was the only genuine issue (the only 'live option,' as William James would have said) in the world I lived in, but my own position with respect to the revolutionary struggle was more dubious than ever. The effect of England upon me, at a moment so critical, was like that of a brake applied to a wheel. It slowed me up, made me ask questions. The questions England suggested were personal ones. They went something like this: Why should you, leading an externally agreeable life under the bourgeois system of society, try to do anything to change it? What does it matter to you if Chinese coolies starve to death, if boys go into the coal mines of Lancashire at the age of twelve, if girls in Germany die by the hundred from tuberculosis and occupational diseases in the chemical factories? What do you care if the steel workers in Pennsylvania are maintained in conditions of life equivalent to slavery? Can't you forget about all that? You'll probably never starve; you can earn enough money with your silly little stories to lead a pleasant life; why not do so? You think revolution is inevitable—or say you do—and why not, then, leave it to other people, workmen, soldiers, Bolsheviks? It's their business, not yours; what have you got to do with it? Are you prepared to give up all the pleasures of modern Western culture, everything from good food and sexual liberty to Bach and Stravinsky, to work for the welfare of other people's grand-children in a world you will never see?

The answer was, decidedly, no. That was what England had done for me in the short space of twenty-one days.

I went to Berlin at the end of October and stayed long enough to complete my arrangements for the winter in Moscow. I was as 'revolutionary' in conversation as ever, but I knew that I did not possess the spirit of self-abnegation required to follow Rayna Prohme in the course that now lay before her. Her letters during October had shown an increasing determination in her purposes. She was on the point of entering the Communist party—not lightly or fashionably, as young men do in Paris and London, but with the intention of sacrificing her personal existence to its service. The whole thing made me unimaginably gloomy, and I could not see even so far as a month ahead, but I did know one thing: that I must make the most valiant attempt to save her, as a person, from absorption into the machine of the party or the Komintern. I no longer cared if this seemed the effort of a vulgar, selfish, lazy and cowardly bourgeois, for England had persuaded me that I was not a Bolshevik and never could be one; the leopard cannot change his spots.

But—by that rule of contradiction which operated upon me all through this time—I could not stop talking about Moscow. I must have been a great bore to everybody I met, and sometimes they did not hesitate to tell me so. I was staying at the Nicolsons' flat in Berlin (Harold had just been appointed Counsellor of the British Embassy there) and consequently met whatever visiting English there happened to be in Berlin at the time. One of them was Mr Drinkwater, whom we took to the Zoo; he seemed a little alarmed at one or two remarks I made, but bore it equably enough. Not so Noel Coward. That singularly prosperous young man thought the whole Communist philosophy was a pack of nonsense and berated me soundly for thinking twice about it. I had a platinum wrist watch, which seemed to him the most conclusive of arguments; he would point to it in scorn and say: 'That shows the kind of Bolshevik you are!'

Sinclair Lewis was in Berlin, too, and his response to my obsession was an incomparable one; I still laugh sometimes when I think of it. Dorothy Thompson, who became Mrs Lewis soon afterwards, asked me to dinner one night with some assorted German countesses and her prospective husband. Lewis—'Red,' we called him—was in fine form, and at his best he was one of the funniest people in the world. I had been particularly tiresome about Moscow that evening, for I was leaving the next day to see the celebration of the tenth anniversary of the Bolshevik Revolution. I kept on telling everybody, including the surprised German countesses, that they ought to go to Moscow for the seventh of November, for the spectacle alone, if for nothing else.

Catching, for about the five hundredth time, the sound of my voice informing some hapless German lady that she had to go to Moscow, Red suddenly burst forth.

'Oh, you must come to Moscow for the seventh of November,' he chanted, giving the sentence the obvious contour of a line by Vachel Lindsay. He went on without a pause, and in five minutes he had recited a whole poem by Vachel Lindsay—all about what was going to happen in Moscow on the momentous day (with a boom, boom, boom!) and how it was imperatively necessary for everybody to go there to see it. When we had recovered from this he went on and did the same thing in three other styles: Longfellow, Swinburne, Tennyson. The rhymes and metres were perfect, the parodies so keen that even the Germans did not need to be told what they were. The Tennyson parody was a triumph of ingenuity and wit, for it is always more difficult to hit off a good poet than a bad one. I have never heard anything like those improvisations; even Red could never do them so well again. They not only delighted their audience, but they performed one of the best offices of parody—showed up an absurdity. The most humourless enthusiast could scarcely have spoken of Moscow on the seventh of November after that.

It seemed that every element in the agreeable existence of Paris,

London, Berlin and New York had to be suggested to me in some way or other during the weeks of my absence from Moscow. Everything I saw, everybody I met, reminded me with irresistible force of my own bourgeois character and past. The different worlds of the American newspaper men in Paris, English intellectuals, Berlin visitors, conflicted in different ways, but all sharply, with the world of Moscow and Rayna Prohme. The duality to which I have referred on other occasions (notably in the first chapter of this history) was never more painful, and it set up an intolerable tension in my mind. How can anybody run with the hare and hunt with the hounds? How is it possible to eat your cake and have it too? How can you so enjoy the pleasures of middle-class life and still feel so profoundly the necessity to destroy them?

Harold Nicolson put me on the train in Berlin, and Rayna met me at the station in Moscow. That was the kind of journey it was —not only a space journey; not even primarily a space journey, although the stations succeeded each other through Germany, Poland and Russia with measured accuracy; it was an idea journey, a trajectory between two worlds. Afflicted, as I was, by a cloud of apprehensions, morbidly awake to every suggestion of the conflict, a hundred insignificant details contributed to the urgency of the crisis. One, for example, was a chance meeting with Ernest Hemingway. When the Paris–Moscow express pulled in to the Friedrichstrasse Bahnhof, and I was just about to climb aboard, Hemingway emerged from it in charming company. He had come to Berlin on his second honeymoon. I got into the train, and for an hour or so I did not think about Berlin or Moscow, one world or another, Rayna or Babylon; I was considering the phenomenon of Hemingway. The chance meeting had called up half-forgotten scenes of Paris a year or so before, people and places, dinners and conversations, that now had changed their sense for me. I had just read a book of Hemingway's and had admired it very much. Here was a highly conscious, deliberate artist, more conscious and deliberate than any American I knew about in our time, who apparently felt no relationship between individual and mass—no necessity to discover a relationship. Why couldn't I (allowing for the general inferiority of my equipment as a writer) do what he did—shut out the whole world and live, both as writer and as human being, in the restricted company of my own kind? (A different kind: but the principle would be the same.) He wrote prose with the precision and power of poetry, upon subjects of the narrowest individual significance—the very special quarrel of a girl and her lover at a railway station; the tragedy of a man who had had his testicles shot away in the war; the mind of a prize-fighter, of a bull-fighter; the loyalty of a jockey to his worthless father. These subjects (except the last) were the fine flower of individualism. They were rare, exceptional subjects, the choice of an artist to whom life was personal and nothing else. Indeed, when he tried to extend his meaning beyond its strict subjectivity —when, for example, he prefaced a novel about himself and his friends with an eminently foolish remark of Miss Gertrude Stein's, 'You are all a lost generation'—he fell into nonsense. His 'lost generation' included few people, and even with regard to them, however brilliantly he filmed their behaviour, he did not seem to understand why they were 'lost.' Yet—a big, resounding yet— this man was the only one I knew who had fulfilled his function in work. He was, of all the writers or artists of this approximate age, the one who had most amply developed and exactly applied the gifts he possessed. You got the impression of finality from even his slightest story—that this was *it;* that it could not be done otherwise, and that if he lived a thousand years he could never improve upon it. The question arose, then: wasn't his way the best way, perhaps the only way, for an American bourgeois writer in the first half of the twentieth century to find his certainties and act upon them? What did he care about Chinese coolies? He had written *My Old Man*.

The train drew in to the October Station in Moscow before noon on November 7th, and Rayna's fiery hair was the first thing I saw on the platform. I had been away from Moscow—far away from Moscow—for a good five weeks.

16

Rayna had taken rooms in a house in the Bolshaya Dmitrovka, number 72, near the centre of Moscow.

'I looked at everything there was,' she said, 'and if you don't like what I found it'll be just too bad. There's a small bedroom and a sitting room with a desk and a couch. I've got a lot of my papers in the desk, but otherwise the place is yours. There's a bathroom, too, but none of the plumbing works.'

'Why do I have to have two rooms?'

'I don't know. I thought you were too grand to live in one room. Anyway, that sitting room is the only place I've seen in Moscow where anybody could do any work. It's all right except for the damned doves—and the landlady. You don't know how hard it is to find rooms in Moscow. Why did it take you so long to get here?'

'I don't know—I had a lot of trouble fixing things up. Has the show begun?'

'It started early this morning, and they've been marching through the Red Square ever since. I've got a ticket for you. We can leave your stuff and go on to the Red Square right away.'

'Where's Trotzky?'

'He was in the street this morning. He tried to speak to the crowd from a window near the Theatre Square, and they shut him up. Some people say he's been arrested. . . . There are a lot of strange things going on just now.'

'Borodin?'

'He arrived about a week ago. He's all right, but of course he's blamed. . . . I wish I knew what was going to happen!'

We found the house in the Bolshaya Dmitrovka and interviewed the large landlady. She spoke copious French, gallons of it at a time, and terrified me from the first moment. Her efforts to explain the history of Russia during the next weeks constituted a steady irritation. 'Monsieur! Vous ne savez pas! Ah, ce que vous ne savez pas!' and so on, in a loud voice, with gestures. The poor woman had once been a dancer and had a grudge against the world because she was no longer young, beautiful and agile. We got away from her as soon as we could and walked down to the Red Square.

We went through several cordons of soldiery before we got into the square.

'That's to keep the masses away from the celebration of their revolution,' I pointed out.

Rayna looked at me, puzzled.

'Something's happened to you,' she said. 'What is it? You didn't talk like that before.'

'I don't know. Let's go see your show. Lucky we've got friends at court, or we'd never be able to get through the guards.'

The passes Rayna held in her hand admitted us to the successive circles around the Kremlin, and at last we stood in the ranks underneath the wall, not far from the tomb of Lenin. The enormous square was filled with marching people. Crowded, disciplined, innumerable, they came into the square under the arch of the Iberian Virgin and rolled across it to the Cathedral of St Basil, where they vanished. For half a day the delegations from all parts of European and Asiatic Russia had been riding or marching through the square, and there were still scores of thousands to come. We found places in the stands and watched for hour after hour. In a high box next to the tomb of Lenin the Russian Communist leaders stood and received the cheers of the uncountable crowd. Stalin was there, in the middle, constantly saluting. It was easy to see how the spectacle now before us, suggesting the tremendous power and density of the Russian mass, would cause the breast of an Old Bolshevik (Stalin, for instance) to swell and glow. The thought of those ten years of desperate struggle made the anniversary seem wholly triumphant to those who were on the right side. But even among Bolsheviks it was hard to forget that Stalin had not dared to call a Congress of the Soviets for a year and a half; that the revolutionary genius who had directed the events of November 17, 1917, was now muzzled and locked away; that with him a whole phalanx of Communist intellectuals, some of the best writers and speakers in the party, were suppressed or about to be suppressed; that the world revolution was abandoned and the actual dictatorship of Russia lodged, not in the proletariat or even in the Russian Communist party, but in a tiny group called the Political Bureau. These reflections were in the air in Moscow on that day; I was by no means the only person out of the hundreds of thousands of people in the Red Square who dwelt upon them. If Trotzky had been enthroned alone above the tomb of Lenin, receiving the homage of the revolution they had made together, he could not have become more conspicuous than he was by his absence. The orderly marchers seemed to me to cheer perfunctorily, by command, and I did not feel—as I had occasionally felt in China—that this mass was fired with a genuine enthusiasm. There were too many rumours afloat, too many dark stories and desperate suppositions. Most of them, as it happened, were untrue, but they had their effect. One of the Chinese Communist delegations had come into the Red Square with the orthodox slogans stamped on their red banners, and suddenly, when they passed in front of Stalin and the remains of the Central Executive Committee, flipped the banners over and disclosed signs reading: 'Long live Trotzky!' They were arrested and put away. (Is this story true or not? I never knew; my Chinese Communist friends said it was, and there was certainly some kind of disturbance, but it was officially denied.) Kamenev had been exiled; Trotzky had been killed; Trotzky had not been killed; Joffe had committed suicide or was trying to commit suicide or had been refused medical attention in the Kremlin Hospital. . . . The Komintern had been reorganized, or was going to be reorganized, its claws cut, its income reduced; all energy in future was to be spent on Russia alone; there was going to be a further retreat towards Capitalism; the Soviet Congress was to be allowed to lapse altogether, the 'constitution' of the Soviet State was gone, and there was nothing left but that small, determined group, the Politbüro. . . .

We stayed in the Red Square until five o'clock on that day, and by then even Rayna's determination to make the best of it was a little worn. She did not agree with me that the demonstration was lacking in spirit, but she did say, with a sudden touch of gloom: 'It was nothing like China. If you had seen what it used to be like in Canton!'

We made our way through the crowds to the Metropol Hotel to call on my former 'relative,' Fanny Borodin. She had arrived in Moscow a few days before, and on this afternoon she was the only person I encountered who seemed much uplifted by the spectacle. She gestured towards the window over the square and said, clasping her hands together ecstatically:

'Isn't it wonnderful? Isn't it wonnderful? When I think of how many years we've worked for this, it all seems like a beautiful dream!'

We went downstairs and dined with Anna Louise Strong, who had come through Mongolia with Borodin and had written a book about it in thirteen days; we wandered about the streets afterwards and ended up at Walter Duranty's house. There was a British Labour M. P. there (the late Frank Wise) who had a sense of humour, and the evening ended cheerfully enough. But throughout that day and for the days that followed I was beset by indefinite and torturing premonitions. They were not correct (what premonitions are?), but they were near enough to what did happen to assume—even at this distance in time—an awful significance. I engaged in a desperate struggle, from that first day onward, to keep Rayna from joining the Communist party.

Of all the contradictions of the period, this was perhaps the worst. The pure flame that gave such light and heat—what was it? The centre towards which I was magnetized, the focus of the world as I saw it, was Rayna Prohme as revolutionary: it was not revolution alone, and it was not Rayna Prohme alone, but Rayna Prohme integrated and set alight by her conviction. This was, in fact, my reason for being in Moscow. And yet from the moment I arrived I fought tooth and nail to get her away from her own essential centre—to recall her, by whatever means, to the half world in which I wanted to keep on living.

When I use such strong words—'desperate' and 'tooth and nail'—I mean everything they mean and more. For six days and nights the struggle continued with hardly a respite. Her room was on the other side of my sitting room, in the adjoining apartment, and when either of us thought of a new argument we kicked on the wall; in two minutes—the time required to take down the innumerable barricades of iron, wood and steel put up by my timorous landlady—we had met and started all over again. We talked until four or five o'clock in the morning sometimes, and the argument was forever renewed, never brought to an end. We neither of us got much sleep, but I was as strong as an ox and did not realize what a terrible strain the whole thing was on her nervous system. No matter how bitterly I may have regretted all this afterwards, it is the fact. When her physical fragility impressed me more than usual, I used it, too, as an argument. She had been having severe headaches for months, and they had lately grown more frequent; aspirin and phenacetin did not help them; sometimes in the midst of the argument a dazed stare would come into her eyes and she would say: 'Wait a minute. I must just be quiet for a minute; it's the headache again.' When it passed, I used to ask her how she proposed to endure the rigours of life as an active revolutionary when her physical resources were so limited. This argument had no effect. She would laugh and say: 'In or out of a revolution, I've got to die sometime, and what does it matter?' Her disregard of her own personal destiny was so complete that nothing I could think of made an impression upon it. The arguments that did reach her were the general ones, those directed at the idea of revolution itself; and one of the most effective of these was the one I had suffered from in London—the opinions of J. M. Keynes as shown in his recent booklet about Russia. I telegraphed to London for that booklet, but it never arrived.

It would be foolish to maintain that there was nothing selfish and personal in all this. There was. I have said that in September I already felt that I could not live without the light and heat that came from this extraordinary flame. In September I had had no doubts; I would have followed her into the Lenin Institute, into the Communist party, to Korea or Japan or anywhere. In October I had been forced to reconsider; I saw, too clearly, my own inadequacies for such a life. In November I was no longer willing to follow her, even in mind, but struggled instead to bring her back from the certainty in which she dwelt to the easier world where men did not die for their beliefs—where they did not, in fact, have any beliefs if they could help it. This endeavour was selfish and personal, based, in the first instance, on a feeling that Rayna Prohme as a completed revolutionary instrument (in a year's time, let us say), would be a stranger to the lazy bourgeois I had recently rediscovered. She would be lost to me and to my world: in the sense of a bourgeois individuality she would be lost altogether, for her intentions were, even for a Communist, extreme.

She had decided to join the party and enter the Lenin Institute to be trained as a revolutionary instrument. When she had completed her training she was to take service in one of the revolutionary organizations, probably in the Pacific Labour Bureau to begin with, perhaps afterwards in direct work for the Komintern. Her special qualification coincided with her own desire, and she would be sure to be sent to the Far East.

No decision in life could be more final. The vows of a nun, the oaths of matrimony, the resolutions of a soldier giving battle, had not the irrevocable character of this decision. Rayna was not taking it lightly; she had had four years of intimate acquaintance with revolutionary work and knew what she was doing. Nothing I could bring up about the nature of the work or its effects made the slightest difference to her, for I found that she had considered it all before.

We knew, for example, that certain workers for the Komintern had been obliged to adopt all sorts of expedients to effect their own escapes and protect the revolutionary organizations in the East. I pressed this point mercilessly.

'Are you prepared to tell lies and forge passports and change your name and even pretend not to belong to the party you work for?'

This kind of thing came nearest to affecting Rayna's certainty, for she was the soul of candour.

'If it is absolutely necessary I will do all that,' she would reply steadily. 'I don't believe it would be necessary or advisable in most cases. But if something important depends upon it, what does it matter if I tell lies? Nothing can be hurt but my own peace of mind, and that isn't important.'

'Are you prepared to obey instructions even when you feel them to be absolutely mistaken?'

'Certainly. If I didn't feel that the experienced Bolsheviks knew more about revolutionary technique than I do, I shouldn't be here.'

I was reduced, again and again, to the simplest forms of impotent argument—attacks upon the emotional nature of the revolutionary, attacks upon Rayna's personal structure.

'Of course, the truth is,' I would say, 'that you derive a personal thrill out of the idea of being a revolutionary worker. It's sheer romanticism. Far more exciting than going home to Chicago and listening to symphony concerts! That's the truth of it. Whether the idea of revolution is correct or not doesn't matter: you've got to have your thrill.'

I never said a thing like this without realizing at once how miserably specious and vulgar it was; but when I had exhausted all the legitimate arguments I could think of, wild stabs were the only form of attack left. Rayna, as it happened, understood the process too thoroughly to be disturbed by it: she knew that a remark of the kind was only a confession of weakness, of intellectual exhaustion, and however weary she might be herself, she never failed to laugh. That laugh was generally accompanied by a polite admonition to use a little rudimentary intelligence, put into this form:

'Don't be a damned fool, Jimmy.'

After seven crowded years this advice sounds as plain and recent as if it had been delivered ten minutes ago. I do not pretend to have acted upon it consistently or even most of the time, but at certain important moments, without preparation in thought or association of ideas, it has suddenly broken through every surrounding circumstance and rung again in my ears, tone and accent and laugh and all, like an actual voice.

The week passed in an argument so intense and unrelieved that it is only by diligent search that I can find out what its external events were. We saw a certain number of other people; the Americans—Anna Louise, Lewis Fischer, and Dorothy Thompson, who came to Moscow that week—and the Chinese. Borodin was busy and worried, and I saw him only two or three times.

Mme Sun Yat-sen had been estranged from Rayna by an unfortunate circumstance that merits recording, and I did not see her for days. The circumstance was this: the New York *Times* had printed on its front page, sometime during October, a story to the effect that Mme Sun Yat-sen was about to marry Eugene Chen, and that the Soviet government was giving them a honeymoon in the Crimea for a wedding present. This story, so silly to anybody with the slightest knowledge of the people involved, presented disastrous alternatives to Rayna: she had either to tell Mme Sun and risk throwing her into a nervous breakdown, or not tell her and risk unpredictable consequences. Mr Chen, as soon as he heard the report, forbade Rayna to mention it to Mme Sun under any circumstances. As she was still ostensibly in the service of the Kuomintang, and directly responsible to Mr Chen (even though without salary), she obeyed. The result was that Mme Sun Yat-sen, returning from a two weeks' rest in the Crimea, met an American on the railway train who bustled up and congratulated her on her approaching marriage to Chen.

She arrived in Moscow in a state of collapse, took to her bed and stayed there. Her nervous system had undergone shock after shock in the service of the highest loyalty she knew—to Sun Yat-sen and the Revolution—and she had sacrificed to that ideal most of the things any Chinese woman holds dearest. To find out, after all this, that it had been useless: that the world at large regarded her flight to Moscow as a vulgar and insignificant elopement—an elopement, moreover, with a man of mixed race, with whom her association had been exclusively political—was a blow of annihilating force. She was ill for three weeks, and during most of that time she refused to see her friends. She was just beginning to recover a little when another stunning blow was delivered, also by means of the newspapers: her young sister Mei-ling was married in Shanghai, with all the display and expensive nonsense of a 'society wedding,' to the illiterate counter-revolutionary, Chiang Kai-shek. Nothing could have hurt her more. Her bravery and dignity were equal to anything, but her physical organization was not. In these dark days, when she was unable to get out of bed, it seemed to her that Rayna, too, had been lacking in loyalty —that Rayna should have told her at once about the story in the New York *Times* and faced it with her. And Rayna's loyalty, so absolute in all matters, did not even permit her to tell Mme Sun that Chen had forbidden it.

This was the situation in the small group of Hankow refugees. They were all at sixes and sevens, and Rayna's actual work— except for some assistance to Borodin in the preparation of a report—had come to a stop. Deprived of the daily association with Mme Sun she turned more and more towards the Chinese and Russian Communists, among whom she had devoted friends, and they certainly had no desire to throw obstacles in the way of the great decision she was now making. All this had taken place before my arrival in Moscow on November 7th, and although Rayna always made valiant efforts to rise above personal considerations, and did rise above them more successfully than anybody else I have ever known, the situation in which she lived just then did not retard, and may even have accelerated, the processes by which she was approaching the final act of immolation.

I am anxious not to exaggerate or generalize the feelings of gloomy tension that weighed down the air of that time in Moscow for me. It is quite possible that large numbers of other people there felt no such thing. In fact, I know that this must be so. One day Dorothy Thompson took me to tea with a foreign ambassadress, and the conversation was—except for a certain amount of talk about funerals and assassinations—light in tone. Dorothy herself was cheerful; most of the press correspondents were the same in Moscow as anywhere else; and even among Bolsheviks and good Soviet citizens the celebrations of the anniversary were not lacking in gaiety. The streets of Moscow are no gloomier than other streets, and among some of the delegations from foreign countries there was a recognizable enthusiasm, an atmosphere of hope. But all external circumstances took a secondary place to the passionate and fatal argument in which I was engaged. In the frame of mind thus set up, dark with apprehension, gloomy with fear, shaken unbearably by the desire to save a human life of the first importance, my imagination seized upon all the sinister rumours afloat in Moscow and worked them into the growing horror with which I regarded the central problem. Among these rumours were innumerable stories about the fate of the leaders of the Communist Opposition, confused theories about the future of the Komintern and of the foreign revolutions (the disposal of the Chinese, for instance), and—perhaps the gloomiest single story of all—the illness and death (or suicide) of Joffe, who had made the original alliance between Soviet Russia and Sun Yat-sen. As the week wore on I took refuge more and more in vodka, for it seemed to me only a question of days before a violent crash of some kind must bring this tension to an end, and whatever the end might be, it could not be contemplated clearly and steadily.

The end I foresaw was the definitive entrance of Rayna into the Communist party and the Lenin Institute, and to this event— which all of my struggles did not seem to be able to postpone— I gave the name, during those days, of 'the end of Rayna Prohme.'

On Friday, November 11th, we argued almost all night long. It was the last argument. At the end of it, when every element in the problem, personal and general, had been gone over a thousand times, and Rayna's resolution was still unshaken, we said good-bye—not too solemnly, of course: there was always some lightness in Rayna's spirit; she could always laugh, even though it was not altogether easy. It was the kind of good-bye I can scarcely explain unless it is instantly apparent. We were to meet again the next day, but in the essential sense it was good-bye just the same. She was to go to the Lenin Institute on the following Monday, and I was going to leave Moscow as soon as I could do so. I asked her to do one trivial thing for me (I do not know what I hoped to prove by it). This was to dress on the following night in the golden dress from China that Soong Ching-ling had given her, to wear Bill's amber necklace, and to dine with me in the most flagrant luxury Moscow had to offer, at the Grand Hotel (Bolshaya Moskovskaya). This was before the Five-Year Plan, of course, and the Metropol had not yet become what it was afterwards: a luxurious establishment for foreigners. Moscow's most bourgeois place just then was the old Grand Hotel, where most of the foreign visitors lived. Since my arrival in Moscow, throughout this week's argument, Rayna had worn the same dress: a wadded green silk dress in Chinese style, the warmest she possessed. We had taken our meals either at the cheap café underneath the Metropol or in workmen's coöperatives, where we could eat for very little, as neither of us had any money. I wanted one 'bourgeois evening' for myself, for the sheer pleasure of it, and to see her once more in that gold dress; but it is possible that I also hoped (madness, of course) that silk and flowers, music and white wine from the south, might accomplish what I had failed to do, and bring her back a little way towards the world she had been born into and was now surrendering forever.

'O.K.,' said Rayna. 'I'll freeze to death in that gold dress, I can tell you, but if I can borrow an overcoat and run like hell when we get out in the street, I'll do it. You shall have your bourgeois evening, but it won't make any difference.'

On the next day (Saturday, November 12th) she went to see Dorothy Thompson at the Bolshaya Moskovskaya and fainted in Dorothy's room. This seemed a little alarming, but by that night it had been forgotten.

'I feel grand tonight,' she said. 'Silly of me to faint like that, but I do feel better now than I have for days. I think I'm going to enjoy the bourgeois evening.'

She looked—as she said—grand. She was only a thin girl, with no particular stature or figure or conventional beauty, but her appearance was at all times lighted up by her expressive eyes and the glory of her hair. The red-brown-gold of her short curls gave her the look of a lighted candle when she wore the gold dress from China. It was cut severe and straight, Manchu style, with a collar, and was made of very plain silk the colour of dull gold. I had seen it only once, on the evening in September when Mme Sun had taken us to the Great Theatre to see *Krassny Mak*.

We went to the Bolshaya Moskovskaya and had our bourgeois evening. We even danced—twice. Dorothy Thompson came and sat with us, and I told her what was happening. She seemed a little startled and incredulous.

'You understand what it is?' I said. 'It's the end of Rayna Prohme. No more Rayna. Finished. Revolutionary Instrument Number 257,849.'

The truth of what I was saying was too much to bear quietly just then, and I turned towards Rayna and pounded her thin shoulders in the Chinese dress.

'The end of Rayna Prohme,' I said. 'The end of Rayna Prohme.'

She moved away, threw back her fiery head and laughed.

'It's the end even of Revolutionary Instrument Number So-and-So,' she said, 'if you don't stop beating me. What do you think I'm made of, anyway?'

The dinner, the gold dress, the certainty of the decision, the gloom of Moscow, the Napareuli wine and vodka, all together had operated to destroy my common sense that night. Even when I was not saying it, I was thinking it, and I said it often enough:

'The end of Rayna Prohme.' That night seemed as final as death itself.

After a while Rayna proposed a bargain.

'I've agreed to the bourgeois evening,' she said, 'and I've carried it out, gold dress and all. Now, don't you think we could end up at the Congress? They're decorating the foreign Bolsheviks tonight, and I'd like to see it.'

We went off to the Congress of Friends of the Soviet Union. It was held in the old Hall of the Nobility of Moscow, a marble palace that had served the ladies and gentlemen of Tolstoy's aristocracy for their splendid entertainments. Now the immense staircase was thronged with Communists and Communist sympathizers from all over the world, and the ballroom itself, as large as the largest opera houses, was filled with proletarian delegates. Great banners strung across the marble halls, and across the ballroom itself, shouted in letters of gold on red, in all the languages: 'Workers of the World, Unite!' On the platform Voroshilov, the head of the Red army, was speaking from the midst of a throng of Russian and foreign delegates, and as we reached our places in one of the galleries he was just about to bestow the Order of the Red Flag on the aged German Communist, Clara Zetkin.

Zetkin, the Frenchman Jacques Sadoul, and the Hungarian Bela Kun, were the heroes of the occasion. Zetkin's appearance was (even to me on that night) impressive. The old woman had spent her whole life in the revolutionary struggle, and her cracked voice trembled with emotion as she thanked Voroshilov for her bit of ribbon and the throng of delegates for their cheers. Bela Kun aroused the thousands of people there to their highest pitch of enthusiasm. He was the only European Bolshevik who had ever succeeded, even for the briefest time, in instituting a Soviet government, and the crowd yelled itself hoarse when he stepped up to Voroshilov to receive his decoration.

I was standing beside Rayna in one of the galleries when this happened. As the roars of the crowd came up to us, crashing in successive, irregular waves like thunder, she looked up at me, and I could see that her eyes were brilliant with tears. I grasped frantically for the nearest weapon and could find only one thing:

'The little fellow looks funny, standing there beside Voroshilov, doesn't he?'

(Voroshilov was tall and thin, Bela Kun short and tubby.)

'Oh, damn you!' Rayna said, wiping her eyes impatiently. 'Can't you feel it at all?'

I did feel it, but I did not want to; and above all the intensity with which she felt it made me, for the moment, almost insane. I left the Hall of the Nobles and went to drink some vodka. When I came back I found Rayna deep in conversation with Comrade Roy, the head of the Far Eastern section of the Komintern. I wandered about the halls for a while, and when I found her again she was surrounded by Chinese Communists. Finally I went away for good, returned to the Bolshaya Moskovskaya, and drank all the vodka I could contain. It was four o'clock in the morning before I went home to the house in the Bolshaya Dmitrovka.

I slept late the next day (Sunday, November 13th), and walked slowly across to the Metropol in the afternoon to see if Rayna was there. As I came up the steps of the hotel, just where I had met Rayna on that evening almost exactly two months before, I ran into Anna Louise Strong and a little Chinese Communist called Chang Ke. Rayna had saved Chang Ke's life in Peking in 1926 by concealing him in the basement of her house, and he was devoted to her.

'Mrs Prohme is very ill,' Chang Ke said in his flat, emotionless voice.

'She's at the Europe,' Anna Louise said, 'and apparently she's fainted. Chang Ke came to get me. We'll have to bring her back here and put her in my room for a while.'

I went along with them to the Hôtel de l'Europe, a small hotel about a square and a half away from the Metropol. Chang Ke led us up the stairs here to a small room, the anteroom to the part of the hotel occupied by the Chinese Labour Delegation. One or two Chinese were sitting there quietly, and Rayna was lying unconscious on a couch.

I picked her up and carried her downstairs and through the streets. She weighed nothing; it was like carrying a child. Once she recovered consciousness enough to speak, asked if she was heavy, and tried to stand up. The people in the streets stared a little and then hurried along on their way. We reached the Metropol quickly, and there Rayna recovered enough to sit up in the lift and apologize for having fainted. But before we got to Anna Louise's room on the top floor she was gone again.

I left her there, in Anna Louise's bed, and went downstairs to see Borodin. He was not in, but I saw Mme Borodin.

'I knew something like this would happen,' she said cheerfully. 'Mrs Prohme works too hard and thinks too much. I never worry! Besides, I expect she doesn't take care of herself. Now you take my advice and make her eat a lot of lemons. There's nothing on earth so good for the system as God's lemon. It's a simple remedy, you may think, but it's a good one. I always say I wouldn't be alive today if it weren't for God's lemon and my rink.'

I did not know what she meant by her rink, but she showed me. It was some sort of contraption worked by gas or electricity, a circular affair on which she was accustomed to cook meals.

'With plenty of lemons and a good rink,' she said, 'nobody ever need be sick. I took my rink with me all across Mongolia; I simply could not live without it. Never trust other people's food! Now, if you insist, I'll telephone for the neighbourhood doctor, and he'll come at once. But believe me, the real remedy is God's lemon.'

She left her rink and her lemons long enough to telephone for the doctor, whose assistant said he would come at once. But whenever I saw Mme Borodin again during the next six days she seized the opportunity to repeat her advice about God's lemon.

I was no good to Anna Louise in taking care of Rayna, and had nothing to do but walk about the town and wait for the doctor. Hours passed before the doctor came. Rayna had recovered consciousness, wholly or partly, and lay silent in the darkened room. Towards evening the 'neighbourhood doctor,' a weary Russian with two assistants and an incredible amount of paraphernalia, arrived and set to work. These gentlemen took possession of the room and started to unpack all their tubes and packs and appliances, which cluttered up the whole floor. I was asked to leave, and did not return for an hour.

By this time Rayna was sleeping fitfully, and I learned that she had been given ether—which, as by chance I happened to know, made her deathly sick. For the rest of that night she was alternately sick and delirious. I thought she should be taken at once to the Kremlin Hospital, and Anna Louise agreed with me, but nothing could be done without the Borodins, and I could not find them.

On the next day Moscow was covered deep in snow. It was bitter cold. The place in the Bolshaya Dmitrovka had become unbearable to me overnight, its every corner filled with the sight and sound of Rayna. I moved to the Savoy that morning. I reached the Metropol in a state of unnamable terror, only to find Rayna rational and able to laugh again. She had passed a dreadful night and was very weak, but she blamed it on the ether. Anna Louise had slept (if at all) on a couch moved into the room. I suggested then that we should take Rayna to the Kremlin, but the patient vetoed this absolutely.

'I'm all right,' she said. 'It's nerves and those headaches, that's all. But I must say I'd like to have a doctor I could trust. We told that fool last night exactly what ether would do to me, and he gave it to me just the same.'

I went off, at this, to look for a doctor. The only person I could appeal to with any confidence just then was Walter Duranty. He was still in bed when I got to his house, but he sat up and put his mind to the problem. While we sat discussing it Bruce Hopper, an American, arrived and joined in. He suggested the German Embassy's doctor, and Walter seemed to agree. Hopper conducted me through the snowstorm to the tram for the doctor's office, and about half an hour later I was talking to Dr Linck. I had no special affection for either doctors or Germans, but that calm, stolid man, so slow and thoughtful in speech, made the fussy brigade of Russians the night before look like so many monkeys. Dr Linck promised to come as soon as he could, and I went back to the Metropol.

We moved Rayna to a room of her own that day. She refused to have a professional nurse or to go to the Kremlin, and Anna Louise Strong and Sonya Vep agreed to take care of her by turns. Sonya—whose real name was Veplinova or Veplinskaya or something of the sort; we had always called her and her husband Vep—

was a gentle, sweet-voiced Russian, the wife of an agitator who had worked in China. Vep himself had been trained as a doctor and was almost as gentle as Sonya. They and Anna Louise did most of what was to be done, for I was hopelessly awkward and incompetent. The only thing I was good for was sitting in the room, and even this (when Rayna was asleep and the room was quite dark) almost drove me mad.

After Dr Linck's visit Rayna became cheerful again. She too had confidence in him. As she felt better the curtains were pulled back, and the room grew light. Many people came to see her—Mme Sun Yat-sen, Borodin, Chang Ke, Scott Nearing, Lewis Fischer and others. Mme Sun's feeling about the New York *Times* incident had evaporated the moment she heard of the illness, and she visited Rayna every day that week. They spoke of plans, and what seemed to me the most hopeful thing of all—the thing that might save everything from wreck—was a possibility of Mme Sun's going to the United States. If she did this she wanted Rayna to go with her, and for two or three days in the middle of that week, in spite of the steady gravity in Dr Linck's eyes when I talked to him, I convinced myself that all the problems could be solved at last.

The week of November 13th was less difficult to get through than the previous week had been. Dr Linck had forbidden political discussion of any kind in Rayna's room, and had made her promise that she would obey his orders. This ukase brought out the patient's laughter.

'Will you tell me,' she said, poking at her pillows, 'what on earth anybody'd ever talk about in Moscow if political discussion was forbidden? What do you suppose we can talk about? I can't remember any other subjects!'

We found the other subjects readily enough, and throughout the week those conversations—never political—were, however difficult it may be to imagine it under the circumstances, a delight. We talked about everything under the sun except politics. She told me long stories about her childhood in Chicago and about a scapegrace younger brother whom she loved. I was never there in the mornings, and when I came in the afternoon she always had a budget of visits to tell me about. Occasionally I had titbits of nonpolitical intelligence to bring her, an account of Mr Theodore Dreiser's latest, a description of a gathering of Communist artists and intellectuals, or the impression of Eisenstein's new film. The week passed almost gaily. After Dr Linck's arrival and the reconciliation with Mme Sun Yat-sen Rayna was in good spirits, sometimes in high spirits, and for months I had not heard her laugh ring out as it did on some of those afternoons. Anna Louise, who had been an invaluable friend all through the week, was nervous and tired towards the end of it, and we thought that between the Veps and myself we could manage without her on Friday.

On that day we must have talked all afternoon and most of the night. Often I wanted to stop talking and let her rest, but she felt better than she had felt for a long time, and it amused her to lie there and recall a thousand stories of her early life, most of which were new and very funny to me. In that whole day the word 'revolution' was mentioned only once. That was when she suddenly recalled Eugene Chen's good-bye to her in Peking two years before. He had said at the door of their office, just as he was about to take wing for Canton:

'The Revolution is grateful,' and then, magnificently: 'The Kuomintang never forgets!'

We both laughed helplessly at this reminiscence.

She also talked a good deal about Bill Prohme, now thousands of miles away in Manila, to whom her affection and loyalty had been constant always. She even dictated a letter to him in which she said she was a little under the weather but would be all right soon.

That night her illness took a turn for the worse, and although none of us yet knew what it was, its seriousness could no longer be concealed. She passed a bad night and was forbidden visitors in the morning. When I was left alone with her for the afternoon on Saturday she spoke to me in a low voice. I had to lean over to hear what she said.

'The doctor thinks I am losing my mind,' she said, 'and that is the worst thing of all. He won't say so, but that is what he thinks. I can tell by the way he holds matches in front of my eyes and tests my responses. He doesn't think I can focus on anything.'

She had spoken vaguely of the fear before, and all I could do was say that I did not believe it was well founded. But on the next day (Sunday, November 20th) she felt certain that this was the case, and it kept her silent and almost afraid to speak, even to me. I sat beside her hour after hour in the dark, silent room, and blackness pressed down and in upon us. Two or three times she raised her voice to say: 'Don't tell anybody.' I knew that this meant her fear that her mind was attacked, and I promised not to tell. Later in the afternoon we talked a little, and she suddenly agreed with a proposal I had made some days before—that when she was able to travel she should go to Germany for treatment. Towards night she said: 'I'll go to sleep for a while now, and when I wake up we can send a cablegram.' I never heard her speak again.

Dr Linck came in the evening and said that a professional nurse must be put on duty at once. The nurse came and sat. Sonya and Vep remained for most of the night in the little ante-room, and Anna Louise returned, too. The place was kept in complete darkness and silence. I was dazed with horror and felt nothing. I came and went; walked in the Red Square; went to the Bolshaya Moskovskaya and drank vodka; returned to the Metropol from time to time to speak to Sonya. During the night Rayna woke up once and asked Sonya for me, but I was across the square. When I reached the room she was unconscious again. She had wanted me, I suppose, to send the cablegram.

On his last visit the doctor said: 'The process I have foreseen has begun. It must take its course.' Although I heard these words clearly, and they were repeated to me by Anna Louise afterwards, they still did not carry their obvious meaning to my dazed intelligence. At three or four in the morning I went around the corner to the Savoy Hotel and went to bed.

At seven o'clock that morning (it was Monday, November 21st) the telephone in my room rang. Anna Louise's voice:

'You'd better come,' it said. 'Rayna is dead.'

17

Rayna Prohme died on Monday, November 21, 1927, and was cremated on the following Thursday, November 24th (Thanksgiving Day). I left Moscow the day after the funeral and have not been there since.

It takes some time for a severe shock to be felt throughout a system, and on the day of Rayna's death I was calm. Anna Louise and I spent the day sending telegrams and letters, talking to the people that came, and arranging, as well as we could in the absence of instructions from Bill, for the funeral. Borodin's secretary in the end took charge of all these arrangements, and I had nothing further to do but wait.

On that night there was a snowstorm, and I was out in it a long time. If I have clearly stated the conflicts that were now so terribly resolved, it can be understood that much more than a person had gone from the world for me with Rayna Prohme. The desolate snowy night suggested this as thought alone could never have done (even if I had been capable of thought); the white snow, the empty night, the cold immensity in which I was lost, unhinged whatever it is that keeps us on our even course as rational human beings. I saw her through the snow as clearly as I see the table now before me, and heard her ringing laugh and the sound of her words: 'Don't be a damned fool, Jimmy.' I made an attempt not to be a damned fool during the next few days, but it was not successful. Sometimes these hallucinations assumed forms as convincing as any of those about us in life, and I carried on long conversations, in my locked room at the Savoy Hotel, with the girl who was to be burned to dust in a day or two. The days passed without bringing these recurrent disorders to an end, and the only hope of not being a damned fool was to leave Moscow as soon as possible.

An autopsy held on November 22d by a group of Moscow professors revealed something that did not surprise me: Rayna had died of encephalitis, inflammation of the brain. It must have begun many months before, and all through this time she had been exactly, literally burning to ashes, just as the shell she had discarded was to be burned to ashes at the crematorium. No human being could so irresistibly suggest the quality of flame without being consumed for it.

On the afternoon of the funeral we all marched for hours across Moscow to the new crematorium. There were delegations of

Chinese, Russian and American Communists, many of whom had never known Rayna. It was very cold, and as I walked along I became conscious of the shivering, bent figure of Mme Sun Yatsen. Her income had been cut off from China; she was too proud to accept the help of strangers; she had no winter clothing at all, and was walking through the dreary, frozen streets in a thin dark cloak. The motorcar loaned to her by the Soviet Foreign Office followed behind the procession; it was at least warm. I tried to persuade her to get into it, but she would not. She walked every step of the way across the city, her lovely face bent down towards her folded arms. She had recovered from her own illness only a few days before, and her pallor was extreme. Even through the cold haze in which everything moved on that day I was aware that Soong Ching-ling was now the loneliest of exiles, shivering through the early dark behind the bier of her most disinterested friend. The band played—out of tune—the revolutionary funeral march, alternating it with Chopin's. The maddening music, its lusty brasses a good half note off pitch, made the long procession hard to endure even for those who had never known Rayna. Eventually—it was dark by now, and the great bells of the nearby convent were ringing for evening service—we came to the modern crematorium outside the city. It was brightly lighted, square and spare. The bier, draped in the Red flag and covered with golden flowers, asters, chrysanthemums, all the flowers of Rayna's own colours, a heap of gold and red and brown, was placed on the platform. There were speeches in Chinese, Russian and English—revolutionary speeches. The English sounded just as meaningless as the Chinese or the Russian. Then a signal was given, a switch was turned, and the golden mass of Rayna, her hair and her bright flowers and the Red flag, sank slowly before us into the furnace.

That night Borodin came to see me. He looked colossal in my narrow room as he walked slowly up and down, speaking. I was on the bed and do not remember having said anything. He had come to say good-bye, he said, and to explain why he had not gone to the funeral. On principle he never went to funerals. The mind must be kept resolutely on its purposes.

His voice was deeply moved, and he controlled it with difficulty.

He did not look at me, but walked from the window to the door and back again.

'I know what this is,' he said. 'I know exactly. But what is needed is the long view. I have come here to ask you to take the long view—China, Russia. . . . A wonderful friend and a wonderful revolutionary instrument have disappeared together. But there is no use in anything unless we take the long view. Remember that. China, Russia . . .'

After a while he shook hands and went away. In the morning I took the train to Berlin.

VII

The Western Cities

It is possible to take 'the long view,' if at all, only by finding a point in time from which events can seem ordered. 'The long view' demands more mastery of the materials of an existence, more control of their significance, than I possessed. At this time I wanted no view at all. I wanted to be submerged again into a life as ordinary as night and day, as familiar as bread and butter, as undramatic as the telephone book. If I never saw beyond the details it could not matter much, I thought. Above all, I did not want to come near the awful alternatives again—the alternatives that seemed to me bound up in the ideas of China and Russia, Revolution, Rayna Prohme. I returned, as rapidly as possible, to the life in which these ideas were least suggested: the life of Paris, London and (at briefer intervals) New York.

A flight so precipitate and complete cannot be explained simply on the basis of cowardice. Cowardice alone might have driven me back to the old cities, but it could not have closed up my mind against all the varieties of thought and feeling that had engaged it for the better part of a year. That operation (the insulation of a mind) was accomplished by the defensive action of nerves and glands, an action so automatic that I did not even know it had occurred until long afterwards. It was, I suppose, the result of a series of stunning blows on the nervous system; I was like one of Professor Pavlov's little dogs, performing according to an arrangement of reflexes over which I had no control. Whether this is a correct statement of the process or not, it resulted in a refusal to contemplate clearly, and still more to discuss, the essential character of the crisis through which I had passed. I could talk for hours about the external details of the Chinese Revolution, and no doubt did. But I was incapable for a long time of speaking of these details in any relationship to myself; the events of the last few weeks in Russia came to be particularly taboo; and unless I was forced to do so I did not mention Rayna's name. So true is this that many of the people who know me best and have known me longest have never heard it. By the time three months had passed these events had been sealed over with a thick layer of ice, the ice of nervous defense, through which it would have been impossible to see even if I had wanted to review (as I have just now done, seven years later) the course of their development.

And once the glacier had closed over, the ice thickened, another strange process took place: the whole of the characters and their interaction moved off into that inconceivable distance at which we regard the movement of a poem. The reality was still there, underneath, sealed in a glacier that could be, and would be, melted in time; but meanwhile the *idea* of these events had assumed the shadowy forms of literary drama. I often doubted if they had taken place at all—even though, at certain critical moments, I could see and hear them again with amazing definition. The kind of psychological puzzle to which I am attempting to give a straightforward explanation is not, perhaps, open to analysis. In an obvious form it has been set forth by Luigi Pirandello in some of his plays; less obviously and more beautifully Mr T. S. Eliot has expressed it in the short poem called *La Figlia che piange*. In it the poet sees two people parting at the head of a stair; he watches them, tells them what to do, and sees them do it; in the end they have done exactly what he would have had them do. The experience has taken place on two planes—the plane of observed reality, and the plane of the creative imagination. He broods over this phenomenon and ends:

> '*Sometimes these cogitations still amaze*
> *The troubled midnight and the noon's repose.*'

It would be nonsense to suggest that the events I have related in the last chapter took place in accordance with any such act of the creative imagination on my part, and yet they were so haunted with premonitions, particularly towards the end, that no single step in the development aroused a feeling of surprise; and when it was all over—long enough over to support the kind of oblique contemplation to which I now refer—they did seem to have been a singularly unified and dramatic progression of events, too unified and too dramatic to be altogether real. They had moved off into another plane, and it was not impossible to ask myself, with the utmost earnestness, whether they had ever taken place at all. The character of Rayna Prohme was (and has remained) unique in my experience of the real; is it not possible that I imagined it upon that other plane? I tried answering this question by writing down some of the events of the last few weeks in Moscow and incorporating them (with considerable differences of names and circumstance) into a bad novel a year or so later, but the experiment only made the peculiar aptness of the events more conspicuous, arousing still further the uneasy feeling that such things do not and cannot happen. That she should have died of inflammation of the brain, thus literally, and all too aptly, burning away; that she should have lain under flowers of gold and flame colours, and sunk with them into the furnace—was this possible in view of the fact that I had always thought of her as a flame? Wasn't it too singly thought out and relentlessly executed to be possible in a world of odds and ends, where nothing matched and nothing ever came to its culmination? Often it seemed that the tragedy bore too much evidence of a plan to have been actual, and that it might have been, rather, a prolonged torture invented by the imagination. But what imagination? My own? Against this alternative (worse than the reality) there was an instinctive rebellion. Besides, I knew, in so far as I knew anything, that these events had taken place. To deny it would have been insane. Postulating (for the sake of continued existence) that I was as sane as anybody, but recognizing also that these events had contained a peculiar inner plan and organized significance beyond anything known to me in experience, I had to fall into a way of thinking about them akin to the mood of certain Pirandello plays or of that short poem of Mr Eliot's—feel them beneath me as a basis of fact, but see them before me as the formal and ordered drama of a world of shadows. Before this contradiction could be resolved much more time had to pass, the ice that covered the realities melt for good, and a view—even, in some measure, a 'long view'—be finally achieved.

Paris and London easily took care of one part of my convalescence from Moscow: they made my recent life seem far off. I knew nobody in the Western capitals who was more than politely interested in China and Russia, but I knew a great many people who were interested in themselves, their doings, and in me as a part of their familiar scene. I could slip back into the life there without an effort, because the assumption of my friends was simply that I had been 'away,' and that I was now back again. Paris and London had been the background of my existence for five or six years, and if I have paid relatively little attention to that background, it is because it often seemed to me, however agreeable, only a place to go away from. Now I had returned to the West with some feeling of permanence, and for a year and a half I fluctuated busily, for no real reasons and without much sense of motive or purpose, between the cities. When I left Moscow I went to Berlin for a week or two, and returned to Paris as soon as I could afterwards.

There existed in Paris in those years a refuge to which I could always repair in difficulty—the Paris *Times*. It was an evening newspaper in English, created by the whim of a millionaire, and edited by a small staff made up of old friends from my earliest days in Paris. The whimsical millionaire did not allow his generosity to run away with him, and there was little money to run the paper with; consequently salaries were tiny, and essential expenses (such as telegraphic service) cut to a minimum. But however small and poverty-stricken, it was a friendly world in which I could always find a place. I had already worked for a month or so on the Paris *Times* a year before; I now returned to it for another two months, and was to return for six weeks or so later in the year. The staff of the paper included some remarkably capable newspapermen. This was a characteristic of the small Paris newspapers in English, which could always draw on a floating population of newspaper reporters who for one reason or another wanted to make a stay in Paris. They were a scapegrace and impractical lot, or they wouldn't have been there; they could all have made much more money in America, and did so whenever the spirit moved them to go home. They included Martin Sommers ('the Merde'),

Hillel Bernstein ('Bernie'), H. E. Monahan ('Mike'), Allen Raymond and a procession of others, presided over and kept in some semblance of order by a bull-like, jovial Franco-English martinet named Gaston Archambault. How that newspaper was daily invented and spread in print upon paper, was daily issued forth to its minute circle of readers, was daily condemned to death and still kept going, was a journalistic phenomenon that amazed us all when we thought of it. We had almost nothing to go on. Sometimes a whole speech by the late lamented Calvin Coolidge had to be made up out of one line of cablegram from America, and you would scarcely believe how accurate the resultant column of type turned out to be. Experienced newspaper men (not I, of course, but those who had worked a lot in America) could write off Mr Coolidge's speeches as soon as they knew the subject. Sometimes no cablegram came from America at all, and the whole newspaper had to be concocted out of what we could dig out of other newspapers. As a conjuring trick the Paris *Times* surpassed anything I have ever seen.

As a way of living it was equally odd. Its staff was tiny, and yet none of its members seemed to see much of anybody else in Paris. We all lived in small hotels near by, and if anybody happened to oversleep (as in my case happened often) he was routed out by the one-eyed office boy and marched to work. When the newspaper had gone to press at four in the afternoon, we congregated in a café downstairs and drank beer. The conversation (like the life) was as aimless as a goat track. We talked about everything and nothing, but it seemed to take up the whole time left over from work.

The extreme restriction of such an existence was not, of course, characteristic of the Paris I knew through the decade. It was characteristic, rather, of the defeated and battered mood in which I then returned to the most familiar of cities. At other times during those years—later and earlier—I knew as wide a range of the forms of life in Paris as most Americans see, and it was exactly this variety, this range and contrast, that gave Paris unique fascination. It was a fascination that wore off. The trees along the river, the gardens of the Luxembourg, the noisy joviality of Montmartre and the spring-like freshness of the Bois afterwards ceased to be objects of wonder to me. The oldest of generalizations about Paris was probably just this: that it was a city of youth. In my case the old tag proved to be as true as it had been for centuries past, and the peculiar fascination faded with the years to which it was most suited to appeal. The chestnut trees and the acacias came to mean no more than so many trees anywhere, and the most they could accomplish was a distinctly second-hand stirring of the sensibilities—a recollection, that is, of the power they once had to excite and to intensify. In the 1920's they were the visible signs of the freest and most variegated life known to me.

2

It was this that I always came back to. From the Rhineland, the Rif, or Persia, from China or Russia or Rome, I always made a bee line, when the work was done and the money gone, for Paris. It happened instinctively, for I never thought much about it. When I thought at all it was of the graver matters with which this book has been concerned. But back to Paris I came, made the *tournée des grands ducs*, explored restaurants with Eugène Rosetti, investigated the decline of manners and morals as shown on the Left Bank, and assiduously cultivated the varieties of humanity known to me in Paris, and in Paris alone. Many of these varieties could never have existed elsewhere, or could have existed only in a stunted and tentative growth. Paris nourished every eccentricity, gave free play to every vice, permitted every exaggeration of individualism. It was international in its own careless way, not industriously international, like a town in Switzerland, but naturally and effortlessly universal. You could find everything there from the pure essence of Illinois to the romanticism of Mürger and DeKock or the exoticism of Foujita. Parallel with these was the continuous life of the old French bourgeoisie, altered in no important particular since the nineteenth century, inwardly unconscious of the existence of the rest of the world. I knew more different kinds of people in Paris than anywhere else—Russian refugees, American journalists, decadent French poets, respectable French families of the middle class, Chinese revolutionaries, drunkards of all nations, ladies and gentlemen of the loosest possible morals and people of the most rigid conventionality, princesses and prostitutes, café owners and politicians. A good deal of this range of acquaintance was professional and was shared by the other American newspaper men; but some of it I owed to my own insatiable curiosity about people, an inexhaustible desire to know as many as possible of the forms of human character. Leaving out the two extremes, the underworld of professional criminals and the upperworld of what is called high Society, I can reasonably believe I had a glimpse or a smattering of almost every kind of Paris life during that decade; and for this —so long as the fascination lasted—I always came back.

If you were to have taken the surface characteristics of the place and time as shown in such things as manners, morals and taste and attempted to put them all together, you would probably have got a result not unlike that of a ballet of Diaghilev. Certainly the ballets of Diaghilev were, whatever their merits as music, painting and dancing, the most contemporary expressive efforts of the age. They were contemporary above all in their determination to be contemporary—in their fluttering from novelty to novelty, and, when novelty failed, from pastiche to pastiche, in the consistent, self-conscious assertion that this was 1924 (or 1926 or whatever year it might be). Diaghilev had lost his greatest dancers and no longer had the Russian State ballet school to draw upon for recruits, but he still had enough trained performers of good quality to help him execute his remarkable synthesis of the spirit of the place and time. He could draw on all Paris for his artists, and did: Picasso, Derain, Marie Laurencin, Chirico, Chelichev and a dozen others designed his settings and costumes; Stravinsky and a host of small fry wrote his music. But his most loyal ally, in the years of this frantic effort to be contemporary, was his audience. Both in Paris and in London it was a hysterically devoted audience, made up of fashionable ladies, ambitious artists or musicians, æsthetic young men and others who, for whatever reason, wished to signalize their consciousness of a break with the past. It was not the largest public (it was never big enough to give the ballets a financial success) but it was the most conspicuous and the most self-conscious public then visible in either of the capitals. And on a Diaghilev first night, what with the excited recognitions and salutes, the scents and jewels, the chatter and affectations of the peacock people, you did certainly get a sort of cinematographic impression of the semi-Bohemian-semi-fashionable bourgeoisie in its period of luxurious decay.

Decay it was, and nobody with any sense of history could deny it. Whatever morality may be—and it seems probable that it was never anything but a series of convenient arrangements —its recognizable influence had vanished from the more conspicuous aspects of life in Paris and London in the 1920's. Every form of self-indulgence flourished and increased *à vue d'œil*. Promiscuity between the sexes, homosexuality, miscegenation and every variety of sexual diversion known to the most learned of German professors could have been studied with ease in the Paris café, night club, theatre or semi-fashionable house. These manifestations of a released libido were accompanied by unlimited indulgence in strong drink, and, often enough, in drugs. What the parents of the time seldom grasped at all was that such wickednesses were not restricted to abandoned Bohemians, creatures of the underworld or of the Paris Left Bank, but were common among their children and their friends' children, however outwardly 'respectable.' My testimony, for what it is worth, would be that my generation had practically no moral sense as that term had hitherto been understood. This is not a judgment: I am in this, as in other respects, an *enfant du siècle*, and have no right or desire to judge anybody's morals; but if we adopt the point of view of history, we must see that these phenomena constitute decay from what preceded. We may like it or not (I like it, at least in preference to bourgeois respectability); but the fact is that the people who were in their twenties in the 1920's were amazingly, perhaps unprecedentedly, immoral. We have to go a long way into the past to find anything to equal their (perhaps I should say our) behaviour.

It was very swift, this decay. When I left the University in 1920 it had scarcely even begun. Five years later it was, so far as I could determine, common among people of my age in the bourgeoisie. Some were more extreme than others; but all had progressed so far that frank conversation with their parents had become an impossibility. I had no parents, and did not face the problem, but again and again in France, England and America I saw my friends struggling with it. The gulf between the generations had suddenly become immense. Even my most respectable American friends—those who lived in happy monogamous marriage—had to hide the liquor, conceal some of the books and exercise a stern control over their conversation when mother came to call. The people I knew may have been better than their parents in some ways, more courageous, more generous, freer from the petty meannesses and crippling prejudices of the nineteenth century, but they had lost all the moral stiffening upon which the bourgeois system had, in its noneconomic aspects, been constructed. It is probably true, as the Marxians would maintain, that decay came when the middle class no longer exercised its economic function—when it ceased, as in my generation, to be the group of active entrepreneurs and became a leisured class—but although this may have been the first cause of the phenomenon, it was powerfully aided by psychological influences (taste, fashion, suggestion) until it spread far beyond the limited number of those who lived without work, affected poor and rich alike and even, so far as I was able to judge, made some superficial inroads upon the moral standards of the workers themselves. In the particular chapter of sexual morality, and the particular example of what Sir Thomas Browne called 'that odd act,' the 1920's worked a swift change in the whole attitude of society. What had been the most serious and unmentionable of processes to our grandparents was now lowered to the level of other diversions, and could be referred to, by one of the typical playwrights of the period, as 'an unpremeditated roll in the hay.'

Paris was, it seemed to me, the centre of the moral revolution. London and New York were not far behind, but Paris was in its usual position as the capital of Western taste, and its cosmopolitan youth influenced all the rest. More than three hundred thousand Americans used to come to Paris every year in the 1920's, the tide reaching its height in the years when the franc was low and the dollar high. Most of them were probably unaffected by anything they saw, but others remained long enough to realize that they liked the new ways better than the old. The same was true of the English. Englishmen still considered themselves licensed to greater freedoms of behaviour in Paris than at home, but a good number of them took their freedom home again. Prohibition may have made some difference in America—increased the process in some measure by arousing instinctive rebellions—but the phenomenon was deeper and wider than anything within the scope of written laws. It was a general crumbling of middle-class morality throughout the West, starting in Paris (the logical centre of Western taste) and reaching to the outposts of bourgeois culture. We can search the literature of the nineteenth century in all the Western countries in vain for any example of the kind of behaviour on view in 1929 at any party in Paris, London or New York. To our grandparents the ordinary manners, conversation, conduct and morals of educated and 'respectable' people would have seemed suitable to the underworld.

The charm of Paris did not, of course, depend upon its moral influence; these were flagrant afterthoughts. Its charm came first, embraced and concealed its moral influence, and would have been analyzed (if we had tried at the time) as the charm of ease, freedom, friendliness and peace. Everything was all right; you did as you pleased; there was always something new to see or do or talk about, and if some of your discoveries were a little startling at first hand, they were easily enough accepted when they were seen to be general and not particular. And quite possibly a further reason why Paris ceased to exercise its peculiar charm upon many people was that this supreme ease, once characteristic of Paris alone, later became a general attribute of the time everywhere.

3

My acquaintance with London was narrower than my acquaintance with Paris, but it was more thorough. I knew few people in England—or few varieties of people—but I knew those few well. The difference was partly conditioned by the obvious differences in the life of Paris and London. The first photograph flashed into any mind by the mention of Paris is that of a street scene, a quai along the river, a café; the first photograph evoked by a mention of London is (for me at least) that of the inside of a comfortable house. London has an outside, but its climate gives it a dimness that causes it to fade easily on the memory. The outside of London is not a place to live in, but a necessary physical transition from interior to interior.

This interiority, so to speak, is not only a trick of my memory or a mere sense impression. It is a general characteristic of such English life as I have seen. Even the most social of Englishmen seemed most at ease in his own house—felt better, thought better, and talked better there; liked to take his psychological shoes off; achieved tranquillity when his own food, drink, books and pictures were within easy reach. There did exist something called Society in England, but I always understood, from such of my friends as knew it, that it was a 'crashing bore.' The evidence seemed to be that Englishmen and Englishwomen regarded large gatherings of their fellow creatures as a necessary evil, and large parties, in particular, as a social duty without immediate recompense in the form of pleasure. That passion for social assembly which characterized so many French and Americans was rare in my experience of the English; and although this may have been partly accidental, it must, when the material is collated over a number of years, indicate a genuine differentiation in national temperaments.

The difference was immediately apparent in the forms taken by conversation on the two sides of the Channel. Conversation was the special art of Paris and London; it had not been developed to the same height anywhere else, and the stupidest Frenchman or Englishman seemed to have inherited some aptitude for easy, graceful talk. But between the two there existed a striking difference of mood, style and direction. Englishmen seemed to talk to themselves, or for one other person, or for two or three other persons; they were dampened by larger numbers. French *causeurs* —at least the best ones, those who knew they talked well and made a point of it—demanded an audience, the larger the better. This could be illustrated by recognizable examples. Jean Cocteau was the wittiest and most various talker I ever heard in Paris, and most people who had the pleasure of listening to him would have said the same thing. But on the few occasions when I witnessed his fireworks I observed that he depended upon his audience, flourished most when he was most observed, was wittiest when he had the largest number hanging on his words. Even the style of his talk seemed suited to space and numbers, as if it had been designed for a kind of theatre in the shape of a dinner table. I never met anybody in London who excelled in the same way. The most famous talker of the period was probably Lady Oxford, but in spite of the brilliance and variety of her conversation, its range, flash and glitter, it did not seem designed for large audiences; it had the quality of an interior monologue, as if its gifted creator had been talking to herself. That low voice and thoughtful manner did not suggest awareness of the listener, and the best things were said almost in an undertone. If Cocteau's talk made a table into a theatre, Lady Oxford's seemed to give it the covered leisure of a book.

England was never really foreign—not as France or Italy was foreign. It was near enough to seem native, comprehensible and comprehending. But in some persistent respects its life could not help appearing, to an American from the Middle West, as strange and remote as the life on one of Mr H. G. Wells's distant planets. I believe the first of these ultra-English (and, therefore, to me, ultra-foreign) characteristics was an inspissated class-consciousness. The divisions and subdivisions of class in England were minute beyond anything Karl Marx ever recorded. It was no use dividing the English (as we could the rest of the world) into bourgeoisie and proletariat; it was no use adding aristocracy to this basic division; and it was no use avoiding economics by classifying them vaguely as upper, middle and lower. Their divisions were far more numerous, more rigid and more irrational than anything known to the rest of the world. However small you might think you had got the class, you would discover, upon investigation, that it was internally subdivided. The hierarchical habit of mind seemed to have penetrated into every order of society, so that, independently of economic position or education, every Englishman felt superior to some groups and inferior to others. It was easy enough to dismiss this phenomenon as 'snobbery,' but the word was only a term of abuse, while the thing was a fundamental and pervasive attribute of the English mind in every aspect under which I had been able to observe it.

Much of this class-consciousness was funny; but once you had

had your laugh you were forced to acknowledge that it was also serious. A case in point: during the General Strike of 1926 a friend of mine, arriving at Paddington with too many bags to carry himself, looked about for a porter. By luck, he found one. As they moved off to find a taxicab the porter said to him:

'The situation is getting a bit difficult, ain't it, sir? Did you see that we had to fire on the lower classes yesterday in Glasgow?'

When you have duly laughed at the episode you cannot help reflecting that this was, essentially, why the General Strike failed. A nation in which the proletariat, under the severest pressure, cannot conceive itself to be one solid class in opposition to the owning and possessing orders is a social curiosity. A domestic crisis is caused because the 'tweenie' (a maid of lower rank than housemaid, parlourmaid, etc.) comes to the servants' table without her apron, exactly as if she were the equal of the cook; a political movement is determined by the fact that certain groups in the proletariat will not surrender their conviction of superiority to (say) the coal miners; a Fascist organization becomes possible when you tell impoverished groups of lower middle-class workers (the petite bourgeoisie) that they must defend their social position against the inroads of the lower orders.

An American could be fascinated by such criteria, could collect them and laugh over them, could be delighted by the rigid and involved character they displayed, but he could never feel altogether at home in a country where social self-consciousness in its extremest form permeated the national culture.

4

Once all this has been said—and said with such detachment as I can command—I confess that certain places in England meant much in my life, more, certainly, than other places in the world. The charm of Paris and the drama of Moscow, the lusty clatter of New York, the poetic stones of Rome, all had their effect upon the processes described in this book; but the most potent of such place-influences were, I think, those to which I was subjected in England. Some places, either through association or suggestion, establish a mood in the mind, but it is not likely that the same place establishes the same mood in all minds. Gordon Square, for instance, is only a rather quiet and old-fashioned square in Bloomsbury, and may suggest nothing more to most of the people familiar with it. To me it was a place of extreme particularity, where the mood of peaceful reflection had been so often established that the same mood, recurring thousands of miles away, could summon it up again tree by tree and door by door. I lived so often in and about that square that the conditioned reflex might reasonably work for almost any mood; I caroused in Gordon square, worked in Gordon Square, was ill in Gordon Square, and made love in Gordon Square; but actually the lasting mood of the place, its particular genius, was that rarest of all—the sessions of sweet solemn thought; even the remembrance of things past. Perhaps because this was a rare mood, a late discovery, perhaps because I could never get over the excitement of finding out that I was able to think, Gordon Square threw the whole geography of London out of joint for me—became a kind of centre upon which the doubtless more important areas, such as Mayfair, Piccadilly and the Strand, were dependent.

Bloomsbury is either a region of cheap hotels and lodging houses, as the writers of detective stories call it; or it is the 'Areopagus of British culture,' as Harold Nicolson once called it (tongue, as always, in cheek). I suppose it may be both. But by a series of accidents it came to be the part of London I knew earliest and best; most of my slender acquaintance in London was to be found somewhere within its limits; and its habit of mind, as I grew to know it better year after year, exercised a moderating influence over my own mutinous impulses. I never lost sight of the difference between myself and the friends who wielded this influence. They were intellectuals and I was not—nor did I want to be. Removed by economic privilege and social security from the ruder struggles of existence (equipped with the advantages Mrs Woolf once described as 'five hundred a year and a room of one's own'), they tended to become a little bloodless, a little too aloof and remote to understand a life in which reason was not, after all, supreme. But I needed a touch of reason. A nature given to too much emotion, too much violence and too little thought, could derive nothing but good from the experience. Bloomsbury and its inhabitants thus took the place in my dilatory education that should have been taken by the University of Chicago, and became, by the time I was thirty, a kind of Alma Mater. The fact that there was something comic in the idea did not make it less true. From the cornfields of Illinois to the shadow of the British Museum was a long journey; but the mind, providing it works at all, has no geography.

I ought perhaps to make some attempt to define what I mean by 'habit of mind' and 'Bloomsbury.' It is not easy, because the work of the best-known writers and artists who lived in that part of the world (Duncan Grant, Vanessa Bell, Roger Fry, Lytton Strachey, David Garnett, Virginia Woolf, J. M. Keynes, E. M. Forster) seems as various and unrelated as possible. But such differences, produced by widely varying individual gifts, could scarcely conceal a sympathetic rapprochement in points of view; and it seemed to me that there was, in fact, almost a single point of view among all these friends and relations, unifying them essentially to a degree that made a single impression inevitable upon anybody who saw them, as I did, from the outside. This single impression (accurate or not) might be summed up in this way: they accepted nothing as true until it had been proved to be true; they acknowledged no standard of good except as it convinced their own minds after examination and reflection; and they attempted to form their own view of the world upon a basis of reason. Whether they always succeeded or not is another question, but it may be seen that such ways of thinking must have exerted a powerful civilizing influence upon the cruder nature I presented to them. A brake could not have been more useful to a runaway set of wheels—or a series of showers more enlivening to a parched potato patch.

One house in the country came to represent, almost to sum up, the imaginative and romantic appeal of England to me, that particular appeal to which I have already given the large name of 'poetry.' I went to Knole for the first time in the autumn of 1926. It was a mournful, wet day, and the trees dripped sadly all through the great park. The grey mass of the house, rising suddenly out of dead leaves and wind and rain, looked like a romantic invention compounded from a thousand books, plays and poems. Eddy Sackville-West, the heir, ghostlike in a brown Inverness cape, took us round the innumerable ghostly corridors and rooms and staircases, explaining with weary patience what needed to be explained. He looked like most of the portraits on the walls (they all look alike in his family, and the centuries seem to make no important difference). In the Venetian Ambassador's room the old grey-pink tapestries swayed out mysteriously beneath the stirring of some unidentified wind. The silver furniture in King James I's bedroom glimmered dully through the gloom, and the great banqueting hall was so dark that only with an effort could I see the roof. The house was, in fact, in one of its most melancholy and romantic moods, and although I saw it in many other moods afterwards, that first day could not easily be forgotten.

In the year after I left Moscow I was often there. In so far as a stranger and a foreigner could be said to know anything about it, I grew to know the house, to feel something of its extraordinary persuasive power as a living thing, and to experience, however indirectly, the emotion it peculiarly evoked: the emotion of visible history. From the time of the first two Tudors to the present was a long sweep, but it seemed to have been telescoped into the halls and staircases, the towers, gardens and park of Knole. The house belonged to the Tudors and was given by Queen Elizabeth to her cousin Thomas Sackville, the Lord Treasurer; from that time onward it remained in the Sackville family and played its part in the long story of that remarkable race; the house and its owners were one. Perhaps to be born in it would be to be overshadowed by it, obsessed by it, particularly in days when so much of its significance has become historical. But to a stranger, a foreigner, a barbarian, it was that rare wonder, a journey of the imagination in time. I should have understood little indeed about England if I had never known it.

5

New York was the least of my cities. I only went there, during these years, to 'make arrangements'—that is, to sign contracts if I could get them, or to perform any of the acts by which we persuade ourselves that we are in control of our lives. Actually, I wasn't—at least, not in New York. It was too big, noisy and pre-occupied to give anything but a headache to a visitor as occasional as I was. It had two disastrous effects on me, both, I suppose, nervous in origin: the first was to make me feel as insignificant as an ant and correspondingly assertive; the second was to make me drink fantastic quantities of alcohol. And since this was the case, I can scarcely pretend to have had any clear notion of New York for most of these years. There was one characteristic of the city, and of everybody I knew in it, that did impress itself then and afterwards: its psychopathic attitude towards what it called 'success.' Success was apparently defined as anything that made money, caused talk or got printed in the newspapers. I never went to New York without being bewildered by a whole crop of new 'successes' of various kinds: great novelists, world-shaking dramatists, stupendous architects or financial geniuses, whose names and achievements were unknown to me. The most charac-teristic example of the New York point of view, I used to think, was the gossip column written in one of the papers by Walter Winchell. It contained titbits of every variety about the private lives of people who, for whatever reason, aroused the interest of the industrious inventor of the system. I made the acquaintance of the Winchell system in the spring of 1928 when I returned to New York. A friend, chuckling jovially, produced the newspaper and pointed out, to my amazement, a line in it about myself. And not only about myself. As nearly as I can remember it, the sentence said that I had returned to New York from China and Russia; that I had started out with Mme Sun Yat-sen, but she '*faw-down*' on the way. Then followed three little dots, like this . . . and then a piece of tremendous information about a chorus girl who was go-ing to have a baby or a saxophone player who was engaged to a débutante, or something of the kind. I was speechless with horror at seeing Mme Sun's name used in this way, but before I had been long in New York I came to see that no harm was meant—that, indeed, the childish inquisitiveness and exhibitionism of the Winchell system were only that and nothing more. The unfor-tunate thing was that the Winchell system of thought and con-versation had an influence on numerous New Yorkers; it represented and magnified a tendency—a clear case of increase of appetite that grows by what it feeds on. It seemed to me during most of these years that New York's triple passion for success, newsprint and private lives made it a hysterical place, unfit for human habitation.

This exaggeration of a natural antipathy had to be corrected, of course. It arose partly from ignorance. There were certainly as many civilized people in New York as among any other seven million you could get together, but my trouble was that I knew almost none of them. It is in such cases that a few good friends save one's life, and I found them, particularly, in that eminent philosopher Martin Sommers (the 'Merde' of Paris, now abetted by a pretty wife), in that eminent pair of philosophers, the Sinclair Lewises, and in Mrs Moskowitz.

The Lewises had bought a farm in Vermont, with two beautiful old houses on it. They owned the whole mountain, led a sylvan life there, and were always ready to take me in when I got to the point of incapacity to endure New York another minute. With Dorothy and Red it was possible to rest, work, talk nonsense and have a good laugh. I think New York had much the same disruptive effect on them that it did on me, and when they were in Vermont they shut it out more successfully than anybody I knew. We used to lead the simple life there, all three working away at something or other and meeting only at meal-times. Red was writing *Dodsworth* when I first went there; he was revising the proofs of *Ann Vickers* the last time. His methods of work stunned me at first, and I used to wonder if writing a good book was actually as arduous as it seemed. It took me a long time to perceive that the marvellous architectural solidity of his novels, their incomparable vitality, depended upon his willingness to work at a book as if he were creating a world. To get a name for a character he would examine and reject thousands of names; to get a street or a house right he would build it, actually construct it in cardboard; to follow one of his characters from point to point in one of his imaginary cities he would make a map. He was the only writer I have ever known who knew exactly what every word meant before he used it. Whether it was classical English or the slang of the Middle West, he was sure of it before he put it down—and being sure of a word does not mean, of course, the mere ability to define it. Red knew where his words came from, what their associations were, how they were variously pronounced, and often just how they had been used throughout the history of the language. He had an infallible ear for words, as can be seen in the dialogue of such books as *Babbitt;* he had an amazing memory, and he had read, I believe, every book ever written in or translated into English. His ruthlessness with his own work was a part of the phenomenon: he thought nothing of throwing away a hundred thousand words, cutting out more than he left in, or abandoning a novel altogether when it did not please him. The spectacle of such volcanic energy under the control of a first-rate artistic conscience was one of the most impressive that could have been offered a lazy youth, and it should have done me far more good than it did. I was not yet ready, however, for the disheartening fact that writing is and must always be hard work; I tried to imagine that Red's methods were suited only to himself, and that good books grew on bushes. As the truth afterwards became apparent, year after year, I was to think often of Red and his extraordinary organized effort, like that of an army in action along an extended front. He was, of course, a man of genius; but no amount of genius could have created the world of his rich, solid and various novels. Once in Bucharest, years later, I met a Rumanian lady who was reading *Babbitt* in French; she enjoyed it, she said, because it was such a brilliant study of the business men she had known at home in Jassy. The universality that could make Zenith and Jassy alike were the qualities of genius, but they took their living form as a result of a no less wonderful organization of plain hard work.

It was not all work in Vermont. Meals were hilarious, and talk was mostly nonsense. Sometimes something would arouse Red's myth-making faculty, and his imagination would go galloping along, miles ahead of the rest of us, constructing a whole story. He could make up ten short stories at breakfast and invent a novel before lunch. The fertility of his imagination never failed to amaze me; it was so curbed and subjected to the observed realities in his books that it came as a surprise to learn that he was actually as inventive, in the easy, effortless story-telling way, as Ouida or

Marion Crawford. Occasionally he made up a short story and presented it to me. The first short story of a more or less professional cast that I ever wrote was one of his, concocted, in the midst of general laughter, at the breakfast table.

Mrs Moskowitz's house was a very different one, much more closely connected with the life of New York. Its animating spirit was 'Mrs M.' herself—the 'Little Corporal'—a woman of the rarest quality. I had met her son Carlos in Normandy in 1926 and was asked to dine at her house one Sunday when I passed through New York on my way to China. From the moment she came into the room, deep-voiced and thoughtful and sure, I was one of her devoted admirers. She had many. Her serene face was still unlined, with a sensitive mouth and dark, thoughtful eyes. She dressed always in black, moved slowly, and spoke—when she spoke at all—in a dark, thoughtful voice that somehow matched her extraordinary eyes. I never heard her raise her voice or lose her temper. In the turmoil in which she lived, particularly during the Presidential campaign of 1928, she seemed as still and sure as a cathedral in a slum.

Mrs Moskowitz had been a reformer, a 'welfare worker,' a closer-up of dance halls and a planner of housing schemes. By the time I knew her her faith in such partial tinkerings with the social system had been weakened. Although she still took a lively interest in some forms of philanthropy, particularly the Jewish charities, she had come to the conclusion that the only way to get anything done was through government. And government being what it is (or was) in America, it was necessary to reach its centres of power by means of a single leader, who would combine honesty, intelligence and the particular quality of hypnotic appeal required to move masses of people and obtain their votes. This ideal political leader for a modern democracy was, Mrs Moskowitz believed, Al Smith. She had an unshakable faith in him. All the last years of her life were devoted to tireless effort towards the great aim—his election to the Presidency. The final disappointment of 1932, when the Democratic party nominated Franklin Roosevelt for a free ride to the White House, was followed a few months later by her death.

For a long time I had no clear idea of Mrs Moskowitz's political rôle. But during the campaign of 1928, when Smith and Hoover were the nominees of the two parties, I saw her at work, and it was a grand spectacle. I wanted Smith to be elected because she wanted it; but otherwise it did not seem to me of much consequence who occupied the office of President in a system afflicted by two parties of indistinguishable opinions and tendencies. I used to see 'Mrs M.'—as the people in the political offices called her—at her desk in the headquarters of the Democratic National Committee, as busy as a general directing an advance, and far calmer. The Democratic National Committee headquarters in 1928 were a kind of madhouse. Ticker tapes and telephones; worried secretaries scurrying about; papers lost and found again; people running in an unceasing hurry from corridor to corridor; antechambers black with Senators—that was the film, with sound effects. In the midst of Bedlam 'Mrs M.'s' office was cool and quiet. She did not allow people to shriek or get excited in her room, and her own slow movements, her deep, thoughtful voice, acted as an anti-hysteria medicine on everybody who came near her. Her official position was that of director of publicity for the National Committee. As a matter of fact she was a great deal more than that. Many people said that she directed the whole campaign. This could hardly have been exact, in a party so afflicted by important personages and great executives. What seems to have been the truth is this: that Governor Smith relied more heavily upon her advice, and upon her systematic work, than upon those of any other one person. As a result her position was magnified in current opinion, and her dislike for personal publicity only increased the word-of-mouth mischief by which all the praise and all the blame of the campaign tended to fall upon her.

On the night of the election in 1928 I set off an hour or so after dinner for the Democratic National Committee's headquarters to get more direct information than could be extracted from the talkative radio. Democratic headquarters were in the General Motors Building. The skyscraper was still surrounded by a mob. Torn-up papers and telephone books lay ankle deep in the streets and in the entrance to the building. The crowds had been rejoicing, in that special New York manner, over the supposed victory of their idol. We got through the police cordons and reached the floor occupied by the National Committee. Here everything was confusion and hysteria. Wading through the débris, we were admitted to Mrs Moskowitz's room by a weeping secretary. There were a score or so of people standing about there, talking lugubriously in hushed voices that somehow sounded noisier than so many shouts. We had come (depending on the belated news from the radio) thinking the victory was assured, but this room did not look like a house of triumph. When we got to Mrs Moskowitz's desk, at the end of the room, she got up to shake hands. Her face was as sad as such dignity as hers could ever permit. She said:

'I'm afraid we've lost New York.'

That was all—she never made a fuss. But it was obvious that if Smith could not carry New York he could never carry the country, and she delivered the inference by the slightest inflection of her voice.

If Smith had been elected either in 1928 or in 1932 it is probable that Mrs Moskowitz would have exercised a vital influence upon the history of our time. As it was, even though her highest goal was not achieved, she did leave traces of her passing all through the social legislation introduced into New York for the first time under Smith's governorship (and developed by his successor). Whatever she did was done by personal power alone. Tammany Hall loathed her; the Roosevelts disliked her; she had no kind of 'organization' or clique to support her view of things, although it could be said that the most intelligent and socially conscious among Smith's advisers were her friends. Smith apparently depended upon her for exactly the same reasons that moved many other people to depend upon her—for her luminous mind, her level-headedness and her lack of selfish interest. Her advice (never given unless asked) was as good in the ordinary affairs of life as it was in politics, and the Governor was by no means the only person in New York who availed himself of it.

6

In the winter of 1928–29 I was initiated (for my sins) into the lecture system of my native land. I did not know much about it, but an amiable manager, who had originally asked me to get his proposals for a lecture tour put before Mme Sun Yat-sen, thought it was time I learned.

It was a harrowing experience. I did it, of course, for money; but by the time I had finished the tour the money had evaporated. At first I could scarcely speak at all. My legs gave way under me, my breath unaccountably failed, and I could not keep my hands still. Mr Alber, the manager, sent me to a 'professor of platform technique' to correct these weaknesses. The professor of platform technique used to stride up and down, gesturing eloquently, advancing and retreating with measured steps, his vast, billowing, political voice filling every corner of the room. I never did credit to his admirable tuition, for lecturers are born, not made; but he did teach me a few tricks about sitting down and standing up, and how to dispose of my awkward limbs. In time, as the engagements succeeded each other and I survived, the experience of public address grew to be less agonizing, but it never became easy or even faintly agreeable. The earlier engagements, before I had been quite stunned into insensibility, were like a foretaste of hell. I used to sweat like a pig and tremble like a leaf. How people could go on year after year lecturing, and even liking it, I never understood. Of the innumerable talents I did not possess, that of making a speech seemed the most mysterious.

The audiences were, on the whole, kind and tolerant. I was supposed to tell them about Morocco or China (they were to choose which). And although they obviously had no interest in either Morocco or China, and I did not possess the power to interest them in such remote subjects, they listened politely and pretended not to notice how incompetent I was at my job. Once in a great while an audience did show impatience, but I could scarcely blame them for it. Once, in a remote village in Idaho, to which I had been summoned as a substitute for somebody who had missed a train, the audience was frankly restive. Some little boys in the first two rows organized a football game while I was talking; a lady farther back calmly changed her baby's diaper just as I was struggling hardest; small children cried out in loud voices. I found that this audience had been lured into the community hall by the promise of an 'entertainment'—specifically, a ventriloquist. The ventriloquist had missed his train, and I had been sent instead.

What all those farmers made of my unintelligible talk, after they had struggled for miles through the snow to be entertained, I never found out. I gave them back their check, for it did seem to me that they had been badly bilked.

The country through which lecturers roamed was as big as the United States and Canada: it seemed that no city was too large, no hamlet too small, to support some kind of lecture course. The notion fostered by self-conscious New Yorkers, that 'the lecture belt' was an area roughly equivalent to the Middle West, was sheer error. New York itself, with its five various boroughs and its innumerable suburbs, absorbed more lectures than any other place in the country. The Old South absorbed least, because it could least afford such luxuries. But it could be taken as proved that numerous Americans of all regions and all classes liked to be talked to by persons who got paid for doing so. The fact that one might not share this taste was no reason for making fun of it, and lecturers who exercised their wits at the expense of the lecturees always gave me an acute pain. If a choice had to be made, it seemed to me that those who submitted to lectures were on the whole preferable to those who inflicted them.

True, there were oddities. The most consistent—so consistent that I could not help thinking it characteristic of all American life, an extension of the Walter Winchell principle—was an interest in persons rather than in subjects. I could talk myself blue in the face about the Chinese Revolution, but when the lecture was over the lady president of the club would tell me I looked like her nephew (or brother or son, or the Prince of Wales or the Pope). The number of persons I was alleged to look like during that tour would have made the late Lon Chaney quiver with envy. By a system of wish-transference that merited the attention of a psychoanalyst, the ladies (and sometimes the gentlemen) of the lecture public imagined their lecturers, however obscure and unimportant, to represent the Great World: and the Great World, to them, meant a number of celebrated persons whose names and photographs appeared constantly in the newspapers—Colonel Lindbergh, the Prince of Wales, and so on. Any male lecturer under sixty, providing he had the usual number and arrangement of features, was instantly thought to look like one of these notables. One lady would tell him he looked like Colonel Lindbergh, the very next lady in the line would say he looked like the Prince of Wales, and it would never occur to anybody that such imaginary resemblances were mutually exclusive. What it depended upon was the secret and perhaps unconscious wish. And as for the Chinese Revolution, it appeared to have passed unnoticed. In the whole tour I cannot remember a single knowledgable question on the subject.

The personal interest of the lecture audience in the lecturer was the essence of the whole matter. It was deliberately excited by all persons who stood to gain in any way out of the business: the manager, his agents, the local clubs and newspapers, and everybody else who had a ticket to sell. The lecturer was, *ipso facto*, a 'celebrity,' and the more celebrated he could be made to seem the better it was for the business. I was as obscure as anybody who has ever set foot on a lecture platform; I knew for a fact that even the publicity agents who tried to make a 'celebrity' out of me had never heard of me; I had no acquaintances outside of New York and Chicago, had written no books that anybody had ever read, and was, all in all, an unknown quantity, a genuine Mr X. And yet—so successful is the artificial stimulation of interest by means of propaganda—no sooner did I arrive in a town than the telephone would begin to ring. People rang up to say that they were my cousins, and the fact that they weren't did not limit their loquacity. The newspapers (urged on by people with tickets to sell) printed interviews. In the largest cities, where the difference between a real and an imitation celebrity was known, this seldom happened, but the rest of the phenomena (personal remarks, imagined resemblances, etc.) were invariable, and did not differ, even in form, from New York to California.

All this seemed to me very bad for the lecturer. Surrounded, for months at a time, by people who kept on telling him he was important, he was in grave danger of beginning to think so himself. The mechanism of the system might have been contrived for that precise purpose. I knew better, but I could ..ot say so for two reasons: first, because the effort to explain the truth had the appearance of affected modesty; second, because my duty to my manager was to pretend as hard as I could. Consequently I had to act as if my opinions on bobbed hair, short skirts, long skirts, and all the other problems with which the usual interview was concerned, mattered enough to be given and printed. The results, in cold type, were so painful to read that after a while I used to make a determined effort to get out of a town without seeing its newspaper.

The lecture system seemed to me to have been fatal to a number of people engaged in it. I met many other lecturers during the two big tours I made for Mr Alber. Some few level-headed and competent people (like Lowell Thomas, for instance) could go through the shattering experience year after year without a twinge of nerves. They could give interviews in their sleep, hand out photographs with the dexterity of a juggler, and treat the whole affair in a calm, businesslike manner, as a means of earning money. But other lecturers, including some notorious ones, were conquered by the system. Nothing was more calculated to make an ass of a man than constant public appearance, constant personal publicity, and on many lecturers of my acquaintance the process was carried to completion. They actually grew to think they were as important and interesting as the ticket sellers had to pretend, and the results, qua human character, were lamentable. After viewing a few of these monsters I came to the conclusion that, even if I had been able to speak in public without agony, it would not be wise to try. I had to make the second tour, a year later, because I had signed a contract and received money on it; but once that contract had expired I was determined never to make another.

Out of the two immense tours, lasting many months, I did at least derive a notion of the United States. Not an accurate notion, perhaps—the lecturer's being rather a bird's-eye view—but a comforting one. I had never liked Americans in Europe, particularly the expatriates; and the more I saw of the country the more I realized that they were not good examples of the American character. The people I met on those tours were as un-European as the Chinese or the Russians. The American type (and whatever anthropology had to say about it, there was such a thing) might have been evolved from a thousand elements, but it did compose into a definite and (to me) likable idiosyncrasy. It was childish in some ways, filled with curiosity and false associations of ideas, and often afflicted by an unfortunate tendency towards display of acquirements (wealth, knowledge, information, clothes, property, wit or accomplishment); but in spite of these defects it seemed to me one of the better types created by Western national capitalism. It was bourgeois from the bone out. But what made this universal bourgeoisie attractive was its lack of secondary class-consciousness, meanness of spirit, and general grubbiness, the dislikable characteristics of the European bourgeoisie. The American type was preëminently generous and friendly: two things that the most ardent apologist could never say of the European middle class. Aside from the obvious difference between rich and poor, American life did not provide machinery for the complicated social differentiations that infest the life of Europe. 'Opportunity,' which figured so largely in the windy speeches of politicians, did actually exist in America to a greater degree than elsewhere, and clever people were not held back in their cleverness by social or economic rigidity. Such facts suggested that the collectivist revolution, when it took place in America, would probably take place in a different way from that established in the technique of Marx, Engels and Lenin. The special American type, which sometimes appeared in the first generation of transplanted Europeans, was remarkably uniform in appearance, tastes and habits of mind; it was not recognizably a civilized type at all, for it placed its emphases quantitatively instead of qualitatively, as savages do; and yet its unique barbarism was a much more comforting spectacle (from the point of view of the future of the human race) than the spectacle of European civilization in decay. The Chamber of Commerce of Key West, Florida, could hang the city's streets with posters declaring that 'Key West was three hundred miles south of Cairo, Egypt,' and expect that this quantitative analysis would induce people to go to Key West instead of Cairo. Such reasoning was, of course, sheer savagery in the anthropological sense—was characteristic, that is, of savage cultures, and could seldom occur among a highly civilized people. The American emphasis upon implements (skyscrapers, machines, engines of all sorts) was again a phenomenon characteristic of the child or the savage. I used to be taken to look at new airports until I was dizzy with information about them; the fortunate possessors of these conveniences had to show them off. The fact that one was exactly like another was not considered. But although I was sometimes bored or nervous under the continual impact of temporary acquaintances, I was never moved to active dislike—the type was, on the whole, too thoroughly decent to arouse such feelings. I liked it partly, of course, because I belonged to it myself (minus the decency), but also because on this extended acquaintance, or rediscovery, it appealed to me as good. It seemed to me that if you could ever get a typical American to understand a problem properly he would do the right thing about it—which was, after all, a high proof of good.

Moreover, in spite of some extraordinary superstitions, such as the notion that America had loaned colossal sums in pure gold to Europe during the war and should now get them back, the American type seemed friendly to the whole world. Throughout the country there was a total absence of the national hatreds that control existence in Europe. But there was much incomprehension. The American type did not understand the question of the war debts at all—at least at that time (1928)—because nobody in authority had ever explained the thing properly. The typical American was always startled to hear that the sum of gold he believed Europe owed him did not exist in the world; even such rudimentary facts were unknown, because American politicians were afraid to state them. Nobody I met in America had an idea what unemployment was: they thought it was caused by the 'dole' (an idea fostered by bankers and politicians), just as they thought the value of currencies depended upon the wealth or poverty of nations. Oddest of all was the typical American attitude towards the national disgrace, the stock market. Everybody speculated, everybody believed 'prosperity' was eternal, and nobody I knew seemed to think that free speculation with the produce of a nation's labour was criminal. I used to have some terrible moments over that question, because Wall Street in 1928 and 1929 made me feel very indignant, and I could seldom keep still about it if the subject arose. There was one evening at Martin Sommers' in New York when I horrified a party by a singularly accurate prediction (not mine, of course, but that of anybody acquainted with

Marxian economics): I said that a crash was inevitable, that it would disclose what had been going on underneath the speculative inflation, a true crisis of overproduction in the Marxian sense, and that this must be followed by wide unemployment and terrible suffering. What I said was only what Karl Marx said a long time ago (typical recurring crisis of capitalism), brought into relation to the existing madness in Wall Street; but to my astonishment it was treated as a rude Bolshevistic attack on the persons in the room. They (being typical Americans) argued in a purely individual way, and if I said (as I did) that free speculation was criminal and Wall Street a national disgrace, they thought I was calling them all criminals. The difference between a system and the persons involved in it was not recognized by their ways of thought, and they believed a prediction of disaster in Wall Street was not only foolish, but impolite.

The greatest curiosity of the time was the failure of educated people to speak out on the question of Wall Street. Thousands of people must have known that a speculative boom of such dimensions would be followed by a terrible crash, and yet, in a country sewn thick with colleges and universities, nobody spoke up loudly. In fact, there was a whole crop of professors who proclaimed (for what payment, who knows?) that the 'prosperity' of 1928 had definitely disproved the 'theories' of Karl Marx—an imbecility of the same general type as the statement that unemployment was caused by the dole. Except for Dorothy and Red Lewis, I cannot remember a single acquaintance of mine in America who perceived the shallowness of the 'prosperity' and the inevitability of the crash. Your typical American didn't. And a rather representative American, Mr Herbert Hoover, was busy all through those two years making speeches that put the cart neatly and competently before the horse. According to Mr Hoover, the American system (Fordizatzia, as the Russians called it—mass production and a prosperity based on turnover) was heading towards the 'abolition of poverty,' whereas in economic principle and historical fact it could only be heading towards a greater crisis of poverty-in-the-midst-of-plenty than national capitalism had ever produced before.

In the spring of 1929, shaken up a good deal by illness and the miseries of the lecture tour, I began to long to get away. As always, I turned towards the East, and specifically towards Palestine. I was not to see the Western cities under the same conditions again, for before I returned the crash had come, and a remarkable change—slow in the beginning, vertiginous in speed after a year or two—passed over the ideas and manners of the Western world. A Londoner has only to remember what parties were like in 1928 to realize how much was altered in a year or two; a New Yorker has only to cast his mind back to the phenomena surrounding a 1928 stockbroker's wedding to see how quickly the thing worked.

I was to like London and New York better afterwards. In the 1920's they were jumping-off places or going-back places, diverting themselves blindly in the midst of the surrounding storm. To perceive the storm it was necessary for them to be overtaken by it. In the 1920's, however pleasant they might be for the intervals between sorties, they were too sheltered, essentially, to convey a sense of relationship to the larger world out of which so much of their wealth and power were derived. I had still, after a year and a half, not acquired anything like the 'long view' Borodin spoke of at our last meeting, but the old impulsions towards some attempt at a view were not dead, and there was no room for them in the Western capitals at this moment of satisfied affluence. The cities of the West, considered either as the flower of capitalism in decay, or as the solid achievement of race-nation-class superiority, were not the world. They scarcely seemed (in spite of their concentrated importance) to belong to, or to be conscious of, the world: they were too safe, too complacent, and still too blind.

VIII

Holy Land

FOR YEARS before 1929 I had thought of making a journey to Palestine. I had long had an exaggerated admiration for the Jewish people, and invested them with all the characteristics of poetic insight, intensity of feeling, and loftiness of motive which seemed to me lacking in the generality of the so-called Christians. This attitude was a kind of anti-Semitism turned wrong side out, I suppose—a product, perhaps, of the extraordinary experience in which I first made the acquaintance of Jews as a freshman in college—but it was, whatever its nature, strong enough to make me gravitate towards the Jews of my acquaintance and submit with eagerness to the influences they (whether they wished to do so or not) could not help exercising. A. B., Rayna Prohme, Borodin, Mrs Moskowitz—these most powerful of personal influences were all, as it happened, Jewish. The point had no importance with regard to their characters, for none of them maintained a self-consciously Jewish attitude towards the rest of the world; but it did show, over so many years, a particular susceptibility on my part to the subtle and intense qualities of the Jewish mind. I was fond of Jewish traditions, Jewish food, the Jewish theatre (when I had access to it) and the society of Jewish friends. The Jewish religion seemed to me less superstitious than other religions, purer than either of its children, Christianity and Islam; my copy of an English version of the Talmud was bought, I remember, as early as 1926. And on a more practical plane I firmly believed in the thesis Romain Rolland set forth at length in a part of *Jean Christophe:* that the Jews of western Europe and America constituted the one international layer of culture, through which everything good in literature, music and art spread from nation to nation and slowly tended to give the Western world a closer relationship between its parts. I was, in short, as thoroughgoing a pro-Semite (if there is such a word) as you could have found anywhere. I remember going once to a large gathering at Mrs Moskowitz's house, where all but I were Jewish. She remarked: 'We're all Jews tonight; the rest of us by birth and you by adoption.' I was inordinately pleased that she could say this word of forgiveness.

Forgiveness was what it seemed to me the Christians had to ask of the Jews—and the only thing they had a right to demand. The more I read of the history of the Jewish people the more I was ashamed of the behaviour of the Christians. The literature of anti-Semitism was nonsense, abounding in the silliest accusations it was possible for minds clouded by hatred to invent (ritual murder, the 'protocol of the elders of Zion,' conspiracy of the Jews to conquer the world, etc., etc.). The literature that recorded the facts was a different affair altogether: the story of a race forever driven and oppressed, surrounded by superstitious hatreds until it was forced to live as the traveller lives on a desert journey, alert and aware of death. Even with the decline of superstition in the nineteenth century, when legal disabilities were removed from the Jews in most civilized countries, a social prejudice remained, the legacy of two thousand years. In my bewildering introduction to the ogre of anti-Semitism I had been conquered by it, but I was determined never to be conquered again. And, in fact, the motives that turned me towards Palestine were not altogether those of interest or curiosity: there was also a perceptible element of militancy, a desire to strike some kind of small blow against race hatred, to help, somehow or other, to *écraser l'infâme*.

But the Palestine journey seemed as far off as ever in the winter of 1929. The only moderately interested person was the lecture manager, Mr Alber, who agreed to supply some of the money I might need for the journey as an advance on a second tour. This would be nothing like enough, but it would be of great assistance if I could interest anybody else in the project.

It was my old friend Hillel Bernstein who solved the difficulty. He was not a Zionist himself, but he knew enough of the Zionist organization to be aware that it sometimes sent writers to Palestine to contribute articles to its own publications. It was Bernie's idea that I might get some such contract, with enough of an advance on it to make a stay in Palestine possible. He pointed out that Zionism was a controversial question, even among Jews, and that it would be well to make some stipulation about it—that I would not write political propaganda, that a description of the country and the Zionist colonies would have to be enough.

I needed more money, much more money, if I was to carry out my plans; I knew nothing about Zionism in politics or about the Zionist Organization; opportunity and ignorance combined to govern the event. By an appointment made through Bernie I went to see the editor of *The New Palestine*, a Zionist publication, and told him what I wanted to do. I suggested that I could do a series of articles on life in the Jewish colonies (my plan being to live as a colonist for a while if possible), and that these articles would have to be noncontroversial and nonpolitical, as I could not bind myself in advance to adopt any particular attitude towards the larger questions. I added that so far as I knew the problems at issue I was already sympathetic to the Zionist views, as I had been for years; but that I could not engage future opinions.

The editor was friendly and polite, but he seemed to regard all this formulation of attitude as unnecessary. 'Don't you worry about that,' he said. 'We don't want people to write propaganda. Propaganda's no good anyway. How much do you want?'

The simplicity of the business delighted me. In fifteen minutes it was all arranged. There followed a delay of some weeks, caused by the deliberations of various persons and committees; but on May 10th I was given the first part of my agreed advance and sailed that night for England. I hoped to begin my acquaintance with Zionism and its organization there, by interviewing the benefactor of the movement, Lord Balfour, and its active president, Dr Weizmann, but I was disappointed. Lord Balfour was ill, very ill; Dr Weizmann was not in London. I waited in London three weeks for the rest of my advance from the editor of *The New Palestine*, but it did not turn up, and at last, on the skeleton of a sufficiency, I went on to Paris, Marseilles and Port Said. On the morning of June 25th (after another delay at Port Said) the Cairo express, containing a rather weary second-class passenger with as little money as possible, arrived in Jerusalem.

2

Jerusalem enchanted me from the beginning by the compactness and precision with which it fulfilled its physical tradition: the Mount of Olives exactly here, the Valley of Jehoshaphat exactly there, The Temple of Solomon (Mosque of Omar) exactly opposite, the Mount of Calvary (Church of the Sepulchre) just up the way, all as sharply marked and visible to the naked eye as are the raised surfaces of a relief map or the bright, sober outlines of a landscape in Italian primitive painting. The contour of the little city and its neighbourhood was remarkably like that of a sacred landscape in Italian pictures, and I was constantly being surprised by a hillside and valley road, or a piece of architecture against a brown descent, that might have been taken straight out of a work by Mantegna. In later painters a knowledge of the physical facts may be suspected: certainly in Raphael's Sposalizio the structure in the background, intended to represent the Temple, resembles the Dome of the Rock too closely to have been painted that way by accident. But Raphael's predecessors arrived at their approximation of the truth without the aid of information, as a minor result of their struggle with the problems of painting. The city was beautiful, particularly when seen from above—a small jewel of a city, white roofs and domes serried in order up and down hills beneath a startlingly clear sky. By day the sky was burning blue, and by night it was so clear that the stars seemed within reach. The Austrian Hospice, where I lived, had a flat roof, and on hot nights it was a particular pleasure to lie there and inspect the floor of heaven, thick inlaid with patines of bright gold —thicker inlaid, and nearer to the view, than in other places.

The Hospice was deep-walled, silent and cool on the hottest days, peaceful in the midst of turmoil. There was a mosque just behind it, and the call of the muezzin used to wake me at unearthly hours until I grew accustomed to it. There were, in fact, mosques everywhere, and Islam's call to prayer haunted the still air of an evening, so that I could scarcely see a photograph of the roofs of

Jerusalem afterwards without hearing the long cry of the muezzin as a part of it.

That was, probably, the first impression I received of walled Jerusalem in the early days: that it was an Arab city. It was as Arab as Cairo or Baghdad, and the Zionist Jews (that is, the modern Jews) were as foreign to it as I was myself. I had expected this, of course. I knew that the old city had not been changed, that the large Zionist population of Jerusalem (an actual majority) lived in new quarters outside the walls, and that Palestine was still predominantly an Arab country. But a fact on paper has not the same effect as its physical configuration. Two days in Jerusalem gave me a clearer perception of the fact than I could have received from a volume of statistics. I had enough political experience to realize that such things as these must determine feeling and action, and from my second or third day in Jerusalem I began to wonder if all was as well between the Arabs and the Jews as I had been led to believe. I knew nothing; but anybody could see, in half an hour, that here were the physical elements of a conflict.

I ignored the conflict as long as I could. I did a little exploring on my own, read what I could, talked to such people as I happened to meet. I had letters to the Palestine Zionist Executive, but most of its members had left the country for the summer. Gershon Agronsky, its press director, was still in Jerusalem, and intended to remain there until the Zionist Congress met at Zurich in August. He was intelligent and friendly, had been prepared by letters from America to receive me, and undertook to help me carry out my plan for studying the life of a Jewish colony. In the meanwhile he introduced me to the Zionist Club and to numbers of his colleagues; best of all, he gave me quantities of his own time and answered any question I had to ask.

I had only one letter to a non-Jew in Jerusalem. That was from E. M. Forster, introducing me to George Antonius. Antonius was an assistant secretary in the Palestine government, and, as it happened, he lived in the Austrian Hospice. He was a Syrian Arab (Christian), educated in Alexandria and at Cambridge, and had been in the British government service for years, first in Egypt and then in Palestine. His rooms in the Hospice had been furnished by himself and his wife and differed sharply from anything else I knew in the country. A big room with high ceilings, hung and strewn with rugs, filled with books and music, was not a usual thing in my experience of Jerusalem, and it constituted, particularly in later weeks, when the atmosphere of the city grew murderous, a personal refuge: it was a connection with the outside world, a reminder that there still existed forms of life in which the miserable antagonisms of an unnecessary struggle could be forgotten. Antonius gave me the range of his books and his gramophone records: a gift of value anywhere; of inestimable value in that unhappy place.

His conversation, too, played an important part in my life in Jerusalem. His intelligence never seemed to be altogether harnessed to one subject, as was the case with everybody else I met in that part of the world. Even people of great gifts (the Grand Mufti, for instance) could not escape the influence of an obsession; even the pleasantest characters (like that of Gershon Agronsky) were somehow turned askew by perpetual concentration upon Palestinian affairs. Antonius was remarkable in many ways, but most remarkable because he kept an even keel, remained interested in the world outside the walls of the city, and remembered his obligation as an intelligent and cultivated human being not to lose his head. I needed some such buttress in my own efforts to retain control and was lucky indeed to find it in him.

It was afterwards suggested before the Parliamentary Commission of Enquiry[1] that the process by which I came to my conclusions in Palestine was influenced by Antonius. That may be true, but if so it must have been by telepathy, for in my earlier weeks in Palestine we had an agreement not to talk Zionism or Palestinian politics. At the outset I had explained to him my exact status, and he had explained his. He believed the Zionist programme was unfair to the Arabs without offering any solution to the Jewish problem; he was convinced it would lead to serious, recurring troubles. Having made ourselves so clear in that first conversation,

---

[1]Minutes of Evidence, Palestine Commission on the Disturbances of August, 1929, questions 10,277–10,282. When I have occasion to refer to this report in future I shall call it Minutes of Evidence. It was published in 1930 by H. M. Stationery Office, for the Colonial Office, and contains the stenographic record of evidence taken by the Parliamentary Commission in forty-seven sittings.

we agreed that we must differ on the Zionist question, and dropped the subject until I had been some weeks in the country and had myself concluded that the situation was full of danger—until, in fact, I had veered towards his own view of the case. After I had broken my connection with the Zionists and had been made apprehensive by a dozen little incidents, the old embargo on political talk broke down, and we discussed Palestinian affairs by the hour. But in the first stages of my stay in the country I talked about Zionism only to Zionists. I was by this time, as anybody who has read the whole of this book must see, amply experienced in the kind of problem I faced in Palestine: the movements of ideas that brought groups or masses of men into conflict. I knew that such movements could only be judged upon their own showing, not upon what they appeared to be to their critics or opponents; and I needed no help, beyond that afforded by the Zionists themselves, in making up my mind about their cause.

3

There has never been a time when some form of Zionism did not exist in the Jewish people. The more I read in the literature of the subject, the more I realized that the nostalgia for Jerusalem was an essential part of the Jewish tradition. But to my amazement I found it had always been a nostalgia and little more. The Jews had been leaving Palestine—had been existing in the 'Diaspora,' or Dispersion—hundreds of years before Christ. Palestine was always a poor country, had never offered sufficient means of livelihood to a growing, energetic race. The yearning for Jerusalem, the literature of the subject from ancient times onwards appeared to show, was accompanied by a desire to live somewhere else.

From this contradiction arose the idea of the 'national home.' In the nineteenth century, as the Jews of Europe came out of their long subjection and took their place as the equals of other citizens of the Western world, they evolved the idea of a 'spiritual centre' for Judaism in Palestine. The Khóvévé Zion (Lovers of Zion) went so far as to send colonies of Jews to live in Palestine. There had always been small colonies of religious Jews in Jerusalem and the other holy cities, supported by contributions from their coreligionists abroad. These groups were now to be augmented, but the basic notion—a 'spiritual centre'—remained the same.

It was the anti-Semitism of continental Europe in the nineteenth century that turned the minds of modern, secular Jews towards the Holy Land and aroused in them the desire to create not only a 'spiritual centre' but a Jewish nation. The founder of modern Zionism was the Viennese journalist Theodor Herzl, who created the Zionist Organization in 1897. He believed that the institution of a Jewish nation in Palestine would solve the Jewish problem, put an end to anti-Semitism, and unite the Jews of all countries in a semi-religious, semi-political homogeneity. His ideas of practical politics were nebulous, and he never seems to have faced the fact that the country was already inhabited by a settled population that had been there for thirteen hundred years. But he did arouse, among modern Jews throughout western Europe and the United States, an enthusiastic response in which it was possible to detect the remains of the old nostalgia, transformed into modern terms. That is, the religious yearning had vanished, but an emotional attachment to Zion remained, even among atheist Jews who regarded the practises of the religion with impatience. Herzl's chief opposition in Jewry came, in fact, from the Orthodox Jews—those who believed it was required of God's people to wait until the coming of the Messiah before restoring the Temple. But it was only in 1917, when the British government, for political reasons, saw fit to issue the Balfour Declaration, that world Zionism became a lively political movement with high hopes for the future.

The Balfour Declaration occupied only one sentence, but it was a masterly one. It was composed by Arthur James Balfour after eighteen months of secret negotiations with the Zionist leaders, and was sent by letter to Lord Rothschild on November 2, 1917. It reads:

His Majesty's Government view with favour the establishment in Palestine of a national home for the Jewish people, and will use their best endeavours to facilitate the achievement of this object, it being clearly understood that nothing shall be done which may prejudice the civil and religious rights of existing non-Jewish communities in Palestine, or the rights and political status enjoyed by Jews in any other country.

Balfour's master hand never did better work than in the rubbery phrases of this sentence. The Arab population of Palestine, outnumbering the Jews then more than ten to one, was referred to only as 'the existing non-Jewish population.' The whole tone of the sentence was that of generosity to both Jew and Arab. The Balfour Declaration seemed to promise the Jews everything and seemed to reserve everything for the Arabs, at one time and with one twist of the pen. I was to learn in Palestine that it had actually given the Jews little, had reserved little for the Arabs, and had achieved one certain purpose only: the installation of the British as the governing power in the country.

4

When I came to Jerusalem the British had been in possession of the city for more than ten years. The Palestine Mandate, under which Britain was to administer the country in trust for the establishment of a Jewish national home, had been in operation for seven years. Arabs and Jews had often been at loggerheads during these years, but the Zionist immigration policy had slowly made progress, so that by the time I arrived in the country there were no longer ten Arabs to every Jew, but only about six—the figures given being, roughly, 750,000 Arabs to 150,000 Jews. Zionist hopes were particularly high in the spring and summer of 1929, for funds were plentiful then, the world was given over to optimism, and the British government, caught between the two fires, seemed on the whole more sensitive to Jewish than to Arab criticism. It was thought that the congress of world Zionists at Zurich, to which representatives of all the non-Zionist Jewish parties and groups had also been invited, would be memorable in the history of Zionism for the advance it would mark in the progress of the cause.

I was aware, as I have said, of the physical material for conflict; I had only to look out my window to see it. But for two or three weeks I made every effort to avoid the signs of trouble. I had come to Palestine to live in a Jewish colony and study its operation, not to write about politics, and I intended to carry out the plan as soon as I had familiarized myself in some measure with the look and feel of the country as a whole. For a while I did an the usual things, visited Bethlehem and the Holy Sepulchre, went down to Jordan, bathed in the Dead Sea, looked at mosaics and was shown round the Hebrew University on Mount Scopus. I was greatly interested in the Hebrew Art Theatre of Moscow, called Habima, which was playing then in Jerusalem. I saw everything I could of their work and met a number of their leading players, some of whom I knew well in Jerusalem and Tel-Aviv. The tone of the press, quarrelsome and vindictive beyond anything known in peaceful countries, was disturbing; there were occasional incidents that caused one to wonder what it was all coming to—every Friday evening at the Wailing Wall, for instance; and conversations sometimes took an unpleasant turn. But on the whole my first weeks in Palestine were calm. I absorbed what I could, listened to everybody, and wrote (on this subject, that is) nothing. I had no intention of writing a word about the country until I had had at least three or four months to observe it. I could not foresee how agitated those three or four months were going to be.

On July 9th I had my first mild jolt. An Arabic newspaper on that day announced that I had come to Palestine, and added, *carrément*, that I was in the pay of the Jews.

There were other comments, but this was the one I attended to carefully. Was I in the pay of the Jews or was I not? If not, why did the statement make me angry? And if I was, what then? It took me about half an hour to see that I must either make up my mind to be, as the Arabic newspaper said, 'in the pay of the Jews,' and to accept any comment that might be made on the subject, or else to break my connection with the Zionists altogether and go my own way.

My diary (which was kept very full, too full, in Palestine) records the results on Thursday, July 11th, in these words:

... Tuesday [the ninth] was distinguished for me by a thing I have never done before. I gave away fifteen hundred dollars. The way of it was this: that morning an Arab newspaper made a sort of attack on me, saying I was in the pay of the Jews. This gave me much food for thought. It depressed me chiefly, I decided, because there was truth in it. Although I've always said I would not allow my opinions to be influenced, how can I be sure? After all,

I have already taken an advance of five hundred dollars and expect fifteen hundred more! All this appears under an entirely different light here. I finally decided that I couldn't do it. I wrote to Weisgal, both in New York and in Zurich, and told him I didn't want any more money and would take no engagement for any Zionist subsidiary. I made it clear that I must write and speak as I please. This relieved my feelings somewhat, although God knows how I shall get along without that money. What's worse is that if I can't write a couple of articles that will suit the Zionists' book I'll have to give back the five hundred I've already received![1]

I suppose that of all the journalists and writers who had been sent to Palestine by the Zionists in the decade after the war, I was the first who had balked at going on with the bargain. My friend Gershon Agronsky had some difficulty in seeing my point of view (he thought, I believe, that there was something more in this than met the eye—that I had been in some way turned against the Zionists); but he accepted it, at any rate, and a few days later I went down to Tel-Aviv with him to join his family. From Tel-Aviv we made a tour of the colonies, with the object of giving me a general idea of their style and differences.

My diary records at length the impressions of these days, describes all the colonies we saw, and concludes:

The most serious and important thing about the tour, to me, was my long conversation (argument? talk?) with Agronsky, beginning at Markenhof. It started when we saw those three babies in their screened cribs. I suppose Gershon saw that I was impressed. At any rate, he said: 'This is Zionism. Those who oppose us oppose this.' I said: 'What on earth do you mean?' He said: 'I mean that these are our standards. Those who oppose us want to see the children of this country brought up in filth and neglect, as you can see in any Arab village. This is the whole Zionist problem, right before you —those babies in their cribs.' I was irritated, but I could scarcely speak out just then. I said: 'You know perfectly well that this isn't the problem at all. When we get away I'll tell you what the problem is, if you really think I don't know.' When we had left Markenhof and got into the car again I said: 'The problem is not one of higher or lower standards. Any fool knows that higher standards of living are preferable to lower standards of living. Nobody could oppose Zionism if it meant simply the improvement of the conditions of life in Palestine. The opposition to Zionism, so far as I can tell—the only reasonable opposition, anyhow—is based upon the fact that Zionism pro-

[1] This five hundred dollars, the original advance, I returned to the editor of *The New Palestine* when I got back to New York, as it was obvious I could never write articles that would be of any use to him.

poses to settle or colonize a country that is already inhabited by another people.' He began to argue that the Arabs had no feeling of nationalism or of resentment against the Zionists, that they were a mercenary people, with no race or nation principles; that they would not and could not oppose Zionism as long as they were paid. I said I had known Arabs in other countries, not Palestine, and that I simply did not believe it. I said: 'If you want to take those babies at Markenhof as the symbols of the Zionist problem, there is one way in which you can do it. Think of them as a problem of life and death. One fine day, if the Zionist programme continues, those babies will have their throats cut by some angry Arabs. It's happened in other countries, and it will happen here. Are you prepared for that?' He baulked at the question for a long time, denying that the Arabs could get so angry; denying that the colonies were weak or defenceless; denying that there was a state of conflict around them. Finally, when he couldn't deny any more, he said flatly, stubbornly: 'All right. If some have to die, they will have to die, Zionism cannot stop and cannot fail.' The argument went on for many hours and was resumed again today. I got rather excited, I am afraid. If he had not tried to make me believe that the Zionist problem was one of higher or lower standards, I should never have talked in that way. But I see it, more and more, every day, as a political problem, and I couldn't allow him to put it into such terms. I am coming, or have already come, to two conclusions: that the difficulty of Zionism is essentially one thing only, its attempt to settle a country that is already settled; and second, that the Balfour Declaration is a document that really guarantees only one thing, the permanence of the British occupation of Palestine.

It may be seen that in three weeks I had already acquired serious misgivings about the wisdom of the Zionist policy. I still knew nothing about the Arabs of Palestine, but I could see them all around me everywhere, and if my long experience in political journalism had taught me anything, it was that one people did not like being dominated or interfered with in its own home by another. These things seemed to me plain, beyond argument. What I wanted to hear was what the Zionists were doing about it; and instead I was given a large number of irrelevant statements about standards of living, etc., etc. Gershon Agronsky was intelligent and brave enough to face the problem when he had to, but I met few ordinary Zionists who were. Their comments on the Arabs took a form that seemed to me invariably stupid, in Palestine or elsewhere: the form of underrating the opponent. Your ordinary Zionist would say, in so many words: 'We don't have to worry about the Arabs. They'll do anything for money.' I knew no Palestine Arabs, but unless they were far different from the Arabs I had known in Morocco, Iraq and Persia, this could not be the truth.

As I retrace, with the aid of my old diary, the steps by which I altered my first opinions of the Zionist experiment, I see that the thing presented itself to me throughout as a practical problem. The steps were small ones, each determined by a fact. For larger ideas—for a consideration of what the whole thing might mean— I had to wait until I had left Palestine behind; no 'long view' was possible in that embittered country. I had arrived on June 25th with a genuine sympathy, however ignorant or romantic, for the Zionist effort. Between June 25th and July 9th I was a little disquieted by the physical configuration of the problem, by the sight and sound of the Arab country in which Zionism was making its effort. On July 9th I received a jolt of a personal nature, and as a result broke my connection with the Zionists and resumed my freedom: all this without consciously turning against the Zionist idea. During the next week I went to Tel-Aviv and the colonies, talked, talked, talked, and listened even more. I saw Jewish islands in an Arab sea: that was what I saw. And on the whole the Jewish disregard for the Arabs seemed to me (from their own point of view) perilous in the extreme. I could not believe that the Arabs of Palestine were so different from other Arabs that they would welcome the attempt to create a Jewish nation in their country.

After July 17th, therefore, I made some attempt to find out what the Arabs of Palestine were like. I remained in touch with the Zionists, visited Tel-Aviv, continued to read Zionist literature and talk to Zionist friends. But I no longer tried to ignore the fact that Palestine was, by the overwhelming majority of its population, an Arab country. It seemed to me important to determine for myself what were the bonds between this population and the land it inhabited. If the bonds were slight—if the Arabs of Palestine had been mere squatters for thirteen centuries—it would still be feasible for the Zionists, by purchase, persuasion and pressure, to get the Arabs out sooner or later and convert Palestine into a Jewish national home. Zionists had pointed out, in conversation and in writing, that the Arabs had plenty of land to go to all around Palestine: Syria, Iraq, Transjordan and Arabia Deserta were all Arab countries. What bound the Arabs of Palestine to Palestine?

My acquaintance with the Arab world in general suggested that the answer would be found in Islamic religious feeling. In the stage of culture represented by most Arab countries—feudal, pastoral or at any rate preindustrial—religious feeling still dominated the acts of life to an extent unknown in the West. I had never known an Arab who was not devout. I had known Moslems who broke the stricter dietary rules of the Prophet (indeed, many); but I had never known a Moslem who did not regard the central doctrines of the Islamic faith with fierce, exclusive devotion. I had to find the religious connection between the Arabs and Palestine – and found it, of course, at five minutes' walk from the Austrian Hospice, in the Haram esh-Sherif.

The Haram esh-Sherif, occupying the traditional Temple Area of the Jews, was one of the great holy places of Islam, ranking immediately after Mecca and Medina. It also contained, as I discovered to my delight, one of the most beautiful buildings in the world. I went there first on Thursday, July 18th. On that and succeeding days I had great difficulty getting beyond the one wonderful building, the Dome of the Rock (Qubbat es-Sakhra). The Dome of the Rock was built over the great black Rock of Abraham's Sacrifice, which once upheld the Altar of Burnt Offerings in the Temple of Solomon. From this rock the Prophet Mohammed ascended into heaven. The Holy of Holies, in the days of the three Jewish Temples, stood somewhere beyond it. But what drew me back to the Dome of the Rock again and again was not its complicated interreligious sanctity, but the incomparable beauty of the structure and the glowing vitality of its ancient mosaics, the oldest of which were composed at the dawn of Islam, in the seventh century. I used to squat on the rugs against the circular walls of the building, stare up at those mosaic arches, and wonder not only at the genius that could have produced them, but at the contradiction between these lofty, exquisite forms and colours and the religious hatreds that clustered round them.

The Dome of the Rock (usually called the 'Mosque of Omar' by Western Christians, because of the mistaken belief that it was built by Omar the Conqueror) was not visited by Orthodox Jews because it was regarded by them as the holiest part of their Temple, and they feared to tread unwittingly upon their Holy of Holies. But Zionists—most of whom, in my experience, were without religious feeling—used to visit it as I did, out of an ordinary æsthetic interest. The Moslems made no objection to such visits. In this and in other respects the Moslems of Palestine were less jealous of their holy places than Moslems elsewhere. I had never been allowed inside a great mosque in Morocco or Persia, but the Haram esh-Sherif, a far holier place to the Islamic world, was open to me or to anybody else all day long.

The same was true of the Mosque of el-Aksa, once a Christian basilica, and of the other parts of the Haram. It would be quite within the facts to say that the Haram esh-Sherif (Noble, or August, Sanctuary), in spite of the religious traditions that made it one of the three holiest spots in Islam, was treated as a public monument, like St Peter's in Rome or the Church of the Holy Sepulchre in Jerusalem. The more I learned about the tradition of the place, the more I was surprised at this. Not only did the Prophet Mohammed visit the place by night (miraculously translated there from Mecca), and ascend to Heaven from Abraham's Rock, but he will come there again on the Day of Judgment, when the Prophet Jesus and the Prophet Mohammed guard the ends of the bridge across the Valley of Jehoshaphat. These and other beliefs, some founded on the Koran and some mere folk-lore, invested the place with a significance stretching through time from the beginnings of the Judæo-Christian-Islamic religion to the last moment contemplated for earthly existence in its philosophy. And nevertheless, so long as one took one's shoes off, it was all right to spend day after day in the place, and even to photograph it.

This being so, it was possible, at first, to assume that the Moslems of Palestine did not regard their holiest shrine with the extreme religious passion characteristic of Moslems elsewhere. The assumption fell in with the Zionist idea that the Arabs of Palestine were, on the whole, a careless and easy-going race. But I had strong doubts, just the same. I could not help remembering that unfortunate Mr Imbrie, the American Consul in Tehran, whom I had once known: he was torn to pieces by the mob for photographing a much less sacred place than this. I remembered stories I had heard in Morocco, accounts I had read of Mecca. It seemed to me more likely that what had happened to the Haram esh-Sherif was due to the Westernized character of life in Jerusalem: this place had fallen under so many different kinds of rule, had experienced such a mixture of invasions and such an assimilation of cultures, that its Moslem leaders were constrained by Western taste and manners to open their great sanctuary to the visits of the infidel. I did not believe that underneath this Europeanization of taste and manners was any slackening of the ardour with which Moslems everywhere regard a place sanctified by the Prophet.

Such considerations—divorced, that is, from current problems, and independently of the 'incidents' that filled the newspapers every week on the subject—would have led me in any case to examine the question of the Wailing Wall.

5

The Wailing Wall was a segment of the southwestern wall of the Haram esh-Sherif. It was called by the Jews 'Ha-Quotel ma-Aravi' (the Western Wall); by the Moslems 'El-Buraq' (from the name of the Prophet's horse, which was tethered there); and by Western Christians the 'Wailing Wall.' It was a short stretch of wall with a pavement in front of it and had been chosen by the Jews centuries ago as a place of lamentation.

The idea of the Wailing Wall was an ancient one, but I was never able to find out why the idea was attached to this particular segment of the wall and not to any other. The idea was, briefly, this: God has seen fit to exile His people from their Temple, and has condemned them to a long period of disaster, to be ended when the Messiah comes to restore them to their rightful place; therefore His people lament and pray before the Temple wall, particularly on the high holy days of the religion, the Day of Atonement and the Day of the Destruction of the Temple.

This idea of a place for lamentation outside the desecrated Temple grew stronger with the passage of centuries and the accretion of tradition. Most religious Jews believed that the old stones of the wall were actually the stones of Solomon's Temple. This was not archæologically correct; the oldest stones in the wall of the Haram were Græco-Roman, of the period of Herod; but the original facts made no difference in religious belief. During these centuries the Western Wall had stood as a representation, a symbol or relic, of the Temple itself. Jews throughout the world who were unable to go there on the Day of Atonement, for instance, paid other Jews to do so for them, and for hundreds of years there had been a small population of religious Jews living in Jerusalem on *Haluka* (sacred doles, for praying). Before the nineteenth century there was no record of trouble at the Western Wall; the Moslems made no attempt to prevent the visits of the Jews there, and a prescriptive right grew up, which was maintained under changing governments thereafter. The only records of an attempt to go beyond the original purposes of lamentation at the Wall were dated 1837 and 1912. In the first document the Egyptian Governor of Jerusalem forbade the Jews to pave the area in front of the wall or to do anything else beyond 'make their visits in accordance with the ancient custom.' In the second document the Jews were forbidden to bring into the Wailing Wall area any of the 'tools or instruments of possession,' such as chairs, screens and the Ark (i.e., the furniture of a synagogue). The Moslem refusal to permit innovations was clearly based upon the fear that, if they did so, the Jews would soon have a synagogue at the wall of the Mosque.

The triumph of Zionism at the end of the war brought a new element into the question. The Zionist Organization was not itself religious, although it possessed a religious (minority and opposition) Right Wing. Its membership professed a wide range of belief in such matters, from agnosticism to orthodoxy, and even included some Jews converted to Christianity; but considered as a whole it was a modern, Western, secular, political body. Still, the advantages to political Zionism of making a test case of the Wailing Wall were obvious. If the Zionists could get new rights at the Wall—better, if they could get absolute possession of the area—they could count on the adherence of a large number of religious Jews who had always been cold to the movement.

PERSONAL HISTORY

An attempt was made in 1919 to buy the Wailing Wall outright.
The Zionists offered (through Sir Ronald Storrs) eighty thousand
pounds; the Arabs refused to sell. From that time onward, at
intervals throughout the period of the British occupation and the
League of Nations mandate, there were 'incidents.' There were
'incidents' from the time I arrived in Palestine until I left, and the
whole of the Palestine question (the national home for the Jews,
the rights of the Arabs, the position of the British) came to be involved in them, so that the Zionist struggle was concentrated upon
the Wailing Wall and the Arab resistance aligned before it. The
question was no longer religious: it had become political and national as well.

It would be tedious indeed to recite these Wailing Wall incidents. Most of them were childish, considered by themselves;
they had to be put all together before any sense emerged from
them. But when the incidents were compared their tendency was
apparent. The struggle, fundamentally, was conceived as being
for ownership. The specific question might be whether the Jews
could bring chairs and a table to the place or not; whether they
could blow the ram's horn (*shofar*) there; whether they could
put up screens to separate the women from the men; whether the
Moslems had a right to walk through the place at hours of Jewish
worship; whether an Arab could drive a donkey through or not.
Such details covered the basic facts of the situation: the Jewish
desire to establish a fixed holy place at the Western Wall, with the
rights of a synagogue, and the Moslem fear that they would succeed in doing so and go on to further encroachments on the
Temple area.

Haj Amin el-Husseini, the Grand Mufti of Jerusalem, whom I
did not know at that time, had been alive to the implications of
the Wailing Wall question for years. There can be no doubt that
some of the steps he took to emphasize the Moslem ownership
of the place gave grave offence to the Jews, and on some occasions
shocked the whole Jewish world, including sections of Jewish
opinion that had never supported the Zionist policy. Haj Amin
was convinced that the Jews would take the Haram area—the
Temple—'if they could,' as he testified later on before the Parlia-

mentary Commission of Enquiry.'[1] The responsible Jewish
authorities, particularly the Va'ad Leumi (Jewish National Council) and the Palestine Zionist Executive, had denied such an intention in official statements both in Palestine and abroad, but
such denials, couched in elastic terms, could have little force in a
conflict involving profound religious passions. The Grand Mufti
was accused by the Zionists of making political capital out of the
Wailing Wall question to consolidate his own position among the
Moslems, but proofs of the contention were lacking. Even if it
had been so—even if the Grand Mufti's motives had been so
improbably petty—the results would have been exactly the same:
he undertook to emphasize the Moslem ownership of the place by
a number of measures that gave offence to the Jews, and they
reiterated their claims with renewed persistence. He restored an
old *ẓawiya*[2] in the Abu Madian Waqf, the Moslem charitable
foundation on whose property the Wailing Wall area stands.
Prayers and a noisy religious service called the *Zikr* took place
in the *ẓawiya* and interfered, it was said, with Jewish prayers in
front of the Wall. The Mufti also undertook various repairs to
the property surrounding the Wailing Wall area and, among
other things, opened a new door in the wall of the Haram itself,
thus converting what had been a blind alley into a thoroughfare
and giving the Moslem crowds from the mosque an access directly
to the pavement in front of the Western Wall.

Opinions might differ widely, and did, as to the Grand Mufti's
reasons for making such a determined stand on the Moslem ownership of the sacred areas thereabouts; but for my part I never could
understand how he, as the religious, political and judicial head of
the Moslems of Palestine, could have done anything else. He had
either to do as he did, it seemed to me, or else see the Jews take
possession of the area and build whatever it was they intended to
build there—synagogue or place of prayer or holy courtyard.

That they did wish to obtain possession of the place was abundantly proved. As His Eminence the Chief Rabbi of the Ashkena-
zim said, they wanted to take it and 'make it beautiful.' As the
young men of Tel-Aviv said: 'The Wailing Wall is ours!' As a

[1] Minutes of Evidence, question 12,903.
[2] Minor shrine or place for prayer.

friend of mine (Jewish but not a Zionist) said: 'What's the sense of a Jewish national home here if we can't even have the Wailing Wall?' As Mr Sacher of the Palestine Zionist Executive said in his speech (not actually delivered, but circulated and given to the press) at the Zionist Congress in Zurich: 'Our rights under the Mandate are more complete and more extensive than those embraced within the principle of the status quo.'

There never was any question in my mind that the Jewish feeling about the Wailing Wall was profound and bitter. Jews who frankly confessed themselves to be without religious belief could not discuss the subject without getting excited. They did not themselves want to go there and pray or lament; they did not think they could put petitions into crevices of the Wall (as Orthodox Jews did) and get them received by the holy spirit of the Temple; they did not want the Wall for themselves at all. But they felt that the Jewish nation in Palestine (as they conceived these minority settlements to be) ought to have possession of one holy place, the relic of the Temple (the only relic, as they somewhat loosely believed), and that the genuinely religious Jews, for the most part not Zionists, should have Zionism to thank for it. The Arabs, for whom they had contempt as an 'uncivilized' race, to whom some of them referred as 'Red Indians' and others as 'savages,' were in possession of a place that signified a great deal to the Jewish world in general. The fact hurt the pride of all Jews, I believe, but oddly enough it was the young agnostics and unbelievers who were most bitterly offended and expressed themselves most loudly. What appeared in everyday talk in Jerusalem was what the *Jewish Chronicle* in London summed up with admirable precision: 'The Wall has come to be regarded as a gauge of Jewish prestige in Palestine.'

But Arab feeling about the Wall was equally profound and bitter. I learned it not only by the evidence in print, the speeches of the authorities, and the fulminations of the press, but also because I had a good many opportunities to speak to Arabs on the subject later on in the year. The Prophet Mohammed had entered the Haram area, on his miraculous visit to Jerusalem, by the Western Gate (the gate in the Western, or Wailing Wall); he had tethered his horse, El-Buraq, at a spot said to be inside the thickness of the Wailing Wall itself. The Archangel Gabriel then conducted him from the Buraq (the Wailing Wall) to the Rock of Abraham, from which they ascended to Heaven. One could never get Jews to take these legends seriously, at least in conversation. In public utterances the Zionists treated Moslem susceptibilities carefully, but in ordinary discussion of these matters, in which the state of mind was most clearly shown, my Jewish friends said: 'The Buraq! What in the world is the Buraq? After all, it's only a legend, and a legend about a horse, at that. How can you compare it to our Temple?' It was no use pointing out that their Temple, in the sense in which the worshippers at the Wall understood it, was equally legendary. After all, the Wailing Wall contained no part of the Temple of Solomon, and there were no parts of the Temple of Solomon anywhere. There were three courses of very old masonry at the Wailing Wall, but those three courses continued for a great distance beyond (the whole southwestern and southern walls contained them). Therefore the idea that the *schechina*, the essential holy spirit of the Temple, was resident particularly in this segment of masonry called the Wailing Wall was just as legendary as the story of the Prophet's horse. Facts made no difference in either case. The Arabs believed one thing and the Jews another. But neither, so far as I could ever discover, made a sincere effort to feel what it was the other believed—to understand it with the imagination, the only instrument we possess for such difficult transactions.

With these beliefs held on both sides, and with neither side fully understanding or crediting the sincerity of the other, the incidents of 1928–29 were sure to make the Wailing Wall a crucial point in the struggle between Jew and Arab. It had become, as the *Jewish Chronicle* said, a 'gauge of Jewish prestige in Palestine.' By July, when the World Congress of the Zionists met at Zurich, the temperature had risen in Palestine to an alarming degree. The speeches and resolutions of that congress did nothing to reassure the Arabs; they did much to fortify the Jews, at least in spirit. On August 6th the new door from the Haram esh-Sherif to the pavement before the Western Wall was opened, and the Jewish press and public in Palestine took on a more agitated tone than ever. Mr Vladimir Jabotinsky's 'Maccabees'—young men who followed the Zionist revisionist leader—vied with their favourite newspaper, *Doar Hayom* (the Hebrew newspaper with the widest circulation), in expressing their vehement dislike for the Moslem authorities, the Palestine government, and the more moderate authorities of the Zionist Organization. The Moslems were so angry that not a Friday passed without some kind of minor 'incident' at the Wailing Wall. The temperature rose throughout the first fortnight of August—you could stick your hand out in the air and feel it rising.

6

I come now to a curious incident. How curious (and, indeed, how horrible) will appear later on in the story. Before relating it I ought to say that the important parts of it were denied under oath before the Parliamentary Commission of Enquiry by the person involved[1] after I had offered them in evidence, also under oath.[2]

On the afternoon of Wednesday, August 14th, I was writing in my room at the Austrian Hospice when one of our ever breathless Tyrolean servants broke in to say that a lady was downstairs to see me. I threw on a voluminous dressing gown and clattered down the great stone staircase to the door. There, to my surprise, I saw a compatriot of mine whom I knew very slightly—a Jewish-American I had met in Zionist circles, chiefly with the Agronskys. What she had to say to me, and what followed that evening, are related baldly in my diary. I shall quote the entry written the next day (August 15th, in the morning), calling the young lady Miss X.[3]

Thursday, August 15. Yesterday was the Eve of Tisha ba'Av (the Ninth of Av), which the Jews of the Galut call Tishabov. Today is the actual fast itself: commemoration of the destruction of the Temple. The day is particularly associated with the Wailing Wall; and with the new Jewish Agency

[1]Minutes of Evidence, pp. 220–23.

[2]Minutes of Evidence, pp. 205–10.

[3]In view of the fact that the poor woman could not have foreseen what these events would lead to, I think I may suppress her name here. Anybody who is sufficiently curious can find it in the Minutes of Evidence containing my account of the incident and her denial of it.

just formed, all the Wailing Wall propaganda going full tilt, the Arabs in a rare state of anxiety, the situation was ripe for anything. Trouble, trouble, and more trouble. There will be plenty. I knew nothing about it at all—didn't even know Tishabov was so near—when Miss X arrived at the Hospice at three in the afternoon, after yesterday's entry in this book was already written. Said she had to go to the Wailing Wall and write a telegram about it for the *Times* (as substitute for Gershon): would I go with her and help? I couldn't understand why, but she said there was going to be a 'bust up.' She had come up from Tel-Aviv especially for this, as Gershon is supposed to be correspondent for the *Times* here, and he is in Zurich. (Did he telegraph her to do this? Must ask.) Anyhow, she said the word had been passed round and hundreds of Haluzim were coming in during the afternoon and evening from the colonies and Tel-Aviv, ready to fight. I simply couldn't believe all this. She said the Haluzim would be armed—'three quarters of them'—and it would be a good thing if there was a row at the Wall, to 'show that we are here.' I didn't believe a damned word of it: too fantastic; but I told her I'd be ready to go along at five o'clock if she would come back. She said there wouldn't be any trouble until sundown, and five o'clock would do. I went along with her when she came back. She was inconceivably cynical and flippant about the whole thing; said a row would be a very good thing for the Zionist cause, arouse world Jews and increase contributions to the new Agency. Before we reached the Wall it was evident that the police were well prepared. There were little clumps of policemen, British and Palestinian, at every turning in the road, and a force of about twenty of them on duty at the Wall itself, half in front of the Grand Mufti's house and half at the other end. There was no excitement whatever, only about half a dozen religious Jews and Jewesses (Oriental) praying and weeping against the Wall. Towards six, a little before, we went away to the Hôtel St John for a glass of beer. Sat there a bit, talking; I couldn't understand her point of view at all, and tried to find out. When we returned to the Wall, a little before seven, everything had changed. There was a dense crowd, made up chiefly of Haluzim, in the little area in front of the Wall. A Yemenite Jew was chanting the lamentations, from the Book, while four other Yemenites sat around him, weeping and rocking themselves back and forth. These seemed to me to be the most sincerely religious manifestants present—they paid no attention to their surroundings, but only to their lament. The rest of that crowd was spoiling for a fight. The crowd I was in, that is. Farther off, at the end of the Wall before the Grand Mufti's house, the service was being read by a Cantor (Sephardic, I believe) who stopped and looked around angrily at the slightest noise. Since noises were continually being made, he was continually stopping, but always had to begin again, as he discovered that the sounds came from zealous but irreverent Haluzim. The number of Jews taking part in this Sephardic group was not more than sixteen. I counted them as well as I could from where I stood, and am pretty sure of the number. This was at the Mufti's house; the other group was at the other end, opposite the Wall itself, sitting on the steps that go down to one of the Moghrabi houses. All the people who choked the area seemed to be either people like myself, who had come out of curiosity or interest, and Haluzim, who were—as Miss X said—'r'arin' to go.' The Yemenites went on weeping and praying throughout; they noticed nobody and nobody noticed them. Strange scene.

Saw Halkin, the poet: very excited. So was everybody I spoke to (Warschawer was there, the most peaceful of people, and even he was angry). What seems to have upset them so is the new door in the Wall. I actually saw one revolver, but don't know who the man was who had it (hip pocket). There were only two actual 'incidents.' In the first a Christian Arab whom I did not see was accused of mocking at the services; I heard cries of 'Notzri!' and saw the Haluzim shoving, but the police took the man out safely. Then there was an Arab in white clothes who walked through the place three times —did nothing, simply walked. I believe he was unmolested the first time, although there were angry murmurs. The second time he came through the Haluzim started to leap on him, but the police took him through without difficulty. The third time he appeared, the police wouldn't let him go on— made him turn back. Very wise of them, for that crowd was in no mood to stand any kind of 'incident' without serious trouble. But in this incident the shouts of the Haluzim must certainly have been far more disturbing to the prayers of the religious Jews than the Arab's progress through the street would have been.

Both the Arabs and the police must have been warned of this invasion from the colonies, for there was evidence of preparation. For instance, the Arabs remained invisible; the Mufti's windows were closed and shuttered at about 7:30 so that he wouldn't have to look at the mob milling around; the police were in force and vigilant. The behaviour of this crowd at the wall of the mosque was, I consider, damned insulting. If I were an Arab I should be angry, very angry, and I don't for a minute think the thing is over.

X was incredibly cynical. I don't believe she's ever seen anybody wounded, or ever seen a street fight; she can't understand the awfulness of the things she said last night. We left the Wall at about nine o'clock. Some time before then Cust[1] came into the area, strode importantly through it, and went out again. We went up to the Bristol Gardens for dinner. X was indescribable— apparently enjoyed the impression of horror she was making on me. Said there was bound to be trouble; if not tonight, tomorrow; 'we have to show we are here'; and 'it won't do a bit of harm if a couple of people get hurt.' I tried to tell her, sitting there under a lemon tree, what this kind of thing meant, what it could lead to. God knows I've seen enough of it in my time. She only laughed. I think she thought I was crazy to take it so hard. According to her, it can't do any harm and will only bring in the shekels. I told her she had definitely killed any remnant of sympathy I had for the Zionist movement. We had a long discussion, argument, and she made a lot of fun of my fears and excitements. I dare say she thinks she's very hard-boiled and I'm a terrible milksop to feel this way about a little bit of danger. However,

[1] I delete an uncomplimentary remark about this official.

HOLY LAND

I've seen it, and she hasn't. Christ! these amateur politicians——! All the time we sat there we could hear the tramp of the Haluzim coming in and marching round the walls. If they were religious at all, if anybody thought they did it for motives of religion, it wouldn't be so terrible. But doing it as they do it, it's bound to come to something pretty bad.

I don't know yet what's happened during the rest of the night and this morning. There were probably minor clashes, but nothing as sensational as these people hoped for. The Arabs shut up their houses and remained invisible, and that's the one thing that saved the situation. X says they had laid in a supply of extra stretchers at the Hadassah Hospital to provide for the casualties expected last night. I must go out and see what has happened.

Later in the same day I added another entry to this:

. . . Jews parading again today. Extreme provocation, but the Arabs are doing nothing. Small army of Haluzim—these precious Maccabees—passed half an hour ago, on their way to the Wall, with a flag, the Zionist national flag, I suppose, but I couldn't see it: it was furled. Shouts and cheers come from down there; the whole thing makes me very nervous. I wish Antonius were here. The young heroes who passed a while ago were guarded heavily by the police; mounted police officers in front of them and behind them, with policemen on foot marching alongside them. The material for an awful three-cornered fight. What an exhibition of imbecility the whole thing is! And if it weren't for the British police I think there would be terrible pogroms. My affection for Zionism has certainly reached the zero point. If this keeps up it will soon go below that and turn into an active antagonism.

This long entry (August 15, 1929) is one of the most puzzling in all the fat volumes of my diary. What did it mean? What could it mean? No sensible human being can believe that the responsible Zionists, like Sacher or Kisch, could have ordered their adherents to make such a show of force at the wall of the Haram esh-Sherif: such a thing would be madness. And yet who did tell the young men to come in from all over the country? I saw them, felt their temperature, knew that they were out for trouble. I had had ample experience in this kind of thing for many years; I had seen mobs and street fights from Chicago to Hankow and back again; I knew the electricity that hatred sets up in the air. And I had seen all the bloodshed I ever wanted to see in my life—all I wanted for a dozen lives, innumerable incarnations. The sight of these angry young men with their *Haluz* energy worked up to such a pitch filled me with alarm. I did not know what I could do about it, but

357

it seemed to me (as is recorded in my diary every day from the 15th to the 23d of August) that we were in for some kind of horror far worse than the young fools could have anticipated. If Miss X was in any way typical, they did not have the slightest conception of the gravity of these issues to the Moslems. Being, themselves, almost completely irreligious, they could not understand the intimate, unreasoning passion with which a Moslem regards his religion and his shrines. I kept thinking of poor Imbrie, torn into shreds by the mob in Tehran—and he had done far less than these people did.

Five years have passed since then, and Palestine seems very remote: pitiful but remote, like an abscess on somebody else's foot. In that tiny, beautiful country, where all the misery of religious obsession has been concentrated for thousands of years in a space too small to accommodate one large idea, I saw many horrors. But of them all, one of the most vivid in my mind is that of my long conversation with Miss X. We sat at a table under a lemon tree in the Bristol gardens. I pulled off leaf after leaf of the lemon tree and crushed it in my fingers—absent-mindedly, never thinking of the lemon tree, smelling the scent that the crushed leaves left on my fingers and never thinking of that either. The lemon leaves had nothing to do with the conversation. And yet that acrid, citric smell is part of the sharply remembered scene; the smell, and the sound of the young men tramping loudly, in measured step, around the walls of Jerusalem. I tried hard to make that woman understand how ghastly her confident desire for trouble could seem to anybody who had actually seen 'trouble' before. She realized nothing, I think; she only laughed at me. I went home that night gloomy, nervous, shaken with apprehension, and as afraid of the ensuing events as if they had been already upon us.

7

If George Antonius had been in Jerusalem I should have gone straight to him with an account of the evening. But he left for Syria on August 10th on his annual holiday. I had met few officials in Jerusalem and felt sure that if I carried such a tale to them their reception of it would have been exactly like my own when I first heard it in the afternoon: flat incredulity. I learned years later that my information would not have been news to them, for there had been several warnings of the same kind. At the time I thought the danger was unknown or unappreciated by the government, as day followed day and the situation grew steadily worse. I wrote out a telegram to Antonius in Syria but tore it up; he was on holiday and would scarcely have welcomed such an agitated call for help. Finally, as there seemed nothing whatever for me to do, I did nothing: sat still and watched the catastrophe approach. The strangest element in the tragedy of August, 1929, is the refusal of persons in authority to believe that the worst would actually come to the worst.

I continue with my diary for the week.

Saturday, Aug. 17th. The Jewish holy day passed off without disaster, but now we are in the midst of a Moslem one, the Prophet's Birthday. Yesterday a big crowd of Moslems came into the Wailing Wall area and tore up the sacred books, pulled petitions out of the stones of the wall, etc. Might have been expected; was, in fact, inevitable. No Jews there; nobody hurt. Jews will be in terrible state of excitement, just the same. Fireworks last night in the Temple area—rather lovely from the roof of the Hospice. All the mosques were illuminated by the Franciscans' electricity, so our current at the Hospice practically vanished. Suffering badly from heat and nerves. Going down to Tel-Aviv tonight.

Sunday, Aug. 18th. Jewish boy hurt in a row between Jews and Arabs yesterday; feeling gets worse all the time. Down to Tel-Aviv last night: it was muggy, like a Turkish bath. Dined with Warschawer and went to Halévy's production of a Hebrew translation of Zweig's *Jeremiah*. This is the Ohel (Tent) players, all proletarian, scenes and costumes made in Tel-Aviv. Shows hard work, even though the players aren't up to Habima standards. Argument with Warschawer about the Wall.

Monday, Aug. 19th. (*Long personal entry, about catarrh, omitted.*) Letter from Weisgal today; seemed surprised at my decision to break off with the Zionists. Thank God I did it when I did! Palestine *Bulletin* says: (*Quotation from P. B.'s account of Moslem demonstration at Wailing Wall on Friday is omitted.*) The same issue of the paper contains a communiqué from the government as follows: 'Misleading reports are being circulated as to the events at the Wailing Wall on the 15th and 16th of August. On the 15th August, during the Fast commemorating the Destruction of the Temple, in addition to the large numbers of Jews who proceeded in the ordinary way to the Wall to worship, some hundreds of young Jews exercised their right of access for purposes not confined to the usual practise of prayer but were associated with the making of a speech and the raising of a flag. At about

1 P.M. on the 16th of August about 2,000 Moslems left the Haram, where they had been celebrating the Prophet's Birthday, and proceeded to the Wailing Wall through streets lying in the Abu Madian Waqf, which also includes the pavement in front of the Wall. A wooden table that was standing on the pavement was overturned by the pressure of the crowd and was broken, and papers containing prayers and petitions lying in the crevices of the Wall were taken out and burnt.'

Palestine *Bulletin* says: 'Moslems penetrated into the pavement of the Wall,' thus supporting the new Jewish contention that the pavement is a holy place, like the Wall itself. Government communiqué makes it clear that it's all Moslem property, and if it's holy, holy to the Moslem owners not to the Jewish visitors. This is what the Jews will never admit nowadays; Zionism makes them insist on more. All this supplies extreme provocation to disorder here, and can make very misleading and inflammatory Zionist propaganda abroad.

Tuesday, August 20th. (Long entry about matters unconnected with Palestine—specifically, a book by Balzac and a book by Tolstoy—omitted.)

Wednesday, August 21st. The Mizrachi boy, who was hurt in the row with Arabs at the Maccabee football field last Saturday, died yesterday. They are going to make a martyr of him, as sure as fate. Haven't yet heard latest developments; must go out and see. Antonius came back last night and I told him about what has been going on. He had heard nothing.[1]

Friday, August 23d. The situation here is awful. Every day I expect the worst. It can't go on like this without an outbreak. The Mizrachi boy— Avrahm Mizrachi was his name—who was stabbed by an Arab after a row in the football field (it seems to have been a row started by the Jewish boys, or so they tell me), died on Tuesday. Wednesday morning was the funeral. Of course, the precious Maccabees had to seize the opportunity: fine chance to link up everything with the Wailing Wall and the general agitation. Two or three thousand of these heroes gathered in procession on the occasion of the funeral. They paraded with flags[2] and tried to head their march through the Jaffa Gate into the Arab city. Feeling has been running so high among the Arabs since these fools raised their flag at the wall of the mosque that anything might have happened. Government apparently decided to keep the Jews out of the Arab town at any cost. Police barred the way, therefore, and the Jews made a rush at their cordon. Police beat them back with clubs. About twenty-five Jews were injured, none very seriously. Feeling all day Wednesday and yesterday intense. Police guard became very obvious all through the city. We even had two guards at the door of this hospice. I don't yet know what today's developments have been, but I am going out to see pretty soon.

---

[1] The entries in my diary in Jerusalem were usually made in the morning, which is why they so often refer to the events of the day before.

[2] It seems that this detail was untrue, but I had been told it on what I thought was good authority at the time.

During the next fortnight I had neither time nor inclination to write in my dairy. The next entry I find was made at Nazareth on September sixth; and it was not until September 18th, in Jerusalem, that I was able to return to the book and write down fully what had happened in the meantime. Relying not only on my memory, but on the entries made in my journal two or three weeks later, I can establish the first sequence of events in something like their chronological order.

After I had finished the last entry in my diary I went downstairs to lunch and heard a new crop of disquieting rumours. At about half-past one I went out to get some cigarettes, and the old Arab porter at the Hospice told me the Grand Mufti had passed a short time before, going out to speak to the crowds around the city walls. Since the Mufti was not given to public appearance—I had never once seen him, although I lived within five minutes' walk of the Haram and his house—this seemed serious. I ran back into the Hospice for my hat, found a friend of mine (a British official), and went out with him to see what was to be seen. We walked up the narrow street, through excited or terrified groups of people, to the Damascus Gate. There we found ourselves in the midst of a mob of country Arabs, who seemed to be in a frenzy of excitement. Long yells of '*Islamiya!*' were going up. We got through these people without trouble—my companion spoke Arabic well—and reached the corner of the street called, I believe, the Street of the Prophet. The mob was gathering directly in front of us, and it was certain that somebody, somewhere, would soon be shedding blood. The houses on the other side of the mob, opposite us, belonged to a group of Georgian Jews, as I afterwards learned; the attention of the crowd was directed towards them. In front of the Jewish houses were ranged six policemen, armed only with short truncheons. The mob gathered with incredible speed—it could not have taken more than two or three minutes for them to get dense in front of us. The long yells that filled the air were enough to curdle one's blood.

A man dressed as a city Arab noticed us standing there and thrust us almost by force into a doorway. 'Stand here, stand here, for God's sake,' he said. 'These fellahin will kill you.' We stood in the doorway, and he took his place in front of us, shouting hoarsely at the mob, telling them to go back, that all was well. They paid no attention to him. They rushed towards the police, who laid about them valiantly with their truncheons; but what good were truncheons at such a time? The fellahin were flourishing sticks, clubs and knives, and, as is the way of mobs, they rushed on regardless of the efforts to stop them. Some rushed under the horses' bellies, others squirmed through between the inadequate six; in another moment we heard smashing and a long scream. There was nothing we could do but run, which we did— up the hill towards the Italian Hospital, where there were British police. We found half a dozen bewildered young fellows up there who were trying to cover a whole area, but at least they had fire-arms. We told them what had happened, and *one* of them set off towards the Georgian houses; it was clear that the police were hopelessly inadequate. Where we stood, in the area at the top of the hill, a mob of Jews in all the stages of terror, fury and despair were assembled. They were held back by some of their own people, but a short time before one of them had thrown a grenade at some of the Arabs coming up the hill, and had killed two.[1] The wretched half-dozen policemen on duty up there did not know whether to leave the mob of Jews and go down towards the mob of Arabs or not. One of the things I remember most clearly out of that agitated quarter of an hour is the appearance of a fat, earnest, anxious Jew in plain clothes, who was, I suppose, a police agent, going fussily up and down in front of the front line of the dense Jewish crowd, saying in Yiddish: 'Alles is fertig, alles is fertig! Sei ruhig, jetzt! Alles is fertig!' His broad, worried face was sweating, and he too obviously knew that *alles* was not *fertig*, but he did his best. The crowd, torn by furious emotions, paid no attention to him.

I returned to the Damascus Gate about a quarter of an hour after I had left it. When I got there the Arab mob had vanished (so little time is required to accomplish the most irrevocable acts); there were shattered glass and torn-up wood, débris of all

---

[1]The evidence as to time shows some conflict, but on the official showing it appears that my information that day was correct—that these Arabs were the first persons killed on Friday.

sorts, in the street, and before the Georgian Jewish houses and on their stone doorsteps there was blood.

8

The Jews of Jerusalem outnumbered the Arabs two to one. It was a matter of common knowledge that the Jews possessed firearms; the Arabs did not. Under these conditions it seemed likely that the Jewish superiority in numbers and equipment, as well as their organization and centralization, would enable them to do great damage among the Arabs for a day or two if they so desired, and from what I had seen and heard the previous week I thought this was probably the wish of a good many among them.

Therefore, on the first day of these troubles the word 'massacre' not only didn't occur in conversation, but never even crossed one's mind. The first casualties, we were told, had been Arabs killed by Jews; the Jews were an armed majority in the city; the Arabs were a minority armed only with sticks and knives. What i⸱ looked like, at about two o'clock on Friday afternoon, was an outbreak of murderous hatred between the two parts of the population—an outbreak that I, at least, had expected for some days; an outbreak caused by the long, exasperating controversy over the Wailing Wall, and precipitated, made inevitable, by the raising of the Jewish national flag at the wall of the Mosque of Omar. I expected the Jews and Arabs to behave more or less as Germans, Chinese, Frenchmen, Moroccans or Americans would behave under similar circumstances, only worse. In short, I thought we were in for a fight—a peculiarly revolting form of fight, in which the Jews would win in Jerusalem, Haifa and Tel-Aviv, and the Arabs would probably get the upper hand elsewhere, and in which neither side would respect the rules of Western civilized murder.

I did what almost any newspaper man or ex-newspaper man would have done: went straight to the post office to send a cablegram to my old office in New York. This was a mistake: my days of sending cablegrams were over, and I should have known it by then; I was no longer callous enough to go through scenes of horror and regard them merely as a 'story' for the papers. I was to learn during the next week, once and for all, that I was no longer a 'newspaper man'—that I couldn't do it and ought never to try to do it again. But on Friday it was my natural response to the situation. I sent a cablegram to the North American Newspaper Alliance, with whom I had a sort of standing agreement to 'cover' any genuinely important situation that might arise during my travels. In the cablegram, without giving details, I said the situation was grave and would get worse, and that I required an RTP (receiver-to-pay) arrangement to send press telegrams to the London office of the N.A.N.A. The RTP privilege had to be arranged at the London end; the Jerusalem post office could not accept press cables on a charge account without instructions. And, of course, it would have taken hundreds of dollars, which I did not possess, to send long press cablegrams and pay for them.

What followed with the New York office was a small irony in the great disasters of the week. The answer I received from New York was: '*How much do you want for articles. Can't you send them by mail?*' At the moment I received that cablegram the terrible murders at Hebron, in which sixty-four Jews, including some American youths, lost their lives, were actually taking place; a crisis of the first magnitude was in progress; troops and ships were on the move; the 'story,' considered simply from a newspaper point of view, as an event of interest, was the most important in the world. But I was asked to 'send it by mail.' I had been up a large part of the preceding night and was already getting into the state of nervous disorder that blotted out subsequent days and nights in Jerusalem. I replied: '*Pay what you like. You are wasting time. Demand RTP immediately*'—which was a peremptory way for a newspaper reporter to speak to his employers.

Eventually, on the third day of these disorders, the Jerusalem post office received instructions to accept my press telegrams on the RTP arrangement, and for three days I worked again as a correspondent. Even as it was, with all these delays and difficulties, mine were still the earliest full accounts of the trouble to reach the English and American newspapers. This was partly due to the difficulties under which my Jewish colleagues laboured—few of them dared circulate in the city, and at the beginning none of them went to the government for information—but also to the

severity of the censorship established at the beginning of the outbreak.

I cannot remember clearly the details of those terrible days. I
scarcely slept at all; I was up at all hours and in all parts of the
city, trying to follow the course of events for professional purposes. I went from Arab quarters to Jewish quarters and back
again, through police lines and about the unguarded parts of the
city. It is a strange thing that nobody ever molested me, for although I did not look particularly Jewish (and certainly not
Arab), angry mobs do not often stop to consider such trifles.
Stranger still, I was not conscious of danger. On all previous occasions of this kind I had been fully aware of the perils that
threatened the curious bystander, and from the time I had first
heard a bullet whiz past in the air, years before, I had retained a salutary fear of death. But in Jerusalem the intensity of
nervous excitement produced, after the first day or two, a kind of
daze in which I lost awareness of my own identity; I could not
have been more unconscious of personal dangers if I had been
invisible. Here again I had ceased to be a rational newspaper man:
I was roaming the streets of Jerusalem at all hours, overworking
fantastically, sleeping scarcely at all, out of sheer nervous horror.
Sometimes I noticed my own existence and was surprised at it:
for example, when an anxious city Arab would attach himself
to me and walk through the streets, as if in protection. This happened several times as I was on my way through the Arab city. I
never knew who the self-appointed bodyguards were—they were
never twice the same—but I suppose they must have been some of
the men the Supreme Moslem Council had sent out to try to keep
order. In the Jewish quarters I neither needed nor received such
escorts, for there I was usually taken to be British; but as I passed
the barricades in those stricken streets I did get many a frown and
a curse, for the British were by no means popular among the
Jewish population during those days.

The disorders of Friday resulted in many deaths among both
Jews and Arabs (the Arabs including Christians as well as Moslems), and the impulse of murder continued for a week. At the
end of the terror the official roll for Jerusalem was: 29 Jews and
38 Arabs killed, 43 Jews and 51 Arabs wounded. Here, as in

Haifa, the Arabs got considerably the worst of it, but it seems clear (and seemed clear even at the time) that the casualties inflicted by Jews were chiefly in self-defence. The government had undertaken to disarm the Jewish police and the Jewish special constables, to avoid giving the Arabs a chance to say that they were being murdered by Jews with official approval; but no government could have disarmed the Jewish population. What surprised me in the roll of dead and wounded was not that Arabs outnumbered Jews, but that they did not outnumber them a great deal more.

The horrors of Friday in Jerusalem were followed by something much worse: the ghastly outbreak at Hebron, where sixty-four Jews of the old-fashioned religious community were slaughtered and fifty-four of them wounded. Hebron was one of the four holy cities of Judaism, and had had a small, constant Jewish population since mediæval days. These were not Zionists at all; a more innocent and harmless group of people could not have been found in Palestine; many of them were Oriental Jews, and all were religious. They had had nothing to do with the Zionist excesses, and had lived in amity with their Arab neighbours up to that day. But when the Arabs of Hebron—an unruly lot, at best—heard that Arabs were being killed by Jews in Jerusalem, and that the Mosque of Omar was in danger, they went mad.[1] The British police force at Hebron was inadequate—indeed, it could scarcely be said to have existed, for there was but one British officer there with a tiny native staff. In spite of the remarkable exertions and courage of this one officer (Mr R. O. Cafferata), the Jewish houses were rushed by the mob, and there was an hour of slashing, killing, stabbing, burning and looting. Among the Jewish victims were some American boys who had arrived only a short time before to study at the rabbinical college. Eight or nine of them died at Hebron, and an equal number suffered severe wounds.

I cannot, at this late date, go through all the story of that week; it has been told over and over again. The horrors of Hebron were not repeated elsewhere, but an Arab mob attack on the religious

[1]The Mosque of Omar was in no danger at any time during the troubles, but Arab rumours throughout the country made it the crux of the matter.

Jews of Safad, on the following Thursday, was sufficiently terrible to be classified as another massacre. In Haifa, where the Jews were predominantly of the modern Zionist type and occupied an excellent strategic position at the top of the hill, the Arabs had much the worst of it. The same was true in some of the colonies; others were almost wiped out. At the end of the disturbances the official British casualty lists showed 207 dead and 379 wounded among the population of Palestine, of which the dead included 87 Arabs (Christian and Moslem) and 120 Jews, the wounded 181 Arabs and 198 Jews.[1]

9

The effort to be an efficient, unemotional newspaper correspondent was difficult to the point of impossibility. Living as I did, without sleep and without rest, eating little, and that at the weirdest hours, I should probably have collapsed in time simply from physical exhaustion. But there was a great deal more in it than that. I was bitterly indignant with the Zionists for having, as I believed, brought on this disaster; I was shocked into hysteria by the ferocity of the Arab anger; and I was aghast at the inadequacy of the British government. I knew that the Moslem authorities were trying to quell the storm, and that the British officials were doing their best against appalling difficulties; I also assumed that the responsible Zionist leaders (none of whom were in Palestine then) had done what they could. But all around me were the visible evidences of their failure. Although I had spent a good part of my life amid scenes of violence and was no stranger to the sight of blood and dying men, I had never overcome my loathing for the spectacle even when it seemed, as in some of the conflicts I had witnessed, compelled by historical necessity. But here, in this miserable little country no bigger, in relation to the rest of the world, than the tip of your finger in relation to your body, I could see no historical necessity whatever. The country was tiny and was already inhabited: why couldn't the Zionists leave it alone? It would never hold enough Jews to make even a beginning towards the solution of the Jewish problem; it would always be a

[1]So far as the Arabs are concerned these figures may be assumed to be incomplete, as Arabs do not always report their dead and wounded.

prey to such ghastly horrors as those I saw every day and every night: religion, the eternal intransigence of religion, ensured that the problem could never be solved. The Holy Land seemed as near an approximation of hell on earth as I had ever seen.

The American consulate-general was one of my regular ports of call during those days. It was crowded with American Jews who had taken refuge there. Like every other official centre in Palestine at the time, the consulate was miserably understaffed and overworked. From the second or third day of the troubles every desk in the place was swamped in cablegrams from America, chiefly from the State Department, for there were two thousand American Jews in Palestine and their relatives at home were anxious. Mr Knabenshue, the consul-general, was working without respite; so was Mr Gilman, the vice-consul; they received no thanks for their efforts. They were accused at the time in Jerusalem, and afterwards in America, of not taking sufficient trouble to protect the American Jews. I saw a good deal of their work and was well aware that the accusation was unfounded. Knabenshue stretched his powers to the utmost. He demanded everything he could possibly demand of the government—police, soldiers, armoured cars. His attitude was very different from that of the Polish consul, whose Jewish *ressortissants* were even more numerous. But the poor man was bombarded with complaints from morning to night. To get his work done at all, Knabenshue had to make a rule that he would not talk to the people who took refuge in the consulate—and that too became a grievance. Some of the American Jews in Palestine were orientalized (I met a few who spoke no English at all). The attitude of such Palestinian-Americans was hysterical, and for a day or two the consulate was not a quiet place.

It was here, I think—in the American consulate-general during the first days—that I made my first acquaintance with a peculiar thing we may call the pogrom heritage, or pogrom complex. It was a state of mind I had never seen before, and it required a powerful effort of the imagination to understand it. It was, briefly, this: that the moment the Jews felt themselves under attack, their lives in danger and their future insecure, they assumed that the world was in league against them—that all persons who did not happen to be Jewish were their enemies. I had seen many people of all nationalities under attack, but I had never seen anybody behave as the Jews did. This was not cowardice and had nothing to do with cowardice. It was often allied to the most courageous conduct. But it took the form of a strange, complete despair. In its simplest form it was the conviction that a Jew had no friend but God. A glaze came over the eyes of every Jew I spoke to—not because I was not friendly: I could not have felt these things more deeply if I had been a Jew myself. But I was not a Jew; therefore I had to be an enemy. This conviction was the heritage of so many generations of persecution that it was hard for a non-Jew, with a different sort of race memory, to understand it.

I saw one Jewish acquaintance who seemed downright heroic during those days. His name was George Hyman, and he was secretary to Dr Magnes, the Rector of the Hebrew University on Mount Scopus. He was a young American of a studious habit of mind, who lived with his pretty young wife somewhere up the hill, and I am sure that neither of them had paid much attention to the political tension that had brought on these disasters. When the outbreak came, Hyman started to work at once. He obtained a rifle and a special constable's brassard, and, armed with these badges of authority, began to move the American Jews in his neighbourhood down the hill to the consulate. He made trip after trip over dangerous roads for two days, and brought many people to safety. I doubt if he could have used his rifle if it had been necessary, for he was not what might be called a military sort of man. But his friends and neighbours were for the most part older than himself, and even less military; he did his best for them. When I saw him at the consulate he was exhausted, nervous, upset; his voice trembled and broke when he tried to speak; his slim young figure looked as if it would crumple at any moment. And yet he went on until he had seen every one of his people down from their exposed and unguarded position on the hill.

I admired Hyman's behaviour more than that of anybody else I saw in Jerusalem during those days. And yet, when I tried to talk to him, I saw the same incomprehensible glaze come over his eyes—the expression that said: 'You are not a Jew; I am a Jew; therefore you are my enemy and I am afraid of you.'

There was one way in which I might have overcome the peculiar attitude I have called the pogrom complex. I might have enrolled as a special constable, obtained a rifle, and taken part in the organized defence of Jewish people or houses. But this was one thing I could not and would not do. I had never fired on a human being in my life and did not intend to begin. However ferocious the Arab mobs might be, however ghastly the results of their fanatical fury, I could never lose sight of the fact that they had been goaded beyond endurance, and I would not take any part in killing them for it. If they had killed me by mistake during these days (as they easily might have done), I should have protested with my dying breath that it was not their fault. No matter how deeply I was moved by the sufferings of the Jews, I had to retain what intelligence nature and experience had given me; and that intelligence represented the present disasters as a plain, inevitable result of the Zionist policy in an Arab country. I was desperately sorry for those who died; for night after night, particularly in the illness that followed, my ears rang with the sound of these horrors; but I was not going to add one drop to the blood that was already spattered over Jerusalem.

10

It was during the first five days of the trouble—my newspaper days; my last—that I made the acquaintance of the British and Arab authorities.

I had known one or two non-political officers who lived in the Austrian Hospice and took little interest in the conflicts of the Palestinian population. Such officers (the auditor for the Palestine government, for instance) paid no attention to politics; by training, habit of mind, and the tradition of the Colonial Civil Service, they left such things to the central government. In the central government I knew only Antonius; I had met Edwin Samuel and Eric Mills, but only briefly, casually, as you meet a man in the street or across a table. I had never seen the Grand Mufti of Jerusalem or any other Arab authority. I had never met the acting High Commissioner—officially called the Officer Administering the Government—and had never been inside the government offices.

When I began to work as a correspondent I had to remedy these deficiencies. On successive days I interviewed everybody who was to be interviewed on the subject in the government offices and the offices of the Supreme Moslem Council. I found the government struggling against difficulties that threatened to overwhelm it. Indeed, the word 'government,' as applied to that harassed handful of young men, seems absurdly pompous. There were five of them—Mr H. C. Luke, the Officer Administering the Government; Mr Mills, the acting Chief Secretary; and three assistant secretaries, Antonius, Moody, and Edwin ('Nebi') Samuel. They had their Palestinian staff, of course, but the responsibility of government fell upon these five, and particularly upon Luke, Mills and Antonius. Antonius was in particular charge of relations with the Arabs, a rôle that kept him busy throughout the day and night. Decisions were made by Mr Luke, but after the first twenty-four hours he was so drowned in trouble that almost any decision he had taken would have been wrong.

For three days this government—if the word be applied with reservations—had to attempt to keep order without military aid. The British police in Palestine numbered about one hundred and seventy men.[1] There was no military garrison. Until troops could be brought from Egypt, and ships from Malta, this tiny force was supposed to keep the whole country quiet—an obvious impossibility. Without power to crush the disorders, the government was obliged to rely heavily on the Moslem authorities themselves to restrain their people, for it became clear after the first day that the Jews were restricting themselves (except in isolated incidents) to self-defense, and that the attacks were for the most part attacks of Arab mobs upon Jews.

The chief of the Arab authorities was the President of the Supreme Moslem Council, Haj Amin el-Husseini, Grand Mufti of Jerusalem. He combined in his person the highest religious and judicial offices of Moslem Palestine, and exercised (through the Arab Executive) an influence also upon the Christian Arab community. Such concentrations of religious, political and judicial authority are common in Arab countries, but perhaps not to the

[1]This was a figure I was given at the time, and I believe it was accurate; I have seen other figures named, both larger and smaller than one hundred and seventy.

same degree: Haj Amin was in an unusually powerful position. I was told from the beginning that he was using his powers to keep the peace and have never seen any evidence against that view. Yet he was held responsible for the whole trouble by the Jewish world, and for years afterwards an ordinary Jewish view of the disturbances was that they were a 'pogrom' carried out under the Grand Mufti's orders.

I found the Mufti an extremely level-headed, deliberate man, mild-mannered and thoughtful. Before I left Palestine I was to know him better, and was to appreciate the simplicity and straight-forwardness of his character in more extended, less formal conversations. He was a patriot, a nationalist, a devout Moslem and an immovable opponent of the Zionist policy. Indeed, in that respect he was as single-minded as anybody I have ever known. Nothing but death could have kept him from opposing Zionism by every means in his power. But Haj Amin was also a humane man, and such tragedies as these could not have come about by his will. My judgment of his character, after considerable opportunity to observe it, would have told me what the evidence afterwards showed: that he had opposed Zionism at every step and had fought the contention of Jewish ownership at the Wall from the beginning, but that his influence in the actual crisis had been used on the side of peace.

The offices of the Supreme Moslem Council, overlooking the Temple area, were not given over to the confusion and hysteria that ruled in other offices in Jerusalem. They were sometimes crowded, but the Mufti's refusal to get excited seemed to have an influence on his immediate followers, and voices were not raised or hands flung in the air in those precincts. True, the Mufti was in little or no danger, but neither were the government officers; and they, I could not help seeing, had allowed the press of events to shatter their composure. All five of the men who made up the government worked like slaves for that week, and I used to see them at all hours of the night struggling with the telephone, with messengers, with orders, communiqués, telegrams, documents. But they were inadequate; they were too few in number to get all their work done properly, and they had almost no actual power in a military sense. The tribes from over Jordan could have swept across Palestine in twenty-four hours. They might have been crushed by military force afterwards, but at the moment the government was feeble beyond belief—the feeblest government I had ever seen. If the Grand Mufti had not supported them it is difficult to imagine how they could have got through the first three or four days at all.

One of the things that wore me down, and contributed, no doubt, to my break-up at the end of the first five days, was the necessity for going everywhere on foot. From eight in the morning until four or five o'clock the next morning I was trudging about Jerusalem. For a lazy man, the strain must have been severe, although I did not notice it then. The factors of physical strain, sleeplessness, excitement and indignation, reached a climax on Tuesday (August 27th). On that day I visited the Jewish hospitals in detail and talked to many of the patients. Every Jewish hospital was full. The doctors and nurses seemed admirably calm, but the relatives of the dead and wounded could not be still. There is nothing more harrowing than Jewish lamentation, particularly if it has a specific origin in such horrors as these. To get into any ward one had to go through halls and staircases where the relatives of the victims sat or stood, giving way to their despair. Sometimes, taking me for British, they would ask for information: 'Have the troops arrived? Is the trouble over?' Once I was asked if the Grand Mufti had been arrested yet.

But the relatives of the victims, however pitiful, faded out of my mind when I visited the victims themselves. They were unhappy beyond anything I had ever seen—not only unhappy because of their pain, their wounds, their suffering, the ghastly scenes they had witnessed during the past few days, but also unhappy with the peculiar misery that is to be found only in Jews: the feeling that they were bereft, betrayed and abandoned, with no friends and no protector but God. This misery surpassed the misery of ordinary wounded men, for it was spiritual as well as physical. It was the kind of thing that caused tears to course down the face of the religious Jew as he leaned his head against the Wailing Wall—an unhappiness beyond personal existence, the remembered unhappiness of a people. The wards were filled with sighing and weeping. I was familiar with the groans of wounded people, but this was something different; it made my hair stand on end. I tried to be as calm as possible, and did succeed in talking quietly to the patients, although my fingers could scarcely hold the pencil with which I made notes. The worst of all was the children's ward. Here I talked for a long time—as long as was considered advisable by the nurse—to an American boy, one of the survivors from Hebron. He could not have been more than twelve or thirteen years old. He was covered in bandages, only his eyes, nose and mouth emerging from them. The list of his wounds was frightful. He had been in Palestine only a short time and was too American to suffer from the peculiar spiritual misery to which I have referred in other cases. In his small, weak voice, without a sign of feeling—just as if he had been telling me something that happened five hundred years ago—he gave me an account of what he had seen in Hebron, how his friends had died and how he had been wounded. His narrative was accompanied throughout by the screams of another child in agony, on the other side of the same ward.

I kept going for the rest of the afternoon and evening, made my necessary visits to the sources of information, the government offices and the American consulate, and sent off my voluminous cablegrams to America. But when I got back to the Austrian Hospice that night (it was a little after two o'clock in the morning, I remember—earlier than usual) I knew that I was finished; I could not go on. My nerves had fallen to pieces altogether, so that I could not hit the right keys on the typewriter and indeed could scarcely pick up a pencil. I had seen too many dead and wounded Arabs being carried silently through the street in front of the Hospice; my ears were ringing with the sounds I had heard in the Jewish hospitals. Worst of all, I could never get out of my head that awful conversation with the lady I have called Miss X, who had told me how desirable 'incidents' would be for the new Jewish agency. I was half crazy with nervous horror and indignation—indignation at the Zionists for bringing on such a catastrophe, at the Arabs for behaving with such ferocity, at the government for its general helplessness. All these things produced a mental derangement unlike anything else I have ever known. I sat at my typewriter all night long, making up cablegrams explaining things to the N. A. N. A. in New York and asking them to release me from further work. The next day the servants found the floor strewn with these cablegrams, none of which was ever sent. Towards seven o'clock in the morning (as I know only by the evidence of my next-door neighbour, the auditor of the government; for my own memory of that night vanished) I stopped trying to write on the typewriter and tumbled into bed. I did not get up again for four days.

The attack, or collapse, or whatever it might be called, kept me from taking an interest in my own affairs. Telegrams poured in from my office in New York: Where was I? What had happened? Why had I stopped sending cables? I did not answer these —scarcely even read them. For the first two days of the time I could not eat or sleep properly, and lay twitching in that darkened room like an old man with palsy. I had just sense enough to realize that if I stayed in bed it would eventually pass. I could not ask for a doctor: the doctors in Jerusalem had more serious matters to take up their time. Occasionally Antonius looked in to see how I was getting along, and I observed on the third and fourth days, as I came a little more to my senses, that he too was near the breaking point. It took nerves of iron and the constitution of a draft horse to do the work he was doing; the sight of him made me ashamed of my own weakness. But being ashamed of it did not cure it. It had to work itself out, as it eventually did.

As I resumed a more normal frame of mind, towards the end of the week I tried again to explain myself to my New York office. I knew, from the Hebrew newspapers—which had resumed publication after some days of suppression—that my dispatches had given grave offense to the Jews. There had been a Zionist demonstration in New York against the *World*, the newspaper that printed my cables; I afterwards learned that this paper had received three thousand letters of protest from Jews in a single day. I was weary unto death of cabling, anyhow, and did not want to get any of my unfortunate newspapers into trouble with their Jewish readers and advertisers. Consequently, I wrote out an account of my bizarre experience in Palestine (not for publication), and asked the N. A. N. A. to release me. This cablegram, afterwards introduced in evidence, was written before I had fully recovered; it might have been couched in more careful language if I had waited another day or two, but except in one respect it was accurate. The inaccuracy was a confusion between the Jewish action at the Wailing Wall on the 14th and 15th of August. I described the earlier visits of the Haluzim as a 'deliberate, organized insult' to the Moslem holy places, whereas the demonstration of the following day was clearly better organized and more insulting. However, the telegram served its purpose, and the North American Newspaper Alliance—puzzled and protesting—had to let me go. I could hardly expect them to believe, and indeed did not ask them to believe, the essential fact about the whole matter, which was that I no longer felt able to maintain the hard-boiled and efficient attitude of a true journalist towards the horrors created by political injustice.

By Sunday, ten days after the beginning of the outbreak, I was able to go out again. The complexion of Jerusalem had changed. The soldiers from Egypt patrolled the streets, and although the Jewish and Arab quarters remained as separate as the camps of opposing armies, within each section the machinery of existence was already tending to take on something like its normal aspect. I went down on Monday to see how the American consulate was bearing up, and found Knabenshue and Gilman more snowed under than ever. Knabenshue showed me a huge sheaf of cablegrams from the State Department, and said: 'My God, what am I to do? I have to report on the safety of every one of these people, and they're scattered all over Palestine! The telephone doesn't work, I have no staff, and I can't leave here myself. I can't send a Jew to investigate: he might be killed. And I can't send an Arab into Jewish settlements: he might be killed. If I get you a car and give you a list of people, will you go out and check up on them? All I need to know is whether they are all right or not and if they need help.'

I agreed to the plan and was glad to have something so definite to occupy my time and mind. Knabenshue and Gilman pieced together a list of the names in which the State Department was interested, and on Tuesday morning, in a large open touring car driven by a garrulous native Christian, I set out for Tel-Aviv.

Tel-Aviv had been fairly safe throughout the troubles, as

might have been expected, but it was not exempt from the apprehensions of the time. My State Department list yielded some interesting characters, including one superb citizen of Brooklyn who wanted to know why the government could not keep the Arabs out of Palestine.

The country was very unsettled, and disorders were still being reported. Consequently I thought it best to fly an American flag on the bonnet of my ramshackle old touring car. When I got to Tel-Aviv I appealed to the ingenuity of the chambermaid in my hotel. We had a long discussion in Yiddish, and she promised to do her best. After I had completed my day's work on the consulate's list and went back to the Palatine for dinner, my friend the chambermaid produced her handiwork: an American flag such as has never been seen before or since, with about seven stripes and an odd few stars, all peculiarly shaped and stuck together, but indubitably red, white and blue. I could scarcely look at this emblem without laughing, but I reflected that the inhabitants of Palestine might not realize its deficiencies, and a comic flag was better than none, particularly as I had stuck to my old principle of going unarmed. The next morning, with the chambermaid's masterpiece gallantly streaming, I started out for the tour of the country.

I visited a large number of colonies and towns during the next four days and checked over the whole of the list I had been given. I found certain peculiarities of citizenship among these: there was one American citizen who had lived in Palestine for twenty years and had forgotten most of his English; there were one or two who could not speak English at all; there were others who did not even claim American citizenship but urged their right to American protection because they had relatives in the United States. It seemed obvious that a good many of these people had no legal right to be American citizens or protégés. However, it was none of my business, so long as the State Department had taken them under its wing. I did what I could in the way of aid and comfort, assured them that all the trouble was over, and took their statements as to their own condition and needs. In most of the colonies I found the apprehensions of the people to be as keen as ever, and in all of them the arrangements for mounting guard and keeping

Arabs out were still in force. I talked to some men who had scarcely slept an hour in the whole preceding week, and their haggard faces showed it.

The scenes when I arrived in some of these places, with that absurd flag stuck up on the car, were irresistibly pathetic. I was not a patriot; I had seen too many of the results of patriotism to regard such impulses with sympathy. And yet there was something rather thrilling in the faith these people put in the ridiculous scrap of red, white and blue. Again and again the chambermaid's flag drew cheers from the Jews (American or not) as it came into sight. In five minutes the car would be surrounded by an eager, chattering, gesticulating crowd, trembling with pleasure at the idea that the American State Department was inquiring about them. This was, I suppose, another aspect of the pogrom psychology: any ordinary American would have taken such inquiries for granted, but the Jews were used to thinking of themselves as abandoned by the world. Young Jews (Zionists) occasionally went to the other extreme and said words to this effect: 'So you want to know how we are? Well, it's about time!' But their elders were touchingly grateful, moved by the sight of the square of coloured cotton. They seemed to have lost faith altogether in the British government, which they believed to be inimical to the Jewish people, and my statement that the government was in control and now had plenty of armed force was greeted, especially in isolated places, with shrugs and stares.

Safad produced one of the striking scenes of that tour. By the time I got there I was used to being welcomed with excitement. In Haifa, for instance, my battered old car was cheered every time it went out—an extraordinary thing, for the Haifa Jews (modern Zionists in the majority) surely must have known that the American State Department could do nothing very effective in a country governed by another power. But in Safad the Jews were Oriental. They had had a dreadful experience the week before—an experience only less dreadful than that of the Jews at Hebron. They too had lost faith in the British for the time being. And as a result I was surrounded by hysterical people from the moment I arrived until I succeeded in getting away. They clung to me so obstinately that it was next to impossible to move. A good many of the Safad Jews apparently could not speak Yiddish, and I was bombarded with stories, complaints and lamentations in Hebrew, which I did not understand. Getting through my list might have been impossible under these conditions if I had not been helped by one of the Hebrew notables who happened along at the right moment. And when I tried to leave Safad numbers of these excited people clung to the running board of my car, still pouring out the complications of their anguish. They were not Americans, and they refused to understand that my task was to deal with Americans only. Apparently they thought—as nearly as I could make out in the noise and confusion of languages—that there existed some mysterious talisman called 'American protection,' which they could claim and thus safeguard themselves against further trouble.

The Arabs, in the areas through which I passed during the week, were sullen and angry, but they did me no harm. Occasionally somebody would yell '*Yahud!*' (Jew) after my car, and at such times the Christian Arab who was driving me wisely speeded up. I had a moment or two of slight apprehension, particularly in the plain near Armageddon and in the streets of Nablus, but nothing serious occurred. In Nablus the Arab boys threw stones at the car, but a few stones more or less could have made no difference to that battered relic. I grew used to the cry of '*Yahud!*' and gave it no attention after the first day.

On my return to Jerusalem Saturday evening (September 7th) I asked the consul's permission to cable an account of this tour to the North American Newspaper Alliance. He said he did not object, and I sent the story off, chiefly to solace my bewildered employers for the suddenness with which I had left their service. It was the last news cablegram I have ever sent—or ever shall send.

11

The tour of the country had given me a memorable picture of Palestine under stress: anxious Jews, sullen Arabs, and stolid British Tommies (Yorkshiremen) who did not know a Jew from an Arab and did not care. The Tommies provided the only element of comedy in the situation, and I never met one who did

not make me laugh, no matter how little I felt inclined to laughter.
I ran into a pair of Tommies with a broken-down lorry in Galilee,
and their account of themselves still makes me chuckle when I
think of it. They were escorting provisions to a Jewish colony,
but they were under the impression that it was an Arab colony,
and in any case they did not know where it was. They had an
Arab driver (Christian) who was laboriously taking the bowels
out of their motor lorry, and they might have been sitting there
yet (and the Jewish colony starving) if my chauffeur had not put
his more efficient hands to the job. Sitting disconsolately in the
midst of the plain, rifles on shoulder, those Tommies must have
found the world a mysterious place: what extraordinary destiny
could it be that thrust them round the world to regulate the
affairs of Jew and Arab, Hindu and Chinese? I am sure they never
knew.

I had written in my diary at Nazareth on the night before I returned to Jerusalem:

Nazareth, Sept. 6. Arrived six tonight. Heavenly place—no hospitals, no
horrors. I wish I could stay here for a month. Past two weeks awful, haven't
been able to write anything in this book. Maybe I can catch up when I go
back to Jerusalem.

The words 'no hospitals, no horrors' summed up my idea of
paradise just then. Jerusalem had been unbearable during the
time of the 'horrors,' but it proved to be just as bad, in another
way, after they had ceased. Special correspondents had started
arriving as soon as the worst was over, and the city was full of
them. Now that the troops were in full control the Hebrew and
Arabic press flourished, and loud accusations filled the air. The
Zionists accused almost everybody of something. The chief
accused were the Grand Mufti, the Moslem and Christian Arab
authorities, the government, Luke, Antonius, Mills, the American
consul-general, the Department of Health, the Christian communities (for not taking arms against the Moslems, presumably) and
the British police. An atmosphere of bitter recrimination was set
up and endured to the end of my experience with the country.

I came in for a certain amount of abuse myself, as my first
cablegrams to America had dated the beginning of the trouble

from the Zionist demonstrations at the Wailing Wall. This view—
which was confirmed long afterwards by a mass of evidence in the
inquiry—had not been put forward by anybody else in the press
of the world, and a good deal of odium fell on me. I was prepared
for it and did not mind.

The antagonism of the Zionists was accompanied by the friendship of the Arabs. I saw the Arab leaders frequently after the
troubles, as I was working on a magazine article about the Haram
esh-Sherif. Occasionally this put me in an odd position. My
old friend Captain Gordon Canning turned up in Jerusalem
early in November. He had been refused admission to Palestine
and then granted it; he was known to be a 'friend of the Arabs,'
as he had been since the days of the Rif. The Arab Executive arranged an impressive festivity for him—a large gathering in a
garden, with speeches and cheers. I went; Canning and I were the
only non-Arabs present, and neither of us understood Arabic; I
felt, I may say, like a complete fool. The Arabs in Palestine and
elsewhere had suffered a good deal from the activities of their
'friends,' I thought—one had only to name Colonel Lawrence and
Miss Bell to show what the best 'friends of the Arabs' could do—
and I never understood why Arabs continued to show such touch-
ing faith in them. With all the will in the world Canning could do
nothing for the Palestine Arabs; neither could I; the Palestine
Arabs, like other members of the human race, could depend in the
last analysis only on themselves; and yet they seemed to love
these manifestations of sympathy, and Canning's noncommittal
little speech was cheered to the echo. With all their individual
charm and intelligence, the Arabs seemed in some respects—
particularly in politics—to be as helpless as children.

My acquaintance with the Arabs during those last two months,
and my investigation of what might be called their 'case'—the
whole tangle of their history, claims, grievances and political
position—led me to regard Palestine as the most flagrant example
of the British betrayal of Arab interests after the war. These Arabs
had no political rights of any kind, no parliament or council or
legislature, and were governed by ukase. The law was whatever
the high commissioner wanted it to be. True, the high com-
missioners had been cautious and just, but the principle of despo-

tism remained the same. All the Arabs had been betrayed by the British, but the Arabs of Palestine were in worse case than any others. Iraq had at least the appearance of independence; Transjordan likewise; Syria worried along under the French but would not have to support them forever. In Palestine, a section of the Arab world where promises of freedom and independence had been scattered generously from 1915 to the end of the war, what had happened? A London promise (Mr Balfour's) was thought to have invalidated all the battlefield promises to the Arabs: Mr Balfour's word was more important than Kitchener's, Sir Henry Macmahon's, Lord Allenby's, Colonel Lawrence's, or anybody else's, and the Arabs of Palestine found themselves handed over to a mandatory régime pledged to the creation of a national home for the Jews. The programme of this national home, clearly expressed by even the moderate Zionists, was to increase its Jewish citizenship by immigration until such time as the Jews should outnumber the Arabs and assume the task of governing. What people would have welcomed such a plan? The populations of Illinois, of Devonshire, of Normandy, would resent being told that they had to make way for a new nation; they would perhaps resent it more than the Arabs, for the Arabs were in normal times a good-natured people; but anybody, Arab or Chinese or American, would resent it. The Arabs had, in this respect, an *absolute* case—that is, independently of personalities or racial distinctions, without respect to circumstances, events or conflicts of interest, the principle involved in the Arab presentation was correct. It would have been correct for any people in any nation at any time. It was, simply, this: that a population has the right to govern itself in such freedom as it can bring about under its own institutions. The Zionist policy denied that elementary right to the Arabs of Palestine—and was obliged to deny it; for the Zionist policy had as its final aim the submergence of the Arabs under a new Jewish nation.

The Zionists had no absolute case at all; what they had was a relative case. That is, if you postulated certain things, certain rather large things, certain other things became relatively true— that is, true for a time and with relation to the other circumstances, but not, in the abstract, true at all. You had to assume that it was desirable and possible to create a secular Jewish nation (something that had never existed even in ancient times); you had to assume that the Jews possessed a moral right to Palestine because of their religious history in the thousand years before Christ; you had to assume that the Arab rights and interests, the accumulation of thirteen hundred years, were of an inferior order to the Jewish rights and interests. Once you assumed all this you could make out a case for Zionism. But in doing so you were obliged constantly to use the terms 'Jew' and 'Arab,' with innumerable other specific expressions such as 'religion' or 'race' or 'Empire' or 'mandate.' You could not possibly state the Zionist case in any large, general form, in any terms that would approximate to a principle of absolute truth.

What was more, you could scarcely get a Zionist to discuss the situation in general terms. The Zionist intellectual attitude was small, specific, even petty. It was directed upon such questions as these: Were the Jews murdered at Hebron mutilated, or not? Did the Grand Mufti 'prepare' the outbreak, or did he only 'order' it? Should he be executed or only deposed? Was the first person killed a Jew or an Arab? Did such-and-such a British official speak offensively of or to such-and-such a Jew? And so on: a host of small controversial questions, argued with the utmost intensity, and raised to such a height of importance in the Zionist mind that they obscured the broader and more permanent bases of the problem altogether.

There was one acquaintance of mine whose conversation never failed to refresh and delight. This was our bishop, the rector at the Austrian Hospice. Monsignor was now second in command to His Beatitude the Latin Patriarch and thus occupied one of the highest positions in the world of the Palestine Christians. I am sure he fulfilled his duties with dignity and competence. But throughout the period of the disorders, when the street in front of us was filled with signs of terror, when one could not go out of doors without seeing the wounded and dying Arabs carried in on stretchers, Monsignor was preoccupied with a problem to which he referred as 'ameliorations.' These ameliorations consisted of new bathrooms and water closets; I think there were two new bathrooms being put in when the troubles began. On the actual day of the outbreak Monsignor was greatly agitated because the Arab workmen could not come to work; he was undoubtedly sorry for the victims of the disorders, but the thing that figured most largely in his talk was the delay caused to his 'ameliorations.' At the beginning of October I went off to Syria and was absent for a week or ten days. When I came back, dirty, unshaven and exhausted, after a long day at Aramageddon and on the road, Monsignor met me in the garden. I remember looking at my bare knees sticking out from beneath my shorts and being startled to see how grimy they were. I wanted a bath and a bed but was nevertheless, as always, happy to see His Grace. His Grace welcomed me back with dignity, bowed, shook hands and said:

'Forgive me—have you the *practique* of the vater closett?'

After a moment's reflection I replied that I had used a good many water closets in my time.

'Then you can tell me,' he remarked with satisfaction. 'I want to know, is it the *practique* among the English and Americans to wash the hands after the use of the vater closett?'

I replied that I believed this was the custom.

The Bishop sighed and looked distressed. His handsome brow was corrugated with an effort of calculation.

'That is bad,' he said. 'That is bad. To install the place to wash the hands will be very expensive. *Also!*'

12

My week of sightseeing in Syria was pleasant enough, and I enjoyed my visit to the Rockefeller 'dig' at Armageddon. But aside from these interludes and an occasional meeting with somebody like the Bishop, my days were spent in an intolerable atmosphere: Zionism and Arab nationalism. Jew and Arab, Balfour Declaration, hatred, accusation, recrimination. I grew weary of it long before my departure. But I stayed on in Jerusalem—stayed for weeks longer than I really wanted to stay—chiefly because of the Parliamentary Commission of Enquiry into the Palestine Disturbances.

The Commission, appointed by the Labour government of the day, consisted of a Conservative, a Liberal and a Labour member of Parliament, presided over by an experienced Colonial official. Its purpose was to find out what had caused the outbreak of August 23d and to make recommendations for the future.

My diary for the latter part of October and November is full of political details that reflect the preoccupations of the time. I had one long talk with the High Commissioner (not for publication) and many with the Grand Mufti, Musa Kazim Pasha and Jemaal el-Husseini. I came into possession of an imperfectly translated and incomplete, but substantially accurate, copy of the correspondence between Sir Henry Macmahon and King Hussein in 1915, promising independence under a Moslem caliph to the Arab people if they would join England in the war against Turkey. Lord Kitchener's, Lord Allenby's and Colonel Lawrence's promises were less amply covered by the documents, but they seemed incontrovertible, just the same. I needed this material for magazine writing, but the more of it I uncovered the more convinced I became that the Arabs of Palestine had been treated disgracefully, and the more sympathetic I grew towards their fundamental claims.

This being the case, when the question of giving evidence for the Arabs came up, I did not hesitate to say I would. I did so with some trepidation. By the end of October I had received a flood of letters from America and knew exactly where I stood with the Zionists. They were prepared to say and believe anything of me; I had irritated them more than if I had been a determined lifelong enemy. The Grand Mufti himself had not been more heartily abused in the Jewish press and in the letters of protest from American Jews to the newspapers. I knew that if I testified for the Arabs I should run into all sorts of difficulties when I got home. But, as my diary shows, I believed it would be inexcusable to allow these things to deter me from giving evidence when I thought it had some historical significance.

The Zionist case before the Commission of Enquiry was prepared with the utmost care. Every available typewriter in Jerusalem was in use for weeks in the preparation of their documents, as I found out to my discomfort (I had to give up the machine I had rented for the period). The chief counsel for the Zionists was Sir Boyd Merriman (afterwards president of the Divorce Court), one of the most accomplished of British barristers. He was assisted by Lord Erleigh (Reading's son), and by a competent Zionist staff fully acquainted with the problems under consideration. The argument Merriman had to present was a simple one: conspiracy by the Arabs, led by the Mufti, to murder innocent and defenseless Jews, aided by culpable negligence and anti-Jewish feeling on the part of the government.

The Arabs were in a position of great inferiority before the Commission. Their counsel—chosen on the advice of some of those self-appointed 'friends-of-the-Arabs' in London—were not at best the equals of Sir Boyd Merriman in ability, and were further handicapped by incompetent, dilatory, haphazard preparation. I knew something of the way they went to work, for they lived in the Austrian Hospice, and I saw them frequently. They had no brief, and long after they should have had the whole affair ranged in their minds, they were still asking questions about the simplest facts. The stenographic record of evidence shows that they remained to the end uncertain of the details among which they had struggled for forty-seven sittings.

The Arab inferiority was indeed so bad that many Arabs wished to boycott the Commission altogether. But the Grand Mufti kept his head; the better I knew him the more I realized that he was a man of remarkable character, extraordinary inner calm and certainty. He never got excited, he was always open to reason, and he never rejected an argument or a suggestion without examining it carefully. His knowledge of Western methods was limited, but he said from the beginning that if the Commission of Enquiry were really interested in getting the truth they would get it no matter what the various barristers did: and he was right.

The Grand Mufti was depressed throughout those weeks—not, I believe, for personal reasons, for he cared little about his personal safety or position. He was depressed by the fatal inferiority of the Arabs in money, in the instruments of Western political struggle, and in what might be called political efficiency. I knew him well and was positive of his disinterested devotion to the cause of the Arabs, for which he would have made any sacrifice. I was not blind to the existence of social and economic problems within the Arab world; I knew enough about the system of Arab feudalism to realize that the lower classes might not fare much better under a government of their own aristocracy than under a government of British and Jews; but I believed, as I had always believed, that the first duty of a popular leader was to obtain the freedom of his people. This sense was the only one in which nationalism had ever appealed to me (as a first stage, that is, and not as an end). And Haj Amin was a singularly devoted, resolute and implacable nationalist. In spite of physical differences, he occasionally reminded me of Abd el-Krim. I know of no higher compliment.

When I said good-bye to Haj Amin he made a remark that has stuck in my memory since. From this particular person—Mufti of Jerusalem almost by inheritance, as his brother, father and grandfather had been before him; president of the Supreme Moslem Council by election for life; and recognized head of his people by the operation of those natural emotions that defy official nomenclature—the words had a certain weight.

'Vous viendrez nous voir encore,' he said, smiling. 'Je serai toujours là.'

13

On November 12th and 13th I testified before the Commission of Enquiry. A futile proceeding: my evidence was immediately denied, it was badly handled and badly given, and I felt that it was not believed. But at least I had done what I could to make the point, and left—with a tremendous *pouf!* of relief—for Cairo on the 14th. I have never been so glad to get out of any place in my life.

I had caught a chill of some kind at the Arab Executive's pow-wow for Gordon Canning. Perhaps it was a consequence of so many long speeches. I thought it was malaria, and the doctor said it was influenza, but whatever it was, it kept me in bed for a week with a fever. I got up to go before the Commission, but I might just as well have spared myself the exertion, for my evidence counted for nothing.

I had agreed to testify to one thing only: the business of Miss X and the gathering at Tishabov. But I had never tried to offer evidence in a court before, and did not realize that it was impossible

PERSONAL HISTORY

to say your one thing and get out. Learned counsel asked me a
variety of questions; counsel for the Arabs wanted me to talk
about the whole Palestine problem, including grievances of which
I knew no more than anybody else; counsel for the Zionists
wanted me to explain my whole personal position, 'sympathies'
and professional status and the rest of it; counsel for the government asked me questions about a press colleague.

The moment I got into the room where the Commission was
sitting I realized that I was in for it. These people had been listening to cautious official evidence ever since their arrival in Palestine
—police reports and the like—and I was the first nonofficial witness to go before them. The Zionist battery, facing me, looked
as if they had seen a ghost; I am sure they did not expect me, at
any rate. The Arab counsel were so far away that I derived no
sense of support from their presence. I was nearest to the Commission itself, and nearest of all to Mr Harry Snell. Mr Harry
Snell was a small, fidgety man with a strong Cockney accent,
which he exercised in a stage whisper at intervals while I was
talking. I was divided between irritation at his discourtesy and
amusement at his comments. He kept saying: '*Ah*ee carnt see
anything in this! *Ah*ee carnt see anything in this! Just a journalist
out for a good story! That's *mah*ee view.' Mr Snell's view could
not have been plainer if he had shouted it through a megaphone,
but it did not make my task easy.

After five minutes in that room my one feeling was: 'Oh, Lord,
how did I ever get into this?' I despaired of making these solemn
lawyers realize that I knew a danger when I saw one. Without
going into the entire history of my life I could never have persuaded them that my view of the behaviour of the Zionist crowds
at the Wailing Wall was just as reliable as the view of their police,
if not more so. I was talking about mood, temper, states of mind,
and they wanted the kind of thing that goes on police reports—
'incidents,' clause A and clause B, dates and details: in short, legal
evidence. The more the difficulties multiplied (and the more Mr
Snell chattered), the more nervous I became, so that before the
first sitting was over I had only one idea in my head: to get it
over as quickly as possible.

What with one thing and another I was a sorry witness, but

388

on the whole I suppose most members of the Commission must have supposed that the central fact (the point I had come there to make) did refer to something. At any rate, they called on Miss X immediately afterwards—and she denied the whole thing! I was told that it was stupidly naïve of me not to expect this, but the fact is that I didn't. Miss X confirmed only those parts of my testimony that could have been confirmed by other witnesses (times, movements, the stretchers at Hadassah Hospital) and denied all the essential parts, those concerned with what she had told me. She further said that she was not a Zionist, saw few people at Tel-Aviv, knew nothing about the Tishabov gatherings, and had not come to Jerusalem on that account at all. Her last and most surprising statement was that when she went to the Wailing Wall she 'generally felt pretty quiet' and did not speak much.

I did not know the details of this evidence for years afterwards. That evening in Jerusalem I only knew that Miss X had denied my evidence under oath, and I had to assume that this disposed of the matter. I had tried to put a rather important point, and if the Commission of Enquiry did not believe me it could not be helped. And in any case it made no great difference to me or to anybody else, for the Commission of Enquiry, whatever it made out of the mass of conflicting evidence before it, could not change the régime in Palestine. The régime, under which an Arab majority had to be governed without representation until such time as a Jewish majority could be pumped into the country from abroad, was regulated by the Balfour Declaration and the Mandate. And with this régime the disturbances of August, 1929, were sure to be repeated from time to time whenever the Zionist policy grew so obviously aggressive as to arouse popular indignation. I was weary of the whole thing, which had never brought anything but trouble and difficulty to me; and it was with the profoundest feelings of relief that I left that wretched little country —the 'Holy Land'—behind.

24

I spent the night in Cairo and took ship at Alexandria the next day for Athens. I was not (for once!) worried about money or time; the editors of *Asia*, the N. A. N. A., my publishers and my lecture manager had, between them, restored my finances, and I was able to break the journey home by a week in Athens, a week in Vienna, a week in London. In Athens Mme Charitaki took me to the Acropolis and the museums, where her own splendid head looked like that of an antique goddess come to life; in Vienna I spoke to nobody but the rotund manager of the old Hapsburger Hof and spent my time in museums or going to hear *Die Meistersinger, Cosi fan Tutte, Die Entführung aus dem Serail;* in England I basked in civilized talk again and renewed my acquaintance with the great yew trees of Knole. By the time I reached New York these influences of a securer world had combined with the passage of time and reflection in tranquillity to drive away—I hoped forever—the small, sharp bitterness given off by men and things in the Holy Land. My judgment of the struggle there was unchanged, but I no longer regarded it as an urgent part of the problem of existence for any but the restricted number of persons engaged in it. That is, I could see with distance and calm what I had never been able to see in Palestine itself: that the Zionist policy was historically without significance. It might delude two or three generations of Jews who would be better employed in other enterprises; it might humiliate and bewilder the Arabs of Palestine and the surrounding Arab provinces; it might give rise to repeated catastrophes of the kind I had just witnessed. But in the end it would be swallowed up in the larger changes through which the world must pass if it was to emerge from chaos and submit to the rule of reason. That is, the Arabs of Palestine would be obliged by history to solve their national problem in relation to the Arabs of the other provinces and to the whole reviving world of Islam; the Jews of Palestine and other countries would have to solve their problem as a part of the general social and economic equation, on terms as wide as the world, as wide as the Jewish race itself. While I was in Vienna there were *numerus clausus* riots in the University: the Gentile students, demonstrating with violence against their Jewish fellows, shouted out in the academic courtyards, 'You've got Palestine, why don't you go there?' The incident brought sharply to mind the existence, on a very large scale, of the Jewish problem, more acutely in some countries than in others, but in every country as acute as hatred and prejudice could make it—and as against that problem what had the Zionists set up? A project for settling a fraction of the world's Jews on land acquired in the midst of an Arab state surrounded by Arab states. Even though the central idea of Zionism came from something profoundly established in the Jewish heart, the ancient nostalgia for Jerusalem, its political expression was trivial. A noble emotion had here been adapted to small, shabby uses and served no ends but those of imperialism.

I was sorry that in coming to these conclusions I had been obliged to give offense to many Jews. Nothing that had happened in Palestine had altered my opinion of the Jewish character in general; I still regarded it as something of special value in the balance of the world's good. The very energies that had raised the temperature of Palestine to fever heat could, if diffused and applied throughout the range of human society on terms of equal association with peoples of a different structure, bring about a powerful acceleration of the processes through which we might hope some day to achieve the dignity of reason. To think of the Jews I had known in China and Russia was to realize that this was possible; they had risen so far above the prison walls of race, religion, nation, tradition, that their Jewishness was altogether lost in their humanity; and their special passion, the purity and intensity in which the best of the Jewish heritage was expressed, burned itself out in a cause from which no human creature was excluded. Only in such freedom, it seemed to me, could the Jewish genius give all it had to give to the developing consciousness of mankind.

I was sorry to have given offense to some Jews; but I would rather have given offense to all Jews than to distort or suppress what I honestly believed to be the truth. One of the pleasant surprises of the next winter was the number of Jewish and part-Jewish audiences that did listen to what I had to say without resentment—displaying again what the hysteria of Palestine had too often obscured, the willingness of the Jewish intelligence to examine and to reflect. But even if this had not been so I should have continued to maintain what the experience in Palestine had abundantly proved: that the Zionist policy belonged not to the forces of light but to the forces of darkness. It kept an Arab population in subjection for the achievement of an end unjustifiable in the logic of history, and in its delusion and obfuscation of the Jewish genius it robbed the general world of what might have been—what still must be—a powerful resource. To fight anti-Semitism on its own ground was the duty of every civilized human being, but that duty could never be fulfilled by attempting to expropriate a part of the Arab world. Two wrongs, in the twentieth as in other centuries, were still two wrongs.

So much was fixed. When you had thought of one particular problem for months, had examined it in every aspect, classed, compared and taken apart its elements, stripped it of circumstance and reduced it to the most general, fundamental expression of which your intelligence was capable, you had at least one fixed point. But what relation did this fixed point bear to total experience? In what way did the shock and disorder to which Zionism had subjected my view of the world affect the general processes, before and afterwards, through which I tried to come by some kind of light in darkness? These questions began to rise in my mind almost as soon as I had left Palestine, and in the first gasp of relief at quitting the unhappy country they were answered with dispatch. I was neither a Jew nor an Arab: that was the quick answer. I would have liked to blot out most of this experience as if it had never been. If the memory could be isolated and controlled, forbidden to play its insidious rôle throughout the whole consciousness, it might be put to work sifting the pieces of my life in Palestine, rejecting the horrors and the hatreds, and leaving, as useful residue, only a set of pleasant pictures like the paintings on a Chinese screen: the lovely, barren, melancholy country, the exquisite Dome of the Rock, the red hills of Moab and the lake of Galilee, a few calm faces and—for the flowers on the screen—a few conversations. There seemed nothing else worth preserving out of an experience too agitated and ugly for contemplation.

But if the view taken in this book is correct such picking and choosing is not within the powers of intelligence. We can choose what we wish to tell, what we prefer to emphasize, or what we believe to be important; we cannot choose what we would like to remember. The Palestine experience was therefore as much a part of my consciousness as my hand was a part of my body. I could neither reject it nor run away from it. And the return of general awareness, the resumption of relationship to a larger world in which Palestine was only a part, had to be accompanied by a process of integration: these things had to enter their place in my life, considered not as a man's unit of time but as a section of the world experience, in accordance with the inner logic that had governed my absorption of such living material from the beginning. That inner logic, not always conscious under the impact of phenomena, but rigid and inevitable after the event, demanded of every experience that it relate the individual to the general life of which he was a segment. The necessity knew no exception and did not permit such evasions as the statement, 'I am neither a Jew nor an Arab.' We are all Jews and all Arabs if we are totally human beings. In the clearest period of my social and historical intelligence, that which ended at a crematorium in Moscow, I had not been given to such pettifogging, and as Palestine receded in space, its meanness and parochiality receded with it. By the time I left Athens for Vienna I already knew that Rayna Prohme had conquered. The argument was over at last, and she had won.

I knew it, I think, on the Acropolis—not that there was any association, direct or indirect, between what I saw there and the idea of Rayna Prohme. But I did have one moment of extraordinarily sensitized vision on the Acropolis, and from then on the events of the previous months tended to take their proper shape and proportion. It was the moment in which I saw, for the first time, the entasis of the columns at the corner of the peristyle of the Parthenon. Thousands of people before me must have had the same vision. I had gone to the Parthenon with no more than the usual interest of a visitor to Athens; I knew nothing much about architecture, and had always been assured by my educated friends, who preferred Ukrainian baroque and Bohemian rococo, that the Parthenon was 'boring'; I thought, on the contrary, that it was very beautiful, but for the first half hour it was no more than that. Then, suddenly, as I stood looking at the brown hills and blue sky of Attica—not at the Parthenon at all, but at the scene beyond—the soft marble of the exquisite shafts, the two at the corner, began to swell and glow in the loveliest line I had ever seen. I did not believe it; I had never heard of the entasis. Startled, almost alarmed, I asked Mme Charitaki if she saw what I saw. She smiled gently and explained: the swelling line was a special achievement of the Athenian architects, and not a mirage or hallucination of my own. The more I looked the more it seemed to live, to frame the brown hills and the blue sky, to compose with them into an incomparable perfection of life preserved through cycle upon cycle of years. The miracle was there to be seen by anybody; I did not imagine it; but to have seen it as I did without foreknowledge of its perfection was to be sure, in a single moment, of duration in the life of man, survival of his best and attrition of his worst, in the unending conflict by which he stretches his powers against time. In this place, where furies as concentrated as those of the Holy Land had perished without a sign, the entasis still embraced, with its living arms, the living hills of Greece. Here you had to take 'the long view'; no other view would do, no other view was possible. Although duration was not in itself a proof of good, the parts of the past that still expressed most vividly the continuous consciousness of man, communicating in a language understanded of the people for century after century, were, like this strange marvel, the best and not the worst parts. And you had to get it in; no view of the world that left it out could be clear or complete; you had to take the Parthenon with the Haram esh-Sherif, the age of Pericles with the age of Wall Street, Zionism and pogroms and capitalist imperialism along with Athene and her temple; you had, somehow, to see the whole thing if you could, by whatever light you could find, before it was too late.

I had known only one long view in my life. Once, for a time, I had perceived human existence to be a coherent struggle towards the reasoned control of its materials and had thought I might have a place, small but exact, in that struggle. Then something had happened: I had first decided I was unfit to participate in the effort, and afterwards lost the most powerful reason I possessed for endeavouring to do so. It was just as clear now as it had been in the long Moscow argument that I was not a revolutionary, could never be a revolutionary. But how did that affect the view? What had happened to the view, anyhow, all this time, and what on earth had I been thinking about?

I went back in two jumps to my argument with Rayna Prohme, resumed it where it had left off, and was vanquished.

'Of course, you fool! Of course! What else did you expect? If you'd asked me I could have told you that Zionism was only a part of the whole thing. It's a little trick, part of the big bag of tricks: capitalism and imperialism. A little special philanthropic and race trimming applied, but essentially the same kind of trick. And useful, too, to the British. The Jewish problem, the Arab problem—what ever put it into your head that they could be solved individually? Wake up, wake up, for God's sake, and look! It's all part of the same thing, and you can't go tinkering away with parts of a rotten old machine. You've got to get a new one. Stop talking nonsense about Jews and Arabs; they can't help themselves whatever they do under this system; the immediate job is to get rid of the present arrangement and contrive a more satisfactory one, without these nation-race-religion tags to help the functioning of capital and empire. They may take a long time to outgrow, but at least under a decent system of society we can avoid emphasizing them, and they won't hurt so much.'

'But I'm not a revolutionary. I can't do anything about getting the new machine. I——'

'You don't have to! All you have to do is talk sense and think sense, if you can. Who ever told you you had to be a revolutionary? Everybody isn't born with an obligation to act. There are some people who can't act, who go to pieces under action, who can only think straight when they have plenty of time and no noise. But if you see it straight, that's the thing: see what's happening, has happened, will happen—and if you ever manage to do a stroke of work in your life, make it fit in. That's all you have to do. You'd be worthless in any other way. Did I ever, at any time, tell you you had to abandon the things you can do (or may be able to do if you try hard enough) and rush out to do things you obviously can't do? Did I?'

'No. But if you are right—and after what I've seen of tinkering in Palestine, I believe you are—it's pretty futile to sit and do nothing about it.'

'Do it in your own way—find your own way.'

'That sounds slow and painful. Or else it does mean doing nothing. They also serve who only stand and wait. Is that it? Well, at least I can do that.'

'You could do worse. You're no good in journalism or politics or any kind of social action unless you can keep your head above water, see where you're going, where you've been and where everybody else is. You can't do that, so don't try. You get carried away, invariably. Standing and waiting is better, if you are in the right place. Find it and stick to it: a solid place, with a view.'

'Easy to say!'

'Well, nothing's easy to do, if you come to that. It won't be easy, but if you don't try you're done for. You see what happens when you abandon the attempt: you get into a nasty little mess like Palestine, all blood and mud. For two years you've tried to forget that you ever saw the human struggle in any really general or comprehensive terms. You've fiddled about with one thing and another, and finally popped off to a miserable fever-spot where people murder each other because they can't see an inch beyond the ends of their noses. Blind as bats, all of them. You have eyes, or used to have, but they'll get pretty myopic if you keep them trained on such things. If you want to relate your own life to its time and space, the particular to the general, the part to the whole, the only way you can do it is by understanding the struggle in its world terms, not in the terms of small fanaticisms and minor hatreds. The Jewish problem is important, but Zionism isn't. And important as the Jewish problem is, it's only one of the complications in the whole system of organized injustice by which few govern many, hundreds of millions work in darkness to support a few thousands in ease, group imposes on group, one nation oppresses another, and the greater part of the human race has to live in filth and starvation to maintain an artificial system of profit. If you can't fight that—and that's a personal thing; knowing what I do of you, I don't think you can—you must at least *see* it. I would have fought it, and did. Your work, if you ever do any that amounts to a damn, will have to be some kind of writing, I suppose; I don't know much about that, but it might be a good idea to try to learn how to write. And if you ever do learn how, the obligation upon you will be just this: to see things as straight as you can and put them into words that won't falsify them. That's programme enough for one life, and if you can ever do it, you'll have acquired the relationship you want between the one life you've got and the many of which it's a part.'

'You didn't say that in Moscow.'

'That's two years ago, and it was personal: it isn't personal any more. That is, there's no question of the you and the me. It's between the subsequent you (of which it's quite possible that some of me has become a part) and the mystery of the subsequent you's relation to existence. It may take you all the rest of your time to establish, and you may never establish it, but if you don't try you're lost. And you've got another birthday coming: remember that. It'll be getting dark pretty soon, and you've fiddled away the whole morning; see that you don't fiddle away the whole afternoon.'

'Harsh words.'

'True words. O. K.?'

'O.K.'

As the train dawdled along through Greece and Yugoslavia, stopping seven whole hours in windswept Belgrade and another six or seven hours at the Hungarian frontier, these discussions accompanied the days and nights of cold and stormy weather. They continued in Vienna through a solitary week in museums and cafés, and did not come to an end for a long time thereafter. In referring to them as discussions I do not mean to suggest that Rayna Prohme actually appeared to me, like a mediæval saint to a flagellant, and held forth. They were discussions, at first, with myself: with a part of myself that had been atrophied for months, buried away under ice, the part to which Rayna Prohme had addressed herself in the successive stages of our conversation. A conversation of this particular kind could not be ended by the death of one of its participants. It was interrupted for a long time, and was resumed at first in Athens in a form difficult to explain: as between myself (1929) and myself (1927); the second step, immediately following, is the one I had recorded here, between myself (1927–1929) and Rayna Prohme. In other words, there still existed a force, a state of mind, an impulse of reason, somewhere in the world about me or in the consciousness with which I faced it, to which I could give the name of Rayna Prohme. That this force or state of mind no longer possessed physical form did not impede its communication. It spoke as clearly as ever, although no longer with a physical voice. There was nothing pseudo-supernatural or spiritistic about this phenomenon: it was a simple consultation of ideas in the world mind. Nobody could deny that there was an idea in the world mind corresponding to what, in books, is called the collectivist philosophy and view of history: this idea spoke to me in the idiom, and with the character, of Rayna Prohme. And in resuming, after the shock and disorder of Palestine, the conversation that had been interrupted by death in Moscow two years before, I discovered that the personal had, indeed, vanished: to talk to Rayna Prohme (to the state of mind I called by this name) was to abandon such terms altogether and to enter upon a transaction in which, whatever the idiom used or the reference made to past personal events, ideas alone confronted each other with the coldness and the purity of stars.

It was in this way that the argument ended and Rayna Prohme won. The conversation did not end, and is not likely to do so until both of its participants have lost physical existence; but the argument was over. I had to admit that she was right, that hers was the only comprehensive view, the nearest thing to a 'long view' that I was likely to know, and that, even if I took no part in the direct struggle by which others attempted to hasten the processes that were here seen to be inevitable in human history, I had to recognize its urgency and find my place with relation to it, in the hope that whatever I did (if indeed I could do anything) would at last integrate the one existence I possessed into the many in which it had been cast.

The decade in which I had pursued such a conclusion through the outer storms had ended, and I was on my way back to a civilization that could never again be so sure of itself, never again so blind.

THE END

An Index of Personal Names

AN INDEX OF PERSONAL NAMES

Ibáñez, Vicente Blasco, 207.
Ibn es-Sa'ud, 8.
Imbrie, Mr., 347.
Imperio, Pastora, 62.
Ishii, Viscount, 79.
Israels, Carlos, 322.

Jabotinsky, Vladimir, 353.
James, William, 277.
Jebb, Gladwyn, 173.
Joffe, Adolph, 284, 290.
Johnson, Hallett, 67, 68, 71, 72, 73, 74.

Kamenev, Leo B., 284.
Kantorovich, A. I., 252, 254, 255, 257, 258.
Kemal, Mustapha, 44, 45.
Keynes, J. M., 275, 286, 317.
Kisch, Colonel, 357.
Kitchener, Lord, 382, 385.
Klems, Joseph. *See* Hadj Alemán.
Knabenshue, Mr., 368, 376.
Kock, de, 308.
Kook, Chief Rabbi, 351.
Kotov, 259–260.
Kun, Bela, 293.

La Cordobesita, Dora, 69.
Lacretelle, Pierre de, 45.
Lamington, Lord, 156.
Lang, Basil, 248.
Lansing, Robert, 79.
Laurencin, Marie, 309.
Law, A. Bonar, 44.
Lawrence, Colonel T. E., 381, 382, 385.
Le May, Alan, 11.
Lemmy, 16, 17–18, 19, 21, 22.
Lenin, Nikolai (Vladimir Ilyich Ulianov), 25, 185, 186, 192, 217, 284.
Lewis, Sinclair, 279, 320, 321, 331.
Li, Phyllis, 227, 242.
Li Chi-sen, 239.
Lili, 45, 46.
Linck, Dr., 296, 297, 298.
Lindbergh, Colonel Charles A., 190, 232, 326.
Lindsay, Vachel, 279.
Li Ta-chao, 225–226, 227, 242.

Litvinov, Madame, 267, 269.
Lloyd George, David. *See* George, David Lloyd.
Lockhart, Frank P., 202, 242, 243, 244.
Longfellow, Henry Wadsworth, 279.
Loraine, Sir Percy, 173.
Lorelei, 45, 46, 81.
Loti, Pierre, 171.
Lucy, 12, 13, 14, 15, 16.
Luke, H. C., 371, 380.
Lyautey, Marshal, 92.

MacDonald, J. Ramsay, 40, 51, 53, 77, 78.
Macmahon, Sir Henry, 382, 385.
Magaz, Admiral de, 84.
Magnes, Dr. Judah, 369.
Magri, Mario, 148, 149.
Mahdani (guide), 122, 123, 125, 126, 127, 128, 129, 130, 131, 133, 135, 145.
Malcolm, 177.
Malvy, 206.
Mantegna, 32.
Maria Cristina, Queen of Spain, 76.
Marx, Karl, 61, 191, 314, 331.
Matisse, Henri, 184.
Matteotti, Giacomo, 53, 60, 61.
Mazzini, Giuseppe, 80.
Mei Lan-fang, 253.
Meller, Raquel, 83.
Merriman, Sir Frank Boyd, 385, 386.
Mills, Eric, 370, 371, 380.
Millspaugh, Dr. A. C., 168, 169, 170.
Milton, John, 276.
Mimoun, Caïd, 93, 94.
Misselwitz, Henry, 213.
Mitchell, Mrs. Mildred, 242, 243.
Mizrachi, Avraham, 360.
Mohammed, Prophet, 346, 347, 352.
Mohammed ben Abd el-Krim, 105, 106, 109, 133, 134–135, 155.
Mohammed Abdullah, 143.
Mohammed ben Haddu, 90, 91, 92, 93, 94, 95, 96, 98, 99, 100, 101.
Mohammed bel-Hadj el-Bukawi, 110, 111, 112–116, 120, 123, 161.
Mohammedi bel Hadj Hitmi, Sidi, 103, 104.

401